Writing Talk

Sentences and Paragraphs
with Readings

Third Edition

Anthony C. Winkler

Jo Ray McCuen-Metherell
Glendale Community College

Prentice
Hall

Upper Saddle River, New Jersey 07458

Library of Congress Cataloging-in-Publication Data

Winkler, Anthony C.
    Writing talk. Sentences and paragraphs with readings / Anthony C.
Winkler, Jo Ray McCuen-Metherell. — 3rd ed.
        p.   cm.
    Includes index.
    ISBN 0-13-097863-9 (text)
    ISBN 0-13-097867-1 (IE)
    1. English language—Sentences—Problems, exercises, etc.
2. English language—Paragraphs—Problems, exercises, etc.
3. English language—Grammar—Problems, exercises, etc.   4. Report
writing—Problems, exercises, etc.   5. College readers.   I. McCuen,
Jo Ray, 1929–   . II. Title.   III. Title: Sentences and paragraphs
with readings.
PE1441.W457   2002
808'.0427—dc21   2002016980

Editor-in-Chief: Leah Jewell
Senior Acquisitions Editor: Craig Campanella
Editorial Assistant: Joan Polk
Production Liaison: Fran Russello
Prepress and Manufacturing Buyer: Ben Smith
Creative Design Director: Leslie Osher
Art Director: Ximena Tamvakopoulos
Cover and Interior Design: Wee Design group
Cover Image: Nicholas Wilton
Marketing Manager: Rachel Falk
Marketing Assistant: Christine Moody

This book was set in 11/13 New Century Schoolbook by
Publications Development Company of Texas and
was printed and bound by Courier Companies, Inc.
The cover was printed by Phoenix Color Corp.

 © 2003, 2000, 1997 by Pearson Education, Inc.
Upper Saddle River, New Jersey 07458

Printed in the United States of America

10   9   8   7   6   5   4   3   2   1

ISBN 0-13-097867-1

Pearson Education LTD, *London*
Pearson Education of Australia PTY, Limited, *Sydney*
Pearson Education Singapore, Pte. Ltd
Pearson Education North Asia Ltd, *Hong Kong*
Pearson Education Canada, Ltd., *Toronto*
Pearson Educación de Mexico, S.A. de C.V.
Pearson Education—Japan, *Tokyo*
Pearson Education Malaysia, Pte. Ltd
Pearson Education, *Upper Saddle River, New Jersey*

Contents

About the Authors

Anthony C. Winkler was born in Kingston, Jamaica, and educated at Mt. Alvernia Academy and Cornwall College in Montego Bay, Jamaica. In 1962, he came to the United States to attend school, and received an A.A. from Citrus College, and a B.A. and M.A. from California State University at Los Angeles.

For seven years, he taught as a part-time evening college instructor while working full time as a book representative first for Appleton Century Crofts, and then for Scott, Foresman.

Winkler began collaborating with Jo Ray McCuen-Metherell in 1973, and became a fulltime freelance writer in 1976. He is the author of numerous textbooks, trade books (including Bob Marley: An Intimate Portrait by His Mother) and screenplays (including The Lunatic, based on his second novel). He lives in Atlanta with his wife and two children.

Jo Ray McCuen-Metherell was born in Belgium and grew up in Europe, coming to the United States for her college education. She received her B.A. from Pacific Union College and her M.A. and Ph.D. from the University of Southern California. While working on her doctorate, Jo Ray was hired to teach English at Glendale Community College, from which she retired in 1996.

A chance meeting in 1973 with Tony Winkler, who was a college textbook sales representative, led to a partnership that has produced fifteen coauthored textbooks used at colleges and universities across the country. "I have reached the place," says Jo Ray, "where I have difficulty remembering what I've said in what book."

Jo Ray has one son, David Cotton, a perinatologist at Wayne State University. When not revising her textbooks and writing new ones, Jo Ray enjoys traveling, reading, opera, snow skiing, and tennis.

Preface to the Third Edition

The third edition of *Writing Talk: Sentences and Paragraphs with Readings,* like its predecessors, takes as its starting point the assumption that grammar for the native speaker is a *built-in skill,* not an added-on one, and that the best sense for grammar in the native speaker is the ear.

People speak the language they hear spoken around them from birth. An English infant raised in a genteel drawing room will emerge from it speaking like an Englishman raised in a genteel drawing room. Transplant that same infant to an urban area like Brooklyn, and he will grow up to speak like someone raised in Brooklyn. We have never seen an exception to this observation. We learn to speak our mother tongue not from a book, but from using our ears.

As English teachers, we know that many of our students neither speak nor write what we have been trained to call "good grammar." Students use fragments; they punctuate badly; they misplace modifiers and garble sentences; they use the wrong case or tense; they speak and write slang. How can we say that a speaker's ear is the best sense of grammar when all around us we have evidence to the contrary?

The answer is simple: Much of the time these are not errors of bad grammar; instead, they are errors of inappropriate usage. If you are raised hearing *ain't* used every day, you will grow using *ain't* in your speaking and writing. But because *ain't* is regarded as nonstandard and unacceptable usage in formal writing, it is our job as English teachers to wean students off that word when the circumstances demand the formality of standard English.

Usage variations aside, it is still a fact that all native speakers, as well as those who have spoken English for years, have within them an ear for grammar that students for whom English is a second language (ESL) do not share.

This assumption was thought by some to make previous editions of this book suitable only for native speakers and to exclude ESL students. But regardless of the differences between native speakers and ESL students, some school systems—many because of budgetary pressures—freely mix both populations in the same classroom, making no distinction between them. The upshot is that many teachers have asked us to include both groups, native speakers as well as ESL students. That is exactly what we have done in this third edition of *Writing Talk: Sentences and Paragraphs with Readings.*

In coping with both audiences, we take a dual approach. We begin with a candid admission that ESL students and native speakers have different strengths. For the native speaker, the advantage is an ear that is finely attuned to the mother tongue. On the other hand, ESL students who come to English as adults or near adults often bring to the table a solid grounding in the grammatical basics of their adopted tongue. Gradually, as they progress in fluency, they will acquire what to the native speaker is a birthright, namely, an ear.

Until that happens, foreign speakers learning English often make mistakes in phrasing that would rarely, if ever, be made by a native speaker. For example, recently we overheard a foreign student say to another student who was about to take a test, "Have a good luck." This sentence is not ungrammatical; it is unidiomatic. But it is also the sort of sentence no native speaker would use. People say to one another, "good luck," all the time. But they never say, "Have a good luck."

On the other hand, a native speaker might write, "The men at the baseball park was talking all throughout the game," confusing the prepositional phrase "at the baseball park" for the subject and making a classic subject verb agreement error. In short, both groups commonly make mistakes in English usage. But they make different mistakes.

With these differences in mind, we have adapted the pedagogy of this book to take into account many of the known difficulties that ESL students have with English as well as many of the common errors that all students make. Where appropriate, we issue an "ESL Advice" notice, alerting students that this particular usage is one that often troubled ESL students.

This dual approach is aimed at both audiences whose superficial differences cannot alter the fact that they have a common goal that this book can help them reach: namely, mastery of English.

There are occasions when, no matter what the background of the student, the ear is at odds with the formal rule and of no help whatsoever in deciding what is right and appropriate. A case in point is the infamous *between you and I.* Although used by a surprising array of prominent men and women in the media, this construction is incorrect. Yet the right form, *between you and me,* often sounds wrong. We flag such cases with a unique feature of the *Writing Talk* series, namely, an Ear Alert warning. We first explain the formal rule for the benefit of both groups, but particularly for the ESL student; we then show how its practice in everyday speech varies from the rule. Finally, the Ear Alert label and distinctive icon in the margin warn everyone that this is a point of grammar on which no one's ear can be trusted.

Writing Talk: Sentences and Paragraphs with Readings is the first book in a series of two, and it has the following features:

- **Common Myths and Standard Written English.** We dispel some common and discouraging myths that students believe about writing. Writing is hard for everybody (no doubt rare exceptions exist, but we can't think of any offhand). We also know that the fumbling and revision that goes with writing is not a sign of ineptness, but a universal condition of the discipline. Many students do not understand how difficult writing is and tend to misinterpret the normal tedium of composing as a sign that they cannot write.
- **Paragraph Writing Instruction from the Beginning.** The emphasis is on sentence skills, but since grammar is neither

taught nor learned in a vacuum, we teach paragraph writing to provide a context for the grammar explanations that follow.

- **Paragraph Writing Assignments in Every Sentence Unit.** Grammar by itself can be a grim, unmerciful, seemingly pointless business. By including paragraph writing assignments at the end of every sentence unit, we emphasize that grammar is a means to an end rather than an end in itself.

Throughout, our explanations of grammar rules

- Emphasize functional problems, not descriptive grammar.
- Use a minimum of terminology.
- Give short, pointed explanations with a light touch.
- Are followed by immediate practice.
- Come with abundant exercises that include paragraphs for editing and sentences for reading aloud.
- Are followed by a short summary of every main point (*In a Nutshell*).

New to This Edition

This edition begins with a new first chapter, "The ESL Student and the Native Speaker," which outlines the differences between these two groups and presents a blueprint of how this book addresses their respective needs. All the well-known features that users of earlier editions particularly liked have been kept: Every chapter still has a *Talk Write Assignment* that gives students practice in translating oral dialogue into its written formal equivalent. Each assignment presents a dialogue that might be overheard in an informal discussion and then asks students to write the equivalent in a more formal style. The new edition ends most chapters with the following four types of exercises:

- A *Unit Test* that tests mastery of the chapter. This is now a feature of virtually every unit.
- A *Unit Talk-Write Assignment* that reinforces the difference between spoken and written language.
- A *Collaborative Writing Assignment* that gives students an opportunity to interact in group sessions and put their ear to use in practicing the contents of the chapter.
- A *Unit Writing Assignment* that gives students a chance to apply the writing principles they have just learned.
- A *Photo Writing Assignment* that asks students to write on a topic suggested by a photograph.

We have made other changes and improvements as well. We have added more exercises throughout the book, but selectively, based on feedback from users. Instructors know the value of repetitive exercises as a learning technique—in this book we call them *Practicings*, but we also understand that exercises and drills walk a fine line between usefulness and tedium. Each chapter now has more numerous and varied exercises that reinforce every concept taught. We have tried to write exercises that are interesting to do and require a variety of responses. Every chapter now ends in a Unit Test, which asks students questions about the major concepts they have learned from the unit.

We've also made some changes, although minor, to the textual explanations. Always, we've tried to be simpler and more direct, and where the opportunity presents itself, to add some humor to what might otherwise seem to the student to be a typically grim exposition of grammatical principles. Teaching grammar is a serious enterprise, but it does not deserve the graveyard sobriety of tone it is so often given.

Finally, we have changed three of the readings. These changes were based on user feedback or because we found a reading that we thought would infuse the book with a freshness and give instructors some new topics. The readings in *Sentences and Paragraphs* are, as before, thematically organized. Some instructors like to teach principles and then show them in practice, exactly what the readings in *Sentences and Paragraphs with Readings* are meant to do. The readings section begins with an essay, "Help for Your Reading," giving practical, nuts-and-bolts advice on techniques of reading. The readings are then grouped into seven categories—*An Object, A Place, An Animal, A Person, An Event, A Problem, and An Argument*—and move from the concrete to the abstract. The readings are multicultural and multiethnic, ranging from the last letter of a Kamikaze pilot to a moving poem by a former president about euthanizing a beloved pet.

Each essay is prefaced by a headnote and followed by comprehension questions (*Understanding What You Have Read*) and thought-provoking questions (*Thinking About What You Have Read*). Finally, two *Writing Assignments* are included for each reading.

Throughout both books, we have tried to make our explanations simple but concise so they will be understandable to both ESL and native students, to explain everything step-by-step, to provide exercises immediately after explaining any rule or principle, and to respect and encourage the student's "ear" for grammar, whether it exists by birthright or was acquired by an accumulated study of English.

Our thanks to Craig Campanella, senior acquisition editor at Prentice Hall, who oversaw this revision, and to the production and manufacturing staff at Prentice Hall.

We would also like to thank the following reviewers: Sally Parsons, The Art Institute of Atlanta and Barbara Brown, Olive Harvey College.

Every writer needs an editor, and over the years it has been our good fortune to have assigned to us editors of sensitivity and insight, who have helped us every step of the way. In this edition, our good shepherd was Sylvia Weber, who stood diligent watch over everything we did and kept at bay the wolves of complacency and carelessness. She guided us in the revision with humor and thoroughness and was there to steady us at every misstep. We gratefully acknowledge her help. Because of her efforts, this new edition is a better book.

Anthony C. Winkler

Jo Ray McCuen-Metherell

Instructor's Teaching Package:

- **Instructor's Edition ~ ISBN 0-13-097867-1.** For the first time WRITING TALK has an Instructor's Edition. The IE contains in-text answers and to help instructors best prepare for class, and a 48-page built-in instructor's guide bound directly into the back of the Instructor's Edition. The Instructor's Guide provides sample syllabi, teaching tips, additional chapter-specific assignments, and selected answers to in-depth exercises from the text. Free to adoptors.
- **Test Bank ~ ISBN 0-13-097869-8.** The WRITING TALK: SENTENCES AND PARAGRAPHS 3E Test Bank provides additional chapter-specific tests for instructors. Available in print or downloadable format. Free to adoptors.

Student's Learning Package:

PH WORDS: An internet-based assessment tool like no other in the Basic Writing market, PH WORDS provides students with summary instruction and practice on each element of basic writing. PH WORDS includes over 100 learning modules covering the writing process, paragraph and essay development, and grammar. For each module, students have access to:

- **Watch** Screens, which provide an audio and animated summary of the content.
- **Recall** Questions, which test student's comprehension of the concept.
- **Apply** Questions, which test student's ability to identify the concepts in existing writing.
- **Write** Questions, which prompt students to demonstrate their knowledge of the concept in their own writing.

    This technology solution frees up class time by allowing students to work on their areas of weakness on their own. The software measures and tracks student's progress through the course with an easy to use management system. PH WORDS is available at a discount when packaged with the text. Contact your local Prentice Hall representative or visit www.prenhall.com/phwords for more information.

Student Answer Key ~ ISBN 0-13-097868-X. For the first time WRITING TALK: SENTENCES AND PARAGRAPHS 3E will have a student answer key available. This answer key will provide answer to selected exercises in the text, and is available free when packaged to the textbook. Contact your local Prentice Hall representative for a package ISBN.

Companion Website ~ www.prenhall.com/winkler. The Companion Website allows students to gain a richer perspective and a deeper understanding of the concepts and issues discussed in WRITING TALK: SENTENCES AND PARAGRAPHS 3/e. This site is free to all students. Features of this site include:

- Chapter objectives that help students organize concepts.

- Online quizzes which include instant scoring and coaching.
- Essay questions that test students' critical thinking skills.
- Built-in routing that gives students the ability to forward essay responses and graded quizzes to their instructors.

The New American Webster Handy College Dictionary, Third Edition ~ ISBN 0-13-032870-7. Your students can receive a **free** *New American Webster Handy College Dictionary* packaged with their text when you adopt *WRITING TALK: SENTENCES AND PARAGRAPHS 3E.* This dictionary has over 1.5 million Signet copies in print and over 115,000 definitions, including current phrases, slang, and scientific terms. It offers more than 1,500 new words, with over 200 not found in any competing dictionary and features boxed inserts on etymologies and language. Ask your Prentice Hall sales representative package ISBN.

English: Evaluating Online Sources ~ ISBN 0-13-049620-0. This completely revised guide, available summer 2002, helps students develop the critical thinking skills needed to evaluate online sources critically. This supplement is available FREE when packaged with the text.

The Prentice Hall ESL Workbook ~ ISBN 0-13-092323-0: This 138-page workbook is designed for use with a developmental English textbook to improve English grammar skills. Divided into seven major units, this workbook provides thorough explanations and exercises in the most challenging grammar topics for non-native speakers. With over 80 exercise sets, this guide provides ample instruction and practice in: Nouns, Articles, Verbs, Modifiers, Pronouns, Prepositions, and Sentence Structures. The PH ESL WORKBOOK also contains: an annotated listing of key ESL internet sites for further study and practice, an answer key to all the exercises so students may study at their own pace, and a glossary for students to look up difficult words and phrases.

The Prentice Hall Grammar Workbook ~ ISBN 0-13-042188-X: This 21-chapter workbook will be a comprehensive source of instruction for students who need additional grammar, punctuation and mechanics instruction. Covering topics like subject-verb agreement, conjunctions, modifiers, capital letters, and vocabulary, each chapter provides ample explanation, examples, and exercise sets. The exercises contain enough variety to ensure student's mastery of each concept. Available to students stand alone or packaged with the text at a discount. Available Fall 2002.

The Prentice Hall TASP Writing Study Guide ~ ISBN 0-13-041585-5: Designed for students studying for the Texas Academic Skills Program test this guide prepares students for the TASP by familiarizing them with the elements of the test and giving them strategies for success. The authors provide practice exercises for each element of the writing and multiple choice portions of exam, and the guide ends with a full-length practice test with answer key so students can judge their own progress.

Ask your local Prentice Hall representative for information about ever-growing list of supplements for both instructors and students.

1

The ESL Student and the Native Speaker

"Having an ear for the language means that you're usually able to tell when something doesn't sound right even though you can't say why."

Language typically consists of two main parts: sounds and rules. Its sounds are the way the language is spoken—its **pronunciation.** Its rules are its **grammar.** Part of learning a language involves mastering the rules. But odd as it may seem, if you are a native speaker you already know, and correctly observe, many rules of the language simply by the way it sounds. For example, do you see anything wrong with this sentence?

> She will speaking with you be later.

Most likely you immediately saw that the verb "be" was out of place. The sentence should have read,

> She will be speaking with you later.

This is just one example of a basic truth: You know more about your language than you think. For instance, did you know that you know how to use the future progressive tense? If you say you don't, you're wrong. The construction "she will be speaking" is in the future progressive tense. If you haven't spoken it today, you probably will later. It is a very complex tense, yet nearly every day you use it flawlessly as you do many other parts of speech. You do not need to know the formal definition of a preposition to correctly use one. Practically no native speaker would make this mistake:

> I put book the table on.

It does not look right. But more important, it just does not sound right. Whether or not you know the formal rule that the preposition comes before the object it modifies, you still practice it. And you do that entirely by the way the construction sounds—strictly by ear.

Differences Between a Native and an ESL Student

We bring this up to help explain the difference that exists between a native speaker of English and the ESL (English as a Second Language) student. Both can learn to master English by using this book. But although both have the same goal—to learn to speak and write English well—they do not begin at the same place and therefore cannot learn English the same way. The main difference between them is this: The native speaker, from having heard English spoken since birth, has an ear for it. Having an ear for a language means that you're usually able to tell when something doesn't sound right even though you can't say why. Nearly all native speakers have this ability. It exists even if they mainly speak a dialect of the language. Most native speakers, for example, will automatically say "If I were you" without knowing the formal rule behind that expression. If an ESL student says, "If I were you," it is most likely because he or she has learned the formal rule of the subjunctive.

ESL students, in short, face different challenges than do native speakers. Indeed, the difficulties most ESL students have with learning English generally fall into these three broad categories: pronunciation, grammar, and idioms.

Pronunciation

Many words in English will take on a different meaning depending on how they are pronounced. From experience, native speakers know, recognize, and use these differences almost instinctively. For example, place the emphasis on the first syllable of the word *present* and it means a gift, as in "Thank you for that terrific birthday present," or a time period as in "There's no time like the present." However, place the emphasis on the second syllable of *present* and it means "to introduce," as in "Ladies and gentlemen, I would like to present the President of the United States." Another example is the word *invalid*. If spoken with an emphasis on the second syllable, this word means "legally no good," as in the sentence, "Her check was invalid." But when the emphasis is on the first syllable, *invalid* means "a sick person."

Here are some other examples of meanings that depend purely on sound:

> The lovely white <u>dove</u> flew from a branch just as I <u>dove</u> into the river.

> Nancy was <u>close</u> to fainting, so the nurse asked that we <u>close</u> the door.

> The <u>wind</u> was so powerful that the sailors could not <u>wind</u> the sails.

Many other examples of words that shift their meanings with sound can be found in English.

PRACTICING 1

Working in a small group, explain the difference in the meanings of the underlined words in the sentences that follow.

1. U.S. farms <u>produce</u> huge volumes of <u>produce</u> every year.
   to create, the results of farming (e.g.vegetables and fruits)

2. Why <u>object</u> to such a beautiful <u>object</u> even though it is old?
   to express disapproval, something that can be seen and felt

3. I <u>refuse</u> to clean the yard because it is full of <u>refuse.</u>
   to decline, garbage

4. The <u>sewer</u> tripped and fell down the <u>sewer.</u>
   a person who sews (e.g., dressmaker), a conduit for carrying sewage or rain water

5. These homeowners <u>lead</u> the campaign to get the <u>lead</u> out of drinking water.
   to direct, a metal

6. There was a <u>row</u> in the third <u>row</u> of seats.
   a quarrel, lineup of seats

7. The bandage was <u>wound</u> around the <u>wound.</u>
   past participle of "wind"—to wrap around an object, injury

8. Please <u>relay</u> the results of the <u>relay</u> to me.
   to pass or send along, a fresh team or crew who relieves another

9. They <u>polish</u> the sign that said they were <u>Polish.</u>
   to render something bright and smooth, belonging to Poland in Eastern Europe

10. The mating stag <u>does</u> a dance when he sees the <u>does.</u>
    performs, female deer

Homonyms

Occasionally two words may sound alike but have different meanings. Such words are called **homonyms.** Here are some examples with the homonyms underlined.

<u>They're</u> much too difficult for the students. <u>Their</u> homes are out of town. Place the book over <u>there.</u>

Give the peach <u>to</u> your brother. He owns <u>two</u> motorcycles. I <u>too</u> love cats.

<u>You're</u> about to win $300. Have you checked with <u>your</u> boss?

In the case of homonyms, however, the spelling always determines the meaning.

PRACTICING 2

Circle the correct homonym in parentheses.

1. The (souls, soles) of his shoes were worn out.

2. We have every (right, write) to complain about so many blackouts.

3. (It's, its) better to have loved and lost than never to have loved at all.

4. They'll simply have to wait for (they're, their) turn

5. I can't see that (theirs, there's) any difference between them.

6. I can't (bear, bare) to face the truth.

7. The students had (sheer, shear) luck on their side.

8. After a long war, finally we had (piece, peace).

9. Every evening for a full year, she took an (our, hour) of conversational French.

10. She told us the story to (lesson, lessen) our grief.

Context

Some words, though spelled and pronounced the same way, still take on different meanings depending on the **context** in which they're used. Consider these examples:

The burglar was *shot* by the police.

After the sales meeting, my whole day was *shot.*

He gave me a *shot* of whiskey.

Most native speakers would immediately grasp from the context the different meanings of *shot* in these sentences. In the first example, *shot* means *gunshot;* in the second, it means *ruined;* in the third, it means *measure* or *portion.* Depending on how much or how little English they know, many students would find these different meanings baffling.

Here are some other examples of words whose meanings change with context:

When he heard the news, he went into shock.
His freckled face was topped by a shock of red hair.

Let me just *lie* here on the green grass.
What that man just told you is a big *lie.*

In the first example, *shock* means a heavy blow of some kind; in the second, it means a thick mass. In its first use, *lie* means to be in a reclining position; in the second, it means an untruth.

IN A NUTSHELL

- Language consists of two main parts: pronunciation and grammar.
- If you're a native speaker, you know more about grammar than you think.
- Native speakers and ESL students face different problems in learning how to write English well.
- Some English words get their meanings from the way they are pronounced.
- Homonyms are words that sound alike but have different meanings.
- Context often determines the meanings of words.

PRACTICING 3

Working with a partner, define the underlined words whose meanings change with context.

1. The foreign student carried a single <u>grip.</u> / Her <u>grip</u> was surprisingly firm.

suitcase, tight hold

2. The bird's <u>wing</u> was broken. / The right <u>wing</u> vote was behind her.

a means of flight (e.g., birds or airplanes), conservative side of politics

3. She said she was <u>fed</u> up. / The dogs were well <u>fed.</u>

figurative language meaning that one has had enough, past participle of
"feed"—to give to eat

4. He <u>spread</u> the bed carefully. / Her ranch was quite a <u>spread.</u>

to distribute over a surface, slang for "living quarters"

5. The team <u>beat</u> us badly. / I love the <u>beat</u> of their latest hit.

to have won by a wide margin, rhythm (as in music)

6. Last year <u>net</u> profits were down. / He caught ten fish with a <u>net.</u>

The money remaining after all necessary deductions have been made, a meshed
network of lines

7. No one is <u>safe</u> around drunk drivers. / I keep my passport in a <u>safe.</u>

Free from danger, a strongbox for storing valuables

8. What a <u>joint</u>! / My knee <u>joint</u> hurt after I played tennis.

Slang for "public dwelling" or "marijuana cigarette"—part of the leg

9. He told her to stop trying to <u>cow</u> him. / My uncle owns a milk <u>cow.</u>

To subdue, mammal that gives milk

> **10.** After nine innings, the score was <u>dead</u> even. / Sundays are
> usually <u>dead.</u>
> *absolutely, lifeless and dull*

Grammar

English grammar is a difficult subject. Even professional grammarians often disagree about its rules, many of which sometimes seem
ridiculous. The native speaker, who may know no more grammar than
the ESL student, at least has the advantage of being able to recognize
the usual and customary place for nouns and verbs in a sentence. It
is the rare native speaker, for example, who would say, "I to the store
now go," putting the verb in the wrong place. Likewise, native speakers are unlikely to make prepositional errors such as saying, "Peggy
stayed her room," leaving out the preposition "in." Of course, native
speakers do make grammatical errors. They're just likely to make
errors of a different kind.

On the other hand, the proper use of prepositions and articles often
baffles ESL students. An ESL student might say, "I must run to store,"
leaving out the "the," an error a native speaker is unlikely to make. Yet
another difficulty often encountered by ESL students is in the use of
pronouns. A pronoun is a word that takes the place of a noun. ESL
students tend to omit pronouns as in the sentence, "The students
shouted when won the football game," leaving out the pronoun <u>they</u>.
Another tendency that ESL students have is to use both a noun and a
pronoun referring to the noun in the same sentence, as in "My boss she
increased my hourly pay." The ear of most native speakers would immediately detect this error.

Many foreign students, especially those from countries like China,
Japan, and Russia, where the grammar of the native language is totally
different from English, find it hard to write English correctly. We have
had students complain in mournful tones, "I go over my writing again
and again so as to make sure that I have corrected all grammar errors,
but my teacher always finds more." Take heart, because millions of
immigrants have arrived in America knowing absolutely no English and
still have mastered it sufficiently not only to survive, but to prosper.

In this book, we will teach English grammar while addressing the
basic differences between the ESL student and native speaker. When
we come across a usage that ESL students are known to have trouble
with, we will issue an ESL Advice warning students to be particularly
careful. We will then follow up that warning with numerous drills.
When the ear is an unreliable guide to a particular item of usage, we
will issue an "Ear Alert," warning the native speaker that the rule
must be mastered.

Both populations should benefit from this dual approach. The native
speaker, who has the ear but probably lacks a grounding in the formal
rules, will benefit from the extra drills. On the other hand, the ESL
student, who may lack the ear but is getting solid training in the
formal rules, will gradually become familiar with ordinary idiomatic
usage. In either case, the goal is the same: to learn to write and speak
English better. And in both cases, whoever you are, if you apply yourself to this book, you will reach this goal.

PRACTICING 4

Using your ear or your grasp of the rules, correct the grammar of the following sentences. If the sentence is correctly written, mark a *C* beside it.

1. Yesterday I went church.   *c*

_____

2. I believe she breaked my skate board.

*I believe she broke my skateboard.*_____

3. Foreign students are special people.   *c*

_____

4. Television in the living room needs fixing.

*The television in the living room needs fixing.*_____

5. He opened up heart to her.

*He opened up his heart to her.*_____

6. He must buy broom.

*He must buy a broom.*_____

7. He said he was lonely and needed friend.

*He said he was lonely and needed a friend.*_____

8. He the book last night tried to read.

*He tried to read the book last night.*_____

9. Come to me, my melancholy baby.   *c*

_____

10. You everything very well understand.

*You understand everything very well.*_____

Idioms

An **idiom** is a phrase or expression that means something different than what it seems to say. For example, the sentence "That guy is a fish out of water" does not mean the person being described actually resembles a beached fish. It means, instead, that the person is in an uncomfortable position. Likewise, to say "I felt my heart leap into my throat" does not mean that the speaker's heart actually moved. Rather, it means that the speaker was terrified. Native speakers immediately get these meanings; ESL students may or may not, depending on their familiarity with such idioms.

To the ESL student, idioms can be a nightmare. The problem is that while there is sometimes a natural logic to an idiom, just as often there is not. For example, to say that someone is a "fifth wheel"—meaning unnecessary—immediately brings to mind an image of uselessness, which is exactly what a fifth wheel would be, giving a natural logic to that particular expression. But what does "kick the bucket," which means *die,* have to do with dying? No doubt, there was once a logical connection between the two. But it has long been lost to most of us. What we are left with is an expression that is common in conversational

English but means something totally different from what its individual words would suggest. That is the trademark of an idiom.

It is not only the colorful phrases of idioms that ESL students find troublesome. What is also hard for them is learning how words are customarily grouped to make up conversational expressions. For example, we heard a foreign student say to another who was about to take a test, "Have a good luck!" What the student meant was clear, and strictly speaking there was nothing ungrammatical about what she had said. It's just that no native speaker would ever phrase it that way. What a native would've said was, "Good luck!" Another example: an ESL student wrote in an essay, "I altered my mind on this question," whereas a native speaker would write, "I changed my mind on this question." The phrase "altered my mind" is not technically wrong; however, it is unidiomatic.

Here, for example, is a letter written by a European travel agent to an American client:

> I have received your dated fax May 3. I communicate to you that we are in accord on the appointment for Friday, May 25. We request you contact us the same day to be at the hour that is convenient. The place of the appointment, if you believe it opportune, can be in our office. Receive a cordial greeting as we transmit our best wishes.
>
> Manuel Ortega

No word in this brief letter is misspelled, and the grammar is not wrong. Still, the letter sounds foreign because the writer has not mastered idiomatic English. Rewritten in everyday English, the letter might sound like this:

> I received your fax dated May 3 and wish to confirm our appointment on Friday, May 25. We ask that you contact us on that day to arrange for a convenient meeting time. If you don't mind, we can meet in our office.
>
> Cordially, sending our best wishes,
>
> Manuel Ortega

Yet as difficult as it might be, with practice and exposure to conversational English, ESL students will gradually gain a mastery over the idioms of their adopted language.

IN A NUTSHELL

- ESL students and native speakers often make different kinds of mistakes.
- Idioms often give ESL students trouble.
- This book takes a dual approach that helps both the ESL student and native speaker.

PRACTICING 5

In the space provided, check the sentence that is in idiomatic English.

1. _____ **(a).** In obedience with the law of New York, we must stop using so much electricity.

✔ **(b).** In accordance with the law of New York, we must stop using so much electricity.

2. _____ **(a).** What a weeping shame that she didn't graduate from Chico High.

✔ **(b).** What a crying shame that she didn't graduate from Chico High.

3. _____ **(a).** If it takes me a thousand years, I'll get even to that thief.

✔ **(b).** If it takes me a thousand years, I'll get even with that thief.

4. ✔ **(a).** By asking her that question, he really put her on the spot.

_____ **(b).** By asking her that question, he really put her in the spot.

5. ✔ **(a).** Henry decided to stick to his guns by telling her not to call him again.

_____ **(b).** Henry decided to make his guns stick by telling her not to call him again.

6. ✔ **(a).** She gives off an air of suffering.

_____ **(b).** She gives off a breeze of suffering.

7. _____ **(a).** He said he would try as difficult as he could.

✔ **(b).** He said he would try as hard as he could.

8. ✔ **(a).** All the effort she made on our behalf came to nothing.

_____ **(b).** All the effort she made in our behalf arrived at nothing.

9. ✔ **(a).** She plays checkers, but she's better at chess.

_____ **(b).** She plays checkers, but she's better in chess.

10. ✔ **(a).** My mother is a treasure.

_____ **(b).** My mother is a fortune.

PRACTICING 6

In the lines provided, write the meanings of the following idiomatic sentences.

1. He's a penny pincher.

He is stingy.

2. When it comes to that question, we're night and day.

When it comes to that question, we have completely different views.

3. She said she had had her nose to the grindstone.

She said she worked hard and diligently.

4. Lately, my friend Jim has been burning the midnight oil.

Lately my friend Jim has been working long night hours.

5. Come into my office and chew the fat.

Come into my office and chat with me.

6. This is a far cry from what you said you'd do.

This is completely different from what you said you'd do.

7. The pitch that he hit for a home run was right in his wheel-house.

The pitch that he hit for a home run was right where he liked it.

8. Things have not been business as usual between us.

We have not continued to do business in the same way as in the past.

9. Our negotiations have hit a stone wall.

Our negotiations have come to a stop.

10. The Wilsons spent a pretty penny remodeling their home.

The Wilsons spent a large amount of money remodeling their home.

 **Unit Test**

From each pair of sentences, check the sentence that is correct.

Example:

 ✔ **(a).** Native speakers often have an ear for correct language but don't know the rules.

 _____ **(b).** Non-native speakers usually have a better ear for correct English than do native speakers.

1. _____ **(a).** The two main parts of language are mind and tongue.

 ✔ **(b).** The two main parts of language are sounds and rules.

2. _____ **(a).** Both the native and non-native speaker begin learning the English language at the same place.

 ✔ **(b).** The native and non-native speakers do not begin at the same place in learning English.

3. ✔ **(a).** The non-native speaker often knows the rules of grammar better than does the native speaker.

 _____ **(b).** It is impossible to teach grown ESL students correct English.

4. ✔ **(a).** Many words in English take on a different meaning, depending on how they are pronounced.

 _____ **(b).** Once you know how to pronounce a word, you will know what it means.

5. _____ **(a).** In the case of homonyms, spelling is unimportant.

 ✔ **(b).** In the case of homonyms, spelling determines the meaning.

6. _____ **(a).** The rules of English grammar are completely consistent.

 ✔ **(b).** Even professional grammarians don't agree on all grammar rules.

7. ✔ **(a).** When your ear fails to give you the correct English, you must memorize the rule.

 _____ **(b).** Always trust your ear to point out the correct English.

8. ✔ **(a).** "I paid top dollar for that coat" is an idiomatic expression.

 _____ **(b).** One should never use idiomatic expressions.

9. _____ **(a).** "I live in the United States" is an idiomatic expression.

    ✔ **(b).** "Let's drum up support" for the candidate is an idiomatic expression.

10. ✔ **(a).** Most foreign students say they find English difficult to learn.

    _____ **(b).** Most foreign students say they find English easy to learn.

Unit Write-Talk Assignment

An ESL student and a native speaker have a talk about English. Correct any mistakes you find in any of the sentences. Rewrite any you think are too idiomatic to be understood by a foreign speaker familiar only with textbook English.

TALK

WRITE

Student No. 1: For me, English it is very difficult

English is very difficult for me

_____

_____

_____

Student No. 2: Nah, man. It's a piece of cake.

No, it's very easy.

_____

_____

_____

Student No. 1: But how can that be? It is not food.

Not idiomatic

_____

_____

_____

Student No. 2: What I mean is that it's a snap. Nothing to it. I could do it in my sleep.

What I mean is that English is so easy, I could do it

In my sleep.

_____

_____

TALK

WRITE

Student No. 1: Do you talk in sleep?

Do you talk in your sleep.

Student No. 2: We're not on the same wavelength, man. You're not with the program.

We're not communicating. We mean different things.

Student No. 1: What program you mean?

What program do you mean?

Student No. 2: No program, dude. You just missing the mark.

You just don't understand me.

Student No. 1: Where is this missing mark?

Not idiomatic.

Student No. 2: You're driving me nuts. I'm trying to tell you something but you keep missing the boat!

You're making me crazy. I'm trying to explain
something to you, but you keep misunderstanding me.

Student No. 1: What exactly you trying say?

What exactly are you trying to say?

Student No. 2: Nothing, man. A big fat zero.

I'm not trying to say anything.

TALK	**WRITE**
Student No. 1: I was saying that for me, English is hard.	*Not idiomatic*
Student No. 2: You got that right! Things are tough all over.	*You're correct. Many things are difficult.*
Student No. 1: What things you mean?	*What things do you mean?*
Student No. 2: Gimme a break, man.	*Let's drop the topic, please.*
Student No. 1: Yes, it is lunchtime.	*Not idiomatic*
Student No. 2: What's cooking in your English class today, man?	*What are you studying in English today?*
Student No. 1: I think prepositions are cooking.	*We are studying prepositions.*
Student No. 2: That's cool.	*That's nice.*

Unit Collaborative Assignment

Get together with three other students. Take turns having one student read the questions that follow aloud to the other three in the group. Listen to how, one by one, each of the three students responds casually to the question, perhaps even using idiomatic expressions. The one who has asked the question will write down the answers given. After all four questions have been answered, sit down with the group and rewrite the answers in formal English, avoiding idiomatic expressions that might be confusing to ESL students.

1. How important is the Internet to the present generation of college students?

2. What is your opinion of people who want to climb Mount Everest when it is known to be so dangerous?

3. What do you think the most popular mode of transportation will be in the year 2100?

4. What do you think of the philosophical admonition "Be yourself; do your best"?

Unit Writing Assignment

Write a paragraph in which you explain what an idiom is. Use examples to clarify your definition.

Photo Writing Assignment

Study this photo of two Westerners engaging in practicing one of the martial arts of the Orient. In groups of three and four students, discuss why activities like this have become so popular among Westerners. After your discussion, come up with the list of reasons to explain the appeal to Westerners of Oriental sports such as karate. What benefits do you think people derive from taking part in these activities? Each item in your list should be a complete sentence.

2

Myths About Writing

"Anyone who's not dead has something to write about."

I f you can "talk" English, you can learn to write it. Indeed, you already know more about writing than you think. If you are like most students, though, you probably believe some common and harmful myths about writing—our own students often do. Most likely, you use these myths to belittle your natural writing skills.

If a myth leads you to think that you write badly, you'll probably try to avoid writing. Practice makes perfect in writing (as in nearly everything else), so if you avoid writing, you won't get any better at it. To think you are naturally bad at writing is to plant a nagging critic inside your head who will scold every sentence you scribble. No one works well with constant scolding; everyone works better if encouraged. Human nature swims on "You can!" and drowns on "You can't!"

We begin, then, with a discussion of some myths about writing and how believing them can stunt your growth as a writer.

Myths About Writing

A **myth** is a popular but false belief. Among the many myths that students believe about writing are the following:

- I have nothing to write about.
- I can't write the way you're supposed to—with big words and long sentences.
- I hate to write because I make too many mistakes.

We will take up these myths, one by one, in order.

I have nothing to write about.

Anyone who's not dead has something to write about. All of us have opinions that can be used as writing topics. The problem is that students often think that only stuffy, academic topics are suitable for college essays.

However, you can write about many topics that are neither academic nor stuffy. You can write about an everyday event in your life, such as dating, or an idea that interests you. You can write about a friend, a hobby, or your job. You can tell about an exciting experience, a favorite teacher, a kindly uncle, or a nasty neighbor. One student we know wrote a funny essay about a goldfish. Another wrote a moving essay about burying a hamster. Everyone alive is interested in something; that something is what you can write about.

To see that you have ideas worth writing about, do the following activity, which we call Practicing. Chances are that everyone in your group will be able to come up with an idea suitable for a paragraph.

PRACTICING 1

Form a group of three or four students. Choose one topic from the list that follows. Everyone in the group should take turns talking about the same topic.

Answers will vary.

1. A movie I recently saw

2. My favorite television show

3. My favorite relative

4. My least favorite relative

5. My last birthday

I can't write the way you're supposed to—with big words and long sentences.

The first aim of any writer is to communicate. If using big words and long sentences will get a message across, a writer will use them. Ask yourself, though, how often do big words and long sentences help anyone communicate? The answer is, almost never. Writers use big words and long sentences only when small words and short sentences will not do the job. Small words and short sentences often make the point as well, if not better, than do big words and long sentences.

Writers mainly want to get a message across, and few people like reading big words clumped together in jaw-breaking sentences. Understanding such writing simply takes too much effort. Look at the following passages, for example. Which one do you think is better written and easier to understand?

> The audience was lachrymose at the termination of the drama, especially expressing a predilection for the heroine's experienced reunification with her long-lost progeny.

The audience was tearful at the end of the play. They especially liked when the heroine was reunited with her long-lost children.

The first passage consists of big words in one python-long sentence; the second uses simple words and two straightforward sentences. The second passage, by being direct and clear, is better than the first because it is easier to read and understand.

Directness and clarity: These are desirable qualities of good writing, not big words and long sentences. This book will teach you how to write clearly, directly, and always understandably.

PRACTICING 2

Get together in a small group. Each student should choose one topic from the list that follows and "talk a paragraph" about it for a minute or less. More than one person in the goup may select the same topic. Be as clear and direct as you can. You might want to write down a few ideas in advance.

1. A cause that has caught my attention

2. How to get to the student union

3. A teacher whom I particularly admire

4. A teacjer whom I particularly dislike

5. A college course I enjoy

Answers will vary.

PRACTICING 3

In the blank provided, check the sentence that is simpler and better.

1. _____ (a). The trees assumed a verdant hue because of heavy precipitation.

   __✔__ (b). The trees looked green because of heavy rainfall last week.

2. __✔__ (a). We are planning to have a quick snack in the student cafeteria

   _____ (b). We are planning to have a quick snack in the student cafeteria.

3. __✔__ (a). Henry was laid off because the garage where he worked went bankrupt.

   _____ (b). Henry experienced an involuntary termination when his place of employment was beset by financial reversals.

4. _____ (a). Can I persuade you to purchase this previously owned automotive vehicle?

   __✔__ (b). Can I talk you into buying this used car?

5. _____ **(a).** This cosmetic product will conceal the blemishes that commonly erupt on the skin of adolexcents.

_✔_ **(b).** This makeup will hide all of the pimples that tend to break out on teenagers' skin.

I hate to write because I make too many mistakes.

Everyone who writes or talks occasionally makes mistakes. We came across this sentence, for example, in a scholarly book about the Civil War's Union General William Tecumseh Sherman:

> When victory was achieved, however, [the army should] stop the bloodshed and destruction immediately and help those in need irregardless of any oaths of allegiance.

Irregardless is not a standard word. If you check your dictionary, you'll see that the author should have written *regardless*.

In speech, every one of us has at one time or another mispronounced a word, addressed someone by a wrong name, or misspoken a common phrase. Mistakes in speech are so common that many even have names. Here, for example, is a **spoonerism**, a mistake where a speaker mixes up the initial letters of words:

> Will someone please hick up my pat?

What the speaker meant was, *Will someone please pick up my hat?*

No one knows everything about the language. Like the rest of us, you have your weaknesses. However, you also have considerable strengths. If you are a native speaker, this book can teach you how to use your natural ear for the language to help your writing. If you are an ESL student, this book will tell you what you need to know about English to write and speak it well.

Let us begin with what you know. Take the following quiz. We think you will be pleasantly surprised to find out how much you already naturally know about English.

PRACTICING 4

Using your ear for the language, make an *X* in the space beside any sentence you think is incorrect. If you think a sentence is correct, leave the space blank.

1. _____ Johnny is bad boy.

2. _____ Atlanta is the capital of Georgia.

3. _____ My mother never go college.

4. _____ You see what I have to put up with?

5. _____ I speak quick because I nervous.

6. _____ You out the door go.

7. _____ Where are you going today?

8. _____ That ticket costed me $5.00.

9. _____ Go to your room.

10. _____ She is a better cook than me is.

Here are the correct sentences:

1. Johnny is a bad boy. (Original omits the *a*.)

2. Atlanta is the capital of Georgia. (Correct as written.)

3. My mother never went to college. (Should be *went to*.)

4. You see what I have to put up with? (Correct as written.)

5. I speak quickly because I'm nervous. (Should be *quickly* and *I'm*.)

6. You go out the door. (Verb *go* in wrong place.)

7. Where are you going today? (Correct as written.)

8. That ticket cost me $5.00. (*Costed* is not a word.)

9. Go to your room. (Correct as written.)

10. She is a better cook than I am. (Not *me is*.)

To sum up, don't approach writing as if it were a kind of communication utterly different from the talking you normally do. See it first as a kind of talking—but on paper. Remember, also, that if English is your mother tongue, you can use your native ear to become a better writer. And if you are an ESL student, you can learn the rules of grammar until you, too, acquire an ear for spoken English.

IN A NUTSHELL

There are three common myths about writing:

- I have nothing to write about.

- I can't write the way you're supposed to—with big words and long sentences.

- I hate to write because I make too many mistakes.

PRACTICING 5

State what you believe to be the three most serious difficulties you have with writing. State each in a separate sentence.

1. _____

Answers will vary.

2. _____

3. _____

PRACTICING 6

Answers will vary.

Form a small group of 3 or 4 classmates and discuss the difficulties you have with writing and what you might do about them. Refer to your answers to Practicing 4. Choose a person to summarize your discussion for the other groups in your class.

Standard English

If you can speak English well, why do you sometimes have trouble writing it? The answer is simple. Writing is, for the most part, done in standard English, which is not the English we commonly speak.

Standard English is English that is universally accepted by dictionaries and respected authorities. It is the English that all people who speak and understand English can use to communicate. Just as plumbing pipes have standardized sizes and fittings, so standard English has a standard vocabulary—no slang or street talk—and a standard grammar. Without standards, English would become so regional that a New Yorker might have a hard time communicating with a Californian or a Georgian. With standard English, however, all who speak the language can make themselves understood, at least on one level.

Consider, for examples, these pairs of sentences, labeled standard and Nonstandard.

Standard: What's happening?

Nonstandard: What's cooking?

Standard: Last night we had fun.

Nonstandard: Last night was a blast.

Standard: Don't try to fool an expert.

Nonstandard: Don't try to lay no boogie-woogie on the king of rock 'n roll.

Realistically, which sentence in each pair do you think, say, a native Russian who speaks only textbook English would more likely understand? The nonstandard sentences would be understandable only to those who have an ear for nonstandard English.

Even if you speak mainly nonstandard English, you also have an ear for standard English. Every day, you hear it in television and radio newscasts and you read it in magazines and newspapers. Even the supermarket tabloids with their alien three-headed babies and prowling bigfoots are written in standard English. In fact, you are more likely to read this standard English headline in a tabloid:

> Bigfoot Spotted by Campers in Yosemite!

than this nonstandard one:

> Campers Scope Bigfoot in Yosemite!

Your ear, however, cannot help you with some finer points of standard English. For example, is this sentence right?

> Between you and I, she can't spell.

The answer is, no. The *I* is wrong. The correct sentence would read,

> Between you and me, she can't spell.

Yet practically every day we hear people say *between you and I*. In standard English, that is wrong.

To sum up, use your ear for the language to help you with your writing, but remember that your ear can sometimes mislead you. To become the best writer you can be, you must also learn certain ground rules for written work. You must learn the rules of capitalization and punctuation and how to use prepositions correctly (*between you and me*), adverbs (*I speak quickly*, not *I speak quick*) and verbs (*cost*, not *costed*). Whether you're a native speaker or an ESL student, learning even a teaspoon of grammar will help your writing.

IN A NUTSHELL

- Standard English is English that is universally accepted by dictionaries and respected authorities.

- Even if you speak nonstandard English, you still have an ear for standard English.

- This ear can usually help you with your writing. When it can't, this book will warn you.

PRACTICING 7

From the following pairs of sentences, check the ones written in standard English.

1. **(a).** _____ You ain't gotta convince me, Joe.

   (b). ___✔___ You don't need to convince me, Joe.

2. (a). ✔ It seems strange that no one has any homework.

   (b). _____ It seems awful fishy that no one has any homework.

3. (a). _____ Mrs. Lopez is tough about discipline; she don't mess around with rude students.

   (b). ✔ Mrs. Lopez is strict about discipline; she doesn't tolerate rude students.

4. (a). ✔ Don't be diffficult.

   (b). _____ Don't be such a sop bucket.

5. (a). ✔ He doesn't care the slightest whether or not I have money.

   (b). _____ He doesn't give a rip about whether or not I have money.

6. (a). _____ I'm fixing to bake a pie.

   (b). ✔ I am getting ready to bake a pie.

7. (a). _____ Old bags like us don't need all that hip shaking no more.

   (b). ✔ Old women like us don't need all that dancing anymore.

8. (a.) _____ Practice hard and you'll be the tall hog at the trough.

   (b). ✔ Practice hard and you'll stand out above the others.

9. (a). ✔ I would appreciate your driving me to the store.

   (b). _____ I'd appreciate it if you'd carry me to the store.

10. (a). _____ We all wish she'd mellow out.

    (b). ✔ We all wish she'd be less nervous.

PRACTICING 8

Below are two paragraphs from a newspaper interview with Tyson Beckford, one of the most popular African-American male models working today. Underline the sentences or phrases that are non-standard English. Then rewrite both paragraphs in standard English.

Answers will vary.
Here is one correct version

I had just dropped out of college, Rockland Community College in Rockland, N.Y. I was just kicking back, no job, nothing. College wasn't for me. . . . I wanted to get into the entertainment field, either entertainment or acting. I never thought of modeling, never that. When that took off, I was like, "Wow." Modeling wasn't known as something masculine, something cool to do.

I had just dropped out of Rockland Community College in Rockland, N.Y. I was

just relaxing, not working or doing anything. College wasn't for me. I wanted to

get into either the entertainment or acting fields. I never thought of modeling.

When that was successful, I was surprised. Modeling wasn't known as something

masculine or acceptable to do.

I was just chillin' in Washington Square Park in New York. And a fashion editor for Source magazine came up to me and asked me to model. I said no. And with some convincing they got me to do it. I didn't think it was real. They just told me where it could lead to, like acting. So I was like, "OK, that's cool, I'll do it." The photo shoot was easy. I was like, "They pay you to do this? I can do this."

I was just spending time in Washington Square Park in New York, and a fashion

editor for Source magazine came up to me and asked me to model. I said no, but

with some convincing, she got me to do it. I didn't really believe her at first. She

told me modeling could lead to acting. So I said, "That would be good. I'll do it." The

photo shoot was easy. I thought, "They pay people to do this? I can do this."

PRACTICING 9

On a separate sheet of paper, write two paragraphs on one of the topics that follow. In the first paragraph, feel free to use nonstandard English. In the second, use only standard English.

1. A person who is not famous that I admire

2. What I like to do in my spare time

Answers will vary.

3. Something memorable that once happened to me

4. Coincidence

5. Superstition

 # Unit Test

In the blank provided, mark *T* if the statement is true, or *F* if the statement is false.

_____F_____ **1.** A myth is the same as a fact.

_____T_____ **2.** If you can talk English, you can learn to write it.

_____F_____ **3.** Even people who are dead have something to write about.

_____F_____ **4.** To write will, you must use big words and long sentences.

_____F_____ **5.** The first aim of a writer is to impress the reader.

_____T_____ **6.** Directness and clarity are desirable qualities of good writing.

_____T_____ **7.** Everyone who writes or talks, occassionally makes mistakes.

_____F_____ **8.** Standard English is what you hear spoken on the streets.

_____T_____ **9.** The purpose of standard English is to have a common way for English-speaking people to communicate.

_____T_____ **10.** When your ear is of no help, you have to go by the rules of standard English.

Unit Talk-Write Assignment

The Talk column on the left side of this page contains sentences from a student's casual conversation with a friend. Many of these sentences use nonstandard phrases, suitable for casual speech but not for formal writing. Rewrite the sentences in the blanks provided under the Write column, converting the nonstandard phrases into their standard English equivalents. If a sentence does not need correcting, leave the space blank.

Answers will vary.

TALK

WRITE

1. Between you and I, Dr. Mudd, my math prof, is, like, a real flake.

   1. *Between you and me, Dr. Mudd, my math professor, is not very smart.*

2. He lets the cute chicks in the class get away with murder, but he shines on all of us guys.

   2. *He lets the attractive women in class do whatever they want, but he criticizes the men.*

3. Math is tough to start with, so when you got a teacher who don't give a crap, how can you learn?

   3. *Math is difficult to start with, so when you have a teacher who doesn't care, how can you learn?*

4. The clue bus came by, but Crud, as we call him, didn't get on.

   4. *"Crud," as we call him, never seems to know what is going on.*

5. He acts like he is the genius dude.

   5. *He acts as if he is a genius.*

TALK

WRITE

6. Last Thursday, I asked him politely to explain the word problem.

6. *Correct* _____

_____

_____

_____

7. Good old Crud reamed me out in front of the whole class, yelling, "If you'd listened, I wouldn't have to waste class time repeating."

7. *Mr. "Crud" criticized me in front of the whole*

class, yelling, "If you'd listened, I wouldn't have to

waste class time repeating."

_____

8. Don't this creep realize how lousy he is?

8. *Doesn't this unpleasant man realize how*

incompetent he is?

_____

_____

9. I mean, gimme a break. A teacher ought to be patient.

9. *A teacher ought to be patient.*

_____

_____

_____

10. I mean, like, you know?

10. *Do you understand what I mean?*

_____

_____

_____

_____

 Unit Collaborative Assignemnt

Get together with a classmate and describe to him or her a job you now or once had and how you feel about it. Then use your discussion to write about the job in standard English.

Unit Writing Assignment

Project ten years into the future. Write about who you would like to be and what work you would like to be doing by then. Stick to standard English.

Here is how one student accomplished the assignment:

> <u>Ten years from now I would like to be a famous costume designer.</u> That is, I would like to be the kind of costume designer that movie studios hire to research what clothes people were wearing at a certain time in history. For instance, the movie <u>Gone with the Wind</u> required female gowns with lace bodices, taffeta petticoats, and broad-brimmed hats. It required male frock coats, stiff shirts, and top hats. I can't imagine a bigger thrill than to have my name called during an Academy Award ceremony and to be asked to walk up to the stage to receive an Oscar for the Best Costume Design. I see myself owning my own design studio, with dozens of helpers to execute my designs. But I would always do the mock-ups myself, to make sure that the details are perfect. This is my dream, but sometimes dreams come true, don't they?

Photo Writing Assignment

The following photo depicts a problem in our society. First discuss the problem in a small group, then, write about how you feel about this problem. Use only standard English.

3

How to Start Writing

Writing is always hardest at the beginning, when the page is blank. We start to write, find the going slow, and imagine our secret fears about our inability to write confirmed.

The truth is that for nearly everyone, writing is hard and slow work. The only solution to the slow start is to get started quickly. Once the words are flowing, self-doubt will give way to the practical business of writing.

In their working habits, writers tend to resemble baseball pitchers. For both, warming up is essential. Pitchers throw practice balls to flex their arms; similarly, writers warm up their writing skills by scribbling words on the page. Indeed, the longer you sit and write, the better you will gradually find yourself getting at it.

There are three things you can do to start yourself writing:

- Freewrite
- Brainstorm
- Cluster

All three activities will help you to warm up, get ideas, and arrive at a suitable writing topic.

Freewriting

A good warm-up exercise for the writer is freewriting. To **freewrite** is to write about a topic for a timed period of about ten minutes. Forget about grammar, spelling, and punctuation. Just sit and write freely. If you have nothing to say, write, "I have nothing to say," until you do say something. The result of such freewriting will be sense mixed with nonsense, but you'll gradually find yourself warming up to the topic.

Here is an example of student freewriting:

> I go to school every day. Then I go to work. I have no time for myself. It's rough. What'd I say now? I can't think of anything to say. That reminds me, I do my best thinking in the bathroom. I like to think in the bathroom because when you are in their you can close the door shut and everyone leaves you alone. I don't know what else to say. The cat keeps out of there and so do the dog. This sounds weird, but I tend to be a weird type of guy with a lot in my head some days. I hate going straight from school to work. I feel like I'm jumping from one planet to another. This is a really, really weird paragraph. I wish I was going to a movie with Maria tonight. She's good for getting my mind off school. But she gotta go to work too. So what can I say?

Notice that the paragraph contains many spelling and grammatical errors. For example, in the sentence, "*I* like to think in the bathroom because when *you* are in *their* you can close the door shut and everyone leaves you alone," the writer misuses *their* for *there*, and shifts the point of view from *I* to *you*. The sentence, "The cat keeps out of there and so *do* the dog," should really read, "The cat keeps out of there and so *does* the dog." These kinds of errors are normal and expected in freewriting.

The writer's thinking might also strike you as jumbled. Some of what he says makes sense—that he does his best thinking in the bathroom, for example—but other sentences seem to hop aimlessly from this to that. In freewriting this mix of sense and nonsense is always a good sign. It shows that you are writing and thinking freely, which is what you are supposed to do in a loosening-up exercise.

Your own attempts at freewriting should be similarly loose. Don't try to correct your mistakes, control your writing, or muzzle your thoughts. Freewriting should be as free and uncontrolled as a pitcher's warm-up tosses. The aim in both cases is the same: to warm up, whether the arm or the brain.

Keeping a Journal

A good way to practice your writing skills is to keep a journal. A **journal** is private writing intended for your eyes only. Regularly keeping a journal teaches some good habits. First, you'll get in the habit of writing freely without fear of criticism or disapproval. Second, keeping a journal can lead to surprising self-discovery. Often, writers do not really know how they feel about a topic until they try writing about it. You, may be surprised when you try to express your feelings in a journal to find out how you really feel about a topic. Finally, keeping a journal will get you into the habit of writing regularly. If you are like most students, you write mainly under pressure, for example, when you have to take a test or do an assignment. Anything done only under pressure can hardly be fun. Journal writing can at least get you used to the idea of writing as a means of relaxation rather than a constant source of stress.

IN A NUTSHELL

- Writing is hardest at the beginning.
- Warming up is critical for the writer.
- You can warm up by freewriting.
- Keeping a journal can help your writing.

PRACTICING 1

Freewrite for five to ten minutes on one of the topics below.

1. A favorite relative
2. Smells
3. A season of the year
4. A scary incident
5. Fantasies
6. Modern music
7. A movie
8. Your career hopes
9. A pet
10. Dating

Answers will vary.

PRACTICING 2

Fill up the freewriting box on page 34 with your own words. Use every line, even if you have to write a filler sentence such as, "I can't think of anything to write." Choose any topic.

Answers will vary.

_____

_____

_____

_____

_____

_____

_____

_____

_____

_____

_____

_____

_____

_____

PRACTICING 3

In this exercise, you're going to talk to yourself on paper, which is another way of saying that you'll be pretending to write a journal. Since you're writing basically for yourself, feel free to experiment and to get your feelings off your chest. Whatever you write will be read by no one else. Get in the habit of writing for yourself regularly, and you'll find it easier to write on more formal occasions.

Answers will vary.

Since this writing exercise is intended only for your eyes, you may say anything you want to and in any way you wish. You may simply tell how the day went, jotting down its highlights and low points. Or, if you can't think of anything to say, you may write your thoughts down about one of these topics:

- Something that was most significant about the day

- Something boring you did

- Something you saw

- An argument you had with someone today

Brainstorming

The aim of freewriting is just to get you writing. Once you're warmed up and ready to write, you need to focus on finding ideas to put down on paper. One especially good technique for finding ideas is brainstorming.

Brainstorming is an exercise in thinking. You list every thought that pops into your head about a subject. Jot down words and phrases. Don't try to write in sentences or worry about logic, style, punctuation, and grammar. Above all, don't judge your ideas as they flow onto the page. Later, after the storm has passed, you can decide which ideas are worthwhile. Here is an example of brainstorming on "my neighborhood":

noisy

lots of traffic

corner stores

people don't know one another

there're few trees

a city worker told me an oak on the corner was a hundred years
    old

most people take the bus to work

a few drive cars

the houses are old

some are 70 years old

my grandparents used to live in our house

we have three bedrooms

a park is down the street

many old people live there

Mrs. Ramirez is 90

Mr. Goldstein is 82

at least my parents own their home

I wished I lived in the country

Brainstorming produces a random list of ideas. When you are finished brainstorming, look over the ideas scribbled on the page and find out what you really think about the topic. As we said earlier, odd as it may seem, many writers learn what they really think about a topic only when they try writing about it.

For example, this student noticed that she kept mentioning the age of her neighborhood in her brainstorming session. Up to then, she hadn't really consciously thought about its age. She decided to write a paragraph on the age of her neighborhood, using as examples its ancient oak tree and elderly homes and residents. Brainstorming will often give you this kind of new slant on a topic.

Brainstorming is the technique of freely jotting down ideas about a topic.

PRACTICING 4

Brainstorm on one or more of the topics below. Don't worry about grammar or logic. Simply write down any idea that comes to mind.

1. Your girlfriend, boyfriend, spouse, child, parent, or sibling

2. Work

3. A favorite book or magazine

4. Winter clothing

5. Your favorite class

6. Why you love (or hate) English class

7. Coping

8. Not coping

9. Favorite sport

10. An ideal vacation

Answers will vary.

Clustering

Clustering is thinking with the help of a diagram. As with brainstorming, you don't worry about grammar or wording. You simply think about your subject or topic, writing down your ideas in circles.

One aim of clustering is to narrow a broad subject into a manageable topic. For some strange reason, it is always harder to find things to say about a big topic than about a smaller one. For example, what can you say about the broad subject of friendship? That it is good, that everyone should have a friend? Everyone already knows and admits all that. On the other hand, try writing about your friend Joe or Pamela and the examples and details will probably gush out of you in a flood: the time Joe helped you to fix your car, or the day Pamela lent you $100.

Clustering is a technique that can help you narrow a broad subject, such as friendship, to a manageable topic, such as your friend Joe. Here is how it works. You begin by writing down the main word of the topic and circling it. From this core word, you draw spokes. Then you write down any other ideas that come to mind. On page 37 is a student cluster about friendship.

Clustering goes a step beyond brainstorming because it groups— clusters—related ideas. You take the big subject in the middle and reduce it to a smaller idea that you put at the end of a spoke. From this smaller idea, you can branch off another idea that is even smaller. Eventually, you will not only find an idea small enough to be a manageable topic, you will also find you have much to say about it. For example, in the clustering diagram below, *"Why Andrea is my best friend"* is a manageable topic. The circles branching off from this topic suggest details you can use in a paragraph or essay on it

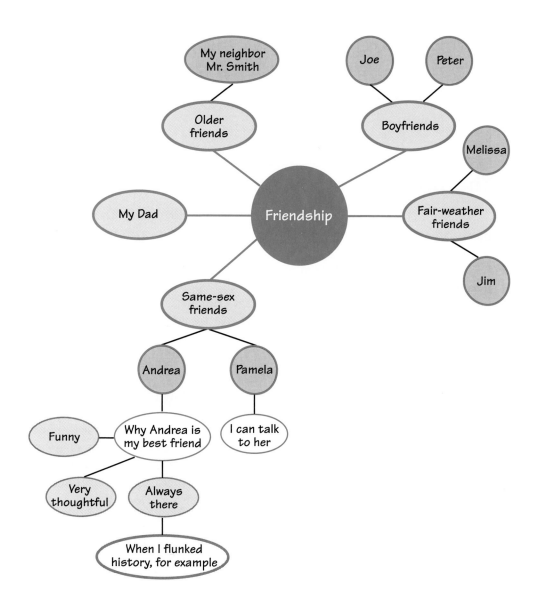

IN A NUTSHELL

Clustering is using a diagram to think about your topic.

PRACTICING 5

Do a cluster on one of the topics below.

1. Lovers
2. Malls
3. Cars
4. Runaway kids
5. Advertising
6. Graduation requirements
7. Instructors
8. Politics
9. Housework
10. Money

The Topic Sentence

You have a topic, some ideas about it, and are now ready to write your paragraph. How do you begin? You begin at the beginning—by writing a topic sentence.

The **topic sentence** is a single sentence that sums up the main point of your paragraph. It is usually the opening sentence and must not be a dry, narrow statement of fact. Rather, it should have a **discussible edge** that gives you something to write about. Here is an example of a weak and a good topic sentence:

Weak: I own a blue Honda Civic.
Good: A Honda Civic is an ideal car for a student.

A weak topic sentence is a dead end and difficult to write about. For example, after you say you own a blue Honda Civic, what else can you say? Nothing comes to mind without head-scratching effort.

On the other hand, notice the momentum in this topic sentence, "A Honda Civic is an ideal car for a student." The question "Why?" immediately comes to mind, and you could easily write a paragraph answering it. You could also write about what you mean by an "ideal car." Many other possibilities exist.

How can you tell if your topic sentence is discussible enough for a paragraph? You tell by using your common sense. If your topic sentence offers nothing to discuss, you'll have trouble writing the paragraph. You'll suffer head-scratching and pen-chewing, and find yourself digging for something to say. The obvious thing to do when you see these signs is to rewrite your topic sentence.

ESL Advice!

Be sure to use the full verb and correct tense in your topic sentence. Don't leave out important articles in front of nouns. (Study Unit 6.)

NOT THIS: My auntie, Pham Phong, live through the hell of watch her village destroyed during the Vietnam War.

BUT THIS: My auntie, Pham Phong, lived through the hell of watching her village being destroyed during the Vietnam War.

NOT THIS: From her home in Darjeeling, I had beautiful view of Kanchenjunga, one of tallest mountains in world.

BUT THIS: From my home in Darjeeling, I had a beautiful view of Kanchenjunga, one of the tallest mountains in the world.

IN A NUTSHELL

The topic sentence of a paragraph should make a discussible point.

PRACTICING 6

Circle the topic sentence in each group that would be easiest to write a paragraph about.

1. **(a).** Hamburger is a surprisingly nourishing food.
   (b). Last week I ate a hamburger.
   (c). That hamburger looks old.

2. **(a).** The primary school is in an adobe building.
   (b). You get out of school what you put into it.
   (c). I went to school yesterday.

3. **(a).** Scouting builds character.
   (b). The Scout told me he was happy.
   (c). I have a Tenderfoot scouting badge.

4. **(a).** The trail goes through the Sierra Madre Mountains.
   (b). Rain falls every day in the Sierra Madres.
   (c). The Sierra Madre Mountains are a hiker's paradise.

5. **(a).** She told me a lie.
   (b). There are three kinds of lies.
   (c). They repeated her lie.

PRACTICING 7

Below are some topics for paragraphs. Write a weak and a good topic sentence on each.

1. Topic: Television shows

Weak topic sentence: _____

I've seen a lot of television shows.

Good topic sentence: _____

Some television shows should not be seen by children.

2. Topic: Credit cards

Weak topic sentence: _____

I have two credit cards.

Good topic sentence: _____

Using credit cards too often can get you into trouble.

3. Topic: Professional athletes

Weak topic sentence: _____

Gregg Maddux is a professional athlete.

Good topic sentence: _____

Professional athletes earn too much money.

4. Topic: Housework

Weak topic sentence: _____

I do housework on Saturdays.

Good topic sentence: _____

Housework can be great exercise.

5. Topic: A Halloween memory

Weak topic sentence: _____

Once I was a clown on Halloween.

Good topic sentence: _____

The year I was ten, my brother gave me the scariest Halloween of my life.

6. Topic: Messy roommates

Weak topic sentence: _____

I had a messy roommate once.

Good topic sentence: _____

Messy roommates can be bad for your love life.

7. Topic: Wearing seat belts

Weak topic sentence: _____

There are laws about wearing seatbelts.

Good topic sentence: _____

It should be our choice whether or not to wear seatbelts.

8. Topic: Junk food

Weak topic sentence: _____

I like junk food.

Good topic sentence: _____

Americans should stop eating so much junk food.

9. Topic: Tattoos

Weak topic sentence: _____

Tattoos are pictures drawn with ink under the skin.

Good topic sentence: _____

People who get tattoos are rebelling against society.

10. Topic: Restaurants

Weak topic sentence: _____

There are good restaurants and bad restaurants.

Good topic sentence: _____

A good restaurant should have good service as well as good food.

Unit Test

Underline the word(s) in parentheses that best completes the meaning of the sentence.

Example: Free writing is writing (free from personal worries/<u>without paying attention to grammar, punctuation, or spelling</u>).

1. Writing is always most difficult when you are trying to find a (<u>beginning</u>/ending).

2. If you want to find ideas for writing, you might use (fiddling with your pencil/<u>brainstorming</u>) as a helpful technique.

3. One helpful way to get started writing is to use a diagram to think about your topic. This technique is called (outlining/<u>clustering</u>).

4. Like most athletes, writers need to (<u>warm up</u>/take vitamin pills).

5. Once your writing flows, (your confidence will decrease/<u>your confidence will increase</u>).

6. The topic sentence of a paragraph (hints at what you have to say/<u>sums up the main point of your paragraph</u>).

7. "A hammer is used for hitting nails" is (excellent/<u>weak</u>) as a topic sentence.

8. The best kind of topic sentence is one (<u>that has a discussible *edge*</u>/ that appeals to you).

9. A weak topic sentence is one that (opens many possibilities for writing about it/<u>leads to a dead end</u>).

10. "Being lost in a foreign city is a frightening experience" makes a good topic sentence because (you need not say anything more/<u>it cries out for further explanation</u>).

Unit Talk-Write Assignment

Answers may vary.

The Talk column on the left contains sentences from a student's conversation with a friend about writing. The selection includes nonstandard phrases and irrelevant material. Re-write the sentences in the blanks provided under Write, making sure that you use standard English and that you stick to the point of what helps writing.

TALK

WRITE

1. I used to think writing was a bummer.

1. *I used to think writing was unpleasant.*

2. But biology is even worse than writing.

2. *Correct but irrelevant*

3. Brainstorming has helped me fight my fear of writing because it's such an awesome feeling suddenly to get ideas that might work.

3. *Brainstorming has helped me fight my fear of writing because it's such a wonderful feeling to get sudden ideas that might work.*

4. When other students whine, "I'm going to crash on this assignment," I tell them to chill cause writing ain't as bad as they think.

4. *When other students whine, "I'm going to fail this assignment," I tell them to relax because writing isn't as bad as they think.*

5. My roommate Jeff, whose a terrific athlete, used to freak out when he had to write an essay.

5. *My roommate Jeff, who's a terrific athlete, used to get very upset when he had to write an essay.*

6. But I showed him how to brainstorm, and now he thinks he's a hot shot writer.

6. *But I showed him how to brainstorm, and now he thinks he's a superior writer.*

TALK	WRITE
7. Brainstorming is better than freewriting because you got to concentrate on one topic.	**7.** *Brainstorming is better than freewriting because you have to concentrate on one topic.*
8. If I freewrite, I don't get nowhere because I blabber all over the place, and I just keep saying, "I can't think of nothing to say."	**8.** *If I freewrite, I don't get anywhere because I write about all kinds of different things, and I also keep writing, "I can't think of anything to say."*
9. Clustering is just flat out too logical and tangled up.	**9.** *Clustering is just too logical and disorganized.*
10. I got me a B on my last essay because I got some good ideas brainstorming on the topic of white lies. I am beginning to kinda like writing.	**10.** *I earned a B on my last essay because I had some good ideas brainstorming on the topic of white lies. I am beginning to like writing.*

Unit Collaborative Assignment

Get together with a partner and brainstorm on two of the subjects listed below.

1. Summertime memories
2. Role models
3. Anger
4. Stress
5. Television commercials

Unit Writing Assignment

Choose one of the above subjects that you brainstormed about and cluster if necessary to produce a manageable topic. Then write about it, beginning with a discussible topic sentence. Here is how one student handled the topic about role models:

Brainstorming Role Models

Mark Rettig is a good choice

he's pretty old, but that's O.K.O

nobody has influenced me more--he's like a grandpa

he grew up during the Depression--attended Catholic school--

made him serious

he used to scrap broken-down cars for salvage metal (always

    carried hammers, axes, picks, and crowbars)

he experimented with crystal radio set

owned a venetian blind shop

Dad and he carved me toys out of scrap lumber

I loved Mark's wife--a sweet, chubby lady--cupboard full

    of candy

they've been married for 52 years.

He should slow down, but he doesn't

dedicated cabinet maker--clock and trunk

his precision and care inspire me still

a real craftsman

Paragraph

    My friend, Mark Rettig, will always be an inspiration to me, no matter what career I choose. He is seventy-four years old and has been like my grandfather. He is a short man, about five feet four with wavy white hair. He is usually wearing a plaid, short-sleeved button-down shirt when I visit him. Mark grew up during the Depression. For most of his life he owned and operated a venetian blind shop. One of my fondest memories is visiting this shop, where Mark and my dad would make wonderful wooden toys from scraps of wood. In his spare time, Mark creates beautiful cabinet work. His living room displays an elegant grandfather clock, which he made. He also restored an old trunk for my family; it now sits proudly in our living room, housing all kinds of pictures and old keepsakes. What continues to inspire me about Mark is the way he carefully explained his methods of woodworking to me. He has taught me to work carefully and painstakingly on all of my projects, whether physical or intellectual. He has inspired me to be a real craftsman.

Photo Writing Assignment

Carefully study the photograph below. Try to get a feel for the way the grandparent and grandchild are interacting. On a separate sheet of paper, brainstorm possible benefits of having caring grandparents.

4

Moving from Sentences to Paragraphs

"What kinds of supporting details do paragraph writers most often use? That depends on the topic sentence."

A typical paragraph consists of two main parts: a topic sentence and supporting details. The topic sentence is the sentence—usually the opening one—that states the main point of the paragraph. Supporting details are sentences that back up this main point with specifics.

Here is a typical paragraph, with the topic sentence underlined:

> <u>The Greek Orthodox Church believes in seven sacraments.</u> They are Holy Baptism, Holy Chrism, Holy Communion, Holy Confession, Holy Marriage, Holy Unction, and Holy Orders. Holy Baptism is the sacrament that cleanses Greek Orthodox Christians of guilt from personal and original sin. Holy Chrism safeguards the baptized against temptations of the future. Holy Communion is the physical intake of the body and blood of Christ. In Holy Confession, done in the church before a priest, the sinner begs for God's forgiveness for sin. Holy Marriage unites a man and woman under the grace of God. Holy Unction is given to the sick and dying, whereas Holy Orders inducts a man into the priesthood. Baptism, Chrism, Communion, and Confession are required of all Greek Orthodox Christians; Marriage, Unction, and Orders, however, are optional.

How important is the topic sentence? Try reading this same paragraph without it.

Without the topic sentence, the paragraph is merely a collection of facts. Without the supporting details, on the other hand, we have merely an unproved sentence:

The Greek Orthodox Church believes in seven sacraments.

The topic sentence and supporting details, then, go hand-in-hand. In the previous unit we talked about the topic sentence. In this one we will discuss supporting details.

Supporting Details

What kinds of supporting details do paragraph writers most often use? That depends on the topic sentence. A good topic sentence suggests the kinds of details needed for its support. Basically, there are five kinds of supporting details:

1. Examples

2. Facts

3. Testimony

4. Reason

5. Personal observation

We'll cover each type of supporting detail separately.

Examples

An **example** is a part used to represent the whole. You say that working at Joe's Diner is hard. Someone asks, "What do you mean by hard?" You say, "Employees must work 12-hour shifts without a break." Working long hours without a break is one example that supports your point.

The example is an effective supporting detail that is used as often by writers as by speakers. Here is an example from a student paragraph on hazing in fraternities:

> Hazing is a dangerous and humiliating ritual. For example, a friend at another university told me about a pledge who was hospitalized with broken ribs after being beaten during hazing. In my own case, I was commanded to drink excessively, appear in boxer shorts at an alumni function, and run stupid late-night errands for brothers. This hazing made me feel so humiliated that I withdrew my pledgeship.

To use examples, simply introduce them with a suitable phrase, such as *for example, for instance,* or *take the case of,* and then spell out the example you have in mind.

Naturally, any example you use should support your point. For instance, Joe's Diner may have a wonderful employee training program, but mentioning that won't support your point that working at Joe's Diner is hard.

PRACTICING 1

Write two appropriate examples that support the following topic sentences. Answers will vary.

1. Topic sentence: Blue jeans have become our culture's fashion statement.

First example: _____

_____

Second example: _____

_____

2. Topic sentence: The pressures to conform are as strong in college as they are in high school.

First example: _____

_____

Second example: _____

_____

3. Topic sentence: Sometimes it hurts to tell the truth.

First example: _____

_____

Second example: _____

_____

4. Topic sentence: Some people are extremely busy.

First example: _____

_____

Second example: _____

_____

5. Topic sentence: Autumn is a beautiful time of year.

First example: _____

_____

Second example: _____

_____

Facts

A **fact** is a statement that is true or can be verified. Anyone who is curious can look up the statement in a proper source and confirm its truth. For instance, the fact that George Washington was born on February 22, 1732, can be confirmed by checking an encyclopedia or any biography of our first president. Some facts are simply accepted by everyone because they have never been proven untrue. That sooner or later all humans die is one such fact.

The opposite of a fact is an **opinion.** Unlike a fact, an opinion is a personal belief, often accompanied by emotion, that cannot be proved either true or false. Here are some examples of facts and opinions:

Accepted Fact: The sun will always rise in the East.

Verifiable Fact: John Steinbeck wrote *Of Mice and Men.*

Opinion: Steinbeck's best book is *Of Mice and Men.*

That the sun rises in the east is a universally accepted fact, and every morning nature again confirms its truth. Anyone can look up who wrote *Of Mice and Men,* and every book consulted will give the same answer: John Steinbeck wrote it. It is not universally accepted that *Of Mice and Men* is Steinbeck's best book. Some readers will argue that *East of Eden* is his best book, whereas others will just as strongly make that claim for *Grapes of Wrath.* The third statement is therefore an opinion because it is not universally accepted like the first nor verifiable like the second.

Here is a paragraph that supports its topic sentence with facts:

> <u>Textbooks at Becky's Bookstore are cheaper than they are at the Student Union.</u> My sociology text at the Student Union store was $35. I found the same text at Becky's Bookstore for $30. The text required for my public speaking class was $19.95 at the Student Union but $17.50 at Becky's. Likewise, I paid $4 less for my Psychology 100 text at Becky's than I would have at the Student Union. These cheaper prices are why I buy my books at Becky's.

Properly cited, facts add believability to a paragraph. Of course, you must always be sure that your facts are indeed facts and not opinions. Ask yourself, can a reader look up this statement and confirm its truth? If not, the statement is an opinion, not a fact.

Unfortunately, writers seldom have at their fingertips all the facts they need to write about a particular topic. Most of the time, writers have to dig up facts before they can begin writing. Digging up facts may involve interviewing specific people or even conducting a mini-survey. Some of your assignments may require you to interview certain professors or your fellow students. If you have access to a computer, the Internet is another rich source of facts.

But overall, the best place for finding facts is the library. Reference books found there, such as encyclopedias, are literally brimming with helpful facts on nearly every topic. Moreover, many libraries are staffed by friendly librarians who can help you find facts on almost anything. All you have to do is ask.

PRACTICING 2

From the pairs of sentences that follow, indicate the sentence that is a fact, not an opinion.
Example:

___✔___ **(a).** My grandmother, who lives with us, was diagnosed as having Alzheimer's, a disease that affects some 4 million Americans.

_____ **(b).** Alzheimer's disease is just the most horrendous, awful curse because it places an unbearable burden on everyone in the family.

1. _____ **(a).** A more enticing place to see than the town market of Ciudad Rodrigo, with its heavenly fresh vegetables, can't be imagined.

___✔___ **(b).** Ciudad Rodrigo sponsors a market every Tuesday in the town square, where the farmers sell baskets of vegetables with the dark, damp soil still clinging to their roots.

2. ___✔___ **(a).** To be called a cathedral, a church must contain a bishop's see and his official throne.

_____ **(b).** Cathedrals are boringly alike all over the world always smelling musky and filled with ugly old crypts.

3. _____ **(a).** Izzy's hamburgers are mouthwateringly delicious and should win a prize for being the best hamburgers in the city.

___✔___ **(b).** Izzy's menu offers four different kinds of hamburgers: mushroom, ground turkey, vegetarian, and pineapple.

4. _____ **(a).** Let's face it, people today don't seem to care at all whether or not they can support themselves once they have retired from work.

___✔___ **(b).** According to the Employee Benefits Research Institute 2001 survey, only 15% of 1,000 adults had $100,000 or more in savings despite a decade-long bull market.

5. ___✔___ **(a).** The Duncan Clark Company is manufacturing and distributing an invisible fence that conditions dogs to stay within a market area by giving them a light shock when they stray.

_____ **(b).** A company that sells some kind of contraption to shock dogs in order to keep them from bothering freshly planted flower beds should be hauled into court.

PRACTICING 3

Support the following topic sentences with at least three facts. You may need to interview or survey classmates or visit your library.

1.   Topic sentence: The students in my English class come from many different backgrounds. (Or, The students in my English class come mainly from the same background.)

First fact: _____

_____

Second fact: _____

_____

Third fact: _____

_____

2.   Topic sentence: The college library has an adequate book collection and excellent facilities. (Or, The college library has an inadequate book collection and poor facilities.)

First fact: _____

_____

Second fact: _____

_____

Third fact: _____

_____

3.   Topic sentence: An automobile is expensive to run and maintain.

First fact: _____

_____

Second fact: _____

_____

Third fact: _____

_____

4.   Topic sentence: Body piercing is an attempt to make a cultural statement.

First fact: _____

_____

Second fact: _____

_____

Third fact: _____

_____

Testimony

Testimony is expert opinion that backs up your topic sentence. The expert may be someone who is recognized in the field or who has had personal experience with your topic. Getting the testimony you need may require you to check a newspaper or interview the right people. Here is a paragraph that has both kinds of testimony—the personal experience and expert opinion.

> <u>If you are stopped by the police for a traffic violation, there are some things you should not do.</u> You should not, for one, get out of your car unless the officer asks you to. My friend Joe was pulled over by the police late one night on a lonely city street and he got out of the car, thinking that it would make him seem friendly. It had the opposite effect on the officer. Joe says she put her hand on her gun and ordered him to get back into the car. He said he was afraid she would shoot him. Officer Yankers of the campus police says a motorist who gets out of the car without being told is considered a threat. Says Officer Yankers, "I'm always cautious when a motorist gets out of the car and walks toward me. I think he's being aggressive."

As testimony, the writer quotes his friend's personal experience as well as the expert opinion of Officer Yankers.

PRACTICING 4

Cite at least two opinions as testimony, supporting the following topic sentences.

Answers will vary.

1. Topic sentence: When you're in college, parents should treat you like an adult, not a child.

First opinion: _____

_____

Second opinion: _____

_____

2.   Topic sentence: To encourage customer loyalty, managers require store clerks and restaurant servers to be more courteous and helpful to customers.

First opinion: _____

_____

Second opinion: _____

_____

3.   Topic sentence: Working your way through college can be a stressful experience.

First opinion: _____

_____

Second opinion: _____

_____

4.   Topic sentence: Children who are not loved are at risk of becoming social misfits.

First opinion: _____

_____

Second opinion: _____

_____

5.   Topic sentence: Patriotism should be quietly felt, not broadcast like a virtue.

First opinion: _____

_____

Second opinion: _____

Reasons

Some topic sentences are best supported by **reasons**—explanations based on common sense, good judgment, clear thinking, and logic. This kind of support is most commonly used when a writer is trying to persuade the reader to change an opinion.

In the following paragraph, reason is used to support the writer's argument that cafeteria food should be prepared on campus and not by off-campus caterers.

<u>Cafeteria food should be prepared in campus kitchens, not trucked in by off-campus caterers.</u> Common sense tells us that a sandwich made to order and served immediately is going to taste

fresher and better than one made miles away and trucked to the campus for sale. Even if the sandwich is prepared elsewhere the same day, it's going to lose some of its taste in being refrigerated and transported. Fresh food tastes better because it's fresh, not half-fresh. If we want better cafeteria food, we should insist that it's prepared on campus, where it is eaten.

Not every topic sentence can be supported by reason. However for those topic sentences that can be—and your common sense should be the judge—reason can be highly effective support.

PRACTICING 5

Use reasons to support one of the following topic sentences.

Answers will vary.

1. Topic sentence: In cases of murder, capital punishment makes sense.

_____

_____

_____

_____

_____

_____

_____

_____

2. Topic sentence: Capital punishment does not stop murder.

_____

_____

_____

_____

_____

_____

_____

_____

Personal observation

Some topics are strictly personal and must be supported mainly by your own personal observation. That old stand-by topic, "Write about how you spent your summer vacation," is a classic example of a personal topic. Unless he or she vacationed with you, no librarian can help you find support for it. You must draw entirely on your own personal observations for support.

Personal observation includes descriptive details and examples. Here is an example of both in a paragraph:

> <u>Last summer I spent a week hiking and discovered that I hate it.</u> To begin with, we got caught in a two-day rain on the Appalachian Trail. The tent turned out not to be waterproof, and for one whole night I tried to sleep with water dripping on my nose. When I moved, it dripped on my belly. I turned over, and it dripped on my butt. I also found out that aside from weather problems, hiking is unhealthy for you. For example, I ate so poorly for the week that I was starving and pigged-out afterward on hamburger and French fries for a month. So I ended up gaining weight. Next time I go camping, it'll be in a Winnebago.

The details this writer uses are not available in any library but come solely from memory. Paragraphs written on such topics as a favorite place, a special friend, or the first day on a new job must be similarly supported by such personal observations.

IN A NUTSHELL

The supporting details of a paragraph typically consist of examples, facts, testimony, reasons, and personal observations.

PRACTICING 6

Answers will vary.

Develop a topic sentence on one of the following subjects and write a paragraph about it, supporting the topic sentence with personal observations.

1. A favorite time of the year for my family

2. My best vacation

3. An incident that changed me in some way

4. My first broken heart

5. A beautiful (or ugly) scene I shall always remember

 **Unit Test**

In the blank provided, place a mark in front of the letter of the phrase that most accurately completes the sentence.

Example: A typical paragraph consists of

    _____ **(a).** a title and an opening sentence.

    __✔__ **(b).** a topic sentence and details.

    _____ **(c).** adjectives and nouns.

    _____ **(d).** details and questions.

1. Supporting details are sentences that

    _____ **(a).** should rarely be used.

    _____ **(b).** confuse the reader.

    _____ **(c).** create a verbal picture.

    __✔__ **(d).** back up the main point.

2. The kinds of details to use depend on

    __✔__ **(a).** what kind of topic sentence you wrote.

    _____ **(b).** how you feel about your subject.

    _____ **(c).** the reader's level of education.

    _____ **(d).** the length of your paragraph.

3. Which of the following is NOT suggested as a kind of supporting detail:

    _____ **(a).** example

    _____ **(b).** fact

    __✔__ **(c).** hint

    _____ **(d).** personal observation

4. Which of the following examples does NOT support this topic sentence: "Climbing a ladder can be dangerous":

    _____ **(a).** One of the rungs in the ladder could break, causing you to fall.

    __✔__ **(b).** Today most ladders are made of metal.

    _____ **(c).** The ladder could be placed on wet ground, causing it to slip.

    _____ **(d).** The ladder may be old and rickety.

5. Which of the following statements is a verifiable fact:

_____ **(a).** Mrs. Smith is a delightful woman.

_____ **(b).** My teacher doesn't know beans about what he's teaching.

_✔_ **(c).** James Garfield served as President of the United States in 1881.

_____ **(d).** Beauty and the Beast is the best cartoon ever made.

6. Expert testimony is a good way to back up a topic sentence because

_____ **(a).** courts like to use it in medical cases.

_____ **(b).** the expert must swear to tell the truth.

_____ **(c).** this kind of testimony is rare and therefore valuable.

_✔_ **(d).** it comes from someone who is recognized in the field.

7. Which of the following is NOT a reason that could be used in support of the topic sentence "Aspirin has long been recognized as having both good and dangerous effects":

_____ **(a).** The history of the aspirin goes back to the year 200 B.C.

_____ **(b).** Aspirin is actually salicyclic acid, which, in its pure form, is capable of burning a hole in the stomach.

_✔_ **(c).** I take aspirin because it helps me when I get a headache.

_____ **(d).** Many pediatricians advise against baby aspirin for their patients because it has been linked to a rare but dangerous condition in children called Reyes syndrome.

8. The topic sentence "My boss is a hard-nosed business man" can probably best be supported by

_✔_ **(a).** personal observation

_____ **(b).** logic

_____ **(c).** good judgment

_____ **(d).** reasoning

9. Which method of support does this topic sentence call for: "No one should complain about giving welfare to people who are handicapped or down on their luck."

_____ **(a).** personal observation

_____ **(b).** facts

_____ **(c).** reason

_✔_ **(d).** all of the above

10. How important is the topic sentence to students who must write?

_____ **(a).** not important except when you use a computer.

_____ **(b).** important only to English majors.

___✔___ **(c).** important because it makes a point the writer can then support.

_____ **(d).** as important as having a readable handwriting. ○

Unit Talk-Write Assignment

In the blanks provided under the Write column, rewrite the Talk column sentences to remove any nonstandard expressions and to include only details that support the topic sentence. Omit any sentence that does not support the topic.

Topic sentence: More and more adults are going back to college in the United States.

TALK

1. I've got to quit goofing off and get this assignment done.

2. According to what I read in the *L.A. Times* last Sunday, the number of students 25 or over has gone up by 10% since 1984.

WRITE

1. *OMIT* _____

_____

_____

_____

_____

2. *Correct* _____

_____

_____

_____

_____

_____

TALK

WRITE

3. After rapping with several older students on campus, I figured out the three main reasons for returning to college later in life: to make more bucks, to make up for losing a job as a result of quick company changes, or just to learn.

3. *After speaking with several older students on campus, I understood the three main reasons for returning to college later in life: to earn more money, to retrain after losing a job as a result of quick company changes, or just to learn.*

4. Well, I have to say that my gut feeling is that these older students generally make the classes more competitive for people like me.

4. *I believe that these older students generally make the classes more competitive for younger students like me.*

5. For instance, a 31-year-old guy in my econ class, who works full time in a bank, told me that he starts his homework around eight every night and hits the books until midnight.

5. *For instance, a 31-year-old man in my economics class, who works full time in a bank, told me that he starts his homework around eight every night and studies until midnight.*

6. Wow! That kind of motivation frosts me because he's going to mess up my A or B by screwing up the grade curve.

6. *That kind of motivation bothers me because he's going to hurt my chances of getting an A or B by raising the grade curve.*

7. Dr. Brenda Fillmore, who is the head honcho of the Foreign Language Department, swears she loves having the older students in her class because they're so gung ho about studying.

7. *Dr. Brenda Fillmore, who is the head of the Foreign Language Department, claims she loves having the older students in her class because they're so enthusiastic about studying.*

TALK	WRITE
8. What else can I say?	**8.** *OMIT* _____
	_____
	_____
	_____
	_____
	_____
9. Well, I guess I gotta admit I really admire these old dudes—and lady dudes—who return to college.	**9.** *I must admit I really admire these older men and*
	women who return to college.
	_____
	_____
	_____
	_____
10. I sure hope these guys will give me a push—I could use it.	**10.** *I hope these people will help me. I could definitely*
	use some help.
	_____
	_____
	_____
	_____

Unit Collaborative Assignment

Get together with two or three students in the class and talk out a paragraph on each of the following topic sentences. Discuss what types of supporting details the topic sentence requires and suggest some specific details that could be used. Make note of what kinds of supporting statements—examples, facts, testimony, reasons, or observations—were suggested in your discussion.

1. Today's new cars incorporate many useful safety features.

2. Students must often write under great pressure.

3. Everyone should play a sport.

4. Doctors are too quick to give people drugs.

5. Pets are a comfort to many people.

6. Some television commercials border on bad taste.

7. Housecleaning should be a unisex chore.

8. American-made cars are not better than foreign models.

9. Good health depends on taking responsibility for yourself.

10. Couples should not marry until they are 25.

 Unit Writing Assignment

Write about one of the topics that follow. Come up with a discussible topic sentence and support it with appropriate examples, facts, testimony, reasons, or personal details. Follow these steps:

1. Choose the topic.

2. Warm up by freewriting.

3. Gather ideas by brainstorming

4. Narrow the subject to a manageable topic by clustering.

If you aren't happy with your topic at this point, put away what you've done and choose another topic and repeat the listed steps.

Then write your topic sentence. Check it by asking these questions:

(a). Is it discussible or is it too dry and narrow?

(b). What kinds of supporting details does it need?

Now write about one of these topics:

1. An exciting place

2. Student jobs

3. The importance of high school GPAs

4. Being a teenager *or* living with a teenager

5. A major league sport

6. My career goals

7. Coping with loneliness or fear

8. The importance of learning geography or a foreign language

9. Local politics

10. Movies

This is how one student completed the assignment:

<u>During my recovery from mononucleosis in junior high, I discovered the power of fantasy to help me handle loneliness.</u> I had to spend lots of time in bed. I felt so weak I could hardly even walk. Every day I got out an atlas and looked up a map of a foreign country. Then I would lie back and imagine myself in that country. Using my imagination, I went on a tiger hunt in India. I went surfing in Australia (even wiping out once). I saw the steppes of Russia during a blizzard, and I went swimming on the beaches of Barbados. My mother used to come in the room, see me lying there staring at the ceiling, and ask me if I felt all right. One day I said to her, "Mom, watch out for the cobra," and she looked worried and asked me if she should call the doctor. That was a long time ago. Nowadays I hardly have time for fantasy. But I know that if I ever have time on my hands again, it'll pass quickly if I just settle back and let my imagination roam.

Photo Writing Assignment

The following photo shows a politician campaigning for office. Write about why you think political campaigns are (or are not) effective in giving voters the information they need to vote for the candidate who will best represent their own political views. Write a discussible topic sentence, then prove it with appropriate details.

5

Writing a Solid Paragraph

"The sentences of a true paragraph always function to make a common point. They are like horses linked together to pull a cart in the same direction."

We write in paragraphs—everyone knows that. What is less well known is that we tend to talk in paragraphs, too. For example, here is a "paragraph" we overheard:

The Redskins outplayed the Cowboys by a mile in yesterday's game. For one thing, the Redskins' defense was great. Emmett Smith didn't even gain 50 yards. Every time he had the ball, he was swarmed by the Redskins' linebackers. Then there was the Redskins' offense. Their running back gained over a hundred yards, and their special team returned two punts to the Cowboys' 20-yard line. I just think Dallas is overrated.

This could be called a spoken paragraph because it does everything a good written paragraph does. First, it announces its topic—the Dallas versus Washington football game—and makes a point about it. Second, it sticks to that point. Third, it tries to prove the point with reasons and examples. Finally, all its sentences are linked together so that it is easy to follow the speaker's train of thought.

To write a solid paragraph, therefore, you should do the following:

- Begin with a discussible point.

- Stick to the point.

- Prove the point; don't merely repeat it.

- Link your sentences to make your ideas easy to follow.

Begin with a Discussible Point

Some clever writers can write a paragraph about anything, even a pin. Most of us, though, need a discussible topic sentence before we can write a good paragraph. Here is an example of a paragraph without a discussible topic sentence:

> The clock in the kitchen is broken. It broke last year. It stopped at 10:25 a.m. My father tried to repair it but couldn't. My mother hit it with a broom. Before it broke, it ran fast. Now it doesn't run at all.

This paragraph is meaningless because the writer has no topic sentence and consequently no point. A discussable point is a statement that immediately calls for further explanation. Here is the rewritten paragraph with a topic sentence added:

> <u>My father and mother react differently to household problems.</u> For example, when the clock in the kitchen broke, my father tried to repair it. He sat down at the kitchen table and took it apart. He worked on it for nearly an hour but couldn't get it to run. So he put it together again and put it back on the wall. My mother, on the other hand, got mad and hit the clock with a broom. Another time she threw her purse at it. Finally, she broke it open with her shoe. Then the two of them went out and bought another clock.

PRACTICING 1

Place a plus (+) beside the sentences that would be good discussible topic sentences and a minus (–) beside those that lead nowhere.

1. __–__ Autumn leaves are often multicolored.

2. __+__ As a child, I always had fun on Sundays.

3. __–__ An F grade means failure.

4. __–__ A travel iron is used to iron clothes while traveling.

5. __+__ My CD player is one of my most valuable possessions.

6. __–__ To memorize means to commit facts to memory.

7. __+__ I have discovered three ways to manage my time.

8. __+__ Extracurricular activities enrich college life.

9. __–__ Bunk beds save space.

10. __+__ The single life has many drawbacks.

PRACTICING 2

Turn each sentence in Practicing 1 that you marked with a minus (–) into a discussible topic sentence.

Answers will vary.

_____

_____

_____

_____

_____

_____

_____

Stick to the Point

A block of print on the page is not necessarily a paragraph just because it looks like one. Consider this example:

> Basketball Coach Burns is the exact opposite of what a good coach should be. The Type A personality is always nervous about something. Sailing is my favorite hobby. My mother saves anything—money, string, even rubber bands. This winter was unusually cold.

This block of print only looks like a paragraph because its first sentence is indented. But it isn't really one. Its sentences do not function like the sentences of a paragraph; they are not linked to make a common point. Rather, each sentence is like a horse galloping in a different direction. The sentences of a true paragraph, on the other hand, always function to make a common point. They are like horses pulling a cart in the same direction.

If you begin to write a paragraph about bass fishing, stick only to bass fishing. Save all your other thoughts for another paragraph. Here is an example of a paragraph that drifts from the point:

> <u>Bass fishing is a popular sport in the South.</u> Fishermen have their own boats and tackle. Some of these boats are very expensive and are bought with prize money. Most have electric trolling motors in addition to a powerful outboard. Personally, I prefer backpacking. My brother, Bob, likes kite building and flying. My sister likes to play chess with her computer. I guess you could say we all have our own way of enjoying ourselves. Bass boats are not cheap and can cost up to $20,000. The electronics that help the fishermen locate bass holes include depth finders and sonar bottom scanners.

It is easy to spot the annoying drift in the above paragraph. Here is the paragraph without it:

<u>Bass fishing is a popular sport in the South.</u> Fishermen have their own boats and tackle. Some of these boats are very expensive and are bought with prize money. Most have electric trolling motors in addition to a powerful outboard. Bass boats are not cheap, and can cost up to $20,000. The electronics that help the fishermen locate bass holes include depth finders and sonar bottom scanners.

With the writer now sticking to the point, the paragraph is sharper, crisper, and easier to read.

PRACTICING 3

Cross out the sentences that stray from the point in the paragraph that follows. The topic sentence is underlined.

<u>Passive smoking is a public health menace.</u> Studies by the Environmental Protection Agency show that people exposed to secondhand smoke are as much as 150 percent more likely to get lung cancer than those who are not. Spouses of inconsiderate smokers have a 30 percent greater risk of getting lung cancer during their lifetimes. ~~Smoking is a bad habit, but drinking alcoholic beverages is also a terrible habit. In my family, my Uncle Irving is a heavy smoker and drinker. I don't know which of his vices is worse, the smoking or drinking. Not only does he smoke, he is also an inconsiderate smoker and is always puffing around my Aunt Elizabeth, who comes down frequently with colds.~~ Because the evidence is so conclusive, several states have passed laws to restrict workplace smoking. More needs to be done to protect people from the bad habits of a few.

Prove the Point; Don't Merely Repeat It

Proving a point is not the same as repeating it. When you prove a point, you add something new to it—an example, a fact, a reason, or an expert's opinion. Look at this paragraph, for example:

<u>The tradition of exchanging gifts at Christmas is practiced differently in different families.</u> Many people practice it differently. Some families do one thing, others do something different. Some families exchange gifts, others don't. In some families, fewer gifts are exchanged. Others go all out. This tradition is a good, wholesome tradition. My family has been practicing this tradition forever.

The paragraph adds nothing to the underlined topic sentence but merely repeats it in different words. Here, on the other hand, is a paragraph that uses examples to support the same topic sentence:

The tradition of exchanging gifts at Christmas is practiced differently in different families. In my family, for example, we exchange wrapped presents on Christmas eve after dinner. On Christmas day, there are also gifts from Santa Claus under the tree for me and my sister. Santa Claus has been bringing such gifts to our house since I was a child, and my sister and I like the tradition so well, that even though we're now grown, we've asked him never to stop. In my husband's family, on the other hand, the gifts are not opened on Christmas eve, but on Christmas day. Santa Claus stopped coming by their house once the children became teenagers. Their gifts to each other, however, are not identified by a tag, so you never know who gave what. Nevertheless, one thing stays the same: Both families enjoy the spirit of Christmas equally, although in their own way.

The writer moves quickly from the tradition of gift exchanging at Christmas to examples of how it is practiced in two families.

IN A NUTSHELL

To write a solid paragraph, you should do the following:

- Begin with a discussible point.
- Stick to the point.
- Prove the point; don't merely repeat it.

PRACTICING 4

Each of the two topic sentences below is followed by ten related sentences. Mark a plus (+) beside the *statements* you think add something specific to the topic sentence and a minus (–) beside those that merely repeat it.

1. **Topic sentence:** Toy manufacturing is a stupendous business.

   1. __–__ Manufacturers are in an enormous enterprise.

   2. __+__ The toy market is an $18 billion market.

   3. __–__ Enormous numbers of manufacturers are involved.

   4. __+__ In 1994 toy manufacturers spent $800 million to advertise their products.

5. __+__ Toy makers in America produce 12,000 different toys every year.

6. __−__ Many toy manufacturers are involved in the business.

7. __+__ Between 5000 and 6000 new toys are introduced each year.

8. __−__ The toy business is really something monumental.

9. __−__ Few people realize how big the toy business really is.

10. __+__ Since my dad is in toy sales, I know the business is bigger than people realize.

2. **Topic sentence:** People who pretend to be what they are not don't usually enjoy the respect of their peers.

1. __−__ You simply can't respect someone who is always putting on a show.

2. __+__ For instance, some of the students on my campus go around bragging about their money.

3. __+__ They love to invite me to drive in their new Honda Civic, just so my mouth will water at their luck.

4. __+__ Social pretenses only serve to turn away potential friends.

5. __+__ I don't even know what the social backgrounds of my best friends are because I don't find them important to our friendship.

6. __+__ The worst social pretenders, though, are students who brag about their grades even though some are close to flunking.

7. __+__ Intellectual pretense really turns people off.

8. __−__ How can you respect someone who lies about his intelligence?

9. __+__ One student in my sociology class insisted that he got an A on a paper; yet, the grade C was clearly written on the first page.

10. __+__ I believe in modesty and honesty.

Link the Sentences

A paragraph is a block of print with all its sentences on the same topic. Consider this example:

> <u>Coach Burns is the exact opposite of what a coach should be.</u> He runs the same old simple plays over and over again so that the other team can easily figure out our game plan. He does not motivate. All he ever does is make his players feel as if they are losers. He points out our weak points, game after game, without a single word of encouragement. He makes the team depressed and angry. He lacks basic kindness. If you play for Coach Burns and have a personal problem, you can't go to him. One day, after a game, I found that someone had stolen the wheels off my car. I went to Coach Burns' office and, practically in tears, said, "Coach, someone stole the wheels off my car." "So," he sarcastically replied, "What do you want me to do about it?"

By our definition, the above is definitely a paragraph. But it is not a good one. The writing is choppy, and the writer's train of thought is hard to follow. Helpful links between its sentences are missing. A paragraph with missing links between its sentences is said to lack **coherence.** Here is the same paragraph rewritten to add sentence links.

> Basketball coach Burns is the exact opposite of what a coach should be. First, he does not even know the game of basketball. He runs the same old simple plays over and over again so that the other team can easily figure out our game plan. Second, he does not motivate. All he ever does is make his players feel as if they are losers. He points out our weak points, game after game, without a single word of encouragement. He makes the team depressed and angry. Finally, he lacks basic kindness. If you play for Coach Burns and have a personal problem, you can't go to him. For example, one day, after a game, I found that someone had stolen the wheels off my car. I went to Coach Burns' office and, practically in tears, said, "Coach, someone stole the wheels off my car." "So," he sarcastically replied, "What do you want me to do about it?" If you ask me, Coach Burns hurts the basketball team more than he helps it.

Now we can easily follow the writer's thinking. The words, *first*, *second*, and *finally* set off the reasons why Coach Burns is a bad coach, and the phrase *for example* introduces the example. Because of these changes, the writing is smooth, not choppy.

To link the sentences of a paragraph writers use the following techniques:

- Transitional words and phrases

- Repeated key words and pronouns

- Similar sentence patterns

Transitional words and phrases

A transition is a word or phrase that links the sentences of a paragraph. In the following paragraphs, the transitions are in bold and the topic sentence is underlined:

> <u>No main dish is simpler to prepare than roast chicken.</u> **Moreover,** there is no more elegant dish for company. To serve two to four people, buy about a three pound roaster or fryer. Buy a fresh bird, not frozen, and look for a plump bird with light gold-colored skin. **When** you get home, take out the giblets that are packaged inside, wash the bird, and pat it dry. Put a couple cloves of garlic and a few slices of lemon inside. **Next,** sprinkle paprika on top; this adds a nice color to the finished chicken. Place the bird breast-down in a shallow pan and cook in a 300 degree oven for 30 minutes per pound. Baste often. The juices add flavor and keep the bird moist. During the last 20 minutes, turn the bird over so it browns evenly. **Then,** all you have to do is present your chicken on a pretty platter and stand back for the compliments.

The writer makes it easy to follow the directions by linking the sentences with transitional words—*moreover, when, next,* and *then.* Here are some other common words and phrases used to link sentences:

after all	also	and	as a consequence	but
finally	for example	however	in addition	in contrast
in fact	in spite of	moreover	nevertheless	next
therefore	moreover	what's more	plus	for instance
so	then	once	first, second	in particular

PRACTICING 5

Link the following sentences to make it easy for the reader to follow the train of thought.

Example: His problem was to make his way to the back of the auditorium without seeming in a hurry. He slowly picked up his jacket and shuffled up the aisle.

Rewritten: His problem was to make his way to the back of the auditorium without seeming in a hurry. <u>Consequently,</u> he slowly picked up his jacket and shuffled up the aisle.

1. My brother can really annoy me sometimes. He keeps pinching me every time he passes by me.

My brother can really annoy me sometimes. For example, he keeps pinching me

every time he passes by me.

2. My math teacher keeps complaining about living in town. He refuses to move.

My math teacher keeps complaining about living in town. However, he refuses to move.

3. Terry had to run errands during lunch. He would not be able to meet Meg for a sandwich.

Terry had to run errands during lunch. As a consequence, he would not be able to

meet Meg for a sandwich.

4. Ann slept through her morning dental appointment. She slept through basketball practice.

Ann slept through her morning dental appointment. In addition, she slept through

basketball practice.

5. The story was filled with violent scenes. The teacher decided not to assign it as reading.

The story was filled with violent scenes. Therefore, the teacher decided not to

assign it as reading.

6. First, we went swimming in the lake. We lay on the grass and rested.

First, we went swimming in the lake. Then, we lay on the grass and rested.

7. Three of his habits annoy me. He leaves dirty dishes on his desk, he leaves wet towels hanging in the bathroom. He never locks the door when he leaves the apartment.

Three of his habits annoy me. First, he leaves dirty dishes on his desk, and second,

he leaves wet towels hanging in the bathroom. Finally, he never locks the door when

he leaves the apartment.

8. The heavy box was about to fall on Jim's head. Bob held it back just in time.

The heavy box was about to fall on Jim's head, but Bob held it back just in time.

9. He weighed 200 pounds. He was extremely fast.

He weighed 200 pounds. However, he was extremely fast.

---

10. I couldn't help feeling lonely. I was in a new neighborhood where I didn't know a soul.

I couldn't help feeling lonely. After all, I was in a new neighborhood where I didn't

know a soul.

Repeated key words and pronouns

Another way to link the sentences of a paragraph is to repeat key words and pronouns. Pronouns are words that take the place of nouns, such as *he* for *Mr. Jones*, or *it* for *the book*. Here is an example:

My Uncle Dan is a good example of a perfectionist. Whenever he sets out to do anything, he always does it right. Once when he was making me a Halloween costume, he stayed up all night sewing until it fit perfectly. If he hangs a picture, he uses a carpenter's level. When Uncle Dan rakes the driveway of leaves, it looks scrubbed when he is finished. Not a single leaf is left behind. Uncle Dan is such a perfectionist that sometimes he drives my Aunt Ida, who is something of a slob, crazy.

The sentences of this paragraph are tightly linked by the repetition of the key words *Uncle Dan* and *perfectionist*, which are used in the topic sentence, and the pronoun *he*.

PRACTICING 6

In the paragraph that follows, underline any noun, pronoun, or key word that is repeated as a link between the sentences.

During the past several years, my home state, Nevada, has been bothered by a band of invading crickets. These horrid little creatures are big; they stink; they're ugly; and they're all over the place. The area most bothered by these bugs is Reno, where entire flower beds and agricultural crops are being chewed up. In fact, entomologists for the Nevada Department of Agriculture are concerned and have called the infestation one of the worst since the 1970's. These crickets tend to multiply fast and are voracious eaters of wheat, barley, alfalfa, garden vegetables, and flowers. Additionally, when they band together, they emit an unpleasant odor. Although their movement is restricted to crawling and hopping, they migrate in groups that can cover as much as a mile a day and up to fifty miles in a summer. How dreadful to think that an army of crickets could ruin the economy of an entire state.

Similar sentence patterns

This linking technique simply means that similar ideas are expressed in similar words. For example, you could use the same sentence patterns to compare places, things, ideas, or people as the writer does below:

My brother Joe and my brother John are completely different when it comes to being neat. My brother Joe is messy; my brother John is neat. Joe comes home and tosses his clothes on the floor. John comes home and neatly folds and puts away his clothes. Joe cooks breakfast and leaves the dirty dishes in the sink. John cooks breakfast and washes every dish afterwards. Joe brushes his teeth and splatters water all over the bathroom mirror. John brushes his teeth and leaves everything bone dry, even his teeth. I love both of them, but I prefer living with John.

Notice the definite pattern used in this paragraph to compare Joe's habits with John's. For each point, the writer first talks about Joe's messiness and then John's neatness, using the same sentence pattern. This technique makes it easy to follow the writer's thoughts.

IN A NUTSHELL

Help your reader follow your train of thought by:

- Using transitions
- Repeating key words and pronouns
- Using similar sentence patternsn

PRACTICING 7

In the following passages, underline the repeated sentence patterns:

Example: Happy is the person who believes in the dignity offered by labor and in the opportunity offered by freedom.

1. We are what we eat as well as what we think.

2. I had no time whatsoever to enjoy good music or to watch good films.

3. This computer is killing me. Whenever I stare at it, my eyes hurt; whenever I type, my hands ache.

4. Here's some good advice: Think before you speak, and read before you think.

5. Money <u>means having power</u>; it <u>means having status</u>, and it <u>means having freedoms</u>. Money isn't such a bad thing.

6. Why is she always <u>here today</u> and <u>gone tomorrow</u>? Please give me the answer to that question.

7. Rick's life has been bumpy: <u>He has known what it is to be hungry</u>, and <u>he has known what it is to eat at the best restaurants</u>.

8. If we don't reward good teachers, teaching will become <u>a lost art</u> and <u>a lost tradition</u>.

9. Most of us prefer to believe <u>what we like</u>, not <u>what we fear</u>.

10. We never became <u>strong friends</u>, but <u>we never became strong enemies</u>, either.

 **Unit Test**

In the blank provided, check the answer that best completes the idea of the sentence.

Example: The sentences of a true paragraph are like

_____ **(a).** oxen carrying a heavy burden

✔ **(b).** horses pulling a carriage together

_____ **(c).** chickens laying eggs

_____ **(d).** snakes crawling through the grass

1. You will write better paragraphs, if you begin with a

_____ **(a).** nice computer font

_____ **(b).** simple sentence

✔ **(c).** discussible point

_____ **(d).** shocking idea.

2. A discussable point is one that

_____ **(a).** is complex

✔ **(b).** calls for further explanation

_____ **(c).** is controversial

_____ **(d).** is one found in your textbook

3. The way you indicate that you have written a paragraph is to

    _____ **(a).** indent the first line of the paragraph five spaces.

    ✔ **(b).** link your sentences so that they make a common point.

    _____ **(c).** compose short, crisp sentences.

    _____ **(d).** make more than one point.

4. You prove your point by

    _____ **(a).** repeating it several times in different words.

    _____ **(b).** making statements with which most people agree.

    _____ **(c).** quoting a famous person, such as a President or a movie star.

    ✔ **(d).** using an example, a fact, a reason, or an expert's opinion to support your point.

5. Which of the following techniques is NOT a way of linking sentences?

    ✔ **(a).** Placing a period between sentences.

    _____ **(b).** Repeating key words and pronouns.

    _____ **(c).** Using transitional words and phrases.

    _____ **(d).** Using similar sentence patterns.

6. Insert an appropriate transitional word to link the sentences in the passages that follow.

    _____ **(a).** Xavier owns a stack of good videos. His friends like to visit him.

    _____ **(b).** The audience laughed continuously in the first act. Many walked out during the second act.

Answers may vary.

7. Check the blank in front of the passage that uses a pronoun as a transition between sentences.

    _____ **(a).** Lynn Dale is a fast runner. Michelle Jaeger is even faster.

    _____ **(b).** Some pop stars shine brighter in the darkness of death than in the daylight of life. Athletes, however, don't seem to get more popular after death.

    ✔ **(c).** When Aaron was a kid, I was already in college. By the time he reached college age, I had kids of my own.

    _____ **(d).** More and more stores are getting websites to make shopping easier. Many direct mail retailers are getting websites, too.

8. Check the blank in front of the passage that uses the repetition of key words to link its sentences.

_____ **(a).** Our school is helping Nelly to win a medal in basketball. The coach gives her personal attention.

_____ **(b).** Twenty-five people come to our house for dinner every Thanksgiving. We have to borrow chairs from our neighbor to be able to seat all our guests.

_____ **(c).** Nature probably has a cure for every disease if we could just discover it. Medical scientists are our explorers.

__✔__ **(d).** Cheap labor is what many employers seek. However, cheap labor is not always the most skilled and trainable labor.

9. Check the blank in front of the passage that uses similar sentence patterns to link its sentences.

__✔__ **(a).** We agree that most drug abusers are losers. We agree that most drug users are troubled. But we do not agree on whether they should be jailed or hospitalized.

_____ **(b).** A fabulously preserved fossil from China all but proves that dinosaurs and birds are closely related. I read a recent newspaper article that explains the connection to those of us who aren't scientists.

_____ **(c).** Tests that elementary school students often have to take at the end of the school year are causing youngsters terrible stress. This anxiety keeps them from succeeding in school.

_____ **(d).** Having been bullied at school is no excuse for shooting other students and teachers. However, parents and teachers should certainly foster self-esteem in children.

Answers may vary.

10. Using whichever of the three linking techniques you think best— transitional words or phrases, repeated key terms, and similar sentence patterns—rewrite the passage that follows to better link its sentences.

Many myths exist about the founding fathers. They were believers in democracy. They were not. They thought unchecked democracy would lead to mob rule that would threaten the social order. Distrust of democracy was common. They merely reflected the thinking of their age.

Many myths exist about the founding fathers. One myth in particular claims that they were

believers in democracy. But, in fact, they were not. To the contrary, they thought unchecked

democracy would lead to mob rule that would threaten the social order. Distrust of democracy

was common among thinkers in the era in which the founding fathers lived. As men of their

time, they merely reflected the thinking of their age.

_____

_____

_____

_____

_____

_____

_____

Answers may vary.
Here is one possibility.

Unit Talk-Write Assignment

In the blanks provided, rewrite the Talk column in standard English, linking the sentences smoothly as necessary. Delete any material that does not stick to the topic sentence.

Discussible topic sentence: Solving crossword puzzles keeps your mind alert and flexible.

TALK

1. Solving crossword puzzles keeps your mind alert and flexible.

WRITE

1. *Correct* _____

_____

_____

_____

_____

TALK

2. One Alzheimer specialist indicates that doing a crossword puzzle daily keeps your memory from choking up.

3. The challenge of trying to think of a synonym for "nimble" forces you to concentrate like crazy until finally you come up with the word *quick*.

4. The word you come up with may not fit into the grid; then you have to come up with another word.

5. It's that heavy-duty concentration that stretches your head and keeps it O.K.

6. The trickier the puzzle, the more your head is exercised and the more it remains young.

WRITE

2. One Alzheimer specialist indicates that doing a crossword puzzle daily keeps your memory sharp.

3. The challenge of trying to think of a synonym for "nimble" forces you to concentrate hard until finally you think of the word "quick."

4. The word you think of may not fit into the grid; then you have to come up with another word.

5. It's the serious concentration that keeps your mind active and strong.

6. The trickier the puzzle, the more your mind works and the more active it stays.

TALK

7. Making friends is important for staying young, too.

8. Most of my friends have a fit when I tell them how much I like crossword puzzles.

9. The beauty of exercise is that you can do it alone and at home, unlike tennis or mountain climbing, which are cool exercises mostly for your physical body and must be done with another person or away from home.

10. If you have never tried doing a crossword puzzle, start now; you'll have a ball while stimulating your brain.

WRITE

7. *OMIT* _____

_____

_____

_____

_____

_____

8. *OMIT* _____

_____

_____

_____

_____

9. *OMIT* _____

_____

_____

_____

_____

_____

10. *If you have never tried doing a crossword puzzle,*

start now; you'll have fun while stimulating your

brain. _____

_____

_____

_____

 ## Unit Collaborative Assignment

Pair up with a classmate. One person should read the following paragraph aloud. Discuss how the paragraph can be improved according to what you have learned in this unit. Check the following:

- Does it have a discussible topic sentence?
- Does it stick to the point?

■ Does it prove the point or merely repeat it?

■ Are all the sentences linked so the reader can easily follow the train of thought?

Revisions will vary.

Then, you and your partner should work together to rewrite the paragraph, making sure that its sentences stick to the point, prove the point, and are smoothly linked.

When I was about five years old, my dream was to be an astronaut and explore unknown paths in space. I can remember, as a little boy, climbing onto the roof of my house to stare at the stars, wishing that I might touch these gleaming lights and hold them in my hands. I wondered what it would be like to travel past the stars. My sights began to turn to new subjects, and this childish dream faded away. ~~I have devoted much time to my studies. I always wanted to make my parents happy with my good grades; it was the reason I looked forward to report card day. I thought that if it was my parents' wish that I go to college, then so be it; I would go.~~ My boyhood dream took on purpose December 7, 1995, when the Galileo space probe plunged into Jupiter's atmosphere. As I watched this historic event on telvision, I decided to study space science and become an engineer or computer specialist. My boyhood dream would become a reality.

Unit Writing Assignment

Choose one of the topics listed below. In your journal, gather ideas about your chosen topic by freewriting, brainstorming, or clustering. On a separate sheet, develop a strong paragraph, observing the following guidelines:

■ Begin with a discussible topic sentence.

■ Support the topic sentence with appropriate examples, testimony, reasons, or personal observations.

■ Stick to your topic sentence.

■ Link your sentences smoothly.

1. A memorable outdoor experience

2. Something about your college you'd like to see changed

3. A significant conflict you had with your parents

4. How luck can be as important as hard work in being successful

5. A time when you felt totally alone and abandoned

6. An experience with racism or prejudice

7. The importance of recycling

8. Your reaction to a recent newspaper headline story

9. Why people jog

10. A Fourth of July (or another holiday) you remember

This is how one student fulfilled the assignment:

<u>Where fashion is concerned, my mother and I live in two different worlds</u>. Mom still lives in the Victorian Age, when women who didn't wear long sleeves and long dresses were considered vulgar. The other day I was leaving our house in a hurry, on my way to geography class, when my mother yelled, "Jessica, your dress barely hides your bottom. Can't you wear something more discreet?" The fact is that my outfit consisted of a pale blue silk skirt, topped by a white cotton tee shirt. The majority of attractive girls in college were wearing outfits just like mine, and these girls aren't sluts. Most of them study hard to get on the honor roll and they avoid lewd behavior with the males on campus. But style is style, and you're either "with it" or you're not. On a hot day, we female students don't want to wear black gabardine pants, which is what Mom loves for me to wear. I told her, "Mom, it's a hot day, and I want to feel cool and comfortable, especially while I'm studying on the campus patio." But Mom has no use for fashion. All that matters to her is that I look "decent." That means looking like the frumpiest, dowdiest person on campus. The really popular girls wear mini skirts that end about ten inches above the knee. But they make sure that they sit with their knees together and they avoid bending over in public; observing these rules is part of the protocol of wearing mini skirts. When Mom kept getting more and more vehement about how "awful" I looked and how I was a "disgrace to the family," I finally roared out of the house and found refuge in my car on the way to school, where my girlfriends would understand my fashion statement.

Photo Writing Assignment

The person in the following picture is obviously trying to make a fashion statement. Write about your reaction to the person's taste. Make sure that your writing has a discussible topic sentence, is supported by appropriate evidence, sticks to the point, and contains smoothly linked sentences.

6

Revising Paragraphs

Do writers generally turn out flawless text on the first try? The answer is a loud and clear no. Over the years, many writers have left behind much testimony about their working habits. We know from this record that nearly all writers repeatedly rewrite their work.

One of our favorite quotations about the importance of rewriting comes from the French writer Antoine de Saint-Exupéry, author of *The Little Prince*:

> Whenever I hear an echo, years later, from an article of mine in . . . a newspaper, it is always, always an article that I rewrote thirty times. When I read a quotation of my own somewhere, it is always, always, always a phrase I rewrote twenty-five times.

The lesson here is simple: If your first draft doesn't satisfy you, don't be disappointed. First drafts are nothing more than a crude beginning. They're not supposed to satisfy. Indeed, if you are totally pleased with your first draft, you're most likely being too easy on yourself. Of course, you could have gotten lucky. It is possible to write a good paragraph on the first try, just as it is possible to be hit on the head by a meteorite. However, neither event is very likely.

What Is Revision?

Imagine you're cleaning your room. How would you logically proceed? First, you'd probably pick up clothes, trash, and dishes coated with dried-up food. Then you'd make your bed and vacuum. The last thing you would do is dust and polish the furniture. In other words, you would do the biggest jobs first and the littlest last.

The same logic applies to rewriting. First comes the big step: checking that you have developed your topic sentence with enough good details, deleting sentences that don't stick to the point, and inserting links between sentences. This big job is the act of revising. Later will come the job of polishing. That is the act of editing, which is correcting the errors in grammar, punctuation, spelling, and capitalization.

We will cover editing later. For now, we want to concentrate on the big job of revising.

The Revising Checklist

Few student writers can afford to rewrite their work 25 or 30 times as Saint-Exupéry did. A more practical goal is three drafts.

The first draft is the original composition. The second draft concentrates on revising—doing the big jobs. The third aims at editing the language for grammar, spelling, and punctuation errors.

To help you revise your paragraphs, use the Revising Checklist found inside the cover.

Notice that the checklist tells you the unit that you need to review if you're unsure of how to answer a particular question. Don't be reluctant to go back and review an earlier unit. Indeed, the practical advice in those units is more likely to sink in only after you actually try to apply it to your own writing. You learn to ride a bicycle in much the same way: not by reading, but by doing.

Using talk skills to revise your work

If you are a native speaker, talking can help with revision. Start by reading the work out loud to a partner or friend. Reading aloud forces you to pay attention to every word and not skip any sentence or passage. It also helps you to tell how your writing might sound to someone else.

To use talk skills to revise your written work, take the following steps:

1. Read your first draft aloud to yourself or to a friend.

2. Ask your friend what you can do to improve it.

3. Apply every question on the Revising Checklist to your first draft.

4. Make changes to the draft as you, or your friend, think of them.

5. If you don't understand a question on the checklist, review the appropriate unit until you do.

Naturally, if you're working with someone in your class, you will have to take turns going over each other's material. Be patient with each other. The mutual give-and-take will help you both learn how to revise.

> **ESL Advice!**
>
> If you have not yet acquired a reliable ear for English, try reading your work to a native speaker.

If you must work alone, follow the same steps given above. If you feel funny about reading your work aloud, do it in private. Reading your work aloud lets you use your speaker's ear to help judge the writing.

Finally, don't be afraid to scribble mercilessly over your first draft. Scratch out and rewrite sentences to your heart's content. First drafts are supposed to look like they've been beaten up. If yours is clean and nice, ask yourself honestly: Have I been hit by a meteorite or am I being too easy on myself?

Here is an example of a paragraph that needs to be revised:

> <u>I keep a pet iguana in my apartment.</u> Her name is Petulia, and she perches on my shoulder whenever I go out. Of course, people who see us together stare at me as if I were crazy. Unfortunately, many people are repulsed at the idea that I actually have a reptile as a pet. Even my roommate screams at me, "Get that horrid critter out of our place." He is especially angry when he sees Petulia climbing the wall of our shower stall just when he wants to take a shower. Most people have this illogical fear of snakes and lizards, probably because they think most of them are poisonous. But if you give an iguana the affection and attention it wants, it will respond by entertaining you and being wonderful company. Petulia is so tame that she waddles alongside me on a leash. My roommate, along with many other people, needs to broaden his mind about what makes a good pet. I wouldn't trade Petulia for any cat or dog I know. Not that I don't like dogs and cats. I do. I used to have a beautiful little Yorkshire who was so smart that at dinner time he would hop on the chair next to me, hoping for a treat.

The student writer applied the Revising Checklist going over the paragraph point by point. She found major problems with this paragraph. First, it has no discussible topic sentence. Second, it lacks unity; some sentences are off the topic. To revise, the student made four changes: (1) she added a topic sentence, (2) she moved up the sentence on why people fear reptiles to where it fits better, (3) she added transitional words to link the final sentence to the rest of the paragraph, and (4) she deleted the material about the Yorkshire because it was off the topic.

Here is the paragraph after these revisions.

> <u>In spite of how people feel about reptiles, I have found that iguanas make great pets.</u> I keep a pet iguana in my apartment. Her name is Petulia, and she perches on my shoulder whenever I go out. Of course, people who see us together stare at me as if I were crazy. Most people have this illogical fear of snakes and lizards, probably because they think most of them are poisonous. But if you

give an iguana the affection and attention it wants, it will respond by entertaining you and being wonderful company. Petulia is so tame that she waddles alongside me on a leash. Unfortunately, many people are repulsed at the idea that I actually have a reptile as a pet. Even my roommate screams at me, "Get that horrid critter out of our place." He is especially angry when he sees Petulia climbing the wall of our shower stall just when he wants to take a shower. My roommate, along with many other people, needs to broaden his mind about what makes a good pet. Despite the negative comments made about her, I wouldn't trade Petulia for any cat or dog I know.

PRACTICING 1

Revisions will vary.

Here are four passages that need revising. Work on them either alone or, if your teacher approves, with a classmate. In either case, read the paragraph aloud and use the Revising Checklist to decide how to revise it.

(1)

"Damn Jap!" Did I hear right? From the scowl on his face, I must have. But I could not understand what I had done to deserve this ugly label. It was incomprehensible to me that someone who did not know me could make such a demeaning comment when I had done nothing. I was stunned. People should not hurt others by using racial slurs. This incident revealed the sheer power that two words can have and their ability to hurt. This was my first experience with racism, and it changed my perception of the world. I grew up in a diverse neighborhood in North Hollywood among African Americans, Caucasians, Latinos, and Asians. I knew that a generation before I was born in the United States, my native country had been at war with Japan, the faraway land from which my mother's parents had come. He might have some lingering prejudices from World War II. But I was just as American as anyone in this melting pot of a country, the U.S.A. I thought of myself as a patriotic American, but obviously this man did not see me that way. It was not the last time that I was to hear a racial slur. The point, though, is that I decided to make sure that I myself would not succumb to stereotyping others. I would work hard at appreciating every individual, separate from his or her stereotype. By the way, I have included ethnic studies in my curriculum so that I can better understand the different cultures that compose our nation. I also work in a Thai restaurant that employs Thai and Latino-Americans, whom I have come to regard as my second family.

(2)

Different people learn lessons about life differently. Many people learn from other people's mistakes, but in my opinion the majority of people learn lessons about their lives from their own mistakes, and some learn from their personal experiences. Every person knows that life is a long journey, and it is filled with experiences that help people to understand more about the meaning of life. I believe everybody in this world has had an incident or an experience that taught him or her an important lesson about life, and I am one who has had a memorable experience, which I shall never forget. It happened while I was baby-sitting the Geyer family's four-year-old child, Wally. While eating, he choked on a green bean. His face turned red, then blue, and he kept gasping for air. In my first aid class, I had learned the Heimlich maneuver, and I used it on Wally—grabbing him from behind and vigorously squeezing below his diaphragm, with the result that he spit up the green bean and started to breathe normally. It felt really good to have learned something so useful in class.

(3)

I have a cousin who loves using our family gatherings to discuss the latest family scandals. She gets a kick out of blabbing about anything bad that has happened to the family. She makes me so mad. At one Thanksgiving dinner, she went on and on about how terrible it was that Uncle Mark was leaving Aunt Gertrude for another woman I was furious with her. We already felt bad enough about the situation without hearing about the secret phone calls he had been caught making and the expensive gifts that showed up on credit card bills. This cousin uses our family reunions as a pulpit to expose any family wrongdoings. She makes me so angry. I think when a member of the family has a personal problem it should stay that way—personal—not broadcast to everyone. Let the people involved work it out themselves or get professional help. Gossiping about the matter only makes it worse. Gossiping is such a bad habit.

(4)

It is difficult to look up to a leader who lies and cheats. George Washington was the founding father of our nation; and Abraham Lincoln liberated the slaves. Richard Nixon never received the full admiration of American citizens after his Watergate affair. If he had just told the truth about breaking into the Watergate apartments to find out what his enemies were up to, he might have recovered his reputation. The television evangelist, Jim Baker, lost all credibility with his audiences once they found out that he had an affair with a prostitute. How could a religious person be seen with a prostitute? For that matter, how can religious leaders be seen with drug peddlers, drunks, and convicted murderers? Even a charismatic leader like John F. Kennedy lost some of his popularity once the newspapers revealed how he had had affairs with various women, including Marilyn Monroe, who happens to be one of my favorite actresses. The public will forgive a popular leader's character faults, but the leader must admit them and show some repentance. Personally, I am not that forgiving.

PRACTICING 2

Reread your Unit Writing Assignment and Photo Writing Assignment from Unit 5 aloud. Pick one of these two assign-ments and revise it, using the Revising Checklist.

☑ Unit Test

In the blank provided, fill in the word that best completes the sentence:

Example: <u>First</u> drafts are nothing more than (a crude beginning).

1. Most writers do not turn out _____*flawless*_____ copy on first try.

2. Does my topic sentence make a _____*discussable*_____ point? (from checklist)

3. Do I support my topic sentence with strong _____*details*_____? (from checklist)

4. Do I _____*stick*_____ to my point? (from checklist)

5. Do I _____*prove*_____ my point or merely repeat it? (from checklist)

6. Do I link the _____*sentences*_____ of my paragraph? (from checklist)

7. Do I use _____*standard*_____ English throughout? (from checklist)

8. Talking can help with revision. Start by reading the work aloud to _____*a partner or a friend*_____.

9. The purpose of reading aloud is to get your speaker's ear to help you _____*judge*_____ your writing.

10. Don't be afraid to mess up your first draft by _____*scribbling*_____ on it.

✐ Unit Talk-Write Assignment

The *Talk* column reflects a conversation between two college women—J and M. Using what you learn from their discussion and ideas of your own on the subject of dieting and diet drugs, draft a paragraph in the *Write* column. Then, using the Revising Checklist on the inside cover, turn the draft into polished form on a separate sheet of paper.

TALK

J: Can you believe they've come out with another diet drug?

M: You mean like fen-phen?

J: You got it! What a drag! Now we can expect some more heart disease or cancer or heaven knows what awful side effects.

M: I have to say, kiddo, I'd love to take a pill that would just burn off the fat. I love to eat and I get so ticked off with my weight!

J: Oh, get off it; you're thin, bordering on sickly looking.

M: Oh yeah? In your dreams. Anyway, What's the new stuff called?

J: Meridia. And I read that instead of boosting the production of seratonin—the way fen-phen did—it slows down the loss of seratonin.

M: I don't understand all the scientific gobblydegook. All I want to know is that it works. Is it Expensive?

J. $3.00 a day.

M: Did you read about any side effects?

J: Yeah; the FDA says it can increase blood pressure.

M: Hmmm, I'd love to try it, but I'm scared. Thin and dead wouldn't be much fun.

J: People oughta just eat moderately and take a 20-minute brisk walk every day and forget about these so-called miracle weight loss pills.

M: At least, I hope the pharmaceutical company that makes Meridia will educate doctors to use it with only patients whose weight is life-threatening.

WRITE

People should use diet pills carefully, and only as a last resort. Diet pills work by changing the way seratonin is produced or maintained. They can be effective, but they can also have dangerous side effects. For example, fen-phen, which was recently taken off the market, caused heart problems in some dieters, and even led to several deaths. Meridia, the latest diet drug, can increase blood pressure. Many people would like to lose weight, but they should first try non-chemical methods, such as eating moderately or taking a 20-minute brisk walk each day. Diet pills should only be used by people whose weight is life-threatening, and they should talk to their doctors about side effects.

Unit Collaborative Assignment

Join with two or three classmates to write a paragraph. First choose one of the topic sentences from the list below:

1. Attending college is a privilege.

2. People love to watch the Academy Awards because they are fascinated by star personalities.

3. Conforming dress styles are the rule in high school.

4. It's OK for men to cry.

Now, do a little brainstorming for details to support the topic sentence. Have one participant write down everyone's ideas. Discuss the ideas and choose the ones that best support the topic sentence. Expand the ideas into complete sentences to write the paragraph. Make sure that each sentence supports the topic sentence without being repetitious. Finally, link your sentences with transitions. After you have developed a written paragraph, read it aloud and apply the Revising Checklist. Revise the paragraph further.

Unit Writing Assignment

Write about the importance of the family, whether consisting of one parent, of grandparents and other relatives, or of a mother and father. You might want to explore the following questions:

1. Was the concept of family important in your upbringing?

2. What are some of your special family memories?

3. What values (e.g., honesty, hard work, tolerance) should a family teach children?

4. What impact has the day care center had on the modern family?

5. According to the 2000 United States census, the traditional family, in which children live with both their mother and father, is now a minority of households. How does this change affect the way you think about the family?

Use the Revising Checklist to make sure that your writing sticks to the point and progresses smoothly, without unnecessary repetition.

Photo Writing Assignment

The following picture portrays a scene from the Special Olympics, which encourages athletic competition among handicapped people. Write about your attitude toward this modern event. Read your paragraph aloud, and then review your work against the Revising Checklist. Revise your paragraph as needed

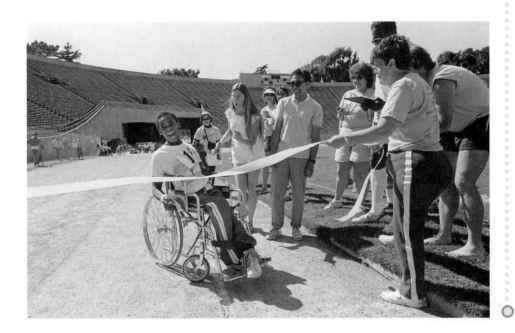

7

The Basic Sentence

"Every sentence—no matter how long and complex—contains a kernel sentence."

A **sentence** is a group of words that expresses a complete thought. This completeness is what your speaker's ear uses to recognize a sentence. If someone said to you, "Leaf," you'd probably reply, "What?" ("What do you mean?") However, if someone said, "A leaf fell," you'd probably reply, "So what?" meaning that you understand but don't care. You responded differently because the second statement is complete enough for you to understand it.

Subject and Verb

To be complete, every sentence must have a subject and a verb. In its simplest form, the **subject** is someone who does something:

> John spoke.
>
> Mary ran.
>
> Jeannie laughed.

John, Mary, and *Jeannie* are the simple subjects of these sentences.

Naturally, the subject of a sentence can also be something rather than someone.

> The plane flew.
>
> The ship sailed.

The house collapsed.

Greed hurts.

The word that tells what the subject does or did is called the **verb**. From the examples above, we know that John *spoke*, Mary *ran*, and Jeannie *laughed*. We also know that the plane *flew*, the ship *sailed*, the house *collapsed*, and greed *hurts*.

PRACTICING 1

In each of these sentences, underline the subject once and the verb twice. In questions, underline both verbs.

Example: The <u>bird chirped</u>. Whom <u>does she fear</u>?

1. The <u>house burned</u>.
2. The <u>car sputters</u>.
3. <u>Jane Alexandra James laughed</u>.
4. Why <u>does Sally dance</u>?
5. The <u>thingamabob spins</u>.
6. <u>Computers crash</u>.
7. How <u>does money talk</u>?
8. <u>Horses neigh</u>.
9. <u>Kings ruled</u>.
10. <u>Elves exist</u>.

Kernel Sentences

Each of these examples is called a **kernel sentence.** A kernel sentence is the smallest sentence possible. Here are some other kernel sentences:

Run!

Halt!

Go!

These kernel sentences are commands. The subject (you) is implied:

[You] run!

[You] halt!

[You] go!

Every sentence—no matter how long and complex—contains a kernel sentence. For example, consider this kernel sentence:

John spoke.

We can add words to it, making it longer and more detailed. It will still have the same basic kernel sentence: John spoke. Here are some examples:

At noon before a crowd of students, *John spoke.*

John, in a red plaid coat and checkered pants, spoke.

Knowing the crowd was against him, *John spoke.*

John spoke at twelve o'clock in the blazing sun.

At twelve o'clock, *John spoke* in the blazing sun.

When we read a sentence, we know who did what or what happened and to whom. Without the subject and verb of the kernel sentence, for example, each of the phrases below is incomplete:

At noon before a crowd of students.	**(What happened?)**
In a red plaid coat and checkered pants.	**(What are you talking about? What did he or she do?)**
Knowing the crowd was against him.	**(Who? What happened?)**
At twelve o'clock in the blazing sun.	**(What happened?)**

To find the subject of a sentence, simply do this: Identify the verb. Then ask "Who?" or "What?" in front of it. The answer will be the subject. For example, in the sentence *John spoke,* we know the verb is spoke. If we ask "Who spoke?" the answer is the subject, John.

This simple test will also help you find the subject of a sentence worded as a question. Consider these examples:

When did John speak?

Did John speak at noon?

Why did John speak at noon?

If we ask, "Who?" before the verb did speak, the answer is the same: John, John, and John.

ESL Advice!

Memorize this test of a subject.

IN A NUTSHELL

- A sentence always expresses a complete thought.
- A sentence always includes a subject and verb.
- A kernel sentence is the smallest sentence possible.

PRACTICING 2

Underline the kernel sentence in each of these sentences.

Example: Clutching her red handbag, the woman ran after the bus.

1. Masako jumped into the pool.
2. Looking hard in the mirror, John smiled proudly.
3. Keisha was happy to be at the party.
4. Jack Horner, a happy grin on his ugly face, ate.
5. Quite by accident, she bumped the chair.
6. The ship hit an iceberg.
7. We skied all day.
8. The trolls played under the bridge.
9. Whether he admits it or not, he often lies.
10. We know plenty about the case.

PRACTICING 3

Sentences will vary.

Write *S* beside any construction you think is a sentence and *NS* if you think the construction is not one. If the construction is not a sentence, turn it into one in the space provided. Remember that a sentence must express a complete thought and contain a subject and verb.

1. _NS_ The green hat.

The green hat belongs to my sister.

2. _S_ Mice squeak.

_____

3. _NS_ The black limousine with shiny tires.

The black limousine with shiny tires pulled up in front of the courthouse.

4. _S_ The bat slept.

_____

5. _S_ Sheila snored.

_____

6. _NS_ Running fast.

We were running fast.

7. _S_ The ocean roared.

_____

8. _NS_ Setting the table.

I was setting the table.

9. _NS_ Made you worried.

The noise of the alarms made her worried.

10. _S_ Hear me, please!

_____

Prepositional Phrases

Sometimes it is easy to spot the subject of a sentence, but sometimes it isn't. For example, what is the subject of this sentence?

> One of Mary's friends gave her a surprise party.

If we apply the test of asking "Who?" before *gave*, we find that *One* is the subject. Because the prepositional phrase *of Mary's friends* comes before the verb *gave,* you might mistake *Mary's friends* for the subject.

A **preposition** is a word that shows the relationship between two things; a **prepositional phrase** is a group of words beginning with a preposition. A preposition always has an **object**—usually a noun or pronoun that follows it. The preposition and its object make up the prepositional phrase. Here is an example:

> He put the book on the table.

Here the preposition is *on,* and the object is *table.* Remember this formula:

PREPOSITION	+	OBJECT	=	PREPOSITIONAL PHRASE
on		the table		on the table
to		the sea		to the sea
of		the college		of the college
from		the store		from the store

Below is a list of the most common prepositions:

about	beside	like	under
above	besides	near	underneath
across	between	of	until
after	beyond	off	up
against	by	on	upon
along	despite	out	with
among	down	outside	within
around	during	over	without
at	except	past	throughout
before	for	since	through
behind	from	inside	
below	in	to	
beneath	into	toward	

One way to avoid mistaking a preposition for the subject of a sentence is to cross out all the prepositional phrases in any sentence whose subject you're trying to find. Here are some examples:

The driver ~~of the car~~ spoke ~~to the officer.~~

The answers ~~to the test~~ were not given.

Every student ~~from our school~~ loves cold weather.

IN A NUTSHELL

- A preposition is a word that shows the relationship between two things; a prepositional phrase is a preposition and its object.

- Don't mistake a word in a prepositional phrase for the subject of a sentence.

- If in doubt, cross out the prepositional phrase.

PRACTICING 4

For each of the following prepositions, create a prepositional phrase. Then write a complete sentence using the prepositional phrase.

Answers will vary.

1. above _____

_____

_____

2. through _____

_____

_____

3. inside _____

_____

_____

4. during _____

_____

_____

5. throughout _____

_____

_____

6. underneath _____

_____

_____

7. without _____

_____

_____

8. toward _____

_____

_____

9. around _____

_____

_____

10. in _____

_____

_____

PRACTICING 5

Exchange your answers to the Practicing 4 exercise with a class-mate. Underline the subject and verb in each of your partner's sentences. If you disagree about the subject and verb of any sentence, discuss it with other classmates.

PRACTICING 6

Cross out the prepositional phrase or phrases in each of the sentences below. Then identify the subject by circling it.

Example: The ⟨box⟩ ~~is on the top shelf in the closet~~.

1. ⟨He⟩ jumped the fence and ran ~~across the field~~.

2. The ⟨son⟩ ~~of Nadia~~ nodded.

3. ~~After the singing,~~ ⟨they⟩ went ~~into the dining room for dinner~~.

4. ⟨I⟩ will be ~~at the library until 4:00~~.

5. ⟨She⟩ is a woman ~~of her word~~.

6. ~~For your love,~~ ⟨I⟩ give everything.

7. ⟨We⟩ sat ~~near Louise, in the back row~~.

8. ⟨We⟩ sailed ~~up the lazy river~~.

9. ⟨You⟩ Put it ~~on the shelf, behind the suitcase~~.

10. ⟨She⟩ backed ~~out of the driveway without looking both ways~~.

Action Verbs and Linking Verbs

Verbs tell us who did what action in a sentence. What action, though, does *is* describe? In fact, it describes no action because *is* is a linking verb.

Indeed, there are two main kinds of verbs: action verbs and linking verbs. **Action verbs** describe an action. They tell us that the subject did a particular something. Here are examples:

Mary jumped off the chair.

Peter threw the ball.

Adam wrote an essay.

Each of these verbs describes a definite action: jumping, throwing, and writing. If someone asked you to mimic any of these actions, you could easily act out someone jumping, throwing, or writing. What if, however, someone asked you to mimic the action behind the verb *is*? You couldn't do it, because *is*, although a verb, describes no action and is instead a linking verb.

A **linking verb** connects the subject to other words that say something about it. Here are some examples:

Cathy is an accountant.

Harry looks tired.

Mary seems happy to be home.

The linking verb *is* connects the subject *Cathy* to the words *an accountant*, which is Cathy's job. Likewise, *Harry* is linked to *tired* by the linking verb *looks*, and *Mary* to *happy to be at home* by the linking verb *seems*. Linking verbs get their name because they link the subject to other words that tell us something about them. These other words are called **complements** because they "complete" the subject by renaming or describing it. So *Cathy* is *an accountant* (another name for Cathy), and *Harry* looks *tired* (describes his appearance).

Here are some other examples of complements:

The whole day was a <u>disaster.</u>

The mayor is his <u>mother.</u>

The milk smells <u>sour.</u>

Granny is the youngest <u>lawyer</u> in the firm.

Old bones become <u>brittle.</u>

Here is a list of some common linking verbs:

am	sound
are	look
has been	appear
is	seem
was	taste
were	smell
feel	

Don't mistake the complement of a sentence for its subject. Remember, to find the subject of a sentence, ask "Who?" or "What?" before the verb. The answer will be the subject. So, for example, in the sentence, *Granny is the youngest lawyer in the firm*, first identify the verb *is* and then ask "Who is?" The answer, Granny, is the subject.

PRACTICING 7

In the space provided, underline the verb and write *AV* beside sentences that contain an action verb or *LV* beside those that contain a linking verb.

1. __LV__   *Little Red Riding Hood* <u>is</u> a famous fairy tale.

2. __LV__   Those years <u>seem so</u> sad to me.

3. __AV__   The students <u>shuffled</u> into the auditorium.

4. __AV__   Jack <u>tripped</u> me on the football field.

5. __AV__   His father <u>handed</u> him the broom.

6. __LV__   The young minister <u>looked</u> awkward.

7. __LV__   All this <u>was</u> most upsetting.

8. __AV__   The colt <u>nuzzled</u> my hand.

9. __AV__   We <u>explored</u> the streams in the winter afternoons.

10. __LV__   The street <u>was</u> filled with potholes.

PRACTICING 8

In each of the following sentences, circle the linking verb and underline the complement.

Example: She ⟨is⟩ <u>lovely</u>.

1. They ⟨were⟩ <u>careful</u>.

2. Otto ⟨is⟩ <u>a St. Bernard</u>.

3. She ⟨was⟩ <u>the team leader</u> both years.

4. Her smile ⟨looked⟩ <u>phony</u>.

5. The judge's memory ⟨was⟩ not <u>clear</u>.

6. Does the cheese ⟨smell⟩ <u>bad</u>?

7. First graders often ⟨feel⟩ <u>lonely</u>.

8. The river ⟨looks⟩ <u>murky</u>.

9. Jealousy ⟨is⟩ <u>a hurtful emotion</u>.

10. Her purse ⟨is⟩ <u>the size of a suitcase</u>.

Helping Verbs

Verbs sometimes need additional words, called **helping verbs**, to express the past, present, and future. In the four sentences below the complete verb is underlined:

The children <u>are eating</u> at noon.   **(present)**

The children <u>will eat</u> at noon.   **(future)**

The children <u>had eaten</u> before the
storm arrived.   **(past)**

The children <u>were eating</u> when he
knocked.   **(past)**

Here, for example, are some of the many forms of the verb *work*.
Notice the many different helping verbs.

works	should have been working	will have worked
worked	can work	would have worked
is working	would have been working	should have worked
was working	will be working	must have worked
may work	had been working	having worked
should work	have worked	did work
will work	has worked	had worked
does work		

Occasionally, words that are not part of the complete verb will come
between the helping verb and the main verb. Here are some examples, with the words underlined:

She has <u>already</u> left.

They could have <u>definitely</u> fallen.

All of us had <u>quickly</u> disappeared.

We will <u>surely</u> help next time.

IN A NUTSHELL

- Action verbs are verbs that describe an action.
- Linking verbs are verbs that link a subject to its complement.
- Helping verbs are words such as *are, will,* and *had* that help
  a verb to express the past, present, and future.

PRACTICING 9

Underline the complete verb in the following sentences.

1. Dimitri <u>had stopped</u> his car a mile from camp.

2. Peter <u>was waiting</u> for her.

3. I <u>will remember</u> that picture.

4. She <u>has begun</u> to make the waffles.

5. They <u>should have gone</u> home earlier.

6. The accident <u>was reported</u> yesterday.

7. If only they <u>had remained</u> quiet!

8. The geese <u>were honking</u> full force.

9. My father <u>is sitting</u> at the head of the table.

10. You <u>should eat</u> more fresh vegetables.

PRACTICING 10

Underline only the complete verb in the following sentences. Do not underline words that come between the helping verb and the main verb.

Example: They <u>had</u> never <u>helped</u> their neighbors.

1. You <u>must</u> occasionally <u>hurry</u>.

2. They <u>have</u> often <u>traveled</u> to a foreign country.

3. Carlos <u>should have</u> deeply <u>regretted</u> his lie.

4. Few people <u>can</u> always <u>smile</u> when they are sad.

5. He <u>must</u> always <u>have been</u> the tallest in his class.

6. He <u>had</u> usually <u>rented</u> an apartment.

7. You <u>could have</u> quickly <u>run</u> across the street.

8. The man <u>should have</u> patiently <u>waited</u>.

9. The party <u>has</u> just <u>been</u> canceled.

10. Carina <u>will</u> never <u>go</u> swimming again.

Verbals

Verbals are words that look like verbs but do not act like verbs. Verbals are of three kinds: gerunds, participles, and infinitives. We'll look at each separately.

Gerunds

Gerunds are words that end in -*ing* and act as nouns, meaning that they can be the subject of a sentence. How can you tell if an -*ing* word is a gerund or a verb? Easy: look for the helping verb. For an -*ing* word to be a verb, it must have a helping verb. Look at these sentences:

We were swimming for fun.	**(were + -*ing* word = verb)**
Swimming is fun.	**(Swimming = subject = gerund)**
He is running in the Boston Marathon.	**(is + -*ing* word = verb)**
Running is good for you.	**(Running = subject = gerund)**

Apply the test for a subject by asking "Who?" or "What?" before the verb. "What" is good for you? Running; running = subject = gerund.

Weeding the garden can be hard work.

"What" can be hard work? Weeding; weeding = subject = gerund.

Another way to spot a gerund is to use the pronoun *it* in place of the suspect *-ing* word. If the *-ing* word is a gerund, this substitution is possible. If it is a verb, the substitution will seem ridiculous.

Swimming is fun.

It is fun.

The substitution makes sense: *swimming* is a gerund.

We were swimming for fun.

We were it for fun.

The sentence is ridiculous: *swimming* as used here is not a gerund.

PRACTICING 11

Rewrite the following sentences by turning the italicized verb into a gerund. As the example shows, you will have to change the original sentence by adding or deleting words and the current subject and the helping verb.

Answers will vary.

Example: Scientists *are finding* cures for many diseases.

Finding cures for many diseases keeps scientists busy.

1. Freddy *has been visiting* his grandparents.

Visiting his grandparents is fun for Freddy.

2. He *was using* a ruler to keep the lines straight.

Using a ruler helps you keep the lines straight.

3. We *were hoping* for sunny weather.

Hoping for sunny weather doesn't always make it happen.

4. The children *were eating* candy.

Eating too much candy can make a person sick.

5. All year I *had been avoiding* my homework.

Avoiding homework is a bad habit.

6. John *was deciding* whether or not to join the team.

Deciding whether or not to join the team was a difficult choice.

7. When was Meg *wearing* a black hat?

Wearing a black hat is not always appropriate.

8. George and Ani *were watching* television.

Watching television can be educational.

9. He *was kicking* the seat to annoy us.

Kicking the seat is an annoying behavior.

10. They had been begging us to paint the house green.

Begging for attention is not a good thing to do.

PRACTICING 12

Mark *V* when the *-ing* word is used as a verb, and circle the helping verb. Mark *G* when the *-ing* word is used as a gerund.

1. __V__   I (am) missing two assignments.
2. __V__   All of us (were) wearing glasses.
3. __G__   Marrying too young is not a good idea.
4. __V__   Ted (is) marrying Maria.
5. __V__   The directions (are) confusing.
6. __G__   Winning the lottery would be nice.
7. __G__   The screaming was eerie.
8. __V__   I (am) counting on him.
9. __V__   The officer (was) enforcing the law.
10. __G__   Driving out West with my sister was fun.

Participles

Participles are words that look like verbs but act like adjectives, meaning that they describe. Present participles end in *-ing*. Past participles end in *-ed*. Here are some examples:

> Jack is dancing with Linda.

Here *dancing* is a verb telling what Jack was doing.

> Jack is a dancing man.

Here *dancing* is a present participle describing the man Jack.

> We barbecued ribs for dinner.

Here *barbecued* is a verb telling what we did to the ribs.

We ate barbecued ribs for dinner.

Here *barbecued* is a past participle describing ribs.

PRACTICING 13

In each of the following sentences, underline the participle.

Example: Jack has on a battered hat.

1. The hissing cat jumped off the table.
2. Howling winds kept us awake all night.
3. The sky looks like a painted wall.
4. My mother's darkened hair makes her look young.
5. None of the running horses belonged to the ranch.
6. Bowing her head, Georgia sighed.
7. The Assembly passed a modified version of the bill.
8. Watching an old movie, he fell asleep.
9. We had an uninterrupted view.
10. Bored neighbors came to watch the dancing.

Infinitives

Infinitives consist of *to* plus a verb. Infinitives never act as verbs; they always serve some other function. Study these examples:

He wanted to disappear.

Here the infinitive *to disappear* tells what he wanted. The verb is *wanted*.

He wanted a place to sleep.

Here the infinitive *to sleep* tells what kind of place. The verb is *wanted*.

He waved to get her attention.

Here *to get* tells why he waved. The verb is *waved*.

Be careful not to confuse an infinitive with the preposition *to* followed by a noun or a pronoun.

Infinitive: Pete wanted to walk.

Preposition: Pete gave the apple to Fred.

- Verbals are words that look like verbs but do not act like verbs.
- Gerunds always end in *-ing* and act as nouns.
- Participles can end in *-ing* or *-ed;* they act as adjectives.
- An infinitive is *to* + a verb.

PRACTICING 14

Underline only the infinitives in the following sentences. Do not underline if the *to* is a preposition.

1. When do you plan <u>to eat</u>?
2. Margie gave her last dime to her sister.
3. Don't expect <u>to see</u> the lions.
4. We prefer <u>to walk</u> in the garden.
5. He whistled to the tune of "Yankee Doodle."
6. He listens only to his stomach.
7. He wanted <u>to play</u> every instrument in the band.
8. Carlita wanted <u>to love</u> her brother but couldn't.
9. Half way to the store, he realized that he'd forgotten <u>to wear</u> his watch.
10. Giving money to his best friend turned out <u>to be</u> a mistake.

PRACTICING 15

In the following sentences, underline the verb and circle the infinitive.

Example: The wind <u>began</u> to (blow.)

1. I <u>am going</u> (to buy) a new suit for my interview.
2. Every single student <u>wanted</u> (to go) to the game.
3. My boyfriend <u>loves</u> (to ski.)
4. I <u>need</u> (to change) the oil in my car.
5. It <u>will be</u> difficult (to be) as cheerful as Olivia.
6. Finally, I <u>have learned</u> how (to drive) a stick shift.
7. Everyone <u>must leave</u> in order (to clear) the hallways.
8. He <u>refuses</u> (to lose) weight.

9. I want <u>to be</u> alone.

10. Why <u>don't</u> you <u>ask</u> her <u>to change</u> your appointment?

Compound Subjects and Verbs

A sentence with more than one subject is said to have a **compound subject**. Here are some examples:

> John and Peter fished.
>
> The man and his son laughed.
>
> My wife and I knew.

In the first sentence, *John* and *Peter* are both subjects of the verb *fished*. In the second the subjects are *man* and *son*. In the third the subjects are *wife* and *I*.

A sentence may also have more than one verb—called a **compound verb**. Here are some examples:

> John fished and hunted.
>
> The man talked and laughed.
>
> I knew and understood.

The compound verbs are *fished* and *hunted* in the first sentence, *laughed* and *talked* in the second, and *knew* and *understood* in the third.

Naturally, compound subjects and verbs may occur in the same sentence:

> John, Peter, Tom, and Harry fished and hunted.
>
> The man and his son talked, laughed, and smiled.
>
> My wife and I knew, understood, and sympathized.

ESL Advice!

Compound subjects take a plural verb in the present tense (i.e., John and his son *talk* about life).

If you are like the rest of us, you often use such compound subjects and verbs in your everyday speech, perhaps without knowing their formal names. Recently a two-year-old we know tearfully blurted out this sentence after an accident:

> I tripped and fell.

When it was pointed out to her that she had just used a compound verb, she was neither consoled nor amused.

■ A sentence with more than one subject has a compound subject.

■ A sentence with more than one verb has a compound verb.

PRACTICING 16

Underline the compound subjects in the following sentences.

1. My teacher and I disagree.

2. My best friend and his wife came to dinner.

3. Fair weather and good company make the time fly.

4. Hope and love are both emotions.

5. Southern women and their diaries tell the story of the Civil War.

6. My dog, cat, and parakeet love one another.

7. Poetry and music are my twin loves.

8. Coffee, tea, and cookies were served.

9. Food and clothing are a big part of my budget.

10. A fool and his money are soon parted.

PRACTICING 17

Underline the compound verbs in the following sentences.

1. My heart sang and rejoiced at the victory.

2. He praised and rewarded my efforts.

3. Many people love and honor their roots.

4. The dog barked and howled all night.

5. She smiled and blew kisses to her fans.

6. I came and saw and conquered.

7. My husband scrimps and saves.

8. She said and did two different things.

9. The reporter talked and pointed to the map.

10. Terry dusted and vacuumed the room.

 **Unit Test**

In the following sentences, underline the subject once and the complete verb twice.

1. The poster showed the beauty of the garden.

2. Carlos had been riding his bicycle for two hours.

3. Do you want to play football?

4. The clouds above the mountains looked white and fluffy.

5. Fifty packed years of experience have taught us much.

6. My whole life has been a miracle.

7. They should have been working.

8. Angie and Dion operate the scoreboard.

9. The car sputtered and stopped.

10. The broken lamp has not been of any use.

In the following sentences, underline the prepositional phrases:

1. We found holes throughout the lace tablecloth.

2. It is difficult to complete college without extra money.

3. There stood Mr. Assadi, hiding behind the door.

From the verbs in parentheses, choose the correct one by underlining it.

1. Playing music (has been, have been) my great joy.

2. He and Marcy (is, are) having trouble communicating.

3. Tina and Josie (asks, ask) him the same question every day.

4. The men in the car (is, are) bothering the neighbors.

5. I often (pretends, pretend) to be rich and famous.

6. Giving the thumbs up sign (mean, means) that everything is fine.

7. What (were, was) you saying when I interrupted you?

8. Living without you (seem, seems) tedious.

9. Grasshoppers on the tree (sing, sings) me to sleep every night.

10. The young owner of the restaurants (speak, speaks) to my class today.

Unit Talk-Write Assignment

Answers will vary.

Underline all the verbals (gerunds, participles, and infinitives) in the *Talk* column. Then, using the sentences in the *Talk* column, write a paragraph in the *Write* column. Most of the sentences need to be rewritten in standard English.

TALK

1. Grandma, who died dirt poor, always made a big deal of <u>having</u> a nest egg for a rainy day.

2. "Don't let <u>spending</u> dictate your finances; let finances dictate your <u>spending</u>," she used <u>to say</u>, <u>pointing</u> her arthritic finger at me.

3. Then she'd dump her famous three rules on me:

4. First, "Don't own a credit card, but if you have <u>to use</u> one, pay it off at the end of every <u>month</u> so you aren't <u>bothered</u> by high interest payments."

5. Second, "Always have an emergency fund, no matter how teensy."

6. Third, "Set up a <u>savings</u> account and put something in it every month, even if it's just a nickel."

WRITE

Grandma, who died very poor, always stressed having money saved for a rainy day. "Don't let spending dictate your finances; let finances dictate your spending," she used to say, pointing her arthritic finger at me. Then she'd recite her famous three rules to me: First, "Don't own a credit card, but if you have to use one, pay it off at the end of every month so you aren't bothered by high interest payments." Second, "Always have an emergency fund, no matter how small." Third, "Set up a savings account and put something in it every month, even if it's just a nickel." Grandma's rules used to really annoy me because she kept repeating them to me. But I must have listened, because now, as a college sophomore, I do have a $100.00 emergency fund, a $1000.00 savings account, and no credit cards. Grandma's warning taught me an excellent lesson. Personal finances can either make you feel crazy or give you a sense of stability.

TALK **WRITE**

7. Grandma's rules used <u>to</u> really <u>drive</u> me nuts cause she kept <u>hitting</u> me over the head with them.

_____

_____

_____

_____

8. But I guess in the back of my mind I listened, because now, as a college sophomore, I do have a $100.00 emergency fund, a $1000.00 <u>savings</u> account, and nix as far as credit cards go.

_____

_____

_____

_____

9. Grandma's <u>warning</u> taught me a super lesson.

_____

_____

_____

10. Personal finances can either drive you bananas or give you a sense of stability.

_____

_____

_____

_____

 ## Unit Collaborative Assignment

Choose a partner to whom you will ask the questions below and who must then write down an answer in a full sentence. Exchange roles and have your partner ask you the same questions, to which you will write your answers in complete sentences. Exchange papers. Circle the subjects and underline the verbs in your partner's sentences, while your partner does the same to yours. Do you agree on all the subjects and verbs? In case of disagreement, ask your instructor.

1. What is your favorite restaurant?
2. Where is it located?
3. Why is it your favorite?
4. What is the decor like?
5. What kind of food does it serve?
6. What are your favorite dishes?
7. How expensive is it?

8. Whom do you go there with?

9. How do the waiters act?

10. How would you sum up your attitude toward this restaurant?

Unit Writing Assignment

Use the sentences you wrote in the Unit Collaborative Assignment to write a paragraph on your favorite restaurant. Use the Revising Checklist to help you revise. Pay particular attention to linking the sentences in your paragraph.

Photo Writing Assignment

Study the following picture of a girls' basketball team. Write about any topic suggested by the picture. For example, you might write about encouraging girls to participate in sports, making sports part of the curriculum in early grades, or teaching cooperation through team sports. Use the Revising Checklist to help you revise your work.

8

Building Sentences

Every sentence must have a subject and a verb: There is no exception to this rule. But not every construction with a subject and verb is a sentence. It could be a dependent clause.

Dependent and Independent Clauses

A **clause** is a group of words with both a subject and a verb. If a clause makes sense on its own, it is called an **independent clause** and is a complete sentence. These are independent clauses and, therefore, complete sentences:

> They will pick up the dry cleaning.
>
> You can always go home for dinner.
>
> We are looking for a renter.

Each of the above has a subject (*they*, *you*, and *we*) and a verb (*will pick*, *go*, and *are looking*). Moreover, as your speaker's ear will tell you, each makes sense on its own.

However, what about the following?

> After you go to the bank.
>
> If it rains.
>
> Who has a steady income.

Each of the above clauses has a subject (*you*, *it*, and *who*) and a verb (*go*, *rains*, and *has*), but none makes complete sense. These are **dependent clauses**—a group of words with a subject and verb that must be connected to an independent clause to make sense.

> Pick up the dry cleaning after you go to the bank.
>
> You can always go to the movies if it rains.
>
> We are looking for a renter who has a steady income.

Your ear for the language is the best judge of whether a clause makes sense or not and is therefore independent or dependent. Most speakers, for example, can immediately hear the differences between the following pairs of clauses:

Dependent:	Since David moved.
Independent:	I haven't been backpacking.
Combined:	Since David moved, I haven't been backpacking.

Dependent:	After they sang.
Independent:	The audience applauded.
Combined:	After they sang, the audience applauded.

Dependent:	Which is my hometown.
Independent:	We stopped in Denver.
Combined:	We stopped in Denver, which is my hometown.

ESL Advice!

If you haven't yet acquired an ear for English, memorize the definition of a sentence.

Many dependent clauses begin with a telltale sign—one of the following words. These words are called **relative pronouns** because they show how a dependent clause is related to a main clause.

who	whose	that
whom	which	

A dependent clause may also begin with one of these words, called **subordinating conjunctions**:

after	even if	once
although	even though	provided that
as if	if	rather than
because	in order that	since
before	now that	so that

than	until	wherever
that	when	whether
though	whenever	while
unless	where	why

Typically, it is these linking words that make a clause dependent. In fact, removing the subordinate conjunction changes a dependent clause into an independent clause. Here are some examples:

Dependent: Since you left me.

Independent: You left me.

Dependent: Because you didn't study.

Independent: You didn't study.

Dependent: While you were on vacation.

Independent: You were on vacation.

The obvious lesson to be learned is this: If you begin a sentence with one of the telltale words that make a clause dependent, be careful not to commit a dependent clause error.

IN A NUTSHELL

- A clause is a group of words that contains a subject and verb.

- An independent clause makes sense on its own; a dependent clause does not.

- Only a clause that can stand by itself is a sentence.

PRACTICING 1

In the blanks provided, write *D* if the clause is dependent and *I* if the clause is independent. For each clause that you mark with a *D*, underline the word that makes the clause dependent.

1. __D__ Who darted across the street like lightning.

2. __I__ New brakes were needed.

3. __I__ The trial will begin in a week.

4. __D__ Because he was sad and depressed.

5. __D__ While she was walking home.

6. __D__ Though the soup was ready.

7. __D__ Since no book can provide all the answers.

8. __D__ That he never looked back.

9. _D_   If war could have solved the problem.

10. _I_   Creative thinkers make good leaders.

11. _D_   <u>Wherever</u> he lived.

12. _D_   <u>Until</u> we meet again.

13. _I_   That quarrel was unnecessary.

14. _I_   Good books contain real treasures.

15. _I_   Loving your enemy will drive him nuts.

PRACTICING 2

In each blank, write an independent clause that could complete the sentence.

Example: Because he was only seventeen, _he could not vote._ _____

1. If you wear a badge with your name on it,_____

2. Before she moved to Idaho, _____

3. _____ , where I found the wallet.

4. Unless you call before 2:00, _____

5. Whenever time passed slowly,_____

6. Mrs. Forsythe, who never spent a dime on Halloween treats, _____

7. Although getting exercise is important,_____

8. Because they won, _____

9. While visiting George, _____

10. Until television arrived, _____

Three Basic Sentence Types

There are three basic sentence types: simple, compound, and complex. All three sentence types are commonly used in writing and talking. We will discuss each separately.

The simple sentence

A **simple sentence** consists of a single independent clause. It is both the first sentence out of the mouth of babes as well as the workhorse of daily writing. First graders routinely write simple sentences such as these:

Bobby fell down.

Sally is my friend.

I like my brother.

The simple sentence is commonly found in the Bible, where its simplicity is surprisingly powerful. Here, for example, is the first sentence of the Bible:

In the beginning God created the heavens and the earth.

The simple sentence, in spite of its name, is not always simply written. Nor is it always short, crisp, and childlike. It can be expanded if it is given more than one subject or verb. Here are some examples:

Simple sentences with singular subjects:

My mother has no ear for music.

My father has no ear for music.

Simple sentences with plural subject:

My mother and father have no ear for music.

The boy and man play together very well.

The children laugh at the monkeys.

They run away from the tigers.

They feed the goats.

Simple sentence with one subject and three verbs:

The children laugh at the monkeys, run away from the tigers, and feed the goats.

Simple sentences with two subjects and one verb:

The teammates and coach rehearse the play.

The women and child enter the room.

The brother and sister often agree.

Simple sentence with three subjects and three verbs:

The man, woman, and children laugh, chuckle, and point.

Another way to expand the simple sentence is to add **modifiers**, which are words that describe and explain the subject or verb. Here are some examples:

Simple sentence: Jim lives in Windsor.

First expansion: Jim, a star basketball player, lives in Windsor.

Second expansion: Jim, a star basketball player and an excellent student, lives in Windsor, Canada, across from Detroit.

IN A NUTSHELL

- The simple sentence consists of one independent clause.
- It can be expanded with multiple subjects and verbs or modifiers.

PRACTICING 3

In the following sentences, underline the subject(s) and verb(s) that make up the kernel sentence.

Example: <u>Alberto and Carmen</u>, who are cousins, <u>play</u> in the school orchestra <u>and sing</u> in the choir.

1. <u>José</u>, who is a new student at school, <u>is</u> a very good striker at soccer.

2. The <u>two dogs and the three cats got</u> along surprisingly well in spite of the heat.

3. A victim of circumstances, the <u>ship went</u> down in the storm.

4. <u>I</u>, like many other people, <u>watch</u> television less and less every year.

5. <u>Carina and Alphonso</u>, who come from different states, <u>are</u> surprisingly alike on political issues.

6. The <u>party fished, caught</u> crabs, <u>played</u> catch, and <u>danced</u> all night long.

7. <u>Alfredo and Juanita</u>, who are both from Guatemala, <u>speak and write</u> English very well.

8. <u>I'm</u> always delighted at the bobbing and weaving of seabirds.

9. The earth <u>shoe disappeared</u> a long time ago.

10. My <u>uncle and aunt</u>, who were both military officers for 25 years, still <u>rise</u> at six every morning.

PRACTICING 4

Expand the simple sentences below by adding subjects, verbs, or modifiers.

Example: My father loves to fish.

Expanded by adding a modifier: My father, a retired firefighter, loves to fish in the stream near his house.

Expanded by adding an additional subject and verb: My father and my uncle like to hike and love to fish.

1. My house is green. _____

_____

2. The man denied the story. _____

_____

3. Many people keep diaries. _____

_____

4. Sailing is fun. _____

_____

5. She is a generous woman. _____

_____

6. The train was late. _____

_____

7. He has a nickname. _____

_____

8. She went shopping. _____

_____

9. I could hardly believe my eyes. _____

_____

10. The room is full. _____

_____

11. John loves to waste time. _____

_____

12. Democracy is based on the will of the people. _____

_____

13. It is never too late to save money. _____

_____

14. The wind blew. _____

_____

15. The good life is inspired by love. _____

_____

The compound sentence

A **compound sentence** consists of two or more simple sentences joined by a **coordinating conjunction**. There are seven coordinating conjunctions: *and, but, for, or, nor, so, yet.* A comma is placed immediately before a coordinating conjunction. The simple sentences in a compound sentence should express ideas of equal importance. Here are some examples:

Simple:	Face-lifts are not always successful. The operation is painful.
Compound:	Face-lifts are not always successful, <u>and</u> the operation is painful.
Simple:	He must pay the fine. He will go to jail.
Compound:	He must pay the fine, <u>or</u> he will go to jail.
Simple:	She was very bright. She didn't study. She got poor grades.
Compound:	She was very bright, <u>but</u> she didn't study, <u>so</u> she got poor grades.

Notice that a comma comes immediately before the coordinating conjunction that joins the sentences.

IN A NUTSHELL

- A compound sentence consists of two or more simple sentences joined by a coordinating conjunction.
- The coordinating conjunctions are: *and, but, for, or, nor, so, yet.*
- A comma is placed immediately before the joining conjunction.

PRACTICING 5

Answers may vary.

Use a coordinating conjunction to join these paired simple sentences into a compound sentence. Don't forget the comma.

Example: My mother hates exercising. My father loves it.

My mother hates exercising, but my father loves it.

1. The band played loudly. The audience enjoyed it.

The band played loudly, but the audience enjoyed it.

2. I spoke to my neighbor. We made a date for lunch.

I spoke to my neighbor, and we made a date for lunch.

3. I went to aerobics class. I did 20 minutes on the treadmill. I'm exhausted.

I went to aerobics class, and I did 20 minutes on the treadmill, so I'm exhausted.

4. Liza ran up the stairs. She made a telephone call.

Liza ran up the stairs, and she made a telephone call.

5. I read the novel last night. I enjoyed it.

I read the novel last night, and I enjoyed it.

6. The dance was enjoyable. The students had a fine evening.

The dance was enjoyable, and the students had a fine evening.

7. Bicarbonate of soda is good for an upset stomach. I often use it.

Bicarbonate of soda is good for an upset stomach, so I often use it.

8. I reserved four tickets. That wasn't enough. I called for two more.

I reserved four tickets, but that wasn't enough, so I called for two more.

9. We met at Luigi's. We had dinner. Molly never showed up.

We met at Luigi's, and we had dinner, but Molly never showed up.

10. The bell rang. We filed out of the class.

The bell rang, so we filed out of the class.

The complex sentence

The **complex sentence** consists of one independent clause joined to one or more dependent clauses. Unlike the compound sentence, which connects two equal ideas, the complex sentence emphasizes one idea over the others. The less important idea or ideas are said to be subordinate. The more important idea is expressed in the independent clause:

> My toe hurts because John stepped on it.

The hurting toe is the main idea; the less important idea is why it hurts—because John stepped on it.

Here is another example of a complex sentence—this one with one independent and two dependent clauses:

> Tea has been shown to be good for you because of an ingredient in the leaf though coffee drinkers dispute the evidence.

The main idea here is that tea is good for you. The less important ideas are that this is so because of an ingredient in the leaf and that coffee drinkers dispute the evidence.

Common sense and your ear for language will help you decide which of two ideas is more important and therefore belongs in the independent clause. If neither idea is clearly more important, you must decide which idea to emphasize. Here are, for example, two sentences:

I drank a cup of hot chocolate. I went to bed.

If you want to emphasize *going to bed,* put it in the independent clause:

After drinking a cup of hot chocolate, I went to bed.

If you want to emphasize *drinking hot chocolate,* put it in the independent clause:

Before I went to bed, I drank a cup of hot chocolate.

Whether you put the independent or dependent clause is a matter of personal style. But the placement of these clauses does affect the punctuation of the sentence. This is the rule: If the dependent clause comes first, it must be followed by a comma; if the independent clause comes first, no comma is needed between clauses. Here are some examples:

Dependent clause first:	While he sat in the dentist's office, Phillip felt nervous. *(Note the comma between clauses.)*
Independent clause first:	Phillip felt nervous while he sat in the dentist's office. *(Note the absence of a comma.)*
Independent clause first:	We could not see the stage because of the dense crowd of people.
Dependent clause first:	Because of the dense crowd of people, we could not see the stage.

Exactly which idea you might choose to emphasize depends on what you want to say. Sometimes, however, it is clear which of two ideas is more important. Consider these two simple sentences:

The *Titanic* sank with a great loss of life. She struck an iceberg.

Common sense suggests that any complex sentence uniting these two ideas should emphasize the loss of life:

After she struck an iceberg, the *Titanic* sank with a great loss of life.

The reason that the *Titanic* sank is secondary and belongs in the dependent clause.

Bear in mind the words that signal a dependent clause. You may wish to review the relative pronouns and subordinating conjunctions on page 118 before you do the exercises.

- A complex sentence consists of one independent clause joined to one or more dependent clauses.

- The more important idea is expressed in the independent clause.

PRACTICING 6

Join the following sentences in a complex sentence, using one of the linking words listed on page 118. Be sure to put the most important idea—or the one you choose to emphasize—in the independent clause.

Example: My mother hates her work. She finds it boring.

My mother hates her work because she finds it boring.

1. She felt sorry for the beggar. She gave him money.

Because she felt sorry for the beggar, she gave him money.

2. The army retreated. It burned the bridges.

As the army retreated, it burned the bridges.

3. We will proceed with the job. You object to the charges.

We will proceed with the job even though you object to the charges.

4. You don't believe me. It is the truth.

Although you don't believe me, it is the truth.

5. You have been gone. I have not been the same.

Since you have been gone, I have not been the same.

6. The headmaster issued the uniforms. There was a complaint against them.

After the headmaster issued the uniforms, there was a complaint against them.

7. You explain your behavior. I will report the incident.

Unless you explain your behavior, I will report the incident.

8. You were gone. The bill collector came.

While you were gone, the bill collector came.

9. You will be admitted to the intermediate level course. You do well in the tests.

You will be admitted if you do well on the tests.

10. The band stopped playing. The program was over.

When the band stopped playing, the program was over.

PRACTICING 7

In the space to the left of each of the following sentences, identify the sentence as simple, compound, or complex.

1. *Simple* — The opera singer, clad in a magnificent costume, shrieked her lungs out during the aria.

2. *Complex* — Baseball is so popular partly because it has a long, storied history.

3. *Simple* — They didn't even ask management's permission to put the idea into effect.

4. *Simple* — The Lifetime channel on cable TV is very popular with women.

5. *Compound* — They ran into trouble from the very start, but they were too foolish to ask for help.

6. *Complex* — Because I'm a birdwatcher, I'm often to be found tromping through the woods.

7. *Simple* — Basking in popularity, the young quarterback became even vainer.

8. *Complex* — Although she is young, she has a surprisingly mature grasp of the stock market.

9. *Compound* — He could not do it no matter how hard he tried, so he threw his hands up in the air and gave up.

10. *Compound* — The streets of Nice, France, are usually littered with dog droppings, yet the streets of Paris, a much bigger city, are surprisingly clean

PRACTICING 8

Answers will vary.

Write a series of sentences on one of your favorite activities— something you really enjoy. Each sentence should be of the specific type listed below.

1. Simple sentence with more than one subject:

_____

2. Simple sentence with more than one verb:

_____

3. Simple sentence with modifiers:

_____

4. Two compound sentences:

(a). _____

_____

(b). _____

5. Three complex sentences:

(a). _____

_____

(b). _____

_____

(c). _____

_____

PRACTICING 9

Exchange papers with a classmate and discuss the sentences you wrote in Practicing 8. Help each other make any necessary corrections.

Answers will vary.

Sentence Variety

Writers seldom write in only one sentence type for the same reason that good cooks season their food with more than just salt. Any sentence pattern that is overused will quickly seem boring. Variety is the key to a good writing style and can be achieved easily if you use a mix of simple, compound, and complex sentences. Here is an example of a ho-hum passage:

> Rap music started during the 1970s. It comes from African chanting. It also comes from chatting. Rap music means "chat music." It contains . . .

This passage consists of a string of simple sentences. Notice how it is immediately improved when the sentences are varied:

> Rap music, which started during the 1970s, comes from African chanting. It also comes from chatting. Rap music means "chat music," and it contains . . .

This sort of sentence variation is exactly what you do instinctively in your everyday speech. It is what you must also try to do in your writing.

For variety, use all three sentence types—simple, compound, and complex—in your writing.

PRACTICING 10

Answers will vary.

Rewrite each paragraph below to eliminate the choppy effect of too many simple sentences. First, read the sentences aloud to determine the relationship between them. Then reduce the number of simple sentences by combining some into compound and complex sentences.

(1)

On Monday nothing seemed right. Friday Linda was pleased with her life. She had called her mother. Her mother had been feeling sick. On the phone she sounded chipper. Linda felt relieved. She decided to go camping in the mountains. Her friend had a cabin there. She would fish all weekend. She would be alone. She liked being alone. The weekend would cost little. She would only have to buy groceries for herself. She had enough money. She had just gotten a paycheck. She would wear old clothes. She would lounge by the river. She would sleep late. There would be no alarm clock. Nobody would bother her. Linda thought, "Everything turns out for the best."

(2)

Most college students juggle the hours in their day. They play sports and go to parties. Many also have jobs. They try to include serving on committees. They perform volunteer work. They go to lectures. The many options do evoke a great deal of anxiety. The choices are unlimited. The hours are limited. Students feel pressured to get good grades. They feel pressured to experience life fully. They have to decide how much time they can spare outside of class and work for general enrichment. That decision is not always easy to make.

 **Unit Test**

1. Write a simple sentence with modifiers about the clothing you are wearing today.

Answers will vary
_____

_____

2. Write a compound sentence by connecting two simple sentences with "but."

Answers will vary
_____

_____

3. Write a complex sentence beginning with "Although." Be sure to place a comma following the dependent clause.

Answers will vary
_____

_____

4. Use the pattern of the following sentence, but change the words to create your own sentence on any topic of your choice: "I will never forget my Aunt Stella because she was my favorite relative." What kind of sentence is this?

Complex
_____

_____

5. Identify each of the following sentences as simple, compound, or complex.

Complex **(a).** When John entered his astronomy class, he was embarrassed to find everyone staring at him.

Compound **(b).** Let's follow the instructions carefully, and then we'll compare what we've done with the picture.

Complex **(c).** If you hurry, you can probably catch her.

Simple **(d).** The umbrella, wet and dripping, stood in the corner of the hall.

Simple **(e).** Our neighborhood block party on Memorial Day is always fun.

Complex **(f).** Because we came late, we couldn't find seats together.

Compound **(g).** I know what it is to be hungry, but I have never been hungry for long.

Complex **(h).** Winning is not always important because sometimes defeat teaches more than winning.

Simple   **(i).** I have discovered how to fool people.

○   _Complex_   **(j).** I don't like to swim unless the water is really warm.

 Unit Talk-Write Assignment

A political science class was asked whether court cases should ever be televised. The reaction was predictably mixed. One student, however, had very strong opinions and was not timid about expressing them. The student's ideas are in the _Talk_ column.

First, study the _Talk_ column to get an understanding of the student's opinion. Second, rewrite every sentence in the _Talk_ column to make it suitable for inclusion in a written paragraph. Third, using a combination of the student's oral remarks and your own opinions, write a paragraph giving your own views on this topic. Check your paragraph against the Revision Checklist.

TALK

1. Court cases on television?

2. How stupid.

3. That may be within the law, but I couldn't care less.

4. Put a witness on the stand before television cameras and lights, and before you know it the Bozo is acting like he's a movie star, cutting up for the director.

WRITE

1. _Should there be court cases on television?_
_____
_____

2. _That is stupid._
_____
_____

3. _That may be within the law, but that doesn't_
matter.
_____

4. _If you put a witness on the stand before_
television cameras and lights, he may begin to
act like a movie star, acting for the director.
_____
_____
_____

TALK

5. The point is, you don't want a system that makes every jerk feel like the world is hanging on to his every word.

6. Take the O. J. Simpson case—what a can of worms!

7. You had the judge carrying on like he was at a circus. You had a defense attorney as concerned about his clothes as his client.

8. And whoever heard of a jury being locked up for a year?

9. The whole thing was like entertainment. Not a life-and-death court case.

10. When a person is on trial, the last thing you need is publicity. I'm totally against televising court cases.

WRITE

5. *It is not good to have a system that makes people feel like the entire world is listening to them.*

6. *For example, the O.J. Simpson case was full of problems.*

7. *The judge behaved as if he was at a circus. The defense attorney was as concerned about his clothes as about his client.*

8. *A year is too long a time for a jury to be sequestered.*

9. *The case became entertainment rather than a murder trial.*

10. *When a person is on trial, publicity is harmful. I'm very much against televising court cases.*

Unit Collaborative Assignment

Get together with two or three classmates to talk about your pet peeves, such as drivers who can't make up their minds, people who refuse to take their turns in lines, and teachers who wait until halfway through the semester to give the first exam. When one student is speaking, the others should write down some of the sentences. When everyone has discussed his or her pet peeve, take turns presenting and classifying the written sentences as simple, compound, or complex.

Unit Writing Assignment

Using the ideas you accumulated during the Unit Collaborative Assignment, write about one of your pet peeves. Make a special effort to use sentence variety, and use the Revising Checklist to revise.

Photo Writing Assignment

The following photo shows a couple dancing. Write about why you think dancing is a waste of time or fun. Again, make a special effort to use sentence variety. Use the Revising Checklist to revise.

9

Avoiding Non-Sentences

"If he blows up the world."
"Fred is a flake no one likes him."
Last night I helped get supper, my potatoes were delicious."

You have already learned that a sentence is the same as an independent clause. It has a subject, a verb, and makes complete sense on its own. Non-sentences can be of two types—fragments and run-ons. We'll discuss fragments first.

Fragments

A **fragment** is only part of a sentence. It is a "wannabe" sentence that lacks either subject or verb and makes no sense; it fails to express a complete thought. Sometimes the omission occurs because the writer is "on a roll." It's fine to write fast and get all your thoughts down in a hurry, but then you must always proofread your work for errors.

Here are some examples of fragments that can occur in the rush of writing:

Has an 8:00 o'clock class.   **(missing subject)**

Joe's sweater.   **(missing verb)**

Especially when she is on a diet.   **(not a complete thought)**

Most of us speak in fragments every day without being misunderstood. Consider, for example, the exchange that follows:

Josh: Get your schedule yet?

Max: Sure did.

Josh: Any 8:00 o'clock classes?

Max: One. Psych.

Josh: Grim.

Max: I know. And with Skrebniski, too.

This conversation in fragments strikes the ear as typical of daily speech. Yet, in spite of the fragments, Max and Josh obviously still understand each other. Their exchange moves along smoothly, and neither interrupts the other for any clarification.

We have learned, however, that formal writing aims for a universal audience and therefore requires the use of standard English—meaning a standard vocabulary and complete sentences. Here is how Max and Josh's exchange would be written in standard English:

Josh: Have you gotten your schedule yet?

Max: Yes, I have.

Josh: Do you have any 8:00 o'clock classes?

Max: I have one—psychology.

Josh: That's grim.

Max: I know. And the class is with Skrebniski, too.

The standard English version may seem a little stiff, perhaps, compared to Max and Josh's informality. However, it is now understandable not only to Max and Josh, but to the millions of people around the world who read standard English.

IN A NUTSHELL

A fragment is a "wannabe" sentence that lacks either a subject or verb and fails to express a complete thought

PRACTICING 1

Identify the fragments in the list of constructions below. Mark *F* for a fragment and *S* for a complete sentence. Using the lines provided, correct all the fragments you find by turning them into complete sentences.

Various answers are possible.

Example: ___*F*___   Went to buy milk. <u>No subject</u>

1. ___*F*___   Hoping to score big. _____

2. ___*S*___   He is a big man on campus. _____

3. ___*S*___   Let me call you sweetheart. _____

4. ___*F*___   To join the army. _____

5. ___F___ Crying all the time. _____

6. ___S___ Give me a few dollars. _____

7. ___S___ I saw you in the garden. _____

8. ___S___ Who's sorry now? _____

9. ___F___ Just in time. _____

10. ___F___ Because it's my decision. _____

Avoiding Sentence Fragments

A fragment can spring from one of several causes. If you learn to recognize these, you will be able to avoid fragments in your own writing.

Fragments caused by a missing subject

In the heat of writing, it is easy to write a verb but forget to write the subject. The result will be a fragment. Here are some examples:

> Kevin handed Marty two tickets for the playoffs. Then watched the look on his face.

> They're getting married in May. But not going on a honeymoon until September.

In these examples, the writer mistakenly thought that the subject of the first sentence also applied to the second group of words. It does—but the second thought must be formally joined to the first by a conjunction, such as *and*. If you forget the conjunction, you must write the two thoughts as separate, complete sentences:

> Kevin handed Marty two tickets for the playoffs and watched the look on Marty's face.

or

> Kevin handed Marty two tickets for the playoffs. Then he watched the look on Marty's face.

> They're getting married in May, but not going on a honeymoon until September.

or

> They're getting married in May. But they're not going on a honeymoon until September.

IN A NUTSHELL

Do not create a fragment by carelessly omitting the subject of the sentence.

PRACTICING 2

Correct the following fragments caused by a missing subject. You can either join the fragment to the sentence preceding it or rewrite it as a separate sentence.

Example: Maybe the universe is younger than we think. And was not caused by the Big Bang.

Joined: Maybe the universe is younger than we think and was not caused by the Big Bang.

Rewritten: Maybe the universe is younger than we think. Maybe it was not caused by the Big Bang.

1. Larry announced that he was going to Finland. Then showed me his ticket.

   Larry announced that he was going to Finland, then showed me his ticket.

2. For plotting to kill Queen Elizabeth I, Sir Walter Raleigh was dropped from the list of the Queen's lovers. Also was beheaded.

   For plotting to kill Queen Elizabeth I, Sir Walter Raleigh was dropped from the list of

   the Queen's lovers. He also was beheaded.

3. Mario learned to ski. And loved the sport.

   Mario learned to ski and loved the sport.

4. They prepared to entertain. But forgot to buy wine.

   They prepared to entertain, but they forgot to buy wine.

5. The car blew a tire. Spun around into a lamppost. And landed in a ditch.

   The car blew a tire, spun around into a lamppost, and landed in a ditch.

6. I find Alice's rudeness to servers irritating. And tell her so.

   I find Alice's rudeness to servers irritating. And I tell her so.

7. Our bookkeeper did the ledger. But didn't do the spreadsheets.

   Our bookkeeper did the ledger, but she didn't do the spreadsheets.

8. Mr. Gibson was always talking about politics. And was himself quite a politician.

   Mr. Gibson was always talking about politics. And he was himself quite a politician.

9. He served a wonderful dinner. But burned the dessert.

   He served a wonderful dinner, but he burned the dessert.

10. Cathy was sorry. Or at least said she was.

    Cathy was sorry. Or at least she said she was.

Fragments due to -ing words

Some fragments are triggered by an *-ing* word, such as *singing*. Here are some examples:

> They celebrated. Dancing in the street.

> The plane landed. Skidding to a halt.

Why beginning with an *-ing* word often leads to a fragment is something of a puzzle. Possibly, the writer mistakes the *-ing* word for a full verb, but it isn't. As you know from Unit 7, an *-ing* word can only be a verb in a sentence if it is paired with a helping verb.

To correct a fragment due to an *-ing* word, either join it to the sentence that went before (use a comma to set off the first part of the sentence), or rewrite it as a separate sentence:

> They celebrated, dancing in the street.

or

> They celebrated. They were dancing in the street.

> The plane landed, skidding to a halt.

or

> The plane landed. It skidded to a halt.

IN A NUTSHELL

Be careful of creating a fragment with an *-ing* word.

PRACTICING 3

Correct the *-ing* fragments by rewriting the sentences below.

Answers may vary.

1. My parents wouldn't let me study the trumpet. Insisting that I should learn to play the piano.

My parents wouldn't let me study the trumpet. They insisted that I should learn to

play the piano.

2. He spent two summers on a farm. Picking vegetables in the heat of the day.

He spent two summers on a farm, picking vegetables in the heat of the day.

3. The coach lifted curfew. Believing the team members could discipline themselves.

The coach lifted curfew, believing the team members could discipline themselves.

4. His handwriting is filled with sharp points and angles. Classifying him as a mean and stingy person.

His handwriting is filled with sharp points and angles. This classifies him as a mean and stingy person.

5. The director carefully observed the dancers. Looking for signs of exceptional talent.

The director carefully observed the dancers, looking for signs of exceptional talent.

6. He loves to read. Spending many hours in an armchair.

He loves to read, spending many hours in an armchair.

7. He attended to his father's business. Working long hours every day.

He attended to his father's business. He worked long hours every day.

8. She was the star of the soccer team. Having scored the most goals.

She was the star of the soccer team, having scored the most goals.

9. He proposed to her one day. Getting down on his knee.

He proposed to her one day, getting down on his knee.

10. Many movies are violent. Appealing to the resentment people feel.

Many movies are violent. They appeal to the resentment people feel.

Fragments due to the incorrect use of infinitives

A third common type of fragment is triggered by the incorrect use of infinitives (*to* + verb). (See Unit 7 to review infinitives.) Here is an example:

I am taking karate lessons. To build up my strength.

John went to a movie. To get his mind off exams.

As before, you can correct this type of fragment by either joining it to the sentence before, or rewriting it as a separate and complete sentence:

Joined: I am taking karate lessons to build up my strength.

Rewritten: I am taking karate lessons. I want to build up my strength.

Joined: John went to a movie to get his mind off exams.

Rewritten: John went to a movie. He needed to get his mind off exams.

Note that you could also make the infinitive and the words around it into a dependent clause that you put either at the beginning or at the end of the combined sentence. If you put the dependent clause at the beginning of the new sentence, be sure to put a comma after it.

To build up my strength, I am taking karate lessons.

To get his mind off exams, John went to a movie.

or

I am taking karate lessons to build up my strength.

John went to a movie to get his mind off exams.

IN A NUTSHELL

Watch out for fragments caused by the incorrect use of infinitives.

PRACTICING 4

Correct the following *to* fragments by either joining them to the sentences before or rewriting them as separate sentences.

1. The students took out state educational loans. To get money at a low interest rate.

The students took out state educational loans. They can get money at a low

interest rate.

2. I, too, would like a wife. To tend to my every want and slightest need.

I, too, would like a wife to tend to my every want and slightest need.

3. We screen our calls through our message machine. To avoid telephone marketers.

We screen our calls through our message machine to avoid telephone marketers.

4. I bought some property outside of Phoenix. To build a cabin some day.

I bought some property outside of Phoenix. I want to build a cabin some day.

5. I used to live in San Antonio, Texas. To make a long story short.

To make a long story short, I used to live in San Antonio, Texas.

6. He took the train home. To avoid the heavy traffic.

He took the train home to avoid the heavy traffic.

7. She read a novel. To wile away the time.

She read a novel to while [or wile] away the time.

8. She took a summer job. To earn money for college.

She took a summer job to earn money for college.

9. You need a key. To start the engine.

You need a key to start the engine.

10. He exercised all summer. To make the football team.

He exercised all summer. He wanted to make the football team.

PRACTICING 5

Turn the following fragments due to incorrect use of –*ing* words or infinitives into complete sentences by adding an independent clause before or after the fragment.

Example: To make sure she got home safely.

Jack picked Carmen up after work every night to make sure she got home safely.

1. Being too tired to go to the theater.

Being too tired to go to the theater, I went to bed.

2. To have her car repaired.

She drove to the service station to have her car repaired.

3. Showing the programmer the operation of the new computer.

Showing the programmer the operation of the new computer, Alice went over the

entire manual with her.

4. Pretending it was otherwise.

Pretending it was otherwise, Jack chose to ignore the dirty kitchen.

5. Investing as a way of life.

She claimed not to understand investing as a way of life.

6. To perform at a higher level of efficiency.

To perform at a higher level of efficiency, the entire team must get more sleep.

7. To fake it for the sake of the show.

The dean of foreign students tried her best to fake it for the sake of the show.

8. Using a substitute for whalebone.

Using a substitute for whalebone, the craftsman carved wonderful trinkets.

9. To laugh at our own weaknesses.

It is healthy to laugh at our own weaknesses.

10. Boiling instead of frying.

The chef was willing to try boiling instead of frying.

Fragments due to dependent words

You have learned about fragments caused by omitted subjects, *-ing* words, and the incorrect use of infinitives. You have also learned two ways of correcting fragments—by joining the fragment to the sentence before or by rewriting the fragment as a separate sentence.

We come now to a fourth kind of fragment. This one is triggered by the misuse of relative pronouns and subordinate conjunctions, both of which we covered in Unit 7. This fourth type of fragment is corrected in only one way—by joining it to the sentence before. Here is a list of relative pronouns that can cause fragments:

who	whose	that
whom	which	

Here are examples of fragments caused by unconnected relative pronouns:

> We inspected the attic. <u>Which</u> had become a dumping ground for excess furniture.

> Next month we must pay tribute to Coach Peters. <u>Who</u> helped us win the trophy.

Here are the corrections:

> We inspected the attic, <u>which</u> had become a dumping ground for excess furniture.

> Next month we must pay tribute to Coach Peters, who helped us win the trophy.

As you can see, both fragments were corrected by joining them to the sentence before. Indeed, both were caused by the writer's use of a period instead of a comma.

Similarly, a fragment can be caused by the misuse of a subordinate conjunction. Here is a list of subordinate conjunctions:

after	although	as if
because	before	even if
even though	if	in order that
now that	once	provided that
rather than	since	so that
than	that	though
unless	until	when
whenever	where	wherever
whether	while	why

Here are some examples of fragments caused by unconnected subordinate conjunctions:

> <u>Even though</u> society seems to be increasingly concerned. Crime keeps rising.

> After the flood subsided. The corn started to grow again.

To correct such fragments, simply join them to the neighboring sentence:

> Even though society seems to be increasingly concerned, crime keeps rising.

> The corn started to grow again after the flood subsided.

Note that if the dependent clause comes first, it is separated from the independent clause by a comma:

Incorrect: Since it was our anniversary. We ordered lobster.

Correct: Since it was our anniversary, we ordered lobster.

But: We ordered lobster since it was our anniversary.

IN A NUTSHELL

Subordinate conjunctions and relative pronouns can trigger sentence fragments. Correct these fragments by joining them to a neighboring sentence.

PRACTICING 6

Correct the following fragments by joining them to a neighboring sentence.

1. We shop at Piggly-Wiggly. Where the prices are lower. Although I prefer Dominick's for meats.

We shop at Piggly-Wiggly, where the prices are lower although I prefer Dominick's

for meats.

2. The words acquired new meaning. When he found out they were spoken by Abraham Lincoln.

The words acquired new meaning when he found out they were spoken by Abraham

Lincoln.

3. Now, let's look at the words *bull* and *cow*. Which are simply male and female equivalents.

Now, let's look at the words bull and cow, which are simply male and female

equivalents.

4. Stop and take a rest. If your breathing becomes labored.

Stop and take a rest if your breathing becomes labored.

5. My favorite restaurant is the Fireside Inn, which is near my grandparents' house. Although it isn't cheap.

Although it isn't cheap, my favorite restaurant is the Fireside Inn, which is near my

grandparents' house.

6. The hills were alive with the voices of people. Whose laughter rang across the valley, where their ancestors have lived for generations.

The hills were alive with the voices of people whose laughter rang across the valley

where their ancestors have lived for generations.

7. He plays several sports. Since he is quite athletic.

He plays several sports since he is quite athletic.

8. I want to leave the hustle and bustle of city life. Where every decision is one more frustration.

I want to leave the hustle and bustle of city life where every decision is one more

frustration.

9. He worked hard and studied until midnight every night. In order to make the Dean's List.

He worked hard and studied until midnight every night in order to make the

Dean's List.

10. Get one large pizza. Rather than two medium ones.

Get one large pizza rather than two medium ones.

Fragments due to added details

Details added to a sentence can also cause a fragment. Beware of the words listed below. They often lead to added-detail fragments.

especially	including
except	not even
also	such as
in addition	for example

Here are three examples of fragments caused by added details:

The entire neighborhood was up in arms. Except the Johnson sisters.

The expedition leader warned of many hardships. Among them freezing weather, lack of food, and difficult terrain.

Pottery made by the Acoma has very bold geometric designs. For example, horizontal and vertical lines, triangles, and diamonds.

To correct a fragment caused by added details, simply attach the details to the previous sentence (using a comma to set off the added details) and add any words necessary to complete the link:

The entire neighborhood was up in arms, except the Johnson sisters.

The expedition leader warned of many hardships, among them freezing weather, lack of food, and difficult terrain.

If the additional detail fragment is long, you can make it into a separate sentence:

Pottery made by the Acoma has very bold geometric designs. These designs feature horizontal and vertical lines, triangles, and diamonds.

IN A NUTSHELL

Details added to a sentence as an afterthought can cause a fragment. Correct the fragment by connecting it to the previous sentence or by turning it into a complete sentence of its own.

PRACTICING 7

Correct the following fragments caused by added details by joining them to the sentence before.

Answers may vary.

1. Some of my favorite people are a little eccentric. For example, the woman who wears an evening gown to feed the pigeons.

Some of my favorite people are a little eccentric, for example, the woman who wears

an evening gown to feed the pigeons.

2. Certain languages are more musical than others. Among them Italian and Spanish.

Certain languages are more musical than others, among them Italian and Spanish.

3. She received many gifts. Tickets to a Hawks game, a
bracelet, and a couple of CDs.

She received many gifts, including tickets to a Hawks game, a bracelet, and a

couple of CDs.

4. No parent always makes the right decision. Not even with
the best intentions.

No parent always makes the right decision even with the best intentions.

5. We encountered some minor difficulties. Including locking
the keys in the car.

We encountered some minor difficulties, including locking the keys in the car.

6. For appetizers we'll have chips and salsa. Also cheese and
vegetables with dips.

For appetizers we'll have chips and salsa. We'll also have cheese and vegetables

with dip.

7. The girls kept getting into trouble at the bus stop. Except
for Mary, an A student.

The girls kept getting into trouble at the bus stop, except for Mary, an A student.

8. Students should be encouraged to become intimate with
their books. Even writing in the margins of pages.

Students should be encouraged to become intimate with their books. They should

even write in the margins of the pages.

9. The Boston Pops always puts on a great July 4th celebration. With fireworks and a cannon.

The Boston Pops always put on a great July 4th celebration with fireworks and a

cannon.

10. A good leader never leaves his followers without hope. Especially in times of serious trouble.

A good leader never leaves his followers without hope, especially in times of serious

trouble.

Run-on Sentences

A **run-on sentence** is actually two sentences mistaken for one. There are two main types of run-on sentences: the fused sentence and the comma splice.

The **fused sentence** consists of two sentences joined—or fused—without any punctuation between them:

> We toured General Grant's home it is in Illinois.

Here is how the sentence should be written:

> We toured General Grant's home. It is in Illinois.

The second type of run-on sentence is the **comma splice**—two full sentences separated by a comma instead of a period:

> The steak was gray and tough, the eggs tasted like rubber.

Here is the sentence, corrected:

> The steak was gray and tough. The eggs tasted like rubber.

PRACTICING 8

In the blanks provided, indicate *FS* if the run-on sentence is fused and *CS* if it is spliced. If the sentence is correct, neither fused nor spliced, mark it with a check.

Example: _CS_ She is beautiful, she is too thin.

1. _✔_ Don't wait another minute to send your money now.

2. _CS_ He must attend class on Wednesday, a test will be given.

3. _CS_ Raspberries are tasty, they are expensive.

4. _FS_ You may be able to live on love you definitely can't retire on it.

5. _FS_ Scorpions are wary they rely on their natural camouflage to protect them from enemies.

6. _✔_ Mark Blumenstein is a modern artist who uses saws, gas nozzles, and scythe blades in his sculptures.

7. _FS_ Get relief from allergies use a steam inhalator.

8. _FS_ It was cold, windy, and dark the fish didn't hit.

9. _✔_ People from all walks of life play softball because it is our most democratic pastime.

10. _FS_ She wore a black turtleneck everyone wanted to know where she had bought it.

Correcting run-on sentences

There are four ways to correct run-on sentences. Take, for example, this one:

> Frank is outgoing Jeff is timid.

To correct it, you can do one of the following:

1. Put a period at the end of the first sentence:

> Frank is outgoing. Jeff is timid.

2. Put a semicolon at the end of the first sentence:

> Frank is outgoing; Jeff is timid.

3. Put a coordinating conjunction (with a comma before it) at the end of the first sentence:

> Frank is outgoing, but Jeff is timid.

4. Use a subordinating conjunction:

> Frank is outgoing though Jeff is timid.

or

> Though Frank is outgoing, Jeff is timid.

IN A NUTSHELL

Two sentences run together as one create a run-on sentence. To correct a run-on sentence, do one of the following:

- Put a period between them.
- Put a semicolon between them.
- Put a coordinating conjunction between them. (Don't forget the comma.)
- Use a subordinating conjunction.

PRACTICING 9

Correct the following run-ons in all four possible ways.

1. He sent a dozen roses she still didn't forgive him.

Insert a period: _____

He sent a dozen roses. She still didn't forgive him.

Insert a semicolon: _____

He sent a dozen roses; she still didn't forgive him.

Insert a coordinating conjunction and comma: _____

He sent a dozen roses, but she still didn't forgive him.

Insert a subordinating conjunction (with comma if needed):____

Although he sent a dozen roses, she still didn't forgive him.

2. I've always wanted a pickup truck it's only a matter of time until I get one.

Insert a period: _____

I've always wanted a pickup truck. It's only a matter of time until I get one.

Insert a semicolon: _____

I've always wanted a pickup truck; it's only a matter of time until I get one.

Insert a coordinating conjunction and comma: _____

I've always wanted a pickup truck, so it's only a matter of time until I get one.

Insert a subordinating conjunction (with comma if needed):____

Because I've always wanted a pickup truck, it's only a matter of time until I get one.

3. It rained all day, the yard was one big puddle.

Insert a period: _____

It rained all day. The yard was one big puddle.

Insert a semicolon: _____

It rained all day; the yard was one big puddle.

Insert a coordinating conjunction and comma: _____

It rained all day, so the yard was one big puddle.

Insert a subordinating conjunction (with comma if needed):____

Since it rained all day, the yard was one big puddle.

4. Bring nametags and pens Mary always forgets them.

Insert a period: _____

Bring nametags and pens. Mary always forgets them.

Insert a semicolon: _____

Bring nametags and pens; Mary always forgets them.

Insert a coordinating conjunction and comma: _____

Bring nametags and pens, for Mary always forgets them.

Insert a subordinating conjunction (with comma if needed):____

Bring nametags and pens because Mary always forgets them.

5. The children looked for shells their mother watched that they didn't wander far.

Insert a period: _____

The children looked for shells. Their mother watched that they didn't wander far.

Insert a semicolon: _____

The children looked for shells; their mother watched that they didn't wander far.

Insert a coordinating conjunction and comma: _____

The children looked for shells, and their mother watched that they didn't wander far.

Insert a subordinating conjunction (with comma if needed):____

While the children looked for shells, their mother watched that they didn't wander far.

6. Our team has talent and trains hard our problem is injuries.

Insert a period: _____

Our team has talent and trains hard. Our problem is injuries.

Insert a semicolon: _____

Our team has talent and trains hard; our problem is injuries.

Insert a coordinating conjunction and comma: _____

Our team has talent and trains hard, but our problem is injuries.

Insert a subordinating conjunction (with comma if needed):____

Although our team has talent and trains hard, our problem is injuries.

7. I love bright colors that doesn't include pea green.

Insert a period: _____

I love bright colors. That doesn't include pea green.

Insert a semicolon: _____

I love bright colors; that doesn't include pea green.

Insert a coordinating conjunction and comma: _____

I love bright colors, but that doesn't include pea green.

Insert a subordinating conjunction (with comma if needed):____

Even though I love bright colors, that doesn't include pea green.

8. People are having dinner on the patio I wish we had an umbrella to avoid the sun.

Insert a period: _____

People are having dinner on the patio. I wish we had an umbrella to avoid the sun.

Insert a semicolon: _____

People are having dinner on the patio; I wish we had an umbrella to avoid the sun.

Insert a coordinating conjunction and comma: _____

People are having dinner on the patio, so I wish we had an umbrella to avoid the sun.

Insert a subordinating conjunction (with comma if needed):____

Whenever people are having dinner on the patio, I wish we had an umbrella to avoid

the sun.

9. We were roommates for one year we got to know each other well.

Insert a period: _____

We were roommates for one year. We got to know each other well.

Insert a semicolon: _____

We were roommates for one year; we got to know each other well.

Insert a coordinating conjunction and comma: _____

We were roommates for one year, so we got to know each other well.

Insert a subordinating conjunction (with comma if needed):____

When we were roommates for one year, we got to know each other well.

10. I often get colds I have some home remedies that really help.

Insert a period: _____

I often get colds. I have some home remedies that really help.

Insert a semicolon: _____

I often get colds; I have some home remedies that really help.

Insert a coordinating conjunction and comma: _____

I often get colds, but I have some home remedies that really help.

Insert a subordinating conjunction (with comma if needed):____

Although I often get colds, I have some home remedies that really help.

PRACTICING 10

In the space before each of the following run-on sentences, mark the error as a fused sentence *(FS)* or comma splice *(CS).* then, correct each sentence.

1. ___FS___   Today is my birthday I still feel young.

Although today is my birthday, I still feel young.

_____

2. ___CS___   Rico wanted to go on vacation, his boss demanded the report by tomorrow.

Rico wanted to go on vacation, but his boss demanded the report by tomorrow.

_____

3. ___FS___   Bright red lipstick looks gaudy it isn't popular this summer.

Bright red lipstick looks gaudy, and it isn't popular this summer.

_____

4. ___CS___   Our plane was delayed, the fog was too thick.

Our plan was delayed because the fog was too thick.

_____

5. ___FS___   Botany is difficult for me it involves much memory work.

Botany is difficult for me because it involves much memory work.

_____

6. ___CS___   A computer is a mystery, I can't even imagine how it functions.

A computer is a mystery. I can't even imagine how it functions.

_____

7. ___CS___   My first date with Felice was a disaster, she wanted to dance and I am a klutz.

My first date with Felice was a disaster. She wanted to dance, and I am a klutz.

_____

8. ___FS___   I made a plum pie it was juicy and sweet.

I made a plum pie, which was juicy and sweet.

_____

9. __FS__   I picked up my coat and ran to the front door my dad was patiently waiting.

As I picked up my coat and ran to the front door, my dad was patiently waiting.

_____

10. __FS__   We had to watch ten minutes of silly trailers the main movie did not begin until 7:15.

We had to watch ten minutes of silly trailers, and the main movie did not begin

until 7:15.

PRACTICING 11

Correct the following run-on sentences.

Answers may vary.

1. Chris has a good sense of humor he often laughs at himself.

Chris has a good sense of humor; he often laughs at himself.

_____

2. Sandra is a striking child, with jet black ringlets framing her face, she looks like her mother.

Sandra is a striking child, with jet black ringlets framing her face. She looks like

her mother.

3. The male butterfly attracts a mate by fluttering around and showing off his strategy doesn't always work.

The male butterfly attracts a mate by fluttering around and showing off, but his

strategy doesn't always work.

4. The police log shows burglaries are down car theft is up, though.

Although the police log shows burglaries are down, car theft is up.

_____

5. Caterpillars are one of nature's great illusions who would ever think that these wormlike creatures become such beauties?

Caterpillars are one of nature's great illusions. Who would ever think that these

wormlike creatures become such beauties?

6. Sherry is totally unreliable, sometimes she arrives an hour or two late.

Sherry is totally unreliable; sometimes she arrives an hour or two late.

7. You cannot avoid cold germs simply by hiding from everyone, a better way is to strengthen your resistance.

You cannot avoid cold germs simply by hiding from everyone. A better way is to

strengthen your resistance.

8. I decided to change my approach I would pretend total indifference to her.

I decided to change my approach; I would pretend total indifference to her.

9. All of us like to show off at times no one is immune to the human need for attention.

All of us like to show off at times. No one is immune to the human need for attention.

10. Lip readers read each word slowly, on the other hand, speed readers drop diagonally down the page to catch the main ideas.

Lip readers read each word slowly; on the other hand, speed readers drop diagonally

down the page to catch the main ideas.

PRACTICING 12

Part A: Revised sentences may vary.

Some of the sentences that follow are correct; others contain fragments or run-ons. If the sentence is correct, write *C* in the blank. If the sentence is incorrect, identify the error by writing *F* for fragment or *R* for run-on in the blank. Then rewrite the sentence to correct the error.

1. _R_ I arrived at the park at noon, the sun was directly overhead and a few random clouds were scattered across the sky.

When I arrived at the park at noon, the sun was directly overhead and a few random

clouds were scattered across the sky.

2. __R__ I brought nothing with me except a pen and notebook for recording my thoughts I did not want to spoil the park's natural beauty with anything from the outside world.

I brought nothing with me except a pen and notebook for recording my thoughts because

I did not want to spoil the park's natural beauty with anything from the outside world.

3. __R__ Other people had also decided to visit the park that day, we paid no attention to each other.

Other people had also decided to visit the park that day, but we paid no attention

to each other.

4. __F__ I stood on a grassy knoll. Where I could observe and absorb everything around me.

I stood on a grassy knoll where I could observe and absorb everything around me.

_____

5. __F__ To the left of me was a small grove of orange trees. Including a tree so gnarled that it looked as if it had been transplanted from a witch's garden.

To the left of me was a small grove of orange trees, including a tree so gnarled that

it looked as if it had been transplanted from a witch's garden.

6. __C__ Everywhere else, all I could see were mountains, mountains, mountains.

_____

_____

7. __C__ As I walked toward the orange grove, I heard different birds calling to one another.

_____

_____

8. __F__ Birds have a freedom that humans do not possess. The freedom to soar above the ground and see the world from a different perspective.

Birds have a freedom that humans do not possess, the freedom to soar above the

ground and see the world from a different perspective.

9. __C__ I picked an orange from a low branch, peeled it, and squeezed the juice into my mouth.

_____

_____

10. ___R___   The sweetness trickled from my lips, it seemed like drops of some magical potion.

The sweetness, which seemed like drops of some magical potion, trickled from my lips.

PRACTICING 13

The following paragraph contains fragments and run-ons. Correct each error by one of the methods described in this unit.

Two years had passed since I had last seen my grandmother. During this time, her condition had worsened, now she was completely bedridden. No longer able to get up and walk. She babbled without making sense, she had no idea who I was. Her gray eyes stared vacantly. As if she were half in another world unknown to me. All I could do was smile at her and hold her hand. Yet, I was struck by the fact that even in this hopelessly deteriorated state, she seemed to want to communicate with me she wanted a human connection. I decided she was still my kind, beautiful grandmother inside, no matter how she appeared on the outside. Today I wonder what it will be like when I am old. Personally, I hope I don't live long enough to be in such a deteriorated condition. Unable to recognize loved ones. How frustrating it must be to be senile. To repeat the same questions and to remember nothing. Still, maybe science will some day find a cure for extreme senility, I hope so.

Unit Test

Revised sentences may vary.

After each sentence write *F* for fragment, *CS* for comma splice, and *FS* for fused sentences. Then correct each error. *(Note: One of the sentences contains two errors.)*

1. Diogenes was not a degenerate or a beggar he was a philosopher and poet. ___FS___

Diogenes was not a degenerate or a beggar; he was a philosopher and poet.

2. Macaroni and cheese are quick and easy meals. Also spaghetti. ___F___

Macaroni and cheese is a quick and easy meal. Spaghetti is quick and easy, also.

3. Political correctness has its down side, it may stop any honest debate about sensitive subjects. ___CS___

Political correctness has its down side. It may stop any honest debate about sensitive

subjects.

4. I love our family farm. Because all of my childhood memories are connected with this piece of land. ___F___

I love our family farm because all of my childhood memories are connected with this

piece of land

5. History teaches us that rebels were often right they were not always crazy or radical. Consider, for example, George Washington, Luther, and Galileo. ___FS and F___

History teaches us that rebels were often right; they were not always crazy or radical.

Some good examples are George Washington, Luther, and Galileo.

6. Most Americans get their news from television they read newspapers only for sports and human interest stories. ___FS___

Most Americans get their news from television. They read newspapers only for sports

and human interest stories.

7. Rollerblading is good exercise you should wear kneepads when you're first learning. ___FS___

Rollerblading is good exercise, but you should wear kneepads when you're first learning.

8. The ice skater gracefully lifted his partner above his head the audience gasped. ___FS___

As the ice skater gracefully lifted his partner above his head, the audience gasped.

9. The health food store closed, I guess it wasn't making money. ___CS___

The health food store closed because it wasn't making money.

10. We drove from Cleveland to Pittsburgh and back. Filling up on gas only once. ___F___

We drove from Cleveland to Pittsburgh and back, filling up on gas only once.

Unit Talk-Write Assignment

Answers will vary.

Two freshman students are talking about the class they hated most in high school. They both agree that it was gym and take turns blasting it as a waste of time. Both students talk in everyday nonstandard English filled with fragments and run-on sentences—the kind of speech you would use with a close friend but unsuitable for an English paper. Using the lines provided in the right column, turn all the fragments into complete sentences that are written in standard English.

TALK	WRITE
Margie: Going to gym! What a waste of time.	*I find gym class a waste of time.*
Cathy: To run up and down the basketball court until you sweat like a pig and doing it everyday.	*Everyday we have to run up and down the basketball court sweating like pigs.*
Margie: You know what I hated the most? Forgetting about the stupid games like golf.	*Do you know what I hated the most, aside from the stupid games like golf?*
Cathy: The way some teachers took it seriously?	*I think you hated the way some teachers took the class so seriously.*
Margie: Not that. Bad enough already. The bowling. I told the teacher I can't do this I just had my nails done you can't expect me to go bowling with these nails. Know what he said?	*I did hate that, but I particularly hated bowling. I explained to the teacher that I'd just had my nails done and couldn't bowl. Do you know what he said?*
Cathy: To forget about your nails?	*He told you he didn't care about your nails?*

TALK

Margie: He said a good bowler will sacrifice her nails for the game. Like I'm a good bowler. To think that about me!

Cathy: Like you care about bowling.

Margie: I said, you know how much these nails cost me you know much a manicure runs these days?

Cathy: Probably as much as a bowling ball. Golf was what got me. Hated that game. Ridiculous running around hitting a stupid ball with a stick into a hole. To take a game like that so seriously!

Margie: To be always hitting the stupid ball into the bushes. And never being able to find them. I told the teacher. Let me throw the ball I can do better that way.

Cathy: Praying for rain everyday so we have to stay inside.

Margie: Gym class—what a joke!

WRITE

He said the good bowler sacrifices her nails for the game. I was surprised he thought me a good bowler.

You don't care about bowling.

I asked him if he knew how much my nails had cost me and how expensive a manicure was these days.

A manicure is probably as expensive as a bowling ball. I hated golf. I thought it was a ridiculous game to play, trying to hit a small ball with that stick. I could never take a game like that seriously.

Golfers are always hitting into bushes. Often they can't find the ball. I told the teacher I would do better at golf if I was allowed to throw the ball.

I'm praying for rain today so we can stay inside.

Gym class is a joke.

Unit Collaborative Assignment

Some of the sentences in the following paragraphs are correct, but some are fragments or run-ons. Correct all the incorrect sentences. Then team up with a classmate, exchange books, and check each other's work. Discuss any sentences about which you disagree.

I am a file clerk in the office of one of Denny's restaurants, I am required to file correctly. While this process may seem easy, it can actually become a real problem. If the proper filing rules are not followed. Nothing is more confusing and time wasting than lost files.

Here are some basic filing rules to follow: First, you need to know the correct order of the letters in the alphabet. Something you should have learned in grade school. Second, a file clerk must know that for each of the 26 letters there is a file cut, the file cut is the label part that extends above the rest of the file. These file cuts are right, left, and middle. Third, before you put files in a filing cabinet, you must take the time to alphabetize them so you don't have to jump back and forth. From drawer to drawer. Fourth, while filing, you must never rush otherwise you are likely to misfile. Which may cause big trouble because lost files are hard to find later.

Finally, the order of filing is important and can be tricky. For instance, you must file by a person's last name. If two people have the same last name, then use the first name to distinguish between them. To stay in proper alphabetical order. For instance, "John Smith," comes after "Agnes Smith." Furthermore, a space in a name is treated as if the space were not there, for instance, "De Lang" precedes "Derring." Following these simple rules lessens the risk of making filing errors, and in the long run they will save you time and energy.

Unit Writing Assignment

Using freewriting, brainstorming, clustering, or any other method of prewriting, write about one of these subjects:

1. The person you are whom others seldom see

2. Your attitude toward practical jokes

3. Someone you think is terribly funny

When you have completed your paragraph, use the Revising Checklist to revise it.

Photo Writing Assignment

The person in the following picture is eating alone. Brainstorm or freewrite to develop a paragraph about why you think the person is alone. Develop a discussible topic sentence, and support it with strong details. Check your sentences carefully to assure that you have avoided fragments, fused sentences, and comma splices. Use the Revising Checklist to revise.

10

Verbs—An Overview

Verbs can be troublesome. Part of the problem is that we don't speak and write verbs the same way. In speech we sometimes drop the tense endings of verbs when we shouldn't, as in this sentence:

She talk too much.

Or, we add an ending when we shouldn't:

They talks too much.

In the first sentence, since *she* is singular, the verb must also be singular—*talks*. In the second sentence, since *they* is plural, the verb must also be plural—*talk*.

You can make these mistakes in everyday speech—we all occasionally do—and be forgiven. You should not, however, make them in writing. The standards for grammar are stricter in writing than in speech, meaning that you must always write verb tenses correctly.

There is good news: You already know more about verb tenses than you realize.

Twelve Tenses

English has 12 tenses. Of these 12 tenses, the most widely used are the simple present, past, and future. Here is a formal list of all the tenses and their functions:

TENSE	HOW IT IS USED	EXAMPLE
Present	For actions that are now and ongoing	I <u>dance</u>. Bill <u>dances</u>.
Simple past	For actions that took place in the past and do not extend into the present	We <u>danced</u> all night.
Future	For actions that will happen some time after now	I <u>will dance</u> at your wedding.
Present perfect	For actions that started in the past and have been completed in the present	I <u>have</u> just <u>finished</u> dancing.
Past perfect	For actions that were completed in the past before another action took place	Amazingly, she <u>had</u> often <u>danced</u> with him before he became president.
Future perfect	For actions that will happen in the future before some other specific future action	The couple <u>will have danced</u> twice before you leave.
Present progressive	For actions that are still in progress	They <u>are dancing</u> in the park.
Past progressive	For actions that were in progress in the past	She <u>was dancing</u> like a gypsy.
Future progressive	For future actions that will take place continuously	He <u>will be dancing</u> with you.
Present perfect progressive	For actions that started in the past and continue into the present	Madame Francois <u>has been dancing</u> lately.
Past perfect progressive	For actions that were in progress in the past before another past action took place	Everyone <u>had been dancing</u> until the music stopped.
Future perfect progressive	For actions that continue to take place before some other future action	The dancing <u>will have been going on</u> a long time before you have to choose a winner.

ESL Advice!

Knowing the formal names of these tenses is unnecessary as long as you learn how to use them correctly.

Scanning this table of tenses should make you appreciate your instinctive sense of grammar—assuming you're a native speaker. Indeed, many people to whom English is the mother tongue cannot name all the 12 tenses but still know how to use them. This is all the more remarkable because many of us rarely, if ever, use some of these tenses. Sometimes months, even years, go by before we use the future perfect progressive. When we do use it, we do so unconsciously. Grammar, as we have said repeatedly in this book, is largely a built-in skill as natural and automatic as walking. Seeing all the tenses listed here should also make us appreciate the effort ESL students must put in to master English as a second language.

Present Tense Endings

In standard English you must use the correct endings with verbs. You cannot use a plural ending with a singular subject, or a singular ending with a plural subject. Here are the correct endings for regular verbs in the present tense:

PRESENT TENSE—SINGULAR

INCORRECT	CORRECT
I walks	I walk
you walks	you walk
he	he
she } walk	she } walks
it	it

PRESENT TENSE—PLURAL

INCORRECT	CORRECT
we walks	we walk
you walks	you walk
they walks	they walk

Present tense problems

There are two kinds of problems that commonly occur with verbs in the present tense.

1. Dropped *-s/-es* endings for *he, she,* and *it.*

Incorrect: She walk home the long way.
Correct: She walks home the long way.

Incorrect: Bob play the piano for relaxation.
Correct: Bob plays the piano for relaxation.

Incorrect: He wash the kitchen floor once a week.
Correct: He washes the kitchen floor once a week.

2. Unnecessary -s/-es for *we, you,* and *they.*

Incorrect: We plays hard every day.
Correct: We play hard every day.

Incorrect: You checks out everything.
Correct: You check out everything.

Incorrect: They watches out for everybody.
Correct: They watch out for everybody.

Problems with dropped and added endings occur, as we said, because we are less precise in our speech than we must be in our writing. If you regularly make such errors in your speech, your ear may not be particularly helpful in catching them. In that case you should simply memorize the correct endings.

PRACTICING 1

Underline the correct verb.

Example: The bus (<u>stops</u>, stop) in front of Mary's house.

1. The waiters (wears, <u>wear</u>) purple suspenders.
2. A big white dog (sit, <u>sits</u>) on the porch swing.
3. All the girls (wants, <u>want</u>) to pierce their ears.
4. The lemons (<u>need</u>, needs) to be grated.
5. Two fleecy clouds (drifts, <u>drift</u>) across the sky.
6. Suzy and I (prefers, <u>prefer</u>) to eat later.
7. We (<u>believe</u>, believes) that country life is better than city life.
8. The schools (<u>deserve</u>, deserves) the most modern libraries.
9. Greg and Karin (promises, <u>promise</u>) to make the punch.
10. Several movie stars (<u>lead</u>, leads) troubled lives.

PRACTICING 2

In the blank provided, mark *S* if the noun is singular and *P* if it is plural. Correct the verb if it does not agree with the noun.

Example: *S* He always whistles in the dark.

1. __P__ Jim and I live on Broadway.

2. __P__ We love baseball.

3. __S__ This restaurant ~~need~~ *needs* remodeling.

4. __S__ Franny ~~own~~ *owns* two cats.

5. __S__ She ~~finish~~ *finishes* her report early.

6. __P__ Women ~~wants~~ *want* good careers nowadays.

7. __S__ I hope Harry washes his car.

8. __S__ My computer ~~save~~ *saves* me lots of time.

9. __S__ Aunt Elsie walks two miles every day.

10. __P__ Jake and Mervin ~~spends~~ *spend* too much time watching television.

PRACTICING 3

In the passage that follows, strike out any incorrect verb and write the correct form above it.

1. Mrs. Farrow, our next-door neighbor, ~~hate~~ *hates* dogs. 2. Anytime she ~~hear~~ *hears* our dog bark, she ~~yell~~ *yells* at him, "Shut up, you ugly mutt." 3. I suppose people like this neighbor ~~dislikes~~ *dislike* pets because they never had a pet of their own. 4. I feel sorry for Mrs. Farrow because she ~~believe~~ *believes* that dogs ~~exists~~ *exist* just to be yelled at and never to be treated as friends. 5. Mrs. Farrow ~~live~~ *lives* alone, and it ~~seem~~ *seems* to me that a dog could be excellent company for her if she would just change her attitude.

PRACTICING 4

In the blanks provided, write the present tense of a verb that would fit into the sentence.   Answers may vary.

1. My dad ___is___ a tall, athletic man. 2. He ___takes___ no guff from anyone. 3. My sister and I ___respect___ my dad and try to please him. 4. Whenever he comes home from work, we ___let___ him read the paper in peace without disturbing him with questions. 5. Some of my friends wonder if my dad and I ___are___ good

friends, and I always insist that we____*are*____ . 6. I ____*know*____ that my dad ____*is*____ stern and strict, but I ___*am*___ also convinced that he basically ____*loves*____ me. 7. The most fun I ____*have*____ with my dad is when we ____*jog*____ together. 8. Then we ____*have*____ good heart-to-heart talks. 9. Dad ____*is*____ always honest and he ____*believes*____ that developing integrity is important. 10. Can you blame me if I ____*admire*____ my dad a lot?

Past Tense Endings

Here are the correct endings for regular singular verbs in the past tense:

PAST TENSE—SINGULAR

INCORRECT	CORRECT
I walk	I walked
you walk	you walked
he, she, it } walk	he, she, it } walked

Here are the correct endings for regular plural verbs in the past tense:

PAST TENSE—PLURAL

INCORRECT	CORRECT
we walk	we walked
you walk	you walked
they walk	he, she, it walked

With both singular and plural verbs, we can be careless in our speech and drop the *-ed* ending. But in writing, you must always use the *-ed* ending with regular verbs in the past tense.

Incorrect: I hike there yesterday.
Correct: I hiked there yesterday.

Incorrect: She bake a pie last week.
Correct: She baked a pie last week.

PRACTICING 5

In the blank at the end of each sentence, write the past tense of the italicized verb.

Example: Only his nose *remain* uncovered. __remained__

1. The giggling clown *twist* his nose. ___twisted___

2. We *decide* to match him dollar for dollar. ___decided___

3. To my deep sorrow, John *believe* a stranger, not me. ___believed___

4. She barely *manage* to wheel her bicycle into the garage. ___managed___

5. They *last* much longer than expected. ___lasted___

6. They *deliver* the paper two days late. ___delivered___

7. Fred and Merv *order* two big pizzas. ___ordered___

8. I *decide* to spare myself much grief by breaking up with Sally. ___decided___

9. Two or three days ago the weather *change* abruptly. ___changed___

10. Disregarding the sign, he *park* in the Disabled Section. ___parked___

PRACTICING 6

In each of the following sentences, change the verb to the past tense if it is in the present tense or to the present tense if it is in the past tense.

Example: I <u>loved</u> my new car. (verb in past tense) I <u>love</u> my new car. (verb now in present tense)

1. She ~~was~~ *is* speaking dreamily of the good old days.

2. The old man ~~remembers~~ *remembered* his youth in Brooklyn.

3. You ~~give~~ *gave* me no choice.

4. Some observers ~~doubted~~ *doubt* that the tribes ~~were~~ *are* really cannibals.

5. On my visit to the zoo, I ~~see~~ *saw* a giant panda.

6. Why ~~didn't~~ *don't* we try again?

7. She ~~asked~~ *asks* what the pacing meant.

8. They ~~hired~~ *hire* a 27-year-old consultant.

9. Some bank robbers ~~are~~ *were* incredibly stupid.

10. Be it ever so humble, there ~~was~~ *is* no place like home.

Problems with -ing verbs

Verbs ending in -*ing* describe an action that is either happening now or is ongoing. As you learned in Unit 7 all -*ing* verbs need a helping verb.

> She is studying in the library.
>
> She was studying in the library.
>
> She has been studying in the library.
>
> She had been studying in the library, but now she studies in her dorm.

Two kinds of problems can occur with -*ing* verbs:

1. *Be* or *been* is used instead of the correct helping verb.

Incorrect:	She be studying in the library.
Correct:	She is studying in the library.

>   or
>
> She has been studying in the library.

Incorrect:	She been studying in the library.
Correct:	She was studying in the library.

>   or
>
> She has been studying in the library.

2. The helping verb is completely omitted:

Incorrect:	They pretending not to know.
Correct:	They are pretending not to know.
	They were pretending not to know.
	They have been pretending not to know.
	They had been pretending not to know.

Both kinds of errors can confuse and mislead a reader. *She has been studying in the library* is more precise than *She be studying in the library*. With the helping verb missing, we can't tell whether an action is ongoing, or has already gone on but is now over. *They pretending not to know* is therefore fuzzier than *They have been pretending not to know*. Be alert to the possibility of both errors.

PRACTICING 7

Rewrite the following sentences to correct the misuse of *be* or *been* or to insert the missing helping verb.

Example: The children be screaming in the room.

_____The children are screaming in the room._____

Example: Macy's having a sale.

_____Macy's is having a sale._____

1. My family be wanting to move to Baltimore.

My family has been wanting to move to Baltimore.

2. She telling her daughter not to marry Bud.

She has been telling her daughter not to marry Bud.

3. Amy putting up with her roommate's messy ways.

Amy has been putting up with her roommate's messy ways.

4. How she be doing at her job?

How is she doing at her job?

5. Frank wishing he were class president.

Frank wishes he were class president.

6. They be listening to the professor lecture.

They have been listening to the professor lecture.

7. Mr. Goldman watching the movie *Working Girls* when the storm hit.

Mr. Goldman was watching the movie Working Girls when the storm hit.

_____

8. Every generation be creating its own music.

Every generation creates its own music.

9. Mitch pushing the idea of creating a band.

Mitch has been pushing the idea of creating a band.

10. We be expecting too much from that motor.

We are expecting too much from that motor.

PRACTICING 8

Underline the correct form of the verb.

1. She (be, <u>has been</u>) studying without proper lighting.

2. Our art class (hoping, <u>is hoping</u>) to go on a museum field trip.

3. The mechanic at the gas station (<u>had been working</u>, working) on Pete's jeep.

4. Most of the children (be, <u>are</u>) asking for hot dogs.

5. Raquel (<u>has been</u>, be) trying out for the swimming team.

6. Whenever the teacher (be, <u>was</u>) reading from his notes, we fell asleep.

7. I (<u>was expecting</u>, expecting) to have to show my ID.

8. Lindsay (be, <u>has been</u>) feeling much better today.

9. We constantly (be, <u>are</u>) hearing that the family is in trouble.

10. Actually, Dad (trying, <u>was trying</u>) to reach you by phone.

Difficult Verbs: Be, Have, Do

Verbs can be hard to master. Few, though, are harder to master than the three verbs we probably use more than any others in the language: *be*, *have* and *do*. Not only are these verbs in their own right, but they are also commonly used as helping verbs. (Try saying a few sentences without *be*, *have* and *do* and see how much you miss them.) We'll treat each one separately.

To be

To be is commonly used both as a verb on its own and as a helping verb. Here is a listing of the forms of the verb *to be*:

PRESENT TENSE—SINGULAR TO BE

INCORRECT	CORRECT
I be, I ain't	I am, I am not
you be, you ain't	you are, you are not
he she it } be/ain't	he she it } is/is not

PRESENT TENSE—PLURAL TO BE

INCORRECT	CORRECT
we be, we ain't	we are, we are not
you be, you ain't	you are, you are not
they be, they ain't	they are, they are not

PAST TENSE—SINGULAR TO BE

INCORRECT	CORRECT
I were	I was
you was	you were
he	he
she } were	she } was
it	it

PAST TENSE—PLURAL TO BE

INCORRECT	CORRECT
we was	we were
you was	you were
they was	they were

As you can see—indeed as you already know from repeated use—*to be* is an irregular verb. As both a verb and a helping verb, it is often incorrectly spoken. All of these sentences below, for example, are wrong, even if your ear tells you otherwise:

EAR ALERT

INCORRECT	CORRECT
I ain't going to do it.	I am not going to do it.
Absence be the reason he gets poor grades.	Absence is the reason he gets poor grades.
You was right about her.	You were right about her.

If you commonly use the incorrect forms in your daily speech, be especially careful not to trust your ear with *to be*. Instead, memorize its correct forms.

PRACTICING 9

The following passage contains several errors in the use of the verb *to be*. Cross out any incorrect use of the verb to be and, in the space between the lines, write the correct form of the verb. (*Hint:* You should find ten errors.)

My car ~~be~~ *(is)* a ten-year-old Chevy. I bought it for $300.00 and I

~~ain't going~~ *(am not)* to sell it because it ~~be~~ *(is)* a great car. Hank, my buddy, and

I worked all last summer to improve the car and make it run. We

~~be~~ *(are)* proud of our work because the car ~~be~~ *(is)* the best in our school.

The paint job ~~be~~ *(is)* bright red. The other kids are jealous of us because

they ~~ain't~~ *(aren't)* smart enough to fix up a car the way we fixed up ours.

Hank ~~be~~ *(is)* the kind of friend who helps me with keeping up this car.

It ~~be~~ *(is)* good to have such a loyal buddy, ~~ain't~~ *(isn't)* that so?

To have

To have, like *to be*, is commonly used both as a verb and as a helping verb. Like *to be*, it is also an irregular verb. Here are its main forms:

PRESENT TENSE—SINGULAR TO HAVE

INCORRECT	CORRECT
I has	I have
you has	you have
he \	he \
she } have	she } has
it /	it /

PRESENT TENSE—PLURAL TO HAVE

INCORRECT	CORRECT
we has	we have
you has	you have
they has	they have

PAST TENSE—SINGULAR TO HAVE

INCORRECT	CORRECT
I has	I had
you has	you had
he	he
she } have	she } had
it	it

PAST TENSE—PLURAL TO HAVE

INCORRECT	CORRECT
we has	we had
you has	you had
they has	they had

Like *to be*, *to have* is so often misused in daily speech that you should be cautious about trusting your ear to judge its correctness. The sentences below, for example, are all incorrect:

> She have a problem.
>
> He have on a new coat.
>
> They has a quarrel yesterday.

Here are the correct forms:

> She has a problem.
>
> He has on a new coat.
>
> They had a quarrel yesterday.

PRACTICING 10

In the following sentences, fill in the correct form of the verb *to have*.

Example: She <u>has</u> to go.

1. Mary <u>has</u> a pet collie.

2. You <u>have</u> to stop saying that.

3. Mr. Ward <u>has</u> the only blue house on the street.

4. You <u>have</u> my only copy, and I must <u>have</u> it back.

5. I <u>have</u> got to let go of her, and she <u>has</u> to understand why.

6. ____Has____ he said anything to you about it?

7. Where ____have____ you been?

8. He ____has____ borrowed my car for the last time.

9. No one ____has____ a right to say that.

10. I ____have____ many friends, but she ____has____ only one.

PRACTICING 11

The following passage contains several errors in the use of the verb *to have*. Cross out the incorrect uses of the verb *to have*, and write the correct form of the verb above each error. (*Hint:* You should find six errors.)

Jimmy ~~have~~ *has* decided to register for English 120 with me. Both

of us ~~has~~ *have* trouble with English because in the past no one ~~have~~ *has*

made us feel that writing is important. We are both football players,

and for us the game means everything while writing correct English

~~have~~ *has* never seemed important. But now we are both motivated

because we want to get good jobs when we finish college. Jimmy

said to me the other day, "O.K., Buddy, we ~~has~~ *have* to prove that we can

change our bad English habits, right?" I slapped him on the back

and said, "Right on, I agree with you." Now we ~~has~~ *have* a new attitude.

To do

The verb *to do*, like *to be* and *to have*, is used both as a main verb and as a helping verb. It is so common to both writing and speech as to be found nearly everywhere. Here are its correct forms:

PRESENT TENSE—SINGULAR TO DO

INCORRECT	CORRECT
I does	I do
you does	you do
he she } do it	he she } does it

PRESENT TENSE—PLURAL TO DO

INCORRECT	CORRECT
we does	we do
you does	you do
they does	they do

PAST TENSE—SINGULAR TO DO

INCORRECT	CORRECT
I done	I did
you done	you did
he	he
she } done	she } did
it	it

PAST TENSE—PLURAL TO DO

INCORRECT	CORRECT
we done	we did
you done	you did
they done	they did

The main problem with *to do* is that it is used in informal speech differently than it is in writing. This common use makes it difficult to judge the correctness of *to do* by ear. All these sentences below, for example, are incorrect:

EAR ALERT

> He don't know what he's saying.
>
> I does what I have to.
>
> She done with him.

Here are the correct forms:

> He doesn't know what he's saying.
>
> I do what I have to.
>
> She is done with him.

If you are used to speaking the incorrect forms, don't trust your ear; instead, memorize the correct forms.

PRACTICING 12

Use the correct form of *to do* in the following sentences.

1. He *does (or doesn't)*   understand the subject.

2. She ____*does*____ carry on, ____*doesn't*____ she?

3. ____*Do*____ you know what the meeting is about?

4. How ____*do*____ you change the sparkplugs?

5. Tiffany always ____*does*____ badly on the tennis court when she plays a match.

6. I ____*do*____ feel a sense of pride.

7. ____*Does*____ she know about the sale?

8. Where ____*do*____ you find such good people?

9. ____*Do*____ not speak to me that way!

10. It ____*does*____ not matter what you are talking about.

PRACTICING 13

The following conversation was overheard in a campus coffee shop. The topic was worrisome problems. Each sentence contains at least one error in the verbs *be, have,* or *do.* Correct each sentence in the lines provided.

1. I be worried about Sue lately.

I am worried about Sue lately.

2. Why? It don't make sense to worry.

Why? It doesn't make sense to worry.

3. She have a car that's always giving her trouble.

She has a car that's always giving her trouble.

4. Why that be your worry?

Why is that your worry?

5. She have a habit of getting in a bad mood when it don't work properly.

She has a habit of getting in a bad mood when it doesn't work properly.

6. Why ain't you fixed it for her?

Why haven't you fixed it for her?

7. I be spending all my time trying to fix it, and Sue just be getting madder and madder at me.

I'm spending all my time trying to fix it, and Sue is just getting madder and

madder at me.

8. Well, you has your problems and I has mine.

Well, you have your problems and I have mine.

9. I guess we be of a different opinion about our problems.

I guess we are of different opinions about our problems.

10. Right. You be in one corner, and I be in the other.

Right. You are in one corner, and I am in the other.

☑ Unit Test

Fill in the blank with the correct form of the verb in parentheses.

1. Yesterday Julie (walk) _____*walked*_____ all the way to Jan's house.

2. My brother (be) ___*is (or was)*___ the best athlete in his class until he sprained his ankle.

3. We are both guitarists, but he (be) _____*is*_____ better than I (be) _____*am*_____.

4. Felix (do) ___*does (or doesn't)*___ take his good looks too seriously.

5. Beverly still (smoke) _____*smokes*_____ like a chimney.

6. Last year Stan (fish) _____*fished*_____ for a whole month in Montana.

7. She (hide) ___*hides (or hid)*___ every time I try to find her.

8. If you (be) _____*are*_____ happy, that's all that matters.

9. The room (have) _____*has*_____ a bad smell.

10. (Do) _____*Does*_____ she always do the best she can?

11. Doris and Jim (have) _____*have*_____ many financial problems.

12. The city (have) _____*has*_____ to protect its citizens from fire hazards.

13. If she (do) _____*does*_____ most of the work herself, it won't be expensive.

14. The winner (take) _____*takes*_____ the entire purse.

15. The furniture (have) _____*has*_____ to be waxed and polished.

Unit Talk-Write Assignment

Answers will vary.

In the Talk column below, a student chatting with a friend expresses his opinion on when teenagers should get their drivers' licenses. His comments are typically phrased in casual talk grammar. Turn them into an appropriatly written paragraph, paying special attention to the correct use of verbs.

TALK

1. My brother's driving scares the living daylights out of me.

2. Yesterday he pile eight kids into my parents' van and burn rubber all the way down our hill to Main Street.

3. My eyes bug out when I seen him.

WRITE

My brother's driving scares me terribly.

_____

_____

_____

Yesterday he had eight people in my parents' van and

sped all the way down our hill to Main Street.

_____

_____

_____

I'm shocked every time I see him.

_____

_____

_____

TALK

WRITE

4. Then I remember how I use to drive just like him.

Then I remember that I used to drive just like he does.

_____

_____

_____

5. Wrapping cars around posts or whamming them into garage doors be almost a badge of honor for us idiots.

Wrapping cars around posts or driving them into

garage doors were things we were proud of.

_____

_____

6. Now I see that we was total jerks.

Now I see that we were foolish.

_____

_____

7. So what? Well I don't think kids should get their license until they turns 18. My parents agrees with me.

This leads me to think that teenagers shouldn't get

their driver's license until they turn 18. My parents

agree with me.

_____

_____

8. I also think teenagers should be on probation for a year before their license be permanent.

I also think teenagers should be on probation for a

year before their licenses become permanent.

_____

_____

_____

9. Kids who shoplifts or paints graffiti should get their probation extended, too.

Teens who shoplift or paint graffiti should have their

probation extended, too.

_____

_____

TALK

WRITE

10. Probies should have their probation extended if they be driving recklessly or with piles of other kids in the car.

Probationers should also have their probation

extended if they are driving recklessly or with too

many other teenagers in the car.

11. And if a guy is busted driving under the influence, that kid loses his probationary license and can't get another one until he be twenty-one.

Furthermore, if a teenage driver is caught driving

under the influence of alcohol, that teen should lose

his or her temporary license and not be allowed to get

another one until he or she is 21.

12. In other words, permanent drivers' licenses should be given only to drivers with good overall records.

In other words, permanent driver's licenses should be

given only to drivers with good overall records.

13. These be sounding like tough rules, but I bet they'd save lives.

These may sound like strict rules, but I believe they

would save lives.

Unit Collaborative Assignment

Do this assignment with a classmate. The sentences that follow have singular subjects. Your classmate should read sentences 1 to 5 aloud. You will then write each sentence in the plural, making sure that the subject and verb agree. Read back the changed sentences and discuss them with your partner.

Then reverse your roles for sentences 6 to 10. Finally, with your partner check all of your written sentences to make sure that the subjects and verbs agree. (*Note:* Sometimes there is more than one verb in the sentence.)

1. Every student needs a healthy breakfast.

_____

2. The train arrived from Philadelphia.

_____

3. He doesn't care about wealth.

_____

4. The woman pants because the hill is steep.

_____

5. A child forgets quickly.

_____

6. She goes to a movie every weekend.

_____

7. Does he live in town?

_____

8. I walk until I drop.

_____

9. That book has a torn cover.

_____

10. My wool sweater has no arms.

_____

Unit Writing Assignment

Write a description of your childhood. Was it carefree? Happy? Lonely? Using brainstorming and freewriting, find a discussible point and support it with well-chosen details. When you have completed your writing, go over it to make sure that all of your verbs are correct. Use the Revising Checklist to revise.

Photo Writing Assignment

Study the following picture. Then brainstorm, freewrite, or cluster until you find a discussible point on the advantages of having a big brother, big sister, or another older relative. Pay particular attention to using regular verbs correctly. Use the Revising Checklist to revise.

11

Regular and Irregular Verbs

"The cat snuck into my bed."
"He brung the book to school."

Very early in life, our ear tells us that the past tense of a verb is usually signaled by *-ed* at the end. At first, we stubbornly apply this rule to every verb. It is not unusual to hear toddlers say, "I sitted on my chair," or "David hitted me with his cup." Later, we learn that the rule applies only to regular verbs, not to verbs that are irregular.

You can usually trust your ear with regular past tenses. However, with irregular past tenses, your ear cannot be trusted. The only solution for both the ESL student and the native speaker is to memorize the irregular verbs.

In this unit you will learn when you can rely on your ear to select the correct verb tenses, and when you should memorize.

Regular Verbs

Verbs are either regular or irregular. Regular verbs form the past tense by adding *-d* or *-ed*. They also form the past participle by adding *-d* or *-ed*. The past participle generally refers to actions in the distant, rather than the immediate, past. It requires a helping verb, either *have*, *has*, or *had*. Here are some examples of common regular verbs:

PRESENT TENSE	PAST TENSE	PAST PARTICIPLE
charge	charged	have/has/had charged
cook	cooked	have/has/had cooked
pack	packed	have/has/had packed

Here are some examples of these words in sentences:

EAR ALERT

Past:	She charged $7 per hour for painting the porch.
Past participle:	She has charged less for simpler jobs.
	She had charged Mr. Jones overtime.

Past:	They packed the books yesterday.
Past participle:	They have packed nearly everything now.
	They had packed until nearly midnight.

Don't let your ear fool you into dropping the *-d* or *-ed* endings of past tense verbs. Although this is a common mistake that we all occasionally make in everyday speech, you must not make it in your writing.

Dropped ending:	We were suppose to meet her at the theater.
	We were use to doing it that way.
Correct:	We were suppose<u>d</u> to meet her at the theater.
	We were use<u>d</u> to doing it that way.

IN A NUTSHELL

- Regular verbs form the past tense by adding *-d* or *-ed*.
- Regular verbs form the past participle with the helping verb to have by adding *-d* or *-ed*.
- Don't be fooled by your ear into dropping the *-d* or *-ed*.

PRACTICING 1

The following sentences are adapted from a Southern woman's Civil War diary. Change the verb in parenthesis to its simple past tense.

1. Sherman's troops (march) past my window.

_____ *marched* _____

2. Of course, we (expect) to sleep through the noise.

_____ *expected* _____

3. They (surround) the campus with their sentries.

_____ *surrounded* _____

4. The southern horizon (reflects) the glare of fire.

_____ _reflected_ _____

5. I (imagine) night being turned into day by the blaze.

_____ _imagined_ _____

6. The men (carry) buckets of water.

_____ _carried_ _____

7. The wounded from the hospital (help) as much as possible.

_____ _helped_ _____

8. The heat (forces) us away from the burning building.

_____ _forced_ _____

9. The flame (approach) from all sides.

_____ _approached_ _____

10. Snipers (fire) at the firefighters.

_____ _fired_ _____

11. The cannon (roar) with unspeakable might.

_____ _roared_ _____

12. The fire (wraps) the campus in the brightness of daylight.

_____ _wrapped_ _____

13. One soldier (apologizes) for the destruction.

_____ _apologized_ _____

14. We (walk) away from him without speaking.

_____ _walked_ _____

15. We all (remember) that dreadful night.

_____ _remembered_ _____

PRACTICING 2

Cross out the italicized regular verb in each sentence, change it to the past participle, and write the new verb above the old one. Remember to use <u>has</u>, <u>have</u>, or <u>had</u>.

               has pumped
Example: Fred ~~pumps~~ gas at an Arco station.

    Fred has pumped gas at an Arco station.

       have parted
1. I ~~*part*~~ my hair on the left side.

              has looked
2. Jamie's father ~~*looked*~~ under the bed.

              has appeared
3. My favorite writer ~~*appeared*~~ on campus.

           had saluted
4. The private ~~*salutes*~~ the general.

       have vacationed
5. We ~~*vacation*~~ in Santa Fe.

        have delivered
6. They ~~*delivered*~~ the furniture.

          have lived
7. The Zunis ~~*live*~~ in pueblos.

            has talked
8. Aunt Susan ~~*talks*~~ about getting a new job.

        have mowed (or mown)
9. The boys ~~*mow*~~ the lawn for a fee.

       have helped
10. You ~~*helped*~~ yourself.

Omitting the helping verb in a past participle

In informal speech, it is common to drop the helping verb in a past participle—an act your ear might even excuse. But dropping the helping verb, whether your ear approves or not, is always wrong in writing. Here are some examples:

Dropped verb: I been a team player.
Correct form: I have been a team player.

Dropped verb: I drawn the picture.
Correct form: I have drawn the picture.

Dropped verb: We driven around for ten minutes.
Correct form: We had driven around for ten minutes.

Dropped verb: Why Fred bought a white Honda?
Correct form: Why has Fred bought a white Honda?

IN A NUTSHELL

In writing, you must always include the helping verb of a past participle.

PRACTICING 3

Insert the omitted helping verb where it belongs, writing it in the line above the sentence.

                  had
Example: Before noon, she spoken to her staff twice.

  Before noon, she had spoken to her staff twice.

               have
1. Most of the children written their parents letters from camp.

    have
2. I been pretty poor all my life.

           have
3. Many people seen cruelty and violence in their families.

             have
4. Farmers in Fresno grown beautiful tomatoes.

         has
5. He said he frozen the bananas to keep them from rotting.

    have
6. Why you broken your promise?

      have
7. Where you left your wallet?

     has
8. He hidden the candy in the bottom drawer.

     has
9. Lupe worn that coat since she was twelve.

       has
10. The snow fallen early this winter.

PRACTICING 4

The paragraph that follows contains many errors in the use of past participles. First, underline each error; second, correct the errors.

Answer is in Instructor's Section.

    What is a real American? Some people have claim that a real American is a person who is loyal, patriotic, and proud to live in the United States. Other people have suppose that a real American is someone who watches football on Monday nights and eats hot dogs. The definition of a real American changes constantly because different generations have experience different problems, such as war or depression. For instance, during the 1950s, when Senator Joseph McCarthy had made everyone paranoid about Communism, a "real American" was someone who was against Communism. Later, in the 1970s, a "real American" was someone who had battle the Vietnamese even though he might have believe that the war was illogical and immoral.

During the later 1970s, a "real American" might have been someone who had purchase an American gas-guzzling car instead of a foreign economical car, just to show that he supported the American economy. Today, the term "real American" is still not easy to define even though on September 11, 2001, we experienced a real war and crisis to pull us together. But this is what I think the term means: "A person who wants to change America for the better and will work to do so."

Irregular Verbs

Verbs are *irregular* if their past tense is not formed by adding *-d* or *-ed*. For example, if the rule for changing tenses were applied to *bring*, its past tense should be *bringed*, which it isn't—it's *brought*. *Bring* is therefore an irregular verb.

There is no single rule for forming the past tense of irregular verbs. Native speaker or ESL student, you simply have to memorize the forms of those verbs that are irregular. In the past, students memorized these forms by chanting them. It is an old technique, but it works.

A list of irregular verbs follows that many of us use practically every day. Remember, the past participle always requires the use of the helping verb *to have*.

PRESENT	PAST	PAST PARTICIPLE
arise	arose	arisen
be	was	been
bear	bore	borne (not *born*)
become	became	become
begin	began	begun
break	broke	broken
bring	brought (not *brung*)	brought
build	built	built
burst	burst (not *busted*)	burst
catch	caught	caught
buy	bought	bought
choose	chose	chosen
cling	clung	clung
come	came	come
dive	dove	dived
do	did (not *done*)	done
drag	dragged (not *drug*)	dragged

PRESENT	PAST	PAST PARTICIPLE
draw	drew	drawn
drink	drank	drunk
drive	drove	driven
eat	ate	eaten
fall	fell	fallen
feed	fed	fed
feel	felt	felt
fight	fought	fought
fly	flew	flown
forgive	forgave	forgiven
freeze	froze	frozen
get	got	gotten
go	went	gone
grow	grew	grown
hang (*clothes*)	hung	hung
hang (*execute*)	hanged	hanged (is a regular verb)
have	had	had
hold	held	held
hurt	hurt (not *hurted*)	hurt
know	knew	known
lead	led	led
lay (*place*)	laid	laid
lie (*rest, recline*)	lay	lain
lose	lost	lost
make	made	made
mean	meant	meant
meet	met	met
pay	paid	paid
put	put	put
read	read (pronounced like *red*)	read (pronounced like *red*)
ride	rode	ridden
ring	rang	rung
rise	rose	risen
run	ran	run
say	said	said
see	saw (not *seen*)	seen
seek	sought (not *seeked*)	sought
sell	sold	sold
set	set	set
shake	shook	shaken

PRESENT	PAST	PAST PARTICIPLE
shine	shone	shone
shrink	shrank	shrunk
sing	sang	sung
sink	sank	sunk
sleep	slept	slept
speak	spoke	spoken
spend	spent	spent
spin	spun	spun
spit	spat	spat
spring	sprang (not *sprung*)	sprung
stand	stood	stood
steal	stole	stolen
sting	stung	stung
stink	stank (not *stunk*)	stunk
strike	struck	struck
strive	strove	striven
swear	swore	sworn
swim	swam (not *swum*)	swum
swing	swung	swung
take	took	taken
teach	taught	taught
tear	tore	torn
tell	told	told
think	thought	thought
throw	threw	thrown
understand	understood	understood
wake	woke	woken
weave	wove	woven
wear	wore	worn
win	won	won
wring	wrung	wrung
write	wrote	written

If you don't know the past tense of an irregular verb, you can always look it up in a dictionary. For example, if you looked up the verb *give*, you would find its past tense listed as *gave* and its past participle as *given*. If the verb is regular, the dictionary will not give its past tense, which means that to form the past tense or past participle you simply add -*d* or -*ed*

IN A NUTSHELL

- Irregular verbs do not form the past tense is not by adding
  -*d* or -*ed*.
- Irregular verbs must be memorized.

PRACTICING 5

Complete the following sentences using the form of the verb
indicated.

Example: Present: I <u>drag</u> my suitcase all over Europe.

   Past: I _____*dragged*_____ my suitcase all over Europe.

   Past participle: I have _____*dragged*_____ my suitcase all
   over Europe.

1. **Present:** I tell the truth

   Past: I _____*told*_____ the truth.

   Past participle: I have _____*told*_____ the truth.

2. **Present:** I hurt.

   Past: I_____*hurt*_____ .

   Past participle: I have _____*hurt*_____ .

3. **Present:** They swim.

   Past: They _____*swam*_____ .

   Past participle: They have _____*swum*_____ .

4. **Present:** The cats spring.

   Past: The cats _____*sprang*_____ .

   Past participle: The cats have _____*sprung*_____ .

5. **Present:** Rains bring hope.

   Past: Rains _____*brought*_____ hope.

   Past participle: Rains have _____*brought*_____ hope.

6. **Present:** The children see.

   Past: The children _____*saw*_____ .

   Past participle: The children have _____*seen*_____ .

7. **Present:** They freeze.

    Past: They _____ froze _____ .

    Past participle: They have _____ frozen _____ .

8. **Present:** The bells ring.

    Past: The bells _____ rang _____ .

    Past participle: The bells have _____ rung _____ .

9. **Present:** The dogs stink.

    Past: The dogs _____ stank _____ .

    Past participle: The dogs have _____ stunk _____ .

10. **Present:** You choose.

    Past: You _____ chose _____ .

    Past participle: You have _____ chosen _____ .

11. **Present:** They spit.

    Past: They _____ spat _____ .

    Past participle: They have _____ spat _____ .

12. **Present:** Poets write.

    Past: Poets _____ wrote _____ .

    Past participle: Poets have _____ written _____ .

13. **Present:** They shrink.

    Past: They _____ shrank _____ .

    Past participle: They have _____ shrunk _____ .

14. **Present:** The rabbits sleep.

    Past: The rabbits _____ slept _____ .

    Past participle: The rabbits have _____ slept _____ .

15. **Present:** The people speak.

    Past: The people _____ spoke _____ .

    Past participle: The people have _____ spoken _____ .

PRACTICING 6

In the following sentences, the past tense of the italicized verb is used incorrectly. Write the correct form of the verb in the space provided.

1. My friend *brung* me to school yesterday. ____brought____

2. I *seen* him playing ball in the gym. ____saw____

3. The cat *sprung* at the bird. ____sprang____

4. You *know* fully well what you *done*. ____did____

5. He *drug* the garbage can down the driveway. ____dragged____

6. I *drawed* a picture of the forest. ____drew____

7. The pipe *busted* in the freezing weather. ____broke____

8. You *stunk* after working in the garage. ____stank____

9. Yesterday we *swum* in the city pool. ____swam____

10. I *freezed* in the chilly water. ____froze____

11. My father *teached* me how to drive a car. ____taught____

12. At our last meet, Cheryl *swum* faster than any other student. ____swam____

13. When he *spit* on the floor, we all looked at him in horror. ____spat____

14. Who *stealed* the alarm clock? ____stole____

15. My sister *woken* me up at 6:00 A.M. ____woke____

PRACTICING 7

Sentences will vary.

Fill in the blank with the past tense of the verb in parentheses. Then, on the line below, write a sentence using the same subject and past participle of the verb. If you are in doubt, check the list of irregular verbs.

Example: She (swim) <u>swam</u> in the lake.

<u>She had swum there often during her childhood.</u>

1. She (hang) _____*hung*_____ her wet bathing suit in a tree nearby.

She has hung out all the laundry.

_____

2. The man (rise) _____*rose*_____ to allow the lady to be seated.

The man has risen already.

_____

3. He (take) _____*took*_____ down the kite from the tree.

He has taken a break.

_____

4. Who (blow) _____*blew*_____ the whistle in the middle of the night?

The wind has blown all afternoon.

_____

5. Was it you who (drag) _____*dragged*_____ the sack of potatoes into the living room?

He has dragged that blanket around since he was two.

_____

6. She (swear) _____*swore*_____ eternal love to him.

She has sworn never to tell his secret.

_____

7. The pigpens (stink) _____*stank*_____ really bad yesterday.

The pens have stunk ever since the weather got hot.

_____

8. Today the birds fly; yesterday the birds (fly) _____*flew*_____ .

The birds have flown south for the winter.

_____

9. Fred (tear) _____*tore*_____ a big hole in his pants.

Fred has torn holes in almost all his pants.

_____

10. Who (lead) _____*led*_____ the opposition last year?

He has led them to victory for three years in a row.

_____

Problems with irregular verbs

Two kinds of problems commonly occur with irregular verbs:

1. We use the simple past instead of the past participle.

Incorrect:	He has ran in two marathons.
Correct:	He has run in two marathons.
Incorrect:	She has just wrote him a letter.
Correct:	She has just written him a letter.

2. We use an incorrect form of the past or past participle.

Incorrect:	She drug him along.
Correct:	She dragged him along.
Incorrect:	He has never wore that before.
Correct:	He has never worn that before.

Beware of these two common errors.

PRACTICING 8

Some of the underlined past participles that follow are correct; others are incorrect. If the participle is correct, place a *C* in the blank; if it is incorrect, write the corrected participle in the blank. If in doubt, check the list of irregular verbs.

Example: Most of the students should have <u>spoke</u> English. *Spoken*

If you had <u>gone</u> to the store, we would have enough milk for dinner. *C*

1. I have <u>ran</u> the Boston Marathon. _____*run*_____

2. She has <u>swore</u> to bring up her grades. _____*sworn*_____

3. One of the rugs she has <u>woven</u> is in the living room.

_____*C*_____

4. The soldiers had <u>dragged</u> the flag through mud and filth.

_____*C*_____

5. Before the party was over, all of the balloons had <u>bursted</u>.

_____*burst*_____

6. Had I <u>knowed</u> then what I know now, I would be rich.

_____*known*_____

7. I have <u>swum</u> from here to the islands with no trouble.

_____*C*_____

8. I have <u>lead</u> in that competition all semester. _____*led*_____

9. She had <u>took</u> much trouble to write a perfect essay.

_____*taken*_____

10. Someone had <u>stole</u> his wallet from the car. _____*stolen*_____

11. She has not yet <u>paid</u> the rent for this month. _____*C*_____

12. The taxi drivers <u>striked</u> the city at four this afternoon.

_____*struck*_____

13. We <u>swinged</u> from the tree in the moonlight. _____*swung*_____

14. They had not <u>understanded</u> the problem. _____*understood*_____

15. She has <u>tore</u> a leaf from that book. _____*torn*_____

PRACTICING 9

Underline the correct form of the verb. Some sentences require the simple past tense, while others require the past participle form.

Example: They (fighted, <u>fought</u>) valiantly at the Battle of Bull Run.

1. We were surprised that the tomato vines had (grew, <u>grown</u>) so tall.

2. If the people had (<u>forgiven</u>, forgave) him, he probably would have survived.

3. Was it you who (<u>brought</u>, brung) the huge dog to church?

4. When was the last time you (driven, <u>drove</u>) Sara's station wagon?

5. The chemistry professor (<u>rode</u>, ridden) in all the way from Manchester.

6. Before he could stop her, she (spit, <u>spat</u>) on the floor.

7. For what reason had the townspeople (rang, <u>rung</u>) the bell?

8. Most of the sweaters had (<u>shrunk</u>, shrank) two sizes.

9. The little rowboat (<u>sank</u>, sunk) into the sea.

10. A large "B" had been (<u>woven</u>, wove) into the rug.

11. The vegetables were rotten and (<u>stank</u>, stunk).

12. If the soldiers had (<u>worn</u>, wore) their helmets, they might have lived.

13. Who would have (thinked, <u>thought</u>) that the woman was only fifty?

14. They (<u>struck</u>, striked) the chair three times.

15. I wish you had (wrote, <u>written</u>) me a note to inform me.

Problem Verbs: Lie/Lay, Sit/Set, Rise/Raise

A few verbs seem to give the entire English-speaking world trouble. They are *lie/lay*, *sit/set*, and *rise/raise*.

Lie/lay

To lie means to rest in a horizontal position like a sleeper. *To lay* means to put or set down something as you might a book. To confuse matters further, the past tense of *lie* is *lay*.

Here are the principal parts of these two verbs:

PRESENT	PAST	PAST PARTICIPLE
lie	lay	lain = to rest in a horizontal position like a sleeper
lay	laid	laid = to set down something, as you might do a book

Lie is always done *by* someone or something; *lay* is always done *to* someone or something. You *lie* down to take a nap, but you *lay* your glasses on the table. You *lie* in your bed, but you are *laid* to rest in your grave. Here are more examples:

TO LIE	TO LAY
I often lie on the floor to watch TV.	He lay the doll on the floor.
She is lying on the floor.	She is laying the doll on the floor.
Yesterday, I lay on the floor.	Yesterday she laid the doll on the floor.
I have lain on the floor.	I have laid the doll on the floor.

PRACTICING 10

Underline the correct verb.

1. "(Lie, Lay) down!" I shouted to my stubborn dog.

2. Tara had been (lying, laying) in bed daydreaming when the phone rang.

3. Within a month the contractor had (lain, laid) all the tile.

4. Yesterday Maxine (laid, lay) in bed with a cold.

5. All she does is (lie, lay) on the living room sofa watching soap operas.

6. Before they had (lain, <u>laid</u>) two miles of track, the mine exploded.

7. She had (lain, <u>laid</u>) her beach towel next to mine.

8. Just to (<u>lie</u>, lay) on the cool, green grass and look at the clouds is heaven.

9. For two weeks Mary conscientiously (lay, <u>laid</u>) napkins on the table for every meal.

10. Yesterday Maxine (lay, <u>laid</u>) a blanket on her bed.

Sit/set

To sit means to rest on your bottom as you might do in a chair. *To set* means to place something somewhere. *To set* always requires an object except when it refers to the sun, which always *sets* but never *sits*.

Here are the principal parts of *sit* and *set*:

PRESENT	PAST	PAST PARTICIPLE
sit	sat	sat = to rest on one's bottom
set	set	set = to place something somewhere

The basic difference is this: Someone or something *sits*; someone or something is *set*. So you *sit* on the floor, but you *set* the glass on the floor.

TO SIT	TO SET
The old man sits by the fire.	The man sets flowers on the table.
He is sitting by the fire.	He is setting the table.
All of us sat in stony silence.	Last year they set a record.
She has always sat in the back row.	Have you set your books down?

PRACTICING 11

Underline the correct verb.

1. I had (sat, <u>set</u>) the books on top of the piano.

2. For two hours, Marie (<u>sat</u>, set) on the bench and waited.

3. It felt to her as if she had (set, <u>sat</u>) there for two days.

4. Who is (setting, <u>sitting</u>) on his right?

5. (Sit, <u>Set</u>) that box down this very moment!

6. We have (<u>sat</u>, set) around twiddling our thumbs long enough.

7. Had they told the truth instead of (setting, <u>sitting</u>) on it, they would have been better off.

8. (<u>Sit</u>, Set) down and listen!

9. He (sat, <u>set</u>) the groceries on the sink.

10. Come and (<u>sit</u>, set) down next to me.

Rise/raise

To rise means to get up or move up on your own; *to raise* is to lift up someone or something or to cultivate or rear something.

Here are the principal parts of *rise* and *raise*:

PRESENT	PAST	PAST PARTICIPLE
rise	rose	risen = to get up or move up on your own
raise	raised	raised = to lift up someone or something

You *rise* from a sitting position or *rise* to the top of your profession. You *raise* your arms or your voice; sometimes, you even *raise* Cain. You always *rise* to the occasion and doing so might get you a *raise* in pay.

Here are some other examples:

TO RISE	TO RAISE
Let us rise and salute the flag.	Let us raise the flag on the pole.
She is rising to greet the man.	I am raising cattle.
The farmers have risen early.	The farmers have raised tons of corn.
The old men rose from the bench.	The old men raised their hands.

PRACTICING 12

Change the italicized word(s) by filling in *rise* or *raise* in the blanks provided. Do not change the tense of the original.

1. India *breeds* beautiful tigers. _____*raises*_____

2. What a thrill to see the sun *come up* over the hilltops!

_____*rise*_____

3. The entire audience had *stood up* to applaud the rock band.

   _____risen_____

4. I *pulled up* the shades to see the tulips in the back yard.

   _____raised_____

5. The manager *has increased* Ellen's pay.   _____has raised_____

6. Lazarus is supposed to *have returned* from his grave.

   _____have raisen_____

7. He *increased* his grade point average this year.

   _____raised_____

8. She will *be equal* to the challenge of chemistry.

   _____rise_____

9. When she walks in, let's *get up* and applaud her.

   _____rise_____

10. When taxes *become higher,* people demand a new president.

    _____rise_____

IN A NUTSHELL

- *To lie* means to rest in a horizontal position; *to lay* means to put something down.
- *To sit* means to rest on your bottom; *to set* means to place something somewhere.
- *To rise* means to get up; *to raise* means to lift up something.

ESL Advice!

These differences in meaning between *lie/lay, sit/set, rise/raised* must be memorized.

Lie/Lay, Sit/Set, Rise/Raise: Does It Really Matter?

If students don't ask the question, "Does it really matter if I say *lie* or *lay*?" they often think it. The answer is, yes, it does matter.

True, if you commanded *Lay down*! instead of *Lie down*! your dog would probably obey just as quickly. Many students might then wonder, "If I'm understood when I incorrectly say *lay* instead of *lie* or *lie* instead of *lay*, what does using the correct form matter?"

However, being understood is no substitute for being correct. Often, being correct is what makes you understandable.

Language does change, and as the years roll by we predict that one day *lie* and *lay* will have the same meaning in grammar books. Until that day comes, though, these differences do matter.

For example, you might scribble this memo to your boss: "Dear Boss, I lay the contract on your desk before I left." Upon reading it your boss might mutter, "No, you didn't. You laid it there. If you can't get that right, how can I trust you with this important contract? I'm giving the account to Nancy." In other words, these little differences are important because they matter to people.

Of course, they don't matter if you work for a dog.

 **Unit Test**

Fill in the blanks with the correct past and past participle of the verb in the left column. Some of the verbs are regular; others are irregular.

PRESENT	PAST	PAST PARTICIPLE
1. bring	brought	brought
2. drink	drank	drunk
3. hunt	hunted	hunted
4. sing	sang	sung
5. speak	spoke	spoken
6. choose	chose	chosen
7. lie	lay	lain
8. decide	decided	decided
9. ride	rode	ridden
10. throw	threw	thrown
11. swim	swam	swum
12. wear	wore	worn

PRESENT	PAST	PAST PARTICIPLE
13. fear	*feared*	*feared*
14. raise	*raised*	*raised*
15. go	*went*	*gone*
16. write	*wrote*	*written*
17. demand	*demanded*	*demanded*
18. study	*studied*	*studied*
19. forgive	*forgave*	*forgiven*
20. eat	*ate*	*eaten*

Unit Talk-Write Assignment

Many college students worry about being overweight. One student expresses her fears in the *Talk* column below. She makes a clear point, but in the slangy, informal English typically used in everyday talk. Your assignment is to use the *Write* column to turn her informal remarks into a paragraph of standard English that supports a discussible point. Correct any errors in verb use.

TALK

1. I have a beef with magazines that write about healthy living.

2. When they claim "healthy living," they really mean "stay twiggy thin."

3. For Pete's sake! Look who they have chose to warn us about anorexia and bulimia.

4. Glamour girls like Bridget Hall or pop stars like Paula Abdul or famous film stars like Hallie Berry.

5. Give me a break!

6. And whose bodies are projected as to die for?

7. Not Rosie O'Donnell's, Oprah Winfrey's, or even Elizabeth Taylor's.

WRITE

There is a something wrong with magazines that write about healthy living. When they claim "healthy living," they really mean, "stay very thin." Look at the models they have chosen to warn us about anorexia and bulimia. They feature glamorous women like Bridget Hall or pop stars like Paula Abdul or famous film stars like Halle Berry. These are not appropriate spokeswomen! Also, look at the bodies the magazines tell us we should want to have. They are not the bodies of Rosie O'Donnell, Oprah Winfrey, or even Elizabeth Taylor. Instead, they show us very thin women like Demi Moore, Kate Winslet, and Sharon Stone. I believe young women who already have relationship problems, self-worth problems, or any

TALK

WRITE

8. No, it's the bodies of skeletons like Demi Moore, Kate Winslet, and Sharon Stone.

9. I'm telling you, kids who already have relationship problems, self-worth problems, or any other psychological baggage get really depressed when they look in the mirror and find they don't look like Helen Hunt.

10. They'll feel like laying down and dying—I'm telling you

11. My mom says that when she was young, the stars that were considered glamorous were sorta round, like Marilyn Monroe and Sophia Loren.

12. Boy, do I wish the round look would come back and women could eat like normal people. Now that would be healthy living.

other psychological problems get very depressed when

they look in the mirror and find they don't look like

Helen Hunt. They may feel like lying down and dying. My

mother says that when she was young, the stars that

were considered glamorous were more full-figured, like

Marilyn Monroe and Sophia Loren. I wish the full-

figured look would become popular again and women

could eat like normal people. Now that would be healthy

living.

_____

_____

_____

_____

_____

Unit Collaborative Assignment

The following paragraph about the human desire for peace contains errors in the past participles of irregular verbs. First, correct the errors. Then team up with a partner, exchange books, and check (correcting if necessary) each other's work. Discuss any mistakes, referring to the list of irregular verbs on pages 192–194 to settle any arguments.

The other day, while I ~~drived~~ *drove* along the freeway, I noticed a bumper sticker. It ~~red~~ *read*, "Aim for peace." I ~~thinked~~ *thought* to myself, "Isn't peace what human beings all over the world want?" How many lives of every generation are ~~drawed~~ *drawn* into the struggle for peace? Will peace be achieved only when millions of additional bodies are ~~lain~~ *laid or lying* in unmarked graves? Martin Luther King, who ~~lays~~ *lies* buried in a Southern cemetery, killed by an assassin's bullet, tried to ~~rise~~ *raise* our consciousness for peace. His idea of peace didn't ~~set~~ *sit* well

with the power structure of his day. Mohandas Gandhi also ~~seeked~~ *sought* peace

for India. He, too, perished at the hand of an assassin who ~~laid~~ *lay* in wait for

him. The wish for peace has obviously not just ~~springed~~ *sprung* up. Human beings

have always craved peace. Getting it, however, has not ~~prove~~ *proved or proven* to be easy. ○

Unit Writing Assignment

Below is a list of commonly seen bumper stickers. Choose one from the list and write about it. Or, choose a bumper sticker that you have on your own car or have seen and write about that. Pay particular attention to verb forms. Use the Revising Checklist to revise.

1. If you want peace, work for justice.

2. Treat me no differently than you would the Queen.

3. The worst day fishing is better than the best day working.

4. I love N.Y. (or some other city or state).

5. Give a damn.

6. I brake for animals.

7. Hand over the chocolate and no one will get hurt.

8. Children are such a great way to start people.

9. Basketball is life. All the rest is details. (or football, baseball, hockey, golf, tennis)

10. Challenge authority. ○

Photo Writing Assignment

The following picture shows an overturned car and rescue workers trying to free trapped passengers in it. Using your imagination to put yourself in the position of an eyewitness, write a paragraph in which you describe the accident you saw that resulted in this wreck. As your topic sentence, use your first impressions of the car as it approached— whether it was speeding, weaving, or etc. Then, as support for the topic sentence, describe the accident as you saw it in your imagination. Pay special attention to using both regular and irregular verbs correctly. Use the Revising Checklist to revise.

12
Subject-Verb Agreement

"Fifi and Rex is well-trained dogs."

Subjects and verbs must agree in number: That is the one rule of subject-verb agreement. A singular subject always takes a singular verb; a plural subject always takes a plural verb. Most of the time this rule is plain and easy to follow, as shown in the following sentences:

> Jane loves John.
>
> The women love John.

Jane, a singular subject, takes the singular verb *loves*. *Women*, a plural subject, takes the plural verb *love*.

We are also likely to come across sentences like these:

> She don't watch much television.
>
> There is four reasons why I bought a Jeep.

She, a singular subject, is incorrectly paired with the plural verb *don't watch*. *Reasons*, a plural subject, is incorrectly paired with the singular verb *is*.

Although such mistakes are common in daily speech, writing demands a greater exactness. Subjects and verbs may disagree as they tumble out of the mouth, but on the page they must agree.

Subject-verb agreement errors are typically caused by some common grammatical situations. They are, in no particular order:

1. *Do, don't, was,* and *wasn't:*

   Incorrect: He don't care about me.
   Correct: He doesn't care about me.

   Incorrect: You was at the party.
   Correct: You were at the party.

2. *Each, every, either/or,* and *neither/nor:*

   InCorrect: Neither of us are going home.
   Correct: Neither of us is going home.

   Incorrect: Either of the cars are available.
   Correct: Either of the cars is available.

3. Prepositional phrase between a subject and verb:

   Incorrect: One of the three cousins are very smart.
   Correct: One of the three cousins is very smart.

4. Sentences beginning with *there/here:*

   Incorrect: There is a lot of chores to do.
   Correct: There are a lot of chores to do.

   Incorrect: Here is the correct answers.
   Correct: Here are the correct answers.

5. Questions:

   Incorrect: Where is the books?
   Correct: Where are the books?

6. Compound subjects joined by *and, or, either/or,* or *neither/nor:*

   Incorrect: The man and his son was smiling.
   Correct: The man and his son were smiling.

   Incorrect: The man or his son were smiling.
   Correct: The man or his son was smiling.

7. *Each, everyone, anybody, somebody,* and *nobody:*
   Incorrect: Everyone in the sociology class like the text.
   Correct: Everyone in the sociology class likes the text.

8. *Who, which,* and *that:*
   Incorrect: Richard is one of those students who works hard.
   Correct: Richard is one of those students who work hard.

We'll take up these situations one by one.

Do, Don't, Was, and Wasn't

Subject-verb agreement errors are often caused by the words *do, don't, was,* and *wasn't.* Here are the correct forms of *to do*:

SINGULAR	PLURAL
I do	We do
You do	You do
He	They do
She } does	
It	

Among the most common subject-verb agreement errors made is the use of *he* or *she* with *do* instead of the correct *does*:

Incorrect: He do his job quite well.

Correct: He does his job quite well.

This error occurs second only to the incorrect use of *don't* with a singular subject:

Incorrect: She don't know what she's talking about.

Correct: She doesn't know what she's talking about.

Was and *wasn't* are also often involved in many subject-verb agreement errors. Here are the correct forms:

SINGULAR	PLURAL
I was	We were
You were	You were
He	They were
She } was	
It	

Here are some examples of errors commonly made with this verb:

Incorrect: You was at the party.

Correct: You were at the party.

Incorrect: You was so nice to me when I was sick.

Correct: You were so nice to me when I was sick.

IN A NUTSHELL

Do, don't, was, and *wasn't* often cause subject-verb agreement errors. Always check to be sure you've used them correctly.

PRACTICING 1

Underline the subject in each of the following sentences and mark *S* in the space to the left if the subject is singular or *P* if the subject is plural. Then underline the form of the verb in parentheses that agrees with the subject.

Example: P   Many of us (was, <u>were</u>) happy when it rained.

1.   *S*   That green chair (<u>doesn't</u>, don't) match the blue table.

2.   *P*   (Wasn't, <u>Weren't</u>) you at home when he arrived?

3.   *S*   The end (<u>doesn't</u>, don't) always justify the means.

4.   *P*   Jimmy and Frank (was, <u>were</u>) both great swimmers.

5.   *S*   She (don't, <u>doesn't</u>) ever deliver what she promises.

6.   *P*   (Was, <u>Were</u>) those the only letters you wrote?

7.   *S*   (<u>Doesn't</u>, Don't) it matter to you that you hurt her feelings?

8.   *P*   Many of the cows (<u>were</u>, was) hungry and diseased.

9.   *P*   There (<u>are</u>, is) many days when I want to stay home.

10.   *P*   Both the sergeant and the corporal (was, <u>were</u>) nice people.

Each, Every, Either/Or, and Neither/Nor

Among some troublesome subjects are the words *each, every, either, either/or, neither,* and *neither/nor*. All take a singular verb. Here are some examples:

> Each pen, pencil, and ruler was (not <u>were</u>) assigned a number.
>
> Every piano and violin is (not <u>are</u>) being used for the performance.
>
> Neither of the students works (not <u>work</u>) very hard.
>
> Either of the cars is (not <u>are</u>) a bargain.

Don't be confused by the prepositional phrase—for example, *of the cars*—that usually follows *each, every, either,* or *neither*. Cross it out, as we suggested in Unit 7, and the verb choice will be clear. If *each* confuses you, and you can't remember whether it's singular or plural, add *one* after it. The *one* is already implied. A *one* is similarly implied in *either* and *neither* used alone. Adding the *one*—whether on the page or in the privacy of your head—will help you remember that *each, either,* and *neither* are always singular.

> Each [one] of the men wore a coat.
>
> Each [one] of the cats had on a pretty collar

Either [one] is as good as the other.

Neither [one] speaks English.

Either/or and *neither/nor* are also troublesome. Here are some examples:

Incorrect: Neither the principal nor the guidance counselor know me by name.

Correct: Neither the principal nor the guidance counselor knows me by name.

Incorrect: Neither the secretary nor the president were to blame.

Correct: Neither the secretary nor the president was to blame.

If one subject joined by *either/or* or *neither/nor* is singular and one is plural, the verb should agree with the nearer subject. Here are some examples:

Incorrect: Either the rats or the raccoon were here.

Correct: Either the rats or the raccoon was here.

Incorrect: Either the raccoon or the rats was here.

Correct: Either the raccoon or the rats were here.

IN A NUTSHELL

Each, every, either/or, and *neither/nor* take singular verbs except when they join two subjects, one singular and one plural, in which case the verb agrees with the nearer subject.

PRACTICING 2

In the following sentences, underline the correct form of the verb in parentheses.

Example: Neither of the boats (are, <u>is</u>) sinking.

1. Each of the girls (<u>has</u>, have) a purple hat.

2. Neither of the books (<u>is</u>, are) written in fine print.

3. Either of them (are, <u>is</u>) suitable for the test.

4. Every house within two blocks (<u>is</u>, are) rented.

5. Each hat and umbrella (<u>was</u>, were) assigned a number.

6. Every car and truck (are, <u>is</u>) available for leasing.

7. Each of the thousand applicants (take, <u>takes</u>) a number.

8. Neither of the boys (<u>understands</u>, understand) the explanation.

9. Either coat (<u>is</u>, are) warm enough for now.

10. Every goose and duck (<u>is</u>, are) playing in the pond.

Phrases Between a Subject and Its Verb

A prepositional phrase that comes between a subject and verb can cause an agreement error. Here is a list of common prepositions:

about	beside	inside	throughout
above	besides	into	through
across	between	like	to
after	beyond	near	toward
against	by	of	under
along	despite	off	underneath
among	down	on	until
around	during	out	up
at	except	outside	upon
before	for	over	with
behind	from	past	within
below	in	since	without
beneath			

Here is a typical agreement error caused by a prepositional phrase coming between a subject and verb:

One of the blue cars were out of gas.

The prepositional phrase *of the blue cars* comes between the subject *one* and the verb *were*. The subject, though, is still *one*, and *one* is always singular. Cross out the prepositional phrase and the subject is immediately clear:

One ~~of the blue cars~~ was out of gas.

An agreement error can be caused by a prepositional phrase that comes between a subject and its verb.

PRACTICING 3

In the sentences that follow, cross out all prepositional phrases. Then circle the subject and underline the correct verb in parentheses.

Example: The (sloop) under the lights (<u>is</u>, are) mine.

1. The (houses) at the end of our block (is, <u>are</u>) old.

2. The (stairs) behind the library (is, <u>are</u>) very steep.

3. That (box) of clothes and books (go, <u>goes</u>) to the garage sale.

4. An (analysis) of the tissues (<u>indicates</u>, indicate) that (disease) is present.

5. Five (stores) in the old alley (shows, <u>show</u>) signs of damage.

6. An (army) of ants (<u>is</u>, are) forming behind the cabinet.

7. This (comment) about The Rolling Stones (<u>explains</u>, explain) their songs.

8. At Ralph's, a (package) of dried bananas (<u>sells</u>, sell) for less.

9. A (quilt) of little blue patches (<u>hangs</u>, hang) on the wall.

10. The (diamonds) scattered on the counter (looks, <u>look</u>) unreal.

Sentences Beginning with There/Here

Subject-verb agreement errors can easily occur in sentences that begin with *there is*, *there are*, *here is*, and *here are*. Here are some examples:

Incorrect: There was two strangers dressed in black.

Correct: There were two strangers dressed in black.

Incorrect: Here is the pencils you asked me to buy.

Correct: Here are the pencils you asked me to buy.

In these examples, the writer is confused by *there* or *here*, which strikes the ear as singular. However, neither *here* nor *there* is the subject of the sentence. If you're confused by such sentences, reword them to make the subject come before the verb and the mistake will quickly become visible:

Two strangers dressed in black were there.

The pencils you asked me to buy are here.

Indeed, many sentences beginning with *there* or *here* can be made crisper and better if they are reworded to avoid such dead openings. Here is an example:

Original: There are many children who go to bed hungry.

Rewrite: Many children go to bed hungry.

The *there is* or *there are* is often unnecessary.

IN A NUTSHELL

Watch out for subject-verb agreement errors in sentences that begin with *there* or *here*. To check the agreement of such a sentence, reword it to place the subject first.

PRACTICING 4

Circle the subject in each sentence. Then underline the correct form of the verb in parentheses

1. There (is, are) the snowcapped (mountains).

2. There (was, were) three (papers) about cats.

3. Here (is, are) a (map) of India, Pakistan, and Bangladesh.

4. There (is, **are**) moments in my life when I would like to be a hermit.

5. Here (is, **are**) the towels you borrowed.

6. There (is, **are**) three dresses hanging in the closet.

7. There (was, **were**) two shacks between the house and the mansion.

8. There (was, **were**) many Italian songs sung that night.

9. There (was, **were**) big iron pots boiling and bubbling on the stove.

10. Here (is, **are**) the autographs you wanted.

PRACTICING 5

Rewrite each sentence below to avoid the *there* or *here* beginning and to make the writing crisper.

1. There is a mountain of laundry to be washed.

A mountain of laundry must be washed.

2. Here are the two diaries for you to read and enjoy.

You will enjoy reading these two diaries.

3. There are certain band players who would prefer to play golf than perform.

Certain band players would prefer to play golf than perform.

4. Here is the computer expert who promised to install your hardware.

This computer expert promised to install your hardware.

5. There are details that need to be added to the paragraph.

Details need to be added to the paragraph.

6. There are many American citizens who never bother to vote.

Many American citizens never bother to vote.

7. Here are some chocolate bunnies and jelly beans to put in the basket.

Put these chocolate bunnies and jelly beans in the basket.

8. There are so many kinds of ball point pens that I don't know which to choose.

I don't know which kind of ball point pen to choose.

9. Here is a map that will tell you how to get to the center of town.

This map tells you how to get to the center of town.

10. There is a whole family story contained in that old stone wall.

A whole family story is contained in that old stone wall.

Questions

Most sentences that we write or speak are statements, such as these:

> The newspaper is here.
>
> The toast is brown.
>
> The coffee is burned.

In these, and in most statements, because the subject comes before the verb, it is easy to spot an agreement error.

However, when we ask a question, the verb typically comes before the subject:

> Where is the newspaper?
>
> What color is the toast?
>
> What happened to the coffee?

With the subject now following the verb, it is easy to make an agreement error:

> Where is John and Mary sitting?

To use the plural verb *are* correctly requires a speaker or writer to know that a plural subject—*John and Mary*—lies ahead. If you're in doubt about the agreement between subject and verb in a question, simply reword it as a statement. For example, we have:

> John and Mary (is/are) sitting here.

It is now evident that the plural *are* is the correct verb since *John and Mary* refer to two people.

To check subject-verb agreement in a question, simply reword it as a statement.

PRACTICING 6

Circle the subject in each question. Then underline the correct form of the verb in parentheses.

1. What (is, <u>are</u>) the (names) of the players?

2. Where on earth (<u>do</u>, does) such (people) live?

3. Where (<u>is</u>, are) (Daddy's) gloves?

4. How many attorneys (do, <u>does</u>) the (defendant) have?

5. What (has, <u>have</u>) the (people) done about it?

6. What (is, <u>are</u>) (Donna's) favorite subjects?

7. Who (is, <u>are</u>) those (strangers) coming up the walkway?

8. (<u>Have</u>, Has) the (tenants) complained to the landlord?

9. What (has, <u>have</u>) (they) said about me?

10. After all, what (<u>do</u>, does) (they) know?

Compound Subjects Joined by And, Or, Either/Or, or Neither/Nor

The sentence that occasionally gives writers trouble is one that looks like this:

SINGULAR NOUN + AND + SINGULAR NOUN

Here are some examples:

The man and the woman was there.

The house and the car is mine.

Time and energy makes a difference.

In all these sentences, the writer was fooled by what seemed to be a singular subject. However, just as one plus one makes two, one singular subject plus another singular subject joined by *and* always makes a subject plural. The sentences should therefore read:

> The man and the woman <u>were</u> there.

> The house and the car <u>are</u> mine.

> Time and energy <u>make</u> a difference.

Just remember that one plus one makes two, and two is plural.

ESL Advice!

ESL students should commit the rule to memory.
Subject + and + Subject = Plural verb

Another test is to substitute a suitable pronoun for the double subject. For example, the sentence,

> The man and the woman was there.

becomes

> They was there.

which should strike your ear as wrong. The correct sentence is therefore

> They were there.

or

> The man and woman were there.

Although two singular subjects joined by *and* always take a plural verb, two singular subjects joined by *or* require a singular verb:

> Burt and Tom are on the team.

but

> Burt or Tom is on the team.

> Joan and Linda are coming.

but

> Joan or Linda is coming.

Of course, two plural nouns joined by *or* take a plural verb:

Usually, captains or co-captains are elected.

What happens when a sentence has two subjects, one singular and one plural, joined by *or*? In that case, the verb agrees with the nearer subject:

The co-captains or the coach <u>is</u> calling a meeting.

but

The coach or the co-captains <u>are</u> calling a meeting.

As we saw earlier in the chapter, the same rule applies with two subjects joined by *either/or* and *neither/nor*: The verb agrees with the nearer subject:

Either the co-captains or the coach <u>is</u> calling a meeting.

but

Either the coach or the co-captains <u>are</u> calling a meeting.

IN A NUTSHELL

- Two singular subjects joined by *and* are plural.
- Two singular subjects joined by *or, either/or,* or *neither/nor* are singular.
- If a singular and plural subject are joined by or, *either/or,* or *neither/nor,* the verb agrees with the closer subject.

PRACTICING 7

In the following sentences, underline the correct form of the verb in parentheses.

1. His bristling eyebrows and large frown (<u>scare</u>, scares) children.

2. Either you or Gus (water, <u>waters</u>) the plants while we're gone.

3. A fool and his money (is, <u>are</u>) soon parted.

4. Neither money nor power (motivate, <u>motivates</u>) him.

5. *Newsweek* and *Time* (is, <u>are</u>) not light reading.

6. Avocado or papaya (<u>is</u>, are) in the salad.

7. London and Paris (<u>attract</u>, attracts) many tourists.

8. Either the president or the sales manager (<u>is</u>, are) going to speak.

9. My mother and father (inspires, <u>inspire</u>) me to achieve.

10. Neither the waiters nor the manager (take, <u>takes</u>) responsibility for the accident.

PRACTICING 8

Complete the following sentences using a correct singular or plural verb form.

Example: Juan or Frederico always <u>*takes out the garbage.*</u>

1. Neither the teacher nor the students _____

2. Love and marriage _____

3. Fighting or screaming _____

4. Either the chef or the owner _____

5. Neither Pat nor I _____

6. Arthritis and other pains of old age _____

7. Two apples or one orange _____

8. The gorilla and the chimpanzee _____

9. Neither that bowl nor those plates _____

10. His favorite books and CDs _____

Everyone, Anyone, Somebody, Someone, Something, None, and Nobody

Everyone, anyone, somebody, someone, something, none, and *nobody* are indefinite pronouns. Indefinite pronouns are so called because they refer to no specific—or definite—person. Such indefnite pronouns as *everyone, anyone, someone* are really blends of *every one, any one,* and *some one,* while *none* is a blend of *no one.* The *one* should warn you that these indefinite pronouns always take singular verbs, as do the following:

another	nobody
anybody	no one
anyone	none
anything	nothing
everybody	one
everyone	somebody
everything	something

Here are some examples:

Everybody has (not <u>have</u>) the right to freedom of speech.

Everyone tells (not <u>tell</u>) a different story.

Nobody knows (not <u>know</u>) the truth better than I do.

Another says (not <u>say</u>) something else.

IN A NUTSHELL

Indefinite pronouns such as *anyone, everybody, everyone, somebody, someone, something, everything, nobody,* and *none* take singular verbs.

PRACTICING 9

Underline the correct form of the verb in parentheses.

1. Everyone (<u>has</u>, have) an opinion.

2. None of the clouds (<u>is</u>, are) below the mountain range.

3. Everybody (<u>loves</u>, love) a beautiful sunset.

4. No one (<u>refuses</u>, refuse) to be in the parade.

5. None of the chocolate (<u>is</u>, are) melted.

6. Anybody who is somebody (<u>knows</u>, know) the mayor personally.

7. One of the actors (<u>wears</u>, wear) a false nose.

8. Somebody (know, <u>knows</u>) who ate my porridge.

9. Everything you say (<u>is</u>, are) a lie.

10. Nobody (<u>knows</u>, know) my name.

Who, Which, and That

Who, which, and *that* are often used to replace nouns in dependent clauses. In such cases, the verb should agree with the closest noun before the *who, which,* or *that.* Consider this example:

Incorrect: John is among the men who thinks we have a problem.

Correct: John is among the men who think we have a problem.

Who stands for the closest preceding noun, which is *men*, not *John*. Therefore, it is *men* that determines the form of the verb. In fact, the sentence is a blend of two smaller sentences:

John is among the men. The men think we have a problem.

If you have trouble with this rule, split the sentence into two smaller sentences, and the subject will become clear.
   Here are other examples:

Jeff or Joe is one of those who are going to Tibet.

Split: Jeff or Joe is one of those. Those are going to Tibet.

Those, not *Jeff* or *Joe*, is the closest noun before *who.* Since *those* takes a plural verb, the *who* that stands for it must also take a plural verb.

Among our daily plagues and troubles is a fly that bites.

Fly, not *plagues* or *troubles*, is the closest noun before *that, so the verb must be singular.*
   Note: Do not be confused by a prepositional phrase that may intervene between the pronouns, *who, that,* or *which* and their antecedents. Here is an example

I admire John because he is the only worker in our offices who cares about other workers.

The antecedent of *who* is not *offices,* which is plural, but *worker,* which is singular. The verb must therefore likewise be singular. Simply disregard the prepositional phrase.

IN A NUTSHELL

Who, which, and *that* used in dependent clauses must agree with the closest preceding noun.

PRACTICING 10

Circle the closest noun preceding *who, which,* or *that* in the following sentences. Then underline the correct form of the verb in parentheses.

1. A (coach) who (allow, <u>allows</u>) personal attacks on an opposing player teaches bad sportsmanship.

2. Bob is one of the (players) who (<u>score</u>, scores) regularly.

3. Peter is the only (student) who (qualify, <u>qualifies</u>) for advanced math.

4. Marie is one of the (dancers) who (hopes, <u>hope</u>) to go to New York.

5. These two (movies), which (contains, <u>contain</u>) pointless violence, should not win Oscars.

6. Betty is among the (students) who (is, <u>are</u>) dissatisfied.

7. His (questions), which (has, <u>have</u>) to do with cost and color, must be answered before we can select the paint.

8. These herb (tablets), which (<u>look</u>, looks) harmless, can cause an upset stomach.

9. The big, billowy (clouds) that (<u>fill</u>, fills) the sky make me feel like singing.

10. He is one of (those) who (<u>object</u>, objects) to the proposal.

Unit Test

Sentences will vary.

Use your imagination to complete the following sentences, making verb and subject agree.

1. One of the dogs that _____

2. Either of the desks _____

3. There is _____

4. The amount of work _____

5. Nobody in this town ever _____

6. Stinginess, among other faults, _____

7. At the edge of town was _____

8. Not only the assistants but the manager _____

9. Talent and hard work _____

10. The paper and the ribbon on this gift package _____

11. Neither his beloved cat nor all four dogs _____

12. Pete by himself or the committee members _____

13. Both the gorgeous pink roses and the silver ribbon _____

14. There are _____

15. Here is _____

16. A sidewalk filled with spring flowers _____

17. Everyone who loves sea animals _____

18. Neither of the two colors _____

19. Every man and woman _____

20. The feathers inside the pillow _____

Unit Talk-Write Assignment

In this exercise a student expresses his opinion on animal cruelty. In the process, he makes several errors in subject-verb agreement. You have two assignments: First, correct all subject-verb agreement errors found in the *Talk* column. Second, using the sentences in the *Talk* column as your starting point, create a standard English paragraph in the *Write* column, beginning with a discussible point and proving it with sufficient details.

TALK

1. I know a man who ~~don't~~ *doesn't* care about animals and always ~~treat~~ *treats* them cruelly.

2. Each of his dogs ~~are~~ *is* dying for affection. Maybe you don't think that's important, but I promise you it is.

3. There ~~is~~ *are* lots of violent criminals who ~~starts~~ *start* out being mean to cats and dogs in the neighborhood. I saw a television program that said criminals ~~was~~ *were* often pet-abusers as children.

4. One of my cousins ~~are~~ *is* that way, too, aways being mean to her pets.

5. Where ~~is~~ *are* the rewards of being mean to an animal who ~~haven't~~ *hasn't* a chance to complain about bad treatment?

6. Nobody ~~make~~ *makes* these mean people stop mistreating animals because they don't want to interfere. Well, interfere.

7. Often, neither the mother nor the father ~~seem~~ *seems* to care if their child ~~tease~~ *teases* an animal.

8. Some people say, "Aw, animal abuse—that's not a real crime." But the TV show said it is a crime in many states. More over, both a scientist and a doctor on the show ~~says~~ *say* it is a proven fact that abusing animals ~~lead~~ *leads* to abusing humans.

9. One of those guys who just ~~get~~ *gets* a tongue lashing for being mean to a pet might be the next serial rapist or killer.

10. The bottom line is this: Everyone of us ~~need~~ *needs* to do our best to stop cruelty to all living creatures if we want to be moral people.

WRITE

Animal abuse is a serious crime and we are all responsible for stopping it. Some people say, "Animal abuse isn't a real crime." But I saw a television program that said it is a crime in many states. Moreover, both a scientist and a doctor on the show say it is a proven fact that abusing animals leads to abusing humans. The TV show said criminals were often pet-abusers as children. There are many violent criminals who start out being mean to cats and dogs in the neighborhood. One of those guys who just gets a warning for being mean to a pet might be the next serial rapist or killer. We all have seen animal abuse in our own neighborhoods. For example, I know a man who doesn't care about animals and always treats them cruelly. Each of his dogs is starving for affection. One of my cousins is that way, too, always being mean to her pets. Children can be very cruel to animals, and often, neither the mother nor the father seems to care if his/her child teases an animal. Nobody makes these mean people stop mistreating animals because they don't want to interfere. Well, we should interfere. Every one of us needs to do our best to stop cruelty to all living creatures if we want to be moral people.

Unit Collaborative Assignment

A. The following paragraph contains errors in subject-verb agreement. Working with a partner, make all the required corrections. Then exchange papers with your partner and discuss your answers.

Old age and youth ~~is~~ *are* different. Whereas children move from childhood to adulthood, what role ~~does~~ *do* senior citizens progress to? In this country there is only two generations, parents and children. A grandmother often ~~do~~ *does* not play an essential role in our society. Instead, she ~~spend~~ *spends* her life feeling unnecessary. No wonder so few of my friends' parents ~~wants~~ *want* to retire, but keep on working past the age of sixty-five. They feel that if they ~~gives~~ *give* up working, they will be ignored and forgotten. Both our young people and the state ~~has~~ *have* a responsibility to help the aged, whose taxes ~~keeps~~ *keep* our economy stable. That does not mean that we should spoil senior citizens by letting them vegetate in comfort. Helping them and caring for them ~~means~~ *mean* finding creative jobs that ~~appeals~~ *appeal* to the elderly. Old people ~~needs~~ *need* solid roles that ~~makes~~ *make* them feel important. To feel useful and to engage in some significant activity ~~gives~~ *give* older people a sense of self-worth.

B. Choose a partner, and talk out a paragraph about a person you admire. This person might be one of the following:

1. A relative, family friend, neighbor, teacher, or coach

2. A political figure

3. A sports personality

4. An entertainer

5. Someone you've read about

Unit Writing Assignment

Write about the person you described in the Unit Collaborative Assignment above. Use the Revising Checklist on the inside cover to revise.

Photo Writing Assignment

Write about how much hard work goes into becoming an artist like the one shown in the following photograph. Begin with a discussible point and make sure that each of your verbs agrees with its subject. If you think about each member of the band as an individual and the entire group working together, you will get practice using both singular and plural subjects in your sentences. Use the Revising Checklist to revise.

13

Problems with Verbs

"Mom fed me an egg, then just ignores me."
"I would of gone if invited."
"A good time was had by all."

If English is a car, then the verb is its engine. Like the engine of a real car, the verb is the part of speech that is most likely to cause problems. In this unit we will cover some common problems with verbs. Specifically, we'll deal with the following:

- Shifts in tense
- Using *would of, could of,* or *should of* instead of *would have, could have, should have,* or *must have*
- Double negatives
- Active and passive voice

Shifts in Tense

If you begin a sentence in the present tense, you must end it in the present tense. If you begin in the past tense, you must end in the past tense. For example, look at this sentence:

Mom fed me an egg and, then just ignores me.

The problem with the sentence is that it begins with a verb in the past tense and ends with a verb in the present tense. Mom is made into

233

a time-traveler—hopping from the past to the present in one breath. To be correct the sentence must read:

> Mom fed me an egg and then just ignored me.   **(all past tense)**

or

> Mom feeds me an egg and then just ignores me.   **(all present tense)**

Your tense use must be consistent. If there is no logical reason for jumping from present to past or past to present, you must not do so. Yet, because we mix up our verb tenses all the time in everyday speech, your ear might mislead you into making the same mistake in writing. Be alert to this possible error. Make sure your verbs in a written sentence all use the same tense.

IN A NUTSHELL

Verbs in the same sentence must all be in the same tense.

PRACTICING 1

Underline the verbs in the following sentences. Then, correct the shifts in verb tense by making both verbs past tense.

1. The thief stole all four wheels and leaves the car hulk on the sidewalk.

The thief stole all four wheels and left the car hulk on the sidewalk.

2. When I told her the package had arrived, she simply shrugs.

When I told her the package had arrived, she simply shrugged.

3. The doctor asks me lots of questions and then gave me a shot of penicillin.

The doctor asked me lots of questions and then gave me a shot of penicillin.

4. When they demanded to see the manager, a secretary tells them to wait.

When they demanded to see the manager, a secretary told them to wait.

5. I had just surfed a wave when an unexpected wave hits me from the back.

I had just surfed a wave when an unexpected wave hit me from the back.

6. The grizzly leaned over and scoops a salmon from the stream.

The grizzly leaned over and scooped a salmon from the stream.

7. On his birthday, Bernie bought a lottery ticket and wins.

On his birthday, Bernie bought a lottery ticket and won.

8. My heart races when I saw the police cruiser behind the billboard.

My heart raced when I saw the police cruiser behind the billboard.

9. My mother recites the poem "Bobby Shaftoe," and we broke up with laughter.

My mother recited the poem "Bobby Shaftoe," and we broke up with laughter.

10. She ran past me and yells, "Hurry up!"

She ran past me and yelled, "Hurry up!"

PRACTICING 2

Correct the shift in verb tense in the following sentences by making both verbs present tense.

1. When the bell rings, all the children assembled in the auditorium.

When the bell rings, the children assemble in the auditorium.

2. She sees the cereal and shouted, "I want that, Mommy!"

She sees the cereal and shouts, "I want that, Mommy!"

3. His friends tried to change his mind, but he still believes he was right.

His friends try to change his mind, but he still believes he is right.

4. He unfurled the sail and starts up the motor.

He unfurls the sail and starts up the motor.

5. My boy loved our rowboat and wants to take it out on the lake.

My boy loves our rowboat and wants to take it out on the lake.

6. The bass were biting well so we do not stop fishing.

The bass are biting well so we do not stop fishing.

7. The landlord is pretending that he wasn't going to raise our rent.

The landlord is pretending that he isn't going to raise our rent.

8. The deer jumps to its feet when it saw the stalking hunters.

The deer jumps to its feet when it sees the stalking hunters.

9. He takes a joke with good humor and often cracked a smile when something funny happened.

He takes a joke with good humor and often cracks a smile when something funny happens.

10. When she was pregnant, her husband is very supportive.

When she is pregnant, her husband is very supportive.

PRACTICING 3

Answers will vary.

Complete the sentences below, using the correct verb tense.

Example: Her mother scolded her and *made her realize her mistake*.

1. I came, I saw, and I *conquered.*

2. The diver checks his oxygen and then *turns on the ignition.*

3. Once the emergency team had her on her back, they _____
proceeded to give her treatment.

4. When Dad had his coffee, Marie *spoke to him.*

5. The violins tune up, the singers hum, and the conductor
begins the concert.

6. You think you're so smart, but you *are really naive.*

7. When he warned them about the road, they *laughed.*

8. Little Red Riding Hood takes her basket of food and _____

walks into the woods.

9. The coyotes howled and *scratched at the door.*

10. The car sputtered, stuttered, and *went dead.*

Would Have, Could Have, or Should Have, and Must Have

Because *have* and *of* sound so much alike in speech, it's easy to begin saying *would of* instead of *would have*. But *would of, could of, should of,* and *must of* are mispronunciations. You should never use *would of, could of, should of,* or *must of* in your writing. Always use *would have, could have, should have,* or *must have.*

EAR ALERT

PRACTICING 4

Correct the use of *would of, could of, should of,* or *must have* in the sentences that follow.

1. I would of come if you had told me.

I would have come if you had told me.

2. Should we of accompanied her to the bridge?

Should we have accompanied her to the bridge?

3. For the right price, she could of bought the car.

For the right price, she could have bought the car.

4. He must of left his keys in the car again.

He must have left his keys in the car again.

5. If he would of reported the crime, the police would of come.

If he would have reported (or had reported) the crime, the police would have come.

6. She never should of promised to move to Connecticut.

She never should have promised to move to Connecticut.

7. She must of been very angry with me that day.

She must have been very angry with me that day.

8. You would of liked Joe, my best friend.

You would have liked Joe, my best friend.

9. Everyone should of shared in the expense.

Everyone should have shared in the expense.

10. If she would of been more patient, Mary wouldn't of broken the zipper.

If she had been more careful, Mary would not have broken the zipper.

Double Negatives

Use only one negative for each idea. Do not use a negative qualifier (*no*, *not*, or *never*) with a negative verb or with the adverbs *hardly* or *scarcely*.

Incorrect: She didn't buy no onions.

Correct: She didn't buy any onions.

Incorrect: I can't hardly wait for spring break.

Correct: I can hardly wait for spring break.

Incorrect: John wouldn't scarcely give her the time of day.

Correct: John would scarcely give her the time of day.

Incorrect: The boys hadn't found no apples.

Correct: The boys hadn't found any apples.

PRACTICING 5

Rewrite each sentence to correct the double negative.

1. Nobody knew nothing about the theft.

Nobody knew anything about the theft.

2. We never play no card games.

We never play any card games.

3. Tom can't hardly wait for the peaches to ripen.

Tom can hardly wait for the peaches to ripen.

4. She never ordered no donuts.

She never ordered any donuts.

5. All of us wouldn't scarcely mention the picnic to her.

All of us would scarcely mention the picnic to her.

6. The storage area didn't contain no usable bicycles.

The storage area didn't contain any usable bicycles.

7. Didn't the police ask you no questions?

Didn't the police ask you any questions?

8. In second grade I hardly spoke no English.

In second grade, I hardly spoke any English.

9. Although they looked at us, they didn't give us no trouble.

Although they looked at us, they didn't give us any trouble.

10. The Olympic judges don't give no scores aloud.

The Olympic judges don't give any scores aloud.

Active and Passive Voice

English has two voices: the active and the passive voice. The **active voice** stresses who did an act. The **passive voice** stresses to whom or to what an act was done. Most of us usually speak in the active voice because it is simpler and more direct.

Active voice: The students greeted the professor.
Passive voice: The professor was greeted by the students.

Because it hides the doer, the passive voice is often preferred by writers who wish to avoid naming names. Here is a case in point:

The oak trees were ordered to be bulldozed to make room for a high-rise office complex.

Who gave this order? The active voice would have told us:

Commissioner Smith ordered the oak trees to be bulldozed to make room for a high-rise office complex.

In writing you should mainly use the active voice. It is livelier, stronger, and more like everyday talk than the passive voice. The passive voice is occasionally used in scientific reporting, where what was done is more important than which researcher did it:

> The bacteria were isolated for further study.

The passive voice is also occasionally used in instances where an act is more important than its cause:

> The village was destroyed by a terrible flood.

The important fact here is the destruction of the village. That it was destroyed by a flood is secondary.

IN A NUTSHELL

Write mainly in the active voice, which is livelier and stronger than the passive voice.

PRACTICING 6

Read the paired sentences aloud and underline the verbs. Place an *A* in the blank beside the sentences in the active voice and a *P* in the blank beside the sentences in the passive voice.

Example: _A_ **(a).** The children <u>opened</u> the door.

   _P_ **(b).** The door <u>was opened</u> by the children.

1.   _P_ **(a).** The vacation <u>was announced</u> by the teacher.

   _A_ **(b).** The teacher <u>announced</u> the vacation.

2.   _P_ **(a).** Students <u>are hurt</u> by the battle for grades.

   _A_ **(b).** The battle for grades <u>hurts</u> students.

3.   _A_ **(a).** Some months Fred <u>owes</u> more money than he earns.

   _P_ **(b).** Some months more money <u>is owed</u> by Fred than <u>is earned</u> by him.

4.   _A_ **(a).** The president of the club <u>deceived</u> its members.

   _P_ **(b).** The members of the club <u>were deceived</u> by its president.

5.   _P_ **(a).** The tenants <u>were told</u> to evacuate the building.

   _A_ **(b).** The police <u>told</u> the tenants to evacuate the building.

6. _A_ **(a).** We <u>found</u> few faults with the house.

   _P_ **(b).** Few faults <u>were found</u> with the house.

7. _A_ **(a).** Never <u>let</u> a fool kiss you.

   _P_ **(b).** Never <u>be kissed</u> by a fool.

8. _P_ **(a).** Three flies <u>were swallowed</u> by the frog.

   _A_ **(b).** The frog <u>swallowed</u> three flies.

9. _P_ **(a).** The miracle <u>must be accepted</u> on faith.

   _A_ **(b).** We <u>must accept</u> the miracle on faith.

10. _A_ **(a).** The Ecological Society <u>chopped</u> down the fir trees.

   _P_ **(b).** The fir trees <u>were chopped</u> down by the Ecological Society.

PRACTICING 7

Rewrite the sentences below to change from the passive to the active voice.

Example: The chili was burned by the cook.

   The cook burned the chili.

1. The point was made by the field-goal kicker.

The field-goal kicker made the point.

2. The plane was struck by lightening.

Lightning struck the plane.

3. The stamps were bought by Ricardo, and the letters were mailed by Luisa.

Ricardo bought the stamps and Luisa mailed the letters.

4. The pictures were taken by my sister.

My sister took the pictures.

5. The contract was signed last week by Mr. Wong.

Mr. Wong signed the contract.

6. The idea was opposed by a vocal minority of students.

A vocal minority of students opposed the idea.

7. Weightlifting is done by the athletes.

Athletes lift weights.

8. The popcorn was popped by Joel.

Joel popped the popcorn.

9. The roof was blown off by the explosion.

The explosion blew off the roof.

10. A deal was struck with management by the truck drivers.

The truck drivers struck a deal with management.

11. A diet was begun by the gymnast.

The gymnast began a diet.

12. The lopsided houses were built by the contractor.

The contractor built the lopsided houses.

13. The sandwiches were fixed by Keisha, and the potato salad was brought by Rujendra.

Keisha fixed the sandwiches, and Rujendra brought the potato salad.

14. The beanstalk is cut down by Jack.

Jack cut down the beanstalk.

15. Tasteless jokes were made by the unfunny comedian.

The unfunny comedian made tasteless jokes.

 **Unit Test**

Underline any errors in each sentence. Then, rewrite each sentence, correcting any mistakes.

1. She could <u>of</u> slept all day.

She could <u>have</u> slept all day.

2. They don't have <u>no</u> time for us.

They don't have <u>any</u> time for us.

3. She scrambled to her feet and <u>looks</u> him in the eye.

She scrambled to her feet and <u>looked</u> him in the eye.

4. All of us should <u>of</u> thanked our guide.

All of us should <u>have</u> thanked our guide.

5. A bone was given to the dog by Mark.

Mark gave the dog a bone.

6. I never promised you <u>nothing</u> whatsoever.

I never promised you <u>anything</u> whatsoever.

7. We don't <u>never have</u> no fun.

We don't <u>ever have any</u> fun.

8. My dad <u>don't never</u> play with me.

My dad <u>doesn't ever</u> play with me.

9. Don't feed me <u>no</u> garbage today.

Don't feed me <u>any</u> garbage today.

10. Fran stopped studying at nine o'clock and <u>goes</u> for ice cream.

Fran stopped studying at nine o'clock and <u>went</u> for ice cream.

11. At the beginning of the movie, the audience laughed, but suddenly they <u>become</u> silent.

At the beginning of the movie, the audience laughed, but suddenly they <u>became</u> silent.

12. We would <u>of</u> all visited her in the hospital if we would <u>of</u> known she was sick.

We would <u>have</u> all visited her in the hospital if we would <u>have</u> known (or had known) she was sick.

13. My neighbors <u>can't</u> hardly wait to find out who won the 120 million dollar lotto.

My neighbors <u>can</u> hardly wait to find out who won the 120 million dollar lotto.

14. Don't you have <u>no</u> manners at all?

Don't you have <u>any</u> manners at all?

15. "Stand by Your Man" was made famous by Tammy Wynette.

Tammy Wynette made "Stand by Your Man" famous.

Unit Talk-Write Assignment

In a brainstorming session for an English composition class, several college students expressed their opinions on telephone answering machine greetings. The students' unedited comments are expressed in the *Talk* column. First, identify the error, if there is one, in each sentence. Second, correct the error in the *Write* column. Third, using the students' comments as background, write a polished paragraph in the space provided at the end of this section about telephone answering machine greetings. Make sure that you avoid shifts in tense, "would of, could of, and should of" errors, and double negatives. Do not use the passive voice where it isn't needed. Be sure to use standard English. Finally, check your paragraph against the Revising Checklist.

TALK

1. My friend bought an answering machine and then puts a really stupid message on it.

2. It griped me that he puts on this long message filled with useless details like "speak slowly and clearly," and "Your call is important to me, so do please leave your name, number, and the date you called. . . ."

3. I know what you mean. A long message is left by my French teacher about how she would of answered the phone, but please leave a message, have a nice life, and eat your vegetables. Then the same long message is repeated by her in French. She must have been drinking. And all I want to tell her was that I'd be absent from the next class.

4. Personally, I don't think no little kids should ever be allowed to leave a message.

5. Yeah, that's a mess, but I think it's just as bad to have some professional voice you can't never recognize. Then you're not sure you have the right number.

WRITE

1. *My friend bought an answering machine and then <u>put</u> a really stupid message on it.*

2. *It griped me that he <u>put</u> on this long message filled with useless details like "speak slowly and clearly," and "Your call is important to me, so do please leave your name, number, and the date you called ..."*

3. *I know what you mean. <u>My French teacher left</u> a long message about how she would <u>have</u> answered the phone, but please leave a message, have a nice life, and eat your vegetables. Then <u>she repeated</u> the same long message in French. And all I <u>wanted</u> to tell her was that I'd be absent from the next class.*

4. *Personally, I don't think <u>any</u> little kids should ever be allowed to leave a message.*

5. *Yeah, that's a mess, but I think it's just as bad to have some professional voice you can't <u>ever</u> recognize. Then you're not sure you have the right number.*

TALK

6. Worse even is some digital voice that sounds like it could of come from the grave.

7. What about funny messages? I get sick of those. The other day I called someone, and the message said, "This is Mary's refrigerator answering. Please leave a message."

8. That reminds me of my uncle's message, which was him singing, "Come be my love" or something. Cuckoo!

9. What about messages that wait so long for the beep to sound that you think there's no beep , so you start leaving a message. Then the beep sounds, and you had to start all over again.

10. People should of realized by now that you don't have to leave no cute messages on answering machines. All you should say was, "Hi, please leave a message."

WRITE

6. *Worse even is some digital voice that sounds as if it could <u>have</u> come from the grave.*

7. *Correct*

8. *Correct*

9. *What about messages that wait so long for the beep to sound that you think there's no beep, so you start leaving a message. Then the beep sounds, and you <u>have</u> to start all over again.*

10. *People should <u>have</u> realized by now that you don't have to leave <u>any</u> cute messages on answering machines. All you should say <u>is</u>, "Hi, please leave me a message."*

Answering machine messages are often more annoying than helpful. For example, my friend bought an answering machine and then put on this long message filled with useless details like "speak slowly and clearly," and "Your call is important to me, so do please leave your name, number, and the date you called . . ." Similarly, my French teacher left a long message about how she would have answered the phone, but please leave a message, have a nice life, and eat your vegetables. Then she repeated the same long message in French. And all I wanted to tell her was that I'd be absent from the next class. Another annoying thing is a message in some professional voice you can't ever recognize. Then you're not sure you have the right number. Even worse is some digital voice that sounds like it could have come from the grave. And certainly little children should never be allowed to leave a message. Some people have annoying messages that are supposed to be funny. The other day I called someone, and the message said, "This is Mary's refrigerator answering. Please leave a message." My uncle once had a crazy message that was him singing, "Come be my love." Finally, some people don't get the timing right. Sometimes you wait so long for the beep to sound that you think there's no beep, so you start leaving a message. Then the beep sounds, and you have to start all over again. People

should have realized by now that you don't have to leave any cute messages on answering machines. All you should say

is, "Hi, please leave me a message."

Unit Collaborative Assignment

A. Working with a partner, read aloud the following paragraph, which contains shifts in verb tense, double negatives, and incorrect use of *would have, could have, should have,* and *must have.* It also uses the passive voice when the active would be more effective. Take turns reading each sentence while the other rewrites it as necessary to correct the errors. When you are through, discuss your rewrites with your partner, referring any points of disagreement to the instructor.

I arrived in Paris and quickly settle into a decent youth hostel. I realize that I was running out of money. "If only I would of spent less money in England," I thought regretfully. My next thought was, "I'd better get a job." The problem was that I didn't have no work permit. No one wanted to hire me since work could not be performed by me legally. Also, French wasn't spoken by me very well. I must of looked terrible because worry was definitely felt by me. My concern would of turned into desperation if I had not met another American at the post office who suggests that I try the American Center situated along the Seine River. Several ads were posted by people who wanted English-speaking nannies. Before long, I found a job, but the hours are long and the kids don't have no respect for adults. I thought I must of been crazy to take such a job. I could of put up with these hardships if I would of received some decent meals. However, the French family I work for ate French bread, cheese, and cabbage day in and day out. So I quit. A few days later, a nanny job was found by me for a four-year-old girl who lived near Versailles. The job was great because the little girl has such a sweet temperament. My six months in Paris helped me become independent both emotionally and financially. It is a great experience and taught me a second language.

B. Discuss with your partner a job you have or once had. Talk out a paragraph on this topic.

Unit Writing Assignment

Write about a job you have or once had, based on your discussion in the Unit Collaborative Assignment above. Use the Revising Checklist to revise.

Photo Writing Assignment

Study the following photo. Think about the people involved in the hustle and bustle of city life. Begin with a general impression. What is their state of mind? Are they happy, excited, stressed, or miserable? Write about your general impression and support it with details from the photo and from your imagination. Write in the active voice. Avoid shifts in verb tense and double negatives. Do not use of for have. Use the Revising Checklist to revise.

14

Using Pronouns Correctly

"Maggie's sister encouraged her to wear her miniskirt."

If writing were baseball, the pronoun would be a relief pitcher whose job is temporarily to relieve nouns, who are the starters. In both speech and writing, the pronoun is a word used in place of a noun.

Here is a paragraph that might be written in a world without pronouns:

> My favorite aunt is my Aunt Ida. Aunt Ida is my mother's sister. Aunt Ida loves to read. Aunt Ida reads everything, especially romance novels. Aunt Ida's house is crammed full of books. One room, which Aunt Ida calls Aunt Ida's library, is filled to the brim with books Aunt Ida has read. Aunt Ida not only reads many books, but Aunt Ida also saves every book Aunt Ida has read. Why? Because, Aunt Ida says, Aunt Ida loves rereading old books Aunt Ida has already read.

This paragraph is repetitious and stiff because it uses no pronouns. Adding a few pronouns makes the writing livelier and more natural:

> My favorite aunt is my Aunt Ida. She is my mother's sister. Aunt Ida loves to read. She reads everything, especially romance novels. Her house is crammed full of books. One room, which she calls her library, is filled to the brim with books she has read. Aunt Ida not only reads many books, but she also saves every book she has read. Why? Because, Aunt Ida says she loves rereading old books she has already read.

All speakers use pronouns by ear, often without even thinking. Although our ear gets them right for the most part, because pronoun use in speech is more informal than in writing, we can't rely on our ear alone. We also need to learn the formal rules of pronoun use. That is what this unit covers.

Here are some common problems associated with pronouns in both speaking and writing:

- Antecedent problems

- Agreement problems

- Shifting point of view

We'll take up these problems in order.

Antecedent Problems

The **antecedent** of a pronoun (also called *the referent*) is the noun it replaces. Consider this sentence:

> John may be shy, but he loves to go to parties.

The pronoun is *he*; its antecedent—the word it refers to—is *John*.

Most of the time, the antecedent of a pronoun is perfectly clear from the context of a sentence. Sometimes, however, it isn't. Sometimes an antecedent is either unclear or altogether missing.

Unclear antecedent

Here are some examples of unclear antecedents:

> Sheila drove Sylvia and her mother to the airport.
>
> Harriett asked Janet if she needed an umbrella.

In the above sentences, the antecedents of the pronouns are unclear. We do not know whether Sheila drove her mother or Sylvia's mother to the airport, or whether it is Harriet or Janet who needs an umbrella. Here are the same sentences rewritten to avoid the unclear antecedent:

> Sheila drove Sylvia and Sylvia's mother to the airport.
>
> Harriett asked Janet if Janet needed an umbrella.

Sometimes the unclear antecedent is not a person, but an action, feeling, or episode.

Unclear: Not only was the fish old, but Sally paid too much, which really made her mad.

Was Sally angry because the fish was old, because she overpaid, or both?

Clear: Not only was the fish old, but Sally paid too much, both of which made her mad.

In the back-and-forth of daily talk, unclear antecedents are cleared up easily. The listener blurts out, "Who?" and gets a clarifying answer. However, in writing we get no chance to ask the writer *who*? If a pronoun does not have a clear antecedent, you risk confusing your reader.

IN A NUTSHELL

Every pronoun must have a clear antecedent.

PRACTICING 1

Rewrite the following sentences so that the pronouns clearly refer to only one antecedent (the word the pronoun stands for).

Answers may vary.

1. Mathilda was planning to share the meat with her dog, but she was so hungry that she ate it.

   Mathilda was planning to share the meat with her dog, but Mathilda was so hungry

   that she ate the meat herself.

2. Betty gave Caroline homemade cookies, which she thought was a nice gift.

   Betty baked cookies for Caroline, which Caroline thought was a nice gesture.

3. We took the curtains off the windows and cleaned them.

   We took the curtains off the windows and cleaned the windows.

4. Bob and Harry started a business that went bankrupt because he always spent money before it was made.

   Bob and Harry started a business that went bankrupt because Bob always spent

   money before it was made.

5. Mary should help Joan, but she should help herself first.

   Mary should help Joan, but Joan should help herself first.

6. My brother was a close friend of our neighbor's son until he left for college.

   My brother was best friends with our neighbor's son until her son left for college.

7. Maggie's sister encouraged her to wear her miniskirt.

   Maggie's sister encouraged her to wear her sister's miniskirt.

8. Professor Jones implied to Jack that he was far too liberal for his own good.

Professor Jones implied to Jack that Jack was far too liberal for his own good.

9. Charlie told Julio that he had been rude.

Charlie told Julio that Julio had been rude.

10. John had the courage to tell his friend that he owed him money.

John screwed up his courage and told his friend that he owed John money.

Missing Antecedents

In both speech and writing, we often use pronouns with missing antecedents. This is especially true of the pronouns *which*, *this*, *that*, *they*, and *it*. Here is an example:

> Even though my mother is a marathon runner, I have no interest in it.

What is the *it*? We have a fuzzy idea that by *it*, the writer means running, but the word *running* does not appear in the sentence.

Usually, the best way to rewrite such a sentence is to omit the pronoun and provide the missing noun.

> Even though my mother is a marathon runner, I have no interest in running.

The best fix for such absent antecedents is simply to supply the noun. Here are some examples:

Missing: At the Emergency Room, they said Mara had broken her ankle.

Who is this mysterious *they* in the sentence?

Clear: At the Emergency Room, the doctor said Mara had broken her ankle.

Incorrect: It says to print your name under your signature.

Correct: The directions say to print your name under your signature.

Now we know the identity of the unnamed *it*.

Unclear: The Coast Guard located the missing boat within an hour and rescued the boys, who said they were not frightened by the experience. This amazed their parents.

What does *this* refer to? We do not know. It could refer either to the boy's rescue, their supposed lack of fear, or both.

Clear: The Coast Guard located the missing boat within an hour and rescued the boys, who said they were not frightened by the experience. The parents were amazed by the Coast Guard's quick response.

Now we know exactly what the writer means. Note that to get around an unclear antecedent, you may need to rewrite the sentence.

Here is yet another example of a pronoun with an unclear antecedent:

Unclear: Sharon arrived late and quietly took a seat in the back row. That was very unlike her.

What is the antecedent for *that*? The antecedent could be that *she arrived late*, that *she quietly took a seat in the back row,* or *both*.

Clear: Sharon arrived late, which was very unlike her, and quietly took a seat in the back row.

The requirement that every pronoun have a specific and clear antecedent is not simply a picky rule. In everyday talk we do not observe such exactness in pronoun use because we can always ask "What?" and get an answer. In writing, though, you have no second chance. Every pronoun must therefore have a specific antecedent.

IN A NUTSHELL

Be alert to the chance of a missing antecedent when using the pronouns *which, this, that, they,* and *it.*

PRACTICING 2

Rewrite the following sentences to clarify the pronoun reference.   Answers will vary.

1. We were standing in line when they informed us that the show was sold out.

We were standing in line when the office managers informed us that the show was

sold out.

2. In the directions, it says to add one cup of flour.

The directions say to add one cup of flour.

3. My sister refused to go to college because she felt they required too much math for graduation.

My sister refused to go to college because she felt the curriculum required too

much math for graduation.

4. My mother's friend and her aunt drove to the airport.

My mother, her aunt, and her friend drove to the airport.

5. It says to change the oil every 3 months or 3,000 miles.

The manual says to change the oil every 3 months or 3,000 miles.

6. Most of my classmates write poems, but I have no talent for it.

Most of my classmates write poems, but I have no talent for poetry.

7. I deposited the money in my bank, but they haven't posted the correct balance.

I deposited money in my bank, but the bank officials haven't posted the correct balance.

8. Mary bragged about her dancing ability although she had never been one.

Mary bragged about her dancing ability although she had never been a dancer.

9. We ordered a large pizza, but they delivered a medium.

We ordered a large pizza, but the restaurant delivered a medium one.

10. Claire said they advised her to have a perm.

Claire said the stylist advised her to have a perm.

Agreement Problems

A pronoun and its antecedent must agree in number. Singular nouns require singular pronouns. Plural nouns require plural pronouns. Some examples follow.

> The widow wanted her land back.
>
> The farmers wanted their land back.

In the first sentence, the singular noun *widow* requires the singular pronoun *her*. In the second sentence, the plural noun *farmers* requires the plural pronoun *their*.

Most of the time pronoun agreement is often not a problem, but it can be when we try to find a pronoun to replace an indefinite pronoun.

An **indefinite pronoun** is a pronoun that refers to no one in particular. Here is a list of common indefinite pronouns that are always singular:

INDEFINITE PRONOUNS

another	either	nobody	somebody
anybody	everybody	no one	someone
anyone	everyone	none	something
anything	everything	nothing	
each	neither	one	

Study these sentences:

Incorrect: Each of the boys has their cap on backwards.

Correct: Each of the boys has his cap on backwards.

(*Each* requires a singular pronoun. Remember, cross out the prepositional phrase if you are confused about the subject.)

Incorrect: Either Tammy or Tina will give me their ticket.

Correct: Either Tammy or Tina will give me her ticket.

(*Either* requires a singular pronoun.)

In both speech and writing, to avoid being sexist we often use the plural *their* to refer to many indefinite pronouns that are singular. We say, for example, and it sounds perfectly right to our ear:

Someone left their coat on the desk.

Technically, this is wrong. *Their* is plural; *someone* is singular. On the other hand, *his*, the singular pronoun, is *sexist*:

Someone left his coat on the desk.

It is sexist because *someone* could be a female, a possibility the pronoun ignores.

The best way to correct an agreement problem is to rewrite. You can change to singular or plural. Both are correct. Here is an example:

Incorrect: Would everyone who ordered chicken raise their hands?

Correct: If you ordered chicken, raise your hand.

Correct: Would all the people who ordered chicken raise their hands?

Here is another example:

Incorrect: Did everyone in class get their seat assignments?

Correct: Did you get your seat assignment?

Correct: Did all students get their seat assignments?

PRACTICING 3

Correct the agreement errors in the following sentences both ways that you've learned—by changing to the singular and changing to the plural.

1. Does everyone in the class have their notebooks?

Correct singular: *Do you have your notebooks?*

Correct plural: *Do all the students in class have their notebooks?*

2. If anyone needs a ride, they should let me know.

Correct singular: *If you need a ride, let me know.*

Correct plural: *If people need rides, they should let me know.*

3. Is anybody taking their camera to the party?

Correct singular: *Are you taking your camera to the party?*

Correct plural: *Are some people taking their cameras to the party?*

4. Did somebody offer their seat to Mr. Kimble?

Correct singular: *Did you offer your seat to Mr. Kimble?*

Correct plural: *Did people offer their seats to Mr. Kimble?*

5. No one will be seated if they arrive after the show starts.

Correct singular: *You won't be seated if you arrive after the show starts.*

Correct plural: *People won't be seated if they arrive after the show starts.*

6. Would everyone please introduce themselves?

Correct singular: *Would you please introduce yourself?*

Correct plural: *Would people please introduce themselves?*

7. If someone has a good barbecue sauce recipe, they should be required by law to share it.

Correct singular: *If you have a good barbecue sauce recipe, you should be required by law to share it.*

Correct plural: *If people have good barbecue sauce recipes, they should be required by law to share them.*

8. Is anyone going to bring their partners to the reunion?

Correct singular: *Are you going to bring your partner to the reunion?*

Correct plural: *Are people going to bring their partners to the reunion?*

9. Everyone should hang their coats in the front closet.

Correct singular: *You should hang your coat in the front closet.*

Correct plural: *People should hang their coats in the front closet.*

10. Nobody should take themselves too seriously.

    Correct singular: *You shouldn't take yourself too seriously.*

    Correct plural: *People shouldn't take themselves too seriously.*

Sexist Use of Pronouns

You have just learned how to avoid sexism with indefinite pronouns. But sexism is even worse when a singular pronoun automatically assigns the male sex to professionals:

> Every doctor should listen to his patients.

The use of *his* in the above sentence suggests that every doctor is a man, which is both sexist and untrue. On the other hand, using *his or her* is correct but clumsy. One solution is to make the whole sentence plural, using the neutral pronoun *their*. Here are the possible nonsexist choices:

    Sexist: Every doctor should listen to his patients.

    Nonsexist: Every doctor should listen to his or her patients.

    Nonsexist: Doctors should listen to their patients.

Their includes both men and women, and it is not as clumsy as *his or her*.

    If you are facing a pronoun agreement problem that you simply cannot rewrite in the plural, then use *his or her*. If the choice is between being sexist or being clumsy, it is better to be clumsy.

IN A NUTSHELL

- Pronouns and their antecedents must agree in number.
- Avoid the sexist use of pronouns.

PRACTICING 4

Rewrite the following sentences to correct the pronoun agreement problem or the sexist bias.

Answers may vary.

1. No student on the social committee was willing to give up their vacation.

The students on the social committee were not willing to give up their vacations.

2. A newspaper reporter often uses his cellular phone.

Newspaper reporters often use their cellular phones.

---

3. A lawyer can lose his case even if the defendant is innocent.

A lawyer can lose his or her case even if the defendant is innocent.

---

4. As soon as a person realizes that they have been insulted, they leave.

As soon as people realize that they have been insulted, they leave.

---

5. A good neighbor mows their lawn regularly.

Good neighbors mow their lawns regularly.

---

6. You may borrow either of these blouses if you promise to iron them.

You may borrow either of these blouses if you promise to iron it.

---

7. One or the other of these girls must admit that they stole the cake.

One or the other of the girls must admit that she stole the cake.

---

8. Each of the nurses will buy their own ticket for the hospital's banquet.

The nurses will buy their own tickets for the hospital's banquet.

---

9. Before someone learns to drive, they have to walk or take a bus.

Before people learn to drive, they have to walk or take a bus.

---

10. Anyone who does not pay their health fee will not be given a flu shot.

People who do not pay their health fee will not be given a flu shot.

_____

PRACTICING 5

Complete the following sentences with the correct pronoun.

Example: Anyone who plans to donate blood must show <u>his or her</u> driver's license or another form of photo identification to the nurse.

1. Another of the women stood up to express ____*her*____ personal opinions.

2. All that was required of either man was ____*his*____ personal assurance to be good.

3. Somebody has left ___*his or her*___ purse in the kitchen.

4. Everybody thinks ___*he or she*___ is right on this issue.

5. An antiquarian is a person who prefers to spend ___*his or her*___ life in the past.

6. Each of the gunmen came to court with ____*his*____ personal attorney.

7. Anyone can become better at sports if ___*he or she*___ works hard.

8. Each of the women felt that ____*her*____ idea was the better one.

9. Anyone who thinks ___*he or she*___ has a better way should share it with me.

10. Neigher of the students knew ____*his*____ way around the campus.

Shifting Point of View

Writing is easier to read if it uses the same point of view throughout. You may choose a first person, second person, or third person point of view:

FIRST PERSON	SECOND PERSON	THIRD PERSON
I	you	he, she, it, one
we	you	they

Here are some examples:

Incorrect: If a <u>person</u> finds a wallet with identification, <u>you</u> should return it to the owner.

Correct: When <u>you</u> find a wallet with identification, <u>you</u> should return it to the rightful owner.

or

When <u>one</u> finds a wallet with identification, <u>one</u> should return it to the rightful owner.

Here is another example containing many shifts:

If <u>you're</u> unhappy, try taking a good hard look at <u>your</u> priorities. When <u>we</u> do that honestly, <u>we</u> can often see imbalances. <u>You</u> can be spending all <u>your</u> time working and not paying attention to the important people in your life. Is <u>one's</u> job really more important than <u>your</u> family? <u>We</u> say no, but then <u>we</u> accept the promotion that means working longer hours and on weekends. Think again about <u>your</u> priorities.

Here is the correction using *you*. *You, we,* or *one* would all be correct as long as the same point of view is used throughout with no shifts from one pronoun to another.

If <u>you're</u> unhappy, try taking a good hard look at <u>your</u> priorities. When <u>you</u> do that honestly, <u>you</u> can often see imbalances. <u>You</u> can be spending all <u>your</u> time working and not paying attention to the important people in <u>your</u> life. Is <u>your</u> job really more important than <u>your</u> family? <u>You</u> say no, but then <u>you</u> accept the promotion that means working longer hours and on weekends. Think again about <u>your</u> priorities.

IN A NUTSHELL

Avoid shifts in pronoun point of view. In other words, be consistent in your use of pronouns.

PRACTICING 6

Correct the pronoun shifts in the following sentences by crossing out the incorrect word or words and writing the correction above them.

Answers may vary.

1. When I first visited the Louvre, ~~you~~ ^I could see all the tourists heading toward the Mona Lisa.

2. Despite the fact that we are loyal and honest, ~~you~~ ^{we} can't count on others being that way.

3. ~~One~~ *A woman* should learn a little tact if ~~they are~~ *she is* a mother-in-law.

4. At our college, students have to study hard if ~~you~~ *they* want top grades.

5. As you enter the building, the personnel office is on ~~one's~~ *your* left.

6. If ~~a person is~~ *people are* going to graduate from college, they must practice good study habits.

7. You have to step back and take an objective look at yourself if ~~a person wants~~ *you want* to get over some bad habit.

8. If ~~one is~~ *you are* traveling to a strange state, you should buy a map.

9. If ~~someone~~ *you* were to invent a cream that would dissolve body fat, you could become a millionaire.

10. We always look forward to the Fourth of July because ~~you~~ *we* can cook out during the day and see fireworks at night.

Unit Test

Rewrite the following sentences to correct the pronoun errors.

1. Tanya told Mary she had to study hard.

Tanya told Mary to study hard.

_____

2. They spread the rumor that Murray was suffering from flesh-eating bacteria.

His coworkers spread the rumor that Murray was suffering from flesh-eating bacteria.

_____

3. Everyone who wants your picture in the yearbook should sign up today.

All students who want their pictures in the yearbook should sign up today.

_____

4. A surgeon should always reassure his patients.

Surgeons should always reassure their patients.

_____

5. In the counseling office they said I needed a cultural diversity course.

The advisors in the counseling office said I needed a cultural diversity course.

_____

6. At the edge of the park it says, "Don't litter."

At the edge of the park, a sign says, "Don't litter."

_____

7. One of the people in line dropped their checkbook.

One of the people in line dropped his or her checkbook.

_____

8. Each of my neighbors put their flags out on the Fourth of July.

All of my neighbors put their flags out on the Fourth of July.

_____

9. Does anyone care about their car getting wet?

Do you care about getting your car wet?

_____

10. Bert paid for Ben and his dad to attend the game.

Bert paid for Ben and Ben's dad to attend the game.

_____

11. I love beautiful flowers that also have a fragrance, making you appreciate them.

I love beautiful flowers that also have a fragrance, making me appreciate them.

_____

12. All of us loved to hang out with Peter and Jim, but then he suddenly left town.

All of us loved to hang out with Peter and Jim, but then Jim suddenly left town.

_____

13. Although my father is an excellent preacher, my brother has no interest in it.

Although my father is an excellent preacher, my brother has no interest in preaching.

_____

14. Neither of the boys care one hoot about sports.

Neither of the boys cares one hoot about sports.

_____

15. Everybody thinks their country is the best.

Everybody thinks his or her country is the best.

_____

Unit Talk-Write Assignment

Answers may vary. Students in a social problems class were asked to discuss their greatest fears about society today. Some students mentioned high divorce rates; others talked about crime and drugs. Several students mentioned terrorism—which became the focus of the discussion. Here are some of their comments, written down more or less the way they were spoken. First correct the pronoun errors in the sentence. If the sentence needs no correction write "C" for "correct." Then write a paragraph about your worst fear for society. When you have finished your paragraph, check it for the correct use of pronouns.

TALK	**WRITE**
1. Terrorism is everywhere, it seems. You never know when you get on a plane whether they might high jack it.	**1.** *Terrorism is everywhere, it seems. You never know when you get on a plane whether terrorists might bomb it.*
2. A person just doesn't feel as safe as you used to. When my friend and her mother flew to Europe last spring, she felt very threatened.	**2.** *People just don't feel as safe as they used to. My friend felt very threatened last year when she and her mother flew to Jerusalem.*
3. Anyone in their right mind should be afraid. Terrorists have killed hundreds of innocent people all over the world.	**3.** *Any people in their right minds should be afraid. Terrorists have killed hundreds of innocent people all over the world.*
4. My mother says that since the September 11 New York and Washington, D.C., terrorists attacks, you don't even feel safe in the United States. It's scary.	**4.** *My mother says that since the September 11 New York and Washington, D.C., terrorist attacks, people don't even feel safe in the United States. Terrorism is scary.*
5. Yeah. And there was other terrorist acts, too. Remember the Unabomber and the bombs found at the Olympic games in Atlanta in 1996?	**5.** *Yes, and there were other terrorist acts, too. Do you remember the Unabomber and the bombs found at the Olympic games in Atlanta?*

TALK

6. My chemistry teacher says that anyone with a little know-how can build a bomb. They don't even need a college degree!

7. We have to find a way to stop sickoes from committing terrorist acts. It has to stop, or they will just get worse and worse.

8. But you can't just let the FBI do electronic surveillance on everyone. Pretty soon everyone becomes a suspected terrorist and their home is bugged.

9. But at least we'd be safe. You wouldn't get blown up just walking along the street.

10. Yeah, it would be a very safe police state. Terrorism is a real problem.

WRITE

6. My chemistry teacher says that anyone with a little know-how can build a bomb. The person doesn't even need a college degree!

7. We have to find a way to stop insane people from committing terrorist acts. Terrorism has to stop, or terrorists will just get worse and worse.

8. However, we can't just let the FBI do electronic surveillance on everyone. After a while all citizens would become suspected terrorists, and their homes would be bugged.

9. At least we'd be safe, though. We wouldn't get blown up just walking along the street.

10. Yes, America would be a very safe police state. Terrorism is a real problem.

Unit Collaborative Assignment

A. Read the following sentences aloud to a classmate, who will catch the pronoun errors and tell you how to correct them. Try to reach agreement on all sentences.

1. Mary told Felice that her boss was too strict.

2. At the Career Center they said Judy should be an architect.

3. Anybody who gets up will lose their seat.

4. If you have your health, one has everything.

5. Not only was the coat much too tight, it was also made of cheap material, which made Irene angry.

6. Merlin walked with a hot dog in one hand and a piece of carrot cake in the other, munching on it as he headed down the steps.

7. It clearly states that you must have a parent's signature.

8. As we walked into the movie, they told us that only the two front rows were unoccupied.

9. Nancy intended to tell her teacher that she had been rude.

10. Everyone wanted his ticket back.

B. Now reverse your roles. Again, try to reach agreement on all sentences.

1. Jane told Marguerite that her cousin would be at the meeting.

2. At the market they said the peaches were ripe.

3. Neither of the girls want to attend the wedding.

4. Every nurse should be gentle with her patients.

5. As one enters the restaurant, it says, "No checks, please."

6. Neither of the grocery checkers ever smile.

7. They have a lot of freeway traffic in Los Angeles.

8. Each of the volunteers takes pride in their service to others.

9. Everyone scored at least 80 on their algebra test.

10. If we are aware of a problem, you should try to help.

Unit Writing Assignment

Write a brief essay about the best or worst job you've ever had. Tell your reader exactly what the job required and what make it so good or so bad, using vivid details to back up your points. Check that you have used all pronouns correctly. Use the Revising Checklist to revise.

Photo Writing Assignment

The photo shows a film star celebrating winning an Oscar. If you could win first prize for something, what would it be? Would you like it to be in sports, entertainment, science, or the arts? Or would you prefer it to be for some humanitarian cause? How do you think winning that prize would make you feel? Answer these questions in a paragraph that begins with a discussible topic sentence and uses strong details. Use the Revising Checklist to check your paragraph.

15

Pronoun Problems

"Him and I are good buddies."

nglish has three cases: subjective, objective, and possessive. Nouns do not change form when they are used as subjects or objects. They change form only in the possessive case:

Larry kissed Nancy.   **(Larry is the subject.)**

Nancy kissed Larry.   **(Larry is the object.)**

Larry's kisses were sweet.   **(The 's added to the noun Larry indicates that they are his kisses. He "possesses" them.)**

If we replace *Larry* with a pronoun, the pronoun is different in all three cases, the subjective, objective, and possessive:

He kissed Nancy.

Nancy kissed *him*.

His kisses were sweet.

If pronouns, like nouns, would only stay the same whether used as subjects or objects, English would be a far easier language to write and speak. Unfortunately, only the pronouns *it* and *you* take the same case and spelling whether they are used as subject or object.

Here are the pronouns in all three cases:

SUBJECT PRONOUNS	OBJECT PRONOUNS	POSSESSIVE PRONOUNS
I	me	my, mine
you	you	your, yours
he	him	his
she	her	hers
it	it	its
we	us	our, ours
you	you	your, yours
they	them	their, theirs

Case Problems

Because pronouns change case depending on how they are used, many of us often make case errors. Typically, we use a subject pronoun for an object pronoun, or the other way around. In the following sections, we will discuss the correct use of subject pronouns, object pronouns, possessive pronouns, and reflexive pronouns.

Subject pronouns

Subject pronouns replace nouns used as subjects. Here are the rules for using subject pronouns correctly:

1. Use a subject pronoun as the subject of a verb.
We usually use subject pronouns correctly, saying *I work at McDonald's*, not *Me work at McDonald's*. But we can run into problems with pronouns used in compound subjects.

> **Incorrect:**   Buddy and me made a pact.
>
> **Correct:**   Buddy and I made a pact.

ESL Advice!

We recommend that ESL students commit the list of pronouns to memory rather than trusting their ears.

Buddy and *I* form the compound subject of the verb *made*.

To test whether you are using the correct pronoun in a compound subject, try the two possible pronouns separately. Your ear will tell you which is right. For example:

Buddy and (I, me) made a pact.

Test: I made a pact.

Me made a pact.

ESL Advice!

This test might not work for you if you don't have a good ear for English. In that case, you should memorize the rule.

Clearly, *Me made a pact* sounds wrong. The correct pronoun is therefore *I*. Try the test with another sentence:

Incorrect: We and them can't get along.

Test: They can't get along.

Them can't get along.

Your ear tells you which pronoun is correct—*they*.

PRACTICING 1

Strike out incorrectly used subject pronouns in the following sentences: If you have trouble deciding which pronoun is incorrect, try letting your ear tell you. Read the sentence aloud using first one pronoun and then the other.

1. Chaney and (me/I) had a class together.

2. She and (he/him) don't get along too well.

3. Howard and (they/them) are always arguing.

4. (She/her) and (he/him) went out to dinner.

5. (She/her) and (I/me) have always been good friends.

6. We and (her/she) went for a long hike together.

7. (She/her) and (he/him) have dated for a long time.

8. You know that (she/her) and (I/me) grew up in the same neighborhood.

9. In December, (she/her) and (I/me) will take a trip to California.

10. (She/her) and (he/him) used to study in the library together.

2. Use a subject pronoun in comparisons.

In sentences using *than* or *as* to make a comparison, the second verb is usually omitted because we know what is meant. For example, in the sentence *Mary is more patient than I*, we really mean,

Mary is more patient than I am patient.

To test whether you're using the right pronoun in a *than* or *as* sentence, simply complete the comparison. Here is another example:

They are as tough as (we, us).

Test: They are as tough as we are tough.
They are as tough as us are tough.

Your ear tells you that *we* is correct.

PRACTICING 2

Underline the correct pronoun in the following comparison.

1. Jane is taller than (me/I).

2. Peter is smarter than (him/he).

3. Martha is as tall as (I/me).

4. They are better in English than (we/us).

5. Do you really think that they can play soccer better than (we/us)?

6. I have never felt that I was a better athlete than (him/he).

7. John is nicer than (him/he).

8. No matter what you think, I know that Hubert can play tennis better than (her/she).

9. Come to think of it, I believe that I am a better chess player than (he/him).

10. They are as determined as (we/us).

3. Use a subject pronoun after the verb to be.

If you rely on your ear to get the pronoun right after the verb *to be*, you will probably get it wrong. Here are some examples:

Incorrect:	It is her speaking.
Correct:	It is she speaking.

Incorrect:	Was it them who swam to the island?
Correct:	Was it they who swam to the island?

The correct sentences probably sound bizarre to your inner grammar ear. After all, most people say *it's me* rather than the grammatically correct *it's I*. In spoken language that usage is fine, but as we have often said in this book, written Standard English requires grammatical correctness.

If you think that the grammatically correct sentences don't sound right, you can always rewrite them to avoid the *it + to be + pronoun* construction. For instance:

Original:	It is she speaking.
Rewrite:	She is speaking.

Original:	Was it they who swam to the island?
Rewrite:	Did they swim to the island?

One good thing about talking or writing in English: You always have a choice.

IN A NUTSHELL

- Use a subject pronoun as the subject of a verb.
- Use a subject pronoun in comparisons.
- Use a subject pronoun after the verb *to be*.

PRACTICING 3

In the blank provided, mark *C* if the italicized pronoun is correct and *NC* if it is not correct. Cross out each incorrect pronoun and write the correct pronoun above it.

Example: ___NC___ It is ~~us~~ who will win in the end.
                we

1. ___NC___ Was that *her* making the decision?
               she

2. ___C___ Yes, it was *I* who baked the cake.

3. ___NC___ If I were *them,* I would pay the fine.
               they

4. _NC_ It was supposed to be *~~them~~* ^{they} who sat at the corner table.

5. _C_ Would you like to be *she?*

6. _C_ Who sent the E-mail? It was *he.*

7. _NC_ To be *~~him~~* ^{he} would mean living in a fish bowl.

8. _C_ If it had to be *they,* it had to be—that's fate for you.

9. _NC_ Yes, it was *~~her~~* ^{she} who wrote the letter.

10. _C_ Is that your mother over there? Yes, it is *she.*

Object pronouns

Object pronouns take the place of nouns used as objects. The object of a verb is the word that receives its action. For example, in the sentence

I kissed Mary.

the object of *kissed* is *Mary,* who received the kiss. If you used a pronoun in place of *Mary,* it would have to be in the objective case.

Correct: I kissed her.
Incorrect: I kissed she.

Although your ear is generally a good guide to the correct use of object pronouns, one trouble spot is the pronoun after a preposition.

Use an object pronoun after a preposition.
A pronoun that follows a preposition becomes its object and must be in the objective case.

Incorrect: I mentioned the problem to she and the landlady.
Correct: I mentioned the problem to her and the landlady.

ESL Advice!

Be very careful with pronouns used after prepositions. This particular usage gives even native speakers trouble.

If you do not know which pronoun to use in a sentence, simply try the pronoun by itself. Your ear will tell you if you've used the correct form. For example:

I mentioned the problem to the landlady and (she, her).

Test: I mentioned the problem to the landlady.
            I mentioned the problem to her.

Your ear will tell you that *her* is correct.

The preposition that probably gives the most trouble with pronoun use is *between*. How many times in everyday speech have you heard these incorrect forms?

INCORRECT	CORRECT
between you and I	between you and me
between John and he	between John and him
between Mary and she	between Mary and her
between you and he	between you and him
between they and the police	between them and the police
between he and she	between him and her

Because the incorrect form is so common in everyday speech, this is one usage where you simply cannot trust your ear. Just remember that *between* is a preposition, and an object pronoun must be used after a preposition. You must observe this ironclad rule of grammar in your writing and should learn to use it in speaking.

EAR ALERT

ESL Advice!

The use of *between* confuses almost everyone. You should memorize the rules about its use.

IN A NUTSHELL

- Use *me, you, him, her, it, us,* or *them* when the pronoun is an object.
- Use an object pronoun after a preposition.

PRACTICING 4

Underline the correct pronoun in parentheses.

1. Legislation now protects (we, <u>us</u>) disabled students.

2. The picture was painted by three of us—Pete, Mabel, and (I, <u>me</u>).

3. For (we, <u>us</u>) nature lovers, the Sierras are like a temple.

4. If it weren't for (he, <u>him</u>) and (I, <u>me</u>), you'd be in trouble.

5. Sitting between (he, <u>him</u>) and Mary, I couldn't move an inch.

6. The volleyball team chose Terry and (she, <u>her</u>).

7. We stood right behind my dad and (they, <u>them</u>).

8. The wealthy aunt gave money to Laura and (he, <u>him</u>).

9. You can't stop us from voting for (they, <u>them</u>).

10. Between Gus and (I, <u>me</u>), we have all the bases covered.

PRACTICING 5

In the sentences that follow, cross out any italicized pronoun used incorrectly, writing the correct form above it. If the sentence is correct, make no changes, but write *C* in the blank preceding it.

_____ **1.** Kira spoke of the trust between (*she* → *her*) and Ricardo.

__*C*__ **2.** Between you and (*me*), the weather is turning ugly.

_____ **3.** The minister spoke to the couple and (*he* → *him*) at great length.

_____ **4.** Watch out! Stand behind Ernesto and (*they* → *them*).

__*C*__ **5.** That is a matter for (*her*) to discuss.

__*C*__ **6.** I told Mr. Faber that I had seen Raoul's letter to the class and (*me*).

_____ **7.** The love between his grandmother and (*he* → *him*) was obvious to everyone.

_____ **8.** She lives right next door to (*I* → *me*).

_____ **9.** The person with (*they* → *them*) arrived from Iran yesterday.

_____ **10.** Let's all vote for (*she* → *her*).

PRACTICING 6

The sentences that follow contain both subjective and objective pronouns some of which are in the wrong case. If the pronouns used in the sentence are correct, mark *C* in the blank. If the pronouns are incorrect, draw a line through the incorrect form and write the correct form above the line.

_____ **1.** Oprah and (~~him~~ → he) gave the books to (she, <u>her</u>).

_____ **2.** Without my uncle and (he → him) as guides, Cheney and (~~me~~ → I) are likely to get lost.

_____ **3.** Willard and ~~(me)~~ *I* have not spoken to ~~(they)~~ *them* for over a year.

_____ **4.** The group invested for ~~(she)~~ *her* a year before ~~(him)~~ *he* knew.

_____ **5.** Candy and (her) *she* told mother that nothing will ever come between you and ~~(I)~~ *me*.

_c_ **6.** "Pretend not to notice," (he) said, "and Joshua and (she) will go way.

_____ **7.** After the storm, Martin and (her) *she* repaired the damage (her) *she* did.

_____ **8.** Without ~~(she)~~ *her*, the house ~~(us)~~ *we* lived in then would never have been painted.

_c_ **9.** The basketball game that (we) played was won by (us).

_c_ **10.** The foreman agreed with (me) that my workers and (I) needed a vacation.

Possessive pronouns

Possessive pronouns are pronouns that show ownership or possession. A list of the possessive pronouns follows.

my, mine

your, yours

his

hers

its

their, theirs

our, ours

your, yours

There are three common possessive pronoun errors:

- *It's/its*: The contraction *it's* (short for *it is*) is sometimes incorrectly used instead of *its* (meaning, belonging to *it*).

    Incorrect: The dog wagged it's tail.
    Correct: The dog wagged its tail.

    You can test the correctness of such a sentence by using the long, rather than the contracted, form of *it's* in a sentence.

    Test: The dog wagged it is tail.

    The mistake is now plainly visible.

■ *Hers'*, *his'*, and *theirs'*: These words do not need an apostrophe. They are already possessive.

Incorrect: That's hers'.
Correct: That's hers.

Incorrect: The tweed coat is his'.
Correct: The tweed coat is his.

Incorrect: The red sports car is theirs'.
Correct: The red sports car is theirs.

■ *Yourn/hisn*: These words are ungrammatical. They are not standard English. The correct forms are *yours* and *his*.

Incorrect: That cup of coffee is yourn.
Correct: That cup of coffee is yours.

Incorrect: That algebra book is hisn.
Correct: That algebra book is his.

IN A NUTSHELL

■ *Its* is a possessive pronoun; *it's* is short for *it is*.

■ Do not use an apostrophe with *hers, his,* and *theirs*.

■ *Yourn* and *hisn* is not standard English.

PRACTICING 7

In the blank, write either *its* or *it's*, whichever is correct. If you have trouble deciding on the correct answer try the "it is test."

1. ___It's___ disgusting to see teenagers smoking.

2. The ramshackle house, with ___its___ broken chimney, makes an excellent postcard.

3. I dialed the restaurant, but ___its___ line was busy.

4. What kind of music is it? ___It's___ jazz.

5. ___It's___ very selfish of her not to visit her grand-mother in the hospital.

6. Why did you say, " ___It's___ going to rain"?

7. From the day of _____*its*_____ first clang, the bell became a

symbol.

8. ___*Its*_____ smooth and powerful engine makes it an

expensive car.

9. When _____*it's*_____ time to go, we'll let you know.

10. Don't worry; _____*it's*_____ only the first draft.

PRACTICING 8

Correct the following sentences, if necessary, crossing out the
incorrect word and writing the correct one in the space above. If
the sentence is correct, leave it as is.

1. The cat licked it's fur.

The cat licked its fur.

2. Its your turn to drive, not mine.

It's your turn to drive, not mine.

3. The hat sitting on the table in the front hall is hers'.

The hat sitting on the table in the front hall is hers.

4. That beautiful motorcycle is theirs'.

That beautiful motorcycle is theirs.

5. I thought that new laptop computer was yourn.

I thought that new laptop computer was yours.

6. Your sister didn't agree with that story of yours.

Correct

7. Isn't that black leather jacket his'?

Isn't that black leather jacket his?

8. Nobody's car is bigger than his.

Correct

9. Its a pity that its such a rainy day.

It's a pity that it's such a rainy day.

10. On a long golf fairway, there is no more beautiful swing than his.

Correct

Reflexive pronouns

A **reflexive pronoun** refers back to the subject in the sentence. It clarifies meaning or adds emphasis.

I bought myself a pair of cowboy boots.	**(I bought the boots not for *him*, but for *me*.)**
He made himself an omelet.	**(He made the omlet for no one else.)**
The architect himself checked the staircase.	**(The architect didn't send his assistant—he did it *himself*.)**

The reflexive pronouns are listed below:

myself
yourself
himself
herself
itself
ourselves
yourselves
themselves

There are two common problems with reflexive pronouns. First, *hisself* is often used for *himself* and *theirself* for *themselves*. These are nonstandard words like *ain't* and don't exist except in slang.

Incorrect: He drives hisself to work.
Correct: He drives himself to work.

Incorrect: They surprised theirself.
Correct: They surprised themselves.

The second common problem with reflexive pronouns is the use of *me* (an objective pronoun) instead of *myself* (the reflexive pronoun).

Incorrect: I bought me a new pair of boots.
Correct: I bought myself a new pair of boots.

Another problem is inappropriate use of *myself* instead of *me*.

Incorrect: If you don't know what to do, be sure to ask Diego or myself for help.

Correct: If you don't know what to do, be sure to ask Diego or me for help

Incorrect: You can send your complaint to myself.

Correct: You can send your complaint to me.

IN A NUTSHELL

- *Hisself* and *theirself* are not standard English words.
- Do not use *me* in place of *myself*.
- Do not use *myself* in place of *me*.

PRACTICING 9

Underline the correct reflexive pronoun in parentheses for each sentence.

1. They blamed (theirselves, <u>themselves</u>) for the dismal outcome.

2. They congratulated (theirself, <u>themselves</u>) on a job well done.

3. I bought (me, <u>myself</u>) a new mattress for my bed.

4. Benny spilled grape juice on (<u>himself</u>, hisself).

5. They (theirselves, <u>themselves</u>) speak highly of the coach.

6. They bought (theirselves, <u>themselves</u>) steak dinners to celebrate.

7. John pulled (<u>himself</u>, hisself) out of the pool.

8. Bring any problems to (<u>me</u>, myself), I told her.

9. Why can't they carve the pumpkin (theirselves, <u>themselves</u>)?

10. He should be thoroughly ashamed of (<u>himself</u>, hisself).

Pesky Pronouns

Some pronouns are pesky—they give everyone trouble. Among the peskiest pronouns are *who/whom, who's/whose, who/which/that.* (For a discussion of *this, that, these,* and *those* see page 311 Unit 16.)

1. Who/whom

Two of the peskiest pronouns are *who* and *whom.*

Use who as a subject pronoun.
Who may be used in place of the following pronouns:

SUBJECT PRONOUNS

I	he	we
you	she	they

Who is in class? (*She* is in class.)

Who is going to speak? (*He* is going to speak.)

Use whom as you would an object pronoun.
Whom, on the other hand, may be used in place of the following pronouns:

OBJECT PRONOUNS

me	us	him
you	them	her

Whom do you love? (I love *him*.)

To whom do I owe an apology? (I owe an apology to *him*.)

If you don't know whether to use *who* or *whom* in a question, try answering the question using *he, she, him, her,* or *them.* For example:

(Who, whom) do you know?

Test: I know him.
I know he.

Because *him* is correct, you know the objective form—*whom*—is therefore correct.
To apply the test to a statement, you have to turn the sentence around:

I know the detective to (who, whom) he confessed.

Test: He confessed to she.

He confessed to her.

Again, because *her* is correct, you know the objective form—*whom*—is correct.

IN A NUTSHELL

Who is always used as a subject; *whom* is always used as an object.

PRACTICING 10

Fill in the blanks below with either *who* or *whom*.

1. ___Whom___ are you referring to?

2. I spoke to a loan officer ___who___ was very helpful.

3. Many of the writers ___whom___ my teacher adores are dead.

4. The game of life is best played by the person ___who___ has the best sense of humor.

5. They knew no one ___who___ matched that description.

6. As to ___whom___ she meant, we could not say for the life of us.

7. Know ___whom___ you are dealing with.

8. I saw a man ___who___ danced with his wife in Chicago.

9. Ask not for ___whom___ the bell tolls.

10. He says he knows many people ___who___ are very stubborn.

11. ___Who___, may I ask, is calling?

12. To ___*whom*___ do you wish to speak?

13. ___*Whom*___ do you trust?

14. ___*Whom*___ do you consider more trustworthy?

15. I don't know; ___*who*___ do you think is more trust-worthy?

2. Who's/whose

Who's is short for *who is*; *whose* shows possession. Here are some examples:

Incorrect: They wondered who's car this was.
Correct: They wondered whose car this was.

Incorrect: I know whose to blame.
Correct: I know who's to blame.

To test *who's/whose*, simply write out *who's* as *who is*:

They wondered who's car this was.

Test: They wondered who is car this was.
            They wondered whose car this was.

Whose is obviously correct.

IN A NUTSHELL

Whose shows possession; *who's* is short for *who is*.

PRACTICING 11

Fill in the blanks with either *who's* or *whose*.

1. ___*Whose*___ ball is this?

2. He's the man at ___*whose*___ house we had dinner and ___*who's*___ responsible for the neighborhood's block party.

3. You may well wonder ___*whose*___ life this is and ___*whose*___ destiny is at stake here.

4. ___Who's___ at the door?

5. He asked for the name of the person ___who's___ the boss.

6. ___Who's___ paying for the birthday cake?

7. ___Whose___ locker is this?

8. The student in ___whose___ wallet the money was found never appeared.

9. Our neighbor, in ___whose___ garage we stored our lawn mower, is moving.

10. I haven't a clue ___whose___ tennis shoes these are.

3. Who, which, and that

Knowing when to use *who*, *which*, and *that* is easy if you remember the following rules:

- Use *who* to refer to people. Do not use *which*. Use *that* to refer to a group of people considered a single unit (like a committee, class, audience, crowd, family).

  Lot's wife was the woman who looked back. (not *which*)

  The people who live across the street have a St. Bernard. (not *which*)

  The jury that convicted him was fair.

  Bob played on the team that won the championship.

- Use *who* with animals that are named. Use *which* or *that* for animals that are unnamed.

  Burt, who is a black lab, loves the water.

  Black labs, which love the water, are my favorite dog.

  If you want a dog that loves water, get a black lab.

- Use *which* or *that* to refer to ideas or things. Use a comma before *which;* do not use a comma before *that* (See Unit 19, p. 359)

  She has patience, which is important in teaching.

  Get the towels that are on the dryer.

IN A NUTSHELL

- Use *who* to refer to people; use *that* to refer to a group of people considered a single unit (like a team or jury).

- Use *who* to refer to animals that are named and *which* or *that* to refer to unnamed animals.

- Use *which* or *that* to refer to ideas or things.

PRACTICING 12

Cross out the inappropriate relative pronoun (*who, which,* or *that*) in the sentences that follow.

1. The man (which/who) spoke at the meeting was quite convincing.

2. (Whom/Who) among you will cast the first stone?

3. Jumping to conclusions (that/which) are wrong won't help.

4. The people (who/whom) helped the most spoke the least.

5. I am monarch of all (which/that) I survey.

6. The chairs, (that/which) both have broken legs, are in the kitchen.

7. My cat, Millie, (that/who) is 14, is starting to show her age.

8. It was an audience (which/that) every performer would love.

9. Treman Park, (that/which) is part of the state park system, has several waterfalls.

10. The committee (which/that) I am on is meeting tonight.

PRACTICING 13

In the blanks insert the pronoun *who*, *which*, or *that* according to the rules that you have just learned.

1. I don't know _____*who*_____ is right, the speaker or her challenger.

2. The panel _____*that*_____ advised the governor was chaired by a woman.

3. My cat, Pookie, _____*who*_____ is sitting on the car, loves to purr.

4. The man _____*who*_____ spoke next was the most convincing.

5. The author, _____*who*_____ is an elderly gentleman, read his work beautifully.

6. Dumbo is an elephant _____*who*_____ is beloved by children.

7. The family _____*that*_____ I liked moved to Atlanta.

8. My sister Jeanne, _____*who*_____ lives in Hawaii, works out every day.

9. Mr. Smith, _____*who*_____ is my father-in-law, takes an interest in my career.

10. The house _____*that*_____ you see perched atop the hill was once owned by a rich lady.

✓ Unit Test

In the blank provided, mark *C* if the sentence is correct and *NC* if there is a pronoun error. Cross out the incorrect pronouns and write the correct form above them.

1. __*NC*__   Narbeh and ~~me~~ *I* decided to climb Mt. Whitney.

2. __*C*__   For whom did she work last year?

3. _NC_   ~~Who~~ *Whom* did you kiss at the prom?

4. _NC_   A long time ago, we mentioned the letter to Mom and ~~she~~ *her*.

5. _NC_   He is the clerk ~~which~~ *who* waited on me.

6. _C_   Between Bob and him, the choice is easy.

7. _C_   I wonder to whom she told that story.

8. _NC_   ~~Who's~~ *Whose* idea was that?

9. _NC_   Juan and ~~him~~ *he* are going to the movies.

10. _NC_   Why did you let him paint the door all by ~~hisself~~ *himself*?

11. _C_   Just between you and me, the Dodgers will lose.

12. _NC_   I bought ~~me~~ *myself* some new shoes.

13. _NC_   He asked Alonzo and ~~myself~~ *me* out to dinner.

14. _C_   They are every bit as disgusted as we.

15. _NC_   I want that lovely vase, but ~~it's~~ *its* side is cracked.

16. _C_   My best buddy and she went out together behind my back.

17. _NC_   My sister has a huge black and white cat ~~who~~ *that* hates me.

18. _C_   With my dark glasses I can't see who's at bat.

19. _NC_   Don't throw out those shoes; they're ~~hers'~~ *hers*.

20. _NC_   Oh yes, it was ~~them~~ *they* for sure.

 # Unit Talk-Write Assignment

Would you rather live a short life in good health or a long life with some of it in bad health? This age old question lies at the heart of the euthanasia (mercy killing) debate. Students were asked to research this topic and present their views to each other in preparation for a writing assignment. One student had really done his homework and held strong opinions. His views are given in the *Talk* column pretty much as he spoke them. Turn his sentences into standard English in the *Write* column, correcting all errors in pronoun reference. Then write a paragraph giving your own views on euthanasia.

TALK

1. Its a bad idea to push euthanasia.

2. My buddy and me have discussed it often. Him and me just can't agree. Come on, let's face it, for most old people, quantity of life is more important than quality.

3. The *Journal of the American Medical Association* published an interesting study in February, 1998. By far the majority of patients between 80 and 98—which are old duffers—said they would not trade living one year in their current condition for living a shorter time without pain.

4. Remember that Dr. Kevorkian? He's the one who finally got sent to jail for mercy killing he did right on TV. I wonder whether he thinks it's such a good idea now?

WRITE

1. *Encouraging euthanasia is a bad idea.*

2. *My friend and I have discussed it often. He and I just can't agree. You must admit, for most old people, quantity of life is more important than quality.*

3. *The Journal of the American Medical Association published an interesting study in February 1998. By far the majority of the patients between 80 and 98 said they would not trade living one year in their current condition for living a shorter time without pain.*

4. *So what's this Dr. Kevorkian frenzy? Who's he to be so popular these days?*

TALK

WRITE

5. Between you and I, helping someone die is pure rubbish. Life is the most precious thing we have, and nobody wants to give it up, not even people which are in a lot of pain.

5. *Between you and me, helping someone die is ridiculous. Life is the most precious thing we have, and nobody wants to give it up, not even people who are in a lot of pain.*

6. A team of researchers at the University of Cincinnati asked 300 people what they thought a relative which was in the hospital would want.

6. *A team of researchers at the University of Cincinnati asked 300 people what they thought a relative who was in the hospital would want.*

7. Twenty percent of them said the person would prefer a shorter but pain-free life to a longer life with pain. But it was them, the relatives, which guessed wrong—completely wrong!

7. *Twenty percent of them said the person would prefer a shorter but pain-free life to a longer life with pain. But it was they, the relatives, who guessed wrong—completely wrong.*

8. Even victims of advanced AIDS, didn't want to trade time for better health.

8. *Correct*

TALK

WRITE

9. My roommate and my girlfriend didn't believe me. I showed the study to him and she and were they surprised

9. *My roommate and my girlfriend didn't believe me. I showed the study to him and her and were they surprised!*

10. I remember my 89-year-old grandfather saying to myself and to my mother and I, "I don't know why—but I'm curious about tomorrow."

10. *I remember my 89-year-old grandfather saying to my mother and me, "I don't know why—but I'm curious about tomorrow."*

11. People which are sick get used to crummy health, and they theirselves don't want to give up life.

11. *People who are sick get used to crummy health, and they themselves don't want to give up life.*

12. I know a woman whom at 103 got leukemia. She kept asking, "Who's idea is it that I don't want to live longer?"

12. *I know a woman who at 103 got leukemia. She kept asking, "Whose idea is it that I don't want to live longer?"*

13. Euthanasia for who?

13. *Euthanasia for whom?*

TALK

WRITE

14. Listen, you guys, no matter who you ask, people want to live.

14. _No matter whom you ask, people want to live._

15. Don't sell life so cheap. Its all we got.

15. _Don't sell life so cheap. It's all we have._

Unit Collaborative Assignment

Get together with a classmate. One of you should read aloud Part A, while the other follows along making corrections. Discuss any points of disagreement. To settle differences of opinion, apply any test you have learned for determining the correct form of a pronoun (substituting *it is* for *it's*, *who is* for *who's* and so on). Exchange places with your partner and do the same for part B.

Part A

One of my favorite activities is biking because I learn from nature, and also *its* good exercise. Last summer, I bought *me* a new mountain bike and took several trips to Colorado. When my friend Fred and *me* first biked to the mountains, I felt as if I had entered a whole new world. The mountains and canyons seemed to tell a very ancient story. For instance, Snow Bird Peak, rising majestically out of the earth, seemed to say that human beings like Fred and *I* are insignificant compared to the power of nature.

[Handwritten corrections above the text: it's (above "its"); myself (above "me"); I (above "me"); me (above "I")]

Part B

At the same time that we were seeing so much beauty, we were also getting good aerobic exercise. *Its* quite challenging to pedal up a steep grade. Between you and *I*, I can't think of another sport that would have allowed Fred and *I* to experience so much beauty and get such good exercise while costing so little money. All college students should take a biking trip and find out for *theirself* what a great experience and good exercise it is.

[Handwritten corrections above the text: It's (above "Its"); me (above "I"); me (above "I"); themselves (above "theirself")]

Unit Writing Assignment

Write a paragraph describing the most unpleasant trip you ever took and what you learned from it. Pay special attention to pronoun use. Use the Revising Checklist to revise.

Photo Writing Assignment

The following photo shows teenagers smoking. Write a paragraph in which you offer your opinion on why teenagers continue to smoke despite all the public warnings. Begin with a topic sentence that expresses your main point. Support that point with appropriate evidence. Use the Revising Checklist to revise.

16

Distinguishing Between Adjectives and Adverbs

"Gertie dances real good."

I f you are a native speaker, using your ear for grammar to help you write is, for the most part, a good strategy. When it comes to the correct use of adjectives and adverbs, however, your ear is likely to be too infected with street-talk to be trusted.

Indeed, adjectives and adverbs are often misused in casual speech. The following are some typical sentences you might overhear in public:

Gertie dances real good.

The Olympic contestants swam terrific.

The guards told us to walk slow.

That remark bothered me considerable.

All of us were real tired.

EAR ALERT

If these sentences sound right to you, your ear is leading you astray. Here are the sentences correctly written:

Gertie dances really well.

The Olympic contestants swam terrifically.

The guards told us to walk slowly.

That remark bothered me considerably.

All of us were really tired.

No matter what your ear tells you, these sentences are grammatically correct. This unit will help you to use adjectives and adverbs correctly in your writing.

Adjectives and Adverbs

Adjectives and adverbs are **modifiers**, words that describe and explain. **Adjectives** describe a noun or a pronoun by narrowing it down to a specific one, such as in the following cases:

I adore that purple hat.	**(Which hat? The *purple* one.)**
She certainly seems happy.	**(What kind of person does she seem? A *happy* one.)**
The milk smells sour.	**(How does the milk smell? It smells *sour*.)**

Adverbs describe verbs, adjectives, and other adverbs in the following ways:

- how
- when
- where
- to what extent

Here are some examples:

She spoke excitedly.	**(*Excitedly* tells how she spoke.)**
I'm going now.	**(*Now* tells when I'm going—describes the verb *going*.)**
I put the book there.	**(*There* tells where the book was put—describes the verb *put*.)**

Orson Welles became excessively fat.

> (***Excessively*** **tells to what extent Welles became fat— describes the adjective *fat*.**)

Many—but not all—adverbs end in *-ly*. Indeed, many adjectives can be turned into adverbs simply by adding *-ly*. Some typical examples follow.

ADJECTIVE	ADVERB
careful	carefully
real	really
most	mostly
forceful	forcefully

However, some of the most commonly used adverbs do not end in *-ly*. Here are some examples:

Walk *fast*.

He is *very* patient.

The lemonade is *too* sweet.

They are *always* late.

She is leaving *tomorrow*.

IN A NUTSHELL

- Adjectives describe nouns and pronouns.
- Adverbs describe verbs, adjectives, and other adverbs.
- Many—but not all—adverbs end in *-ly*.

PRACTICING 1

Underline the correct modifier in parentheses—adjective or adverb—in each sentence below.

1. The old man crossed the railroad tracks (slow, <u>slowly</u>).

2. His fingernails looked (real, <u>really</u>) dirty.

3. He (nimble, <u>nimbly</u>) climbed down the mine shaft.

4. The birds flew away, chirping (angry, <u>angrily</u>).

5. He (most, <u>mostly</u>) ignored the letters.

6. He had a bad cold and was feeling (miserable, <u>miserably</u>).

7. John examined the roof (careful, <u>carefully</u>).

8. My friend felt (complete, <u>completely</u>) alone in his poverty.

9. He flies (frequent, <u>frequently</u>) on business.

10. The engine hummed (smooth, <u>smoothly</u>).

PRACTICING 2

Complete the sentences below with an appropriate modifier—either an adjective or an adverb—from the following list. Each word should be used only once.

sadly	immediately
popular	slowly
silently	dreadful
terribly	hot
playful	most

In the parentheses at the end of each sentence, identify the modifier as an adjective or adverb.

1. The telephone company hired Byron *immediately*.
(*adverb*)

2. My bath water was *hot*. (*adjective*)

3. It was a *dreadful* call. (*adjective*)

4. Soccer is a *popular* sport. (*adjective*)

5. The next mile of the road was *terribly* rough.
(*adverb*)

6. We approached the intersection *slowly*.
(*adverb*)

7. The   waitress   looked   _____*silently*_____   at   the   rain.
(_____*adverb*_____)

8. The   _____*playful*_____   puppies   romped   in   the   grass.
(_____*adjective*_____)

9. She _____*sadly*_____ picked up her suitcase and walked away.
(_____*adverb*_____)

10. Tom complained _____*most*_____ often. (_____*adverb*_____)

PRACTICING 3

Change the italicized adjective to an adverb; you will need to
rewrite the sentence.

Answers may vary.

Example: Have you noticed her *elegant* walk?

Answer: Have you noticed how *elegantly* she walks?

1. Mark is *happy* to speak.

Mark speaks happily.

2. Dogs can be *noisy* barkers.

Dogs bark noisily.

3. His performance was *admirable*.

He performed admirably.

4. What a *tight* jacket!

The jacket fit tightly.

5. He's a *slow* walker.

He walks slowly.

6. He wrote a *poor* essay.

He wrote the essay poorly.

7. The man was a *glib* talker.

The man talked glibly.

8. Her arrival was *unexpected*.

She arrived unexpectedly.

9. He gave her an *intimate* hug.

He hugged her intimately.

10. It was a *quiet* moan.

He moaned quietly.

Past participles used as adjectives

The past participles of verbs may also be used as adjectives. Consider the verb *mash*:

Please mash the potatoes.	(*mash* = present)
I mashed the potatoes yesterday.	(*mashed* = past)
I have mashed the potatoes every day.	(*have mashed* = past participle)
These mashed potatoes are good.	(*mashed* = adjective)

Here are other examples of past participles used as adjectives:

broken bones

forgotten key

rented car

frozen food

torn jacket

A common problem with using past participles as adjectives is dropping the *-d/-ed* or *-n/-en* ending. We do this so often, especially in rapid speech, that the mistake usually goes unnoticed. A dropped ending in writing, however, is always obvious. Look at these examples:

Dropped ending: We ate mash potatoes with butter.
Correct: We ate mashed potatoes with butter.

Dropped ending: I was sad to see those broke toys.
Correct: I was sad to see those broken toys.

IN A NUTSHELL

Don't let your ear trick you into dropping the *-d/ -ed* or *n/ -en* ending when you write a past participle.

PRACTICING 4

Correct the misused past participles in the sentences that follow.

1. He wept about his dash hopes. _____*dashed*_____

2. Watch out for the broke glass! _____*broken*_____

3. His pants were tore. _____*torn*_____

4. The potatoes are all peel. _____*peeled*_____

5. The eraser of the pencil looked chew. _____*chewed*_____

6. He had not practice enough. _____*practiced*_____

7. That's not an excuse absence. _____*excused*_____

8. He seemed confuse by all the noise. _____*confused*_____

9. He said the fish was fresh-froze. _____*fresh-frozen*_____

10. I'll have two hard-boil eggs, please. _____*hard-boiled*_____

11. Dad wore a borrow tie. _____*borrowed*_____

12. They quarreled over some spoke words. _____*spoken*_____

Comparisons

Adjectives and adverbs are often used to make comparisons between two things. The rules for making comparisons are straightforward:

- For an adjective or adverb of one syllable, add *-er.*

My uncle Bob is *rich.*
Uncle John is *richer.*   **(one-syllable adjective)**

He spoke *fast.*
She spoke *faster.*   **(one-syllable adverb)**

- For an adjective or adverb of more than one syllable that does not end in *y,* add *more.*

This is an *affordable* car.
This is a *more affordable* car.   **(adjective of more than one syllable)**

Comparative adverbs are usually formed by placing *more* before them, but sometimes by adding *-er* to the positive form:

When my sister graduated from college with honors, my mother praised her *more enthusiastically* than she had praised me years earlier.

The man snored *loudly.* His wife, however, snored *louder.*

- For an adjective or adverb that ends in *y,* drop the *y* and add *-ier* in the comparative.

The road to the farm was *icy.*
The road to the mountains was *icier.*

PRACTICING 5

Write the comparative form of each word listed below. Use the comparative form in a sentence.

Example: feverish   <u>more feverish</u>
The sick child was more feverish in the morning.

fresh   <u>fresher</u>
The fish at Jake's Gormet Fish Shop is fresher than the fish at the supermarket.

1. ugly   <u>uglier</u>

_____

2. hateful   <u>more hateful</u>

_____

3. junky   <u>junkier</u>

_____

4. marvelous   <u>more marvelous</u>

_____

5. hot   <u>hotter</u>

_____

6. silly   *sillier*

_____

7. silent   *more silent*

_____

8. lucky   *luckier*

_____

9. spicy   *spicier*

_____

10. thorough   *more thorough*

_____

Double comparisons

A common mistake often heard in everyday speech is the **double comparison**, using both *-er* and *more*.

Incorrect: Janet's writing is more neater than Mary's.
Correct: Janet's writing is neater than Mary's.

Incorrect: I spoke more louder than you.
Correct: I spoke louder than you.

PRACTICING 7

Rewrite the following sentences to correct the comparisons.

1. You carry the more heavier suitcase.

You carry the heavier suitcase.

2. If I study hard, I should do more better in math.

If I study hard, I should do better in math.

3. She was more angrier than I've ever seen her.

She was angrier than I've ever seen her.

4. Who was the more nicer of the two?

Who was the nicer of the two?

5. The wind was terrifyinger than the rain.

The wind was more terrifying than the rain.

6. The cheese is more fresher than the salami.

The cheese is fresher than the salami.

7. My brother was more badlier hurt than my sister.

My brother was more badly hurt than my sister.

8. When can you give me a more better answer?

When can you give me a better answer?

9. Working at three jobs was difficulter than I thought.

Working at three jobs was more difficult than I thought.

10. The cut was more deeper than the doctor expected.

The cut was deeper than the doctor expected.

Using Superlatives

The comparative form of adjectives and adverbs is used to express a difference between two things.

> The brown suitcase is strong.
>
> The black suitcase is stronger.   **(comparative)**

To express differences among three or more things, you must use the superlative form of an adjective or adverb.

> The brown suitcase is strong.
>
> The black suitcase is stronger.   **(comparative)**
>
> The blue suitcase is strongest.   **(superlative)**

ESL Advice!

To use the correct forms of the comparative and superlative, memorize these rules

The rules for changing adjectives and adverbs into the superlative form follow:

- For an adverb or adjective of one syllable, add *-est*.

    wild → wilder → wildest

    glad → gladder → gladdest   **(Note that the "d" is doubled.)**

    tall → taller → tallest

    She was saddest of all the relatives there.

- For an adverb or adjective that ends in *y*, drop the *y* and add *-iest*.

    silly → sillier → silliest

    tiny → tinier → tiniest

    pretty → prettier → prettiest

    He was the luckiest of them all.

- For an adjective or adverb of two or more syllables that does not end in *y*, add the word *most*.

    dreadful → more dreadful → most dreadful

    cheerful → more cheerful → most cheerful

    interesting → more interesting → most interesting

    She is the most cheerful person in the morning.

PRACTICING 7

In the blanks provided, write the correct superlative forms of the words below. Use each superlative form in a sentence.

Example: luck   *luckiest*

When she played blackjack, she was the *luckiest* person alive.

1. funny *funniest*

_____

2. disappointed *most disappointed*

_____

3. meek *meekest*

_____

4. rich   *richest*

_____

5. pushy   *pushiest*

_____

6. snappy   *snappiest*

_____

7. regretful   *most regretful*

_____

8. ripe   *ripest*

_____

9. short   *shortest*

_____

10. slick   *slickest*

_____

Problems with superlatives

When you use superlatives, watch out for these two common errors of everyday speech:

- Use the superlative only when you are speaking of *more than two* things.

  Incorrect: She is the most beautiful of the two sisters.
  Correct: She is the more beautiful of the two sisters.

  Incorrect: This is the riskiest of the two choices.
  Correct: This is the riskier of the two choices.

- Do not use both an *-est* or an *-iest* ending and *most*.

  Incorrect: She is the most unkindest person.
  Correct: She is the most unkind person.

  Incorrect: He is the most trendiest dresser.
  Correct: He is the trendiest dresser.

IN A NUTSHELL

- Use a comparative adjective or adverb to compare two things.
- Form most comparatives by adding *-er, -ier,* or *more.*
- Use a superlative adjective or adverb to compare three or more things.
- Form most superlatives by adding *-est, -iest,* or *most.*

PRACTICING 8

Rewrite the following sentences to correct the problems with the superlatives.

1. This is the most beautifulest rose I have ever seen.

This is the most beautiful rose I have ever seen.

_____

2. That movie is the fascinatingest one I've seen this year.

That movie is the most fascinating one I've seen this year.

_____

3. Give the piece of pie to the most biggest football player.

Give the piece of pie to the biggest football player.

_____

4. Briana was the smartest of the two sisters.

Brianna was the smarter of the two sisters.

_____

5. Just because she is the most oldest, my sister gets more spending money.

Just because she is the oldest, my sister gets more spending money.

_____

6. Have you chosen the most fastest runner yet?

Have you chosen the fastest runner yet?

_____

7. Maggie is definitely the interestingest of the three girls.

Maggie is definitely the most interesting of the three girls.

_____

8. Jake is the most stingiest roommate he ever had.

Jake is the stingiest roommate he ever had.

_____

9. Of the two choices, that is the wisest.

Of the two choices, that is the wiser.

_____

10. Go down Maxwell Street, and you'll find the most poorest people you have ever seen.

Go down Maxwell Street, and you'll find the poorest people you have ever seen.

_____

PRACTICING 9

For the following sentences, first decide if a comparative or superlative form is needed. In the blank to the left of the sentence, write *C* if the comparative form is correct, *S* if the superltive form is correct. Then write the correct form.

Example: __C__ All of us wanted to climb the (tall) taller of the two towers.

___S___ **1.** It was the (frightening) *most frightening* story I have ever heard.

___C___ **2.** Of the two deans, Smith was the (reasonable) *more reasonable*.

___S___ **3.** My high school graduation was the (long) *longest* day of my life.

___C___ **4.** Ann's wedding was (expensive) *more expensive* than Mary's.

___C___ **5.** The desert is much (dry) *drier* than the beach.

___C___ **6.** Of the two wrestlers, Moe was the (big) *bigger*.

_S_   **7.** Aunt Ethel is the (generous) _most generous_ person in our family.

_S_   **8.** Get the (large) _largest_ cake they have.

_S_   **9.** What was the (nice) _nicest_ experience you had in elementary school?

_C_   **10.** Sardines are (oily) _oilier_ than salmon.

Using Good/Well and Bad/Badly

Most adjectives and adverbs follow the basic rules for forming comparatives and superlatives that we have just described. A few, however, have irregular forms. The most troublesome are *good/well* and *bad/badly.*

	COMPARATIVE	SUPERLATIVE
good	better	best
well	better	best
bad	worse	worst
badly	worse	worst

Good is an adjective; *well* is an adverb (unless you are talking about someone's health). Here are examples.

Correct:	This is a good bicycle.	(***Good*** **is an adjective describing** ***bicycle.***)
Incorrect:	She rides good.	
Correct:	She rides well.	(***Well*** **is an adverb telling how she** ***rides.***)
Incorrect:	I don't feel good.	
Correct:	I don't feel well.	(**Use** ***well*** **to describe someone's health.**)

Bad is an adjective; *badly* is an adverb. A common mistake made in everyday speech is to use *badly* to describe emotions when *bad* should be used.

Incorrect:	I feel badly that we were late.
Correct:	I feel bad that we were late.

To say *I feel badly* is to mean that your sense of touch is bad—perhaps your fingers are numb.

There is no such word as *bestest* or *worsest*. The correct form is either *best* or *worst*.

IN A NUTSHELL

- *Good* is an adjective; *well* is used as an adverb unless you're talking about someone's health.
- *Bad* is an adjective; *badly* is an adverb.
- To say *I feel badly* means something is wrong with your sense of touch.

PRACTICING 10

Write either *good* or *well* in the blanks provided.

1. All the sophomores on the team swam _____*well*_____ .

2. Even the honor students did not do _____*well*_____ on the final test.

3. His coat was made of _____*good*_____ leather.

4. It was obvious that she was not feeling _____*well*_____ .

5. This cream is _____*good*_____ for your complexion.

6. I have been _____*good*_____ to you lately.

7. You must try to do _____*well*_____ on your final exam.

8. He lied _____*well*_____ , but he gave us _____*good*_____ advice.

9. You know very _____*well*_____ what I mean!

10. You will do _____*well*_____ if you try your best.

PRACTICING 11

In the blanks below, insert either *bad* or *badly*.

1. He felt _____*bad*_____ about eating the last piece of pie.

2. She felt _____*bad*_____ for her father.

3. I felt _____*bad*_____ that we lost the game.

4. His manners are very _____*bad*_____.

5. The crew sailed the first leg of the race _____*badly*_____.

6. I'm _____*badly*_____ sick with the flu.

7. The flu shot made me feel _____*bad*_____.

8. They hoisted the flag very _____*badly*_____.

9. No matter how _____*bad*_____ you feel, you must go.

10. My heart was _____*badly*_____ broken.

This/that and these/those

The four demonstratives—*this/that* (singular) and *these/those* (plural)—are generally used to point to or single out something.

I just love *this* book.   **(A particular book is singled out.)**

Don't you dare eat *those* cookies.   **(Particular cookies are singled out.)**

This and *these* refer to something nearby, whereas *that* and *those* refer to something farther away.

I love petting *this* cat.

but

Would you mind walking across the room to bring me *that* blanket?

ESL Advice!
Memorize the rules for using *this, that, these,* and *those.* Native speakers usually know them from long usage.

Note that when a demonstrative is paired with a noun, it becomes an adjective:

I won't buy *those* plums.
These books are mine.

On the other hand, a demonstrative that stands alone functions as a pronoun:

The plums are *those.*
The books to be flied are *these.*

Two kinds of problems can occur in the use of *this/that* and *these/those.* The first is putting *here* or *there* after *this* or after *that.*

Incorrect: This here boat belongs to my neighbor.
Correct: This boat belongs to my neighbor.

Incorrect: That there house belongs to my uncle.
Correct: That house belongs to my uncle.

The second problem is using *them* in place of *these* or *those.* Unlike *these* and *those,* which can function as an adjective or a pronoun, *them* is always a pronoun, never an adjective. It is incorrect to use a pronoun in place of an adjective:

Incorrect: Them doughnuts are fattening.
Correct: Those doughnuts are fattening.

or

These doughnuts are fattening.

Incorrect: Them weeds are hard to kill.
Correct: These weeds are hard to kill.

or

Those weeds are hard to kill.

IN A NUTSHELL

- Never use *them* in place of *these* or *those.*
- Never use *here* or *there* after *this* or *that.*

PRACTICING 12

Underline the correct word in parentheses.

1. (Those, them) ducks are quacking nonstop.

2. Please take (this/that there) package to Mrs. Jones.

3. (This, this here) suitcase is too heavy to carry.

4. Did Peter borrow (them, <u>those</u>) roller skates?

5. Marcos, would you please take (<u>that</u>, this here) painting across the street to (this, <u>that</u>) house.

6. (<u>That</u>, that there) piano needs tuning.

7. Take (this here, <u>that</u>) one right next to me.

8. If (that there, <u>this</u>) present weather continues, you'd better buy a raincoat.

9. Be polite to (these, <u>those</u>) women standing over there.

10. (<u>That</u>, that there) rug was woven in India.

 **Unit Test**

Correct the following sentences.

1. Mary's essay is the bestest in the class.

Mary's essay is the best in the class.

_____

2. She scribbled her signature quick on that there check.

She scribbled her signature quickly.

_____

3. The beggar looked envious at the mountain of food.

The beggar looked enviously at the mountain of food.

_____

4. John was the most patient of the two men.

John was the more patient of the two men.

_____

5. The fish was froze.

The fish was frozen.

_____

6. Billy folded his blanket most carefulliest.

Billy folded his blanket most carefully.

_____

7. It is best for you to walk home rather than ride.

It is better for you to walk home rather than ride.

_____

8. Feeling badly that she had lost the ring, Fran wept.

Feeling bad that she had lost the ring, Fran wept.

_____

9. Them there carrots taste too salty.

The speech was the worst he had ever given.

_____

10. Mark said them apples are too sour to eat.

Mark said his cold was gone, and he was now feeling well.

_____

11. Jamie feels badly about what happened last night.

Jamie feels bad about what happened last night.

_____

12. It was the most fastest race he had ever run.

It was the fastest race he had ever run.

_____

13. Those hands were the most dirtiest you could imagine.

Those hands were the dirtiest you could imagine.

_____

14. My uncle tells the amazingest stories.

My uncle tells the most amazing stories.

_____

15. She is much more fussier about her room than I am.

She is much fussier about her room than I am.

_____

16. Every day they asked for mash potatoes at breakfast time.

Every day they ask for mashed potatoes at breakfast time.

_____

17. Why is she limping so bad?

Why is she limping so badly?

_____

18. Let's stay home because the sky looks horrible dark.

Let's stay home because the sky looks horribly dark.

_____

19. The mechanic said the fanbelt was wore out.

The mechanic said that the fan belt was worn out.

_____

20. It's real stupid to bite the hand that feeds you.

It's really stupid to bite the hand that feeds you.

_____

Unit Talk-Write Assignment

This unit's *Talk* column is a dialogue between two students, Lisa and Frank, who have opposing points of view on being famous. Your assignment is to rewrite their comments as complete sentences and in standard English. Be sure to correct all adjective and adverb errors. Then, decide how you feel about what it means to be famous and express your thoughts in a polished paragraph. Check carefully for errors in adjective-adverb use.

Answers will vary.

TALK

L: You couldn't pay me enough to be rich and famous, it would be like living in a fishbowl.

F: Are you serious? I can't think of anything more better.

WRITE

L: You couldn't pay me enough to be rich and famous. It would be like living in a fishbowl.

_____

_____

F: Are you serious? I can't think of anything better.

_____

_____

TALK

L: Oh, sure. Hound by the paparazzi, maybe stalk by some nut, and constantly crush by crowds of people trying to touch you. Yuck!

F: You're missing the point. Fame gives you the mostest money and money is power. Power to do anything you want.

L: Yeah, and fame brings tragedy, too, what about Princess Diana, who was killed in a car chase by the paparazzi?

F: No way. She died because of a drunk chauffeur who was driving reckless.

L: What about John Lennon, who was murdered by an obsess fan?

F: You just have to take precautions. It's a small price to pay for living good and having hot cars, and mansions.

L: Think of poor Madonna, having to hide her baby girl for fear she will be kidnap.

F: Sure, poor Madonna with her millions. Don't cry too loud for her, Argentina.

WRITE

L: *Think about it. You would be hounded by the tabloids, maybe stalked by some crazy person, and constantly crushed by crowds of people trying to touch you. That sounds terrible.*

F: *You're missing the point. Fame gives you the most money, and money is power, power to do anything you want.*

L: *Yes, and fame brings tragedy, too. What about Princess Diana, who was killed in a car chased by the tabloid press?*

F: *That's not the way it happened. She died because of a drunk chauffeur who was driving recklessly.*

L: *What about John Lennon, who was murdered by an obsessed fan?*

F: *You just have to take precautions. It's a small price to pay for living well and having hot cars and mansions.*

L: *You should think about poor Madonna, having to hide her baby girl for fear she will be kidnapped.*

F: *You call her poor Madonna, but she has millions. Don't cry too loudly for her, Argentina.*

TALK

L: Arnold Schwarzenegger had to sue some pushier photographer to stop him from badgering the Schwarzenegger kids. Them kids don't know how lucky they are.

F: Yeah, yeah—the Terminator has the most pitifullesst life. Tell that to some hungry and froze homeless person. That there man isn't suffering, lemme tell you.

L: Well, I definitely would feel badly if I became famous and lost my privacy, I don't care what you say.

F: And I'd sure give up some privacy in return for a closetful of the most beautifullest clothes and a Cadillac in my driveway.

WRITE

L: Arnold Schwarzenegger had to sue some aggressive photographer to stop him from harassing the Schwarzenegger kids.

F: I don't really believe the Terminator has the most pitiful life. You should tell that to some hungry and frozen homeless person.

L: I definitely would feel bad if I became famous and lost my privacy. I don't care what you say.

F: I'd certainly give up some privacy in return for a closetful of the most beautiful clothes and a Cadillac in my driveway.

Paragraphs will vary.

Unit Collaborative Assignment

The following paragraph is about leasing versus buying a car. Work with a partner to fill in the blanks with appropriate adverbs or adjectives from the list of words below. Talk through, and agree on, the possible choices.

also	strongly	cheaper
definitely	smart	better
thriftiest	smarter	more economical
busiest	major	constantly

1. Because cars are so expensive, leasing is often _more economical_ than buying.

2. In a number of states, it is actually _smarter_ to lease a car than to own one.

3. Leasing a car is _better_ because the lessee does not have to worry _constantly_ about trade-in values or maintenance costs.

4. Leasing appeals to some of the _thriftiest_ and _busiest_ people I know. They want their money's worth, and they don't want to spend a lot of time taking care of a car.

5. Many people are _also_ leasing other goods besides cars.

6. For instance they're leasing such _major_ appliances as freezers, dishwashers, washers, dryers, and air-conditioners.

7. These people see "temporary use" rather than "permanent ownership" as the _better_ choice.

8. Next year the lease on my car will be up, and I _definitely_ plan to lease a brand new car.

9. I _unquestionably_ like driving a new car rather than an _old_ car, and it's _cheaper_ to lease than buy.

10. Furthermore, I _truly_ believe that leasing helps a person get rid of the curse of possessions.

Unit Writing Assignment

Beginning with one of the topic sentences listed below, develop a paragraph that is vivid and clear. Pay special attention to your use of adverbs and adjectives. Use the Revising Checklist to revise.

1. Our love for machines lessens our love for human beings.

2. Preserving the wilderness is our hope for planet Earth.

3. People who don't have pets are missing a lot.

4. I have found that failure teaches me more than success.

5. I have learned that it is not wise to burn your bridges.

Photo Writing Assignment

The following photo shows people relaxing. Brainstorm about the value of leisure time. Compare the sunbathing in the picture with other leisure activities. Come up with a discussible topic sentence and support it with convincing details. Once you have completed your writing, make sure that all of your adjectives and adverbs follow the rules in this unit. Use the Revising Checklist to revise.

17

Dangling and Misplaced Modifiers

*"After watching the movie, the sky turned black
and began to rain."*

A modifier is a word or phrase that describes—you learned that in Unit 16. Modifiers are either adjectives or adverbs, or words or phrases that function as adjectives or adverbs. What a modifier describes in a sentence depends not only on what it says, but also on where it is located.

Dangling Modifiers

Panting, the bus pulled away.

Here *panting* is a modifier, but because of its place in the sentence, it modifies *bus* rather than *Mary*. Such a modifier is said to *dangle*. **Dangling modifiers** consist of a word or phrase that modifies a word not plainly stated in the sentence. In this particular sentence, the dangling modifier makes the bus pant as it pulls away. Here are some other examples:

Dangling: Walking home that day, the sun seemed unusually warm.

Dangling: Having reached the age of six, my grandfather marched me off to grade school.

Dangling: Aggressive, the job was perfect.

321

Because of its misplacement, the modifier in each of these sentences is attached to the wrong word, making a ridiculous sentence. In the first sentence, the sun is walking home. In the second, the grandfather is six years old; and in the third, the job is aggressive.

There are two ways to correct these sentences. You can simply place the word being modified *immediately* after the modifier. Or, you can rewrite the sentence.

Correct: Walking home that day, I thought the sun seemed unusually warm.

or

As I walked home that day, the sun seemed unusually warm.

Correct: Having reached the age of six, I was marched off to school by my grandfather.

or

My grandfather marched me off to school when I reached the age of six.

Correct: The job was perfect for Paul, who is agressive

or

Paul was suited to the job perfectly because he was aggressive.

IN A NUTSHELL

Correct dangling modifiers by rearranging or adding words so that the modifier clearly refers to the right word.

PRACTICING 1

Answers may vary.

Rewrite these sentences, each of which contains a dangling modifier.

1. Having no time to waste, the article was left unread.

Having no time to waste, I left the article unread.

_____

2. Having finished all the chores, the baseball game was turned on.

Having finished all the chores, we turned on the baseball game.

_____

3. Worn out from hiking, the alarm clock didn't wake me up.

Because I was worn out from hiking, the alarm clock didn't wake me up.

---

4. Being newly painted, $4,000 was not bad for the car.

I did not mind paying $4,000 for the car because it was newly painted.

---

5. As a mother of twins, my washing machine is always running.

I am a mother of twins, so my washing machine is always running.

---

6. After taking our seats, the Ice Capades started off with a waltz.

After we took our seats, the Ice Capades started off with a waltz.

---

7. Jumping through fiery hoops, everyone in the audience went wild.

The audience went wild over the circus dogs jumping through fiery hoops.

---

8. When shredded and salted, you will enjoy the taste.

You will enjoy the taste of Russian cabbage when it's shredded and salted.

---

9. The test was not taken, having not studied enough.

Having not studied enough, I did not take the test.

---

10. Flying to New York, the Empire State Building gleamed below.

As we were flying to New York, the Empire State Building gleamed below.

Misplaced Modifiers

A **misplaced modifier** changes the meaning of a sentence because it is not placed next to the word it is supposed to describe. Misplaced modifiers, like dangling modifiers, do not communicate what the writer meant. Unlike dangling modifiers, which are always found at the beginning of a sentence, a misplaced modifier occurs later in the sentence. For example, notice how the meaning of the following sentence changes as we move the modifier *only*.

She went into the pool wearing her only bikini.	**(She owned only one *bikini*. Only is modifying *bikini*.)**
She went into the pool wearing only her bikini.	**(She wore nothing else but a bikini. *Only* is modifying *wearing*.)**

Sometimes a modifier is misplaced because it is too far from the word it is meant to modify. In this case, the result is often an unintended, funny meaning. Here are some examples:

Misplaced: We could watch the stars sitting on the balcony.

Misplaced: My grandmother showed us how to sew a quilt with an encouraging smile.

Misplaced: I stood in the cold stream and caught a fish without waders.

Because of a misplaced modifier, we have *stars sitting on the balcony, quilts with an encouraging smile*, and *a fish without waders*. A misplaced modifier can be corrected only one way: by rewriting the sentence. You must reword the modifier or move it closer to the word it modifies. Here are possible corrections:

Correct: Sitting on the balcony, we could watch the stars.

Correct: With an encouraging smile, my grandmother showed us how to sew a quilt.

Correct: I stood without waders in the cold stream and caught a fish.

or

Without waders, I stood in the cold stream and caught a fish.

To avoid the confusion of misplaced modifiers, always place a modifier immediately *before* the word it is meant to modify. This is especially true of one-word modifiers such as *only, just, almost, even,*

Communicate clearly by placing modifiers as close as possible to the words they describe.

hardly, nearly, and *often.* Because these words limit what follows, where they occur in a sentence is important. Remember the bikini example at the beginning of this section.

PRACTICING 2

For each of the following pairs of sentences, tell how the meaning of the sentence changes when the modifier is moved.

Example: He just washed the dishes.

He did it a moment ago.

He washed just the dishes.

He didn't do the pots.

1. Francine did only 20 sit-ups.

Francine did not do more than 20 sit-ups, although she may have done other exercises.

Francine only did 20 sit-ups.

Francine only did 20 sit-ups, and no other exercises.

2. Rico was just eating dinner, when the phone rang.

Rico had just begun dinner.

Just Rico was eating dinner, when the phone rang.

Only Rico was eating dinner.

3. She even drinks Coke for breakfast.

She drinks Cokes at all times including breakfast.

Even she drinks Coke for breakfast.

Everyone drinks Cokes for breakfast, including her.

4. He just said that he would be late.

That is all he said.

He said that just he would be late.

He is the only one who will be late.

5. The mechanic said only the front brakes need to be tightened.

The rear brakes don't need to be tightened.

The mechanic said the front brakes only need to be tightened.

The only thing wrong with the front brakes is that they are loose.

PRACTICING 3

First, underline the misplaced modifier in each sentence below. Then rewrite the sentence so that the modifier is correctly placed.

Example: I borrowed a ballpoint pen to write a letter <u>that didn't</u> work.

Answer: <u>To write a letter, I borrowed a ballpoint pen that didn't work.</u>

1. Mimi fed her dog on the porch <u>she had received for Christmas</u>.

Mimi fed the dog she had received for Christmas on the porch.

_____

2. A pilot since World War II <u>in 1995</u>, he received an award for long service.

A pilot since World War II, he received an award for long service in 1995.

_____

3. The waiters served French pastries <u>to customers</u> on expensive bone china.

The waiters served French pastries on expensive bone china to customers.

_____

4. Caroline could not attend the dance in her lovely new off-the-shoulder gown <u>with a broken foot</u>.

With a broken foot, Caroline could not attend the dance in her lovely new off-the-

shoulder gown.

5. He <u>nearly</u> exercised every morning.

He exercised nearly every morning.

_____

6. John Henry School needs volunteers to read to their students <u>badly</u>.

John Henry School badly needs volunteers to read to their students.

7. Peter is canvassing the neighborhood for voters <u>dressed in an Uncle Sam costume</u>.

Dressed in an Uncle Sam costume, Peter is canvassing the neighborhood for voters.

8. We saw many deer <u>driving to the country</u>.

Driving to the country, we saw many deer.

9. We drank ten gallons of cranberry juice <u>with enjoyment</u>.

With enjoyment, we drank ten gallons of cranberry juice.

10. At 10:00 A.M. the students heard that an earthquake had hit <u>on television</u>.

At 10:00 A.M. the students heard on television that an earthquake had hit.

PRACTICING 4

A. Underline the dangling and misplaced modifiers in the following paragraph. Then rewrite those sentences correctly in the spaces below. You should find four errors.

Answers may vary.

An Afternoon by the Lake

It was July, and we were out of school. <u>Having finished our chores and changed into our bathing suits</u>, the lake seemed to invite us to come down and feel its coolness. My mind was <u>only</u> fixed on two things—swimming and what fun we would have. We ran to the lake and plunged into the cool water. We stayed until past dinner. <u>But after explaining how much fun we had</u>, my mother didn't punish me. To this day, I connect beautiful vacations with a lake <u>in my mind</u>.

1. *When we had finished our chores and changed into our bathing suits, the lake seemed to invite us to come down and feel its coolness.*

2. *My mind was fixed on only two things—swimming and what fun we would have.*

_____

3. *But after we explained how much fun we had, my mother didn't punish me.*

_____

4. *To this day, in my mind I connect beautiful vacations with a lake.*

_____

B. Underline the dangling and misplaced modifiers in the following paragraph. Then rewrite those sentences correctly in the spaces below. You should find four errors.

The Gift of Music

Like a beautiful butterfly or a rainbow, a person who loves music finds it healing. Our neighbor, who has constant back pain, almost listens to an entire Beethoven symphony every day. He says the music keeps him alive. My closest friend listens to the radio driving to a job twenty miles from his home. He tells me that because of the music, he actually looks forward to the drive. I can't imagine my life without music. With a lifetime ahead, music will be my trusted companion and gracious friend.

Answers may vary.

1. *A person who loves music finds it healing, like a beautiful butterfly or a rainbow.*

_____

2. *Our neighbor, who has constant back pain, listens to an entire Beethoven symphony almost every day.*

3. *My closest friend listens to the radio while he drives to a job twenty miles from his home.*

4. *During my lifetime ahead, music will be my trusted companion and gracious friend.*

 **Unit Test**

The following sentences contain either a dangling or a misplaced modifier. Correct the sentences by rewriting them.

Answers may vary.

1. Having already waited an hour for the traffic to die down, our car wouldn't start.

After we had already waited an hour for the traffic to die down, our car wouldn't start.

2. After sticking my card key into the slot, the gate opened automatically.

After I stuck my card key into the slot, the gate opened automatically.

3. Purring, I stroked the cat on the table.

I stroked the purring cat on the table.

4. Driving down the country road after the rain, a lovely rainbow arched across the sky.

As we were driving down the country road after the rain, a lovely rainbow arched across the sky.

5. We finally found her ring during our lunch break in the desk.

We finally found her ring in the desk during our lunch break.

6. Rolling on wheels, I steered the suitcase down the hill.

I steered the suitcase, rolling on wheels, down the hill.

7. Thinking about this poem, the meaning was unclear.

When I was thinking about this poem, the meaning was unclear.

8. Drifting to sleep, my plaid sheets felt clean and cool.

As I was drifting to sleep, my plaid sheets felt clean and cool.

9. Mr. Smith took the broken pipes to the dump in his truck.

Using his truck, Mr. Smith took the broken pipes to the dump.

_____

10. Do not eat the brownie until completely baked.

Do not eat the brownie until it is completely baked.

_____

Unit Talk-Write Assignment

Students were asked to discuss the problems of their age group. Older students talked about combining school and a job and sometimes even a family, too. Some younger students talked about their parents' lack of understanding; others described problems with relationships or said that college made them feel isolated. But one student saw her worst problem as acne. Rewrite her comments in complete sentences and Standard English. You should also find four dangling and four misplaced modifiers. Then write a paragraph on what you consider the most difficult problem for your age group. Use the Revising Checklist to help you improve your paragraph.

Answers may vary.

TALK

1. Have you ever had acne? Well, looking in the mirror, my acne is really awful.

2. Having no patience, the job was impossible to do.

WRITE

1. *Have you ever had acne? Well, when I look in the mirror, my acne is really awful.*

_____

_____

2. *Since I have little patience, the job of clearing up my complexion seemed impossible.*

_____

TALK

WRITE

3. Desperately wanting to look decent, your skin suddenly explodes into a field of zits, zits, zits.

3. *Just when you are desperately wanting to look decent, your skin suddenly explodes into a field of blemishes, blemishes, blemishes.*

4. Going to a party last week my face looked terrible—like I had measles!

4. *When I went to a party last week, my face looked terrible—as if I had measles!*

5. My date could see all those red spots sitting next to me on the couch.

5. *Sitting next to me on the couch, my date could see all those red spots.*

6. I kept wondering whether even he heard anything I was saying or whether he was fixating on my face.

6. *I kept wondering if he even heard anything I was saying or if he was fixating on my face.*

7. My doctor prescribed a drug, but then I was told it can cause severe depression and that even some kids had committed suicide.

7. *My doctor prescribed a drug, but then I was told it could cause severe depression and that some young people had even committed suicide.*

8. Nice choice. Depressed from the zits or depressed from the medication.

8. *It isn't any fun to have to choose between depression from blemishes or depression from medication.*

TALK

WRITE

9. Experiencing some form of acne, pimples can be really painful as well as embarrassing.

9. *When you are experiencing some form of acne, pimples can be really painful as well as embarrassing.*

10. Please, can we find just a medication that will put an end to our pain and embarrassment without having us committing suicide?

10. *Please, can we find a medication that will just put an end to our pain and embarrassment without having us commit suicide?*

Unit Collaborative Assignment

Pair up with a partner. Each of you should alternate reading a sentence while the other corrects it, if necessary, in the space below. Decide what kind of error you have found. You should find four dangling or misplaced modifiers.

Children should live free from fear. Fear in a child's life has no redeeming qualities; it does not make a child stronger, nor does it teach the child how to be more independent. One of a child's worst fears comes from watching parents fight. Arriving home from work, little Freddy is afraid that Dad will start a fight with Mom. So Freddy whispers a silent prayer that his parents will be peaceful under his breath. Children not only fear quarrels between their parents, they also fear snakes and spiders. For instance, if little Suzy is in bed, ready for sleep, but sees a black spider crawling out of the corner of her eye, she may panic and have terrible nightmares the rest of the night. Again, fear of this kind is not good for the child's development. Perhaps a child's worst fear is the fear of abandonment. To feel safe, secure, and protected by one's parents is crucial to a child. Some children only feel secure when they finally grow up and have children of their own. When bringing up children, fear must be removed by parents.

1. *In a child's life, fear has no redeeming qualities.*

2. *When Dad arrives home from work, little Freddy is afraid that Dad will start a fight with Mom.*

3. *So Freddy whispers a silent prayer under his breath that his parents will be peaceful.*

4. *When bringing up children, parents must remove fear.*

Unit Writing Assignment

Write a paragraph agreeing or disagreeing with the idea that "College is not for everyone." Begin with a discussible topic sentence and support it with appropriate facts and examples. Check your writing for misplaced or dangling modifiers. Use the Revising Checklist to revise.

Photo Writing Assignment

After studying the following picture, use brainstorming, freewriting, clustering, or any other method of gathering ideas to write a paragraph answering the question, "What are the benefits of a good library system?" Use the Revising Checklist to revise.

18

Using Prepositions

A **preposition** is a word that shows the relationship between two things. In the example above, the prepositions show the relationships between a plane and a cloud. Indeed, one informal definition of the preposition is anything an airplane can do to a cloud. This, however, is not a complete definition, as our list of common prepositions makes clear:

about	beneath	in	since
above	beside	into	through
across	besides	inside	throughout
after	between	like	to
against	beyond	near	toward
along	by	of	under
among	despite	off	underneath
around	down	on	until
at	during	out	up
before	except	outside	with
behind	for	over	within
below	from	past	without

Some prepositions consist of more than one word. Here is a list of the most common multiword prepositions:

along with	in place of
because of	in spite of
due to	instead of
except for	on account of
in addition to	out of
in case of	up to
in front of	with the exception of

PRACTICING 1

Without consulting the above lists, place a check mark next to each preposition. (If you're uncertain about a word, try the plane-cloud test.) Leave the other kinds of words unchecked.

1. ✔ behind

2. _____ house

3. ✔ for

4. _____ too

5. _____ singing

6. _____ certainly

7. ✔ in

8. ✔ underneath

9. _____ a

10. ✔ below

11. _____ lightly

12. _____ however

13. ✔ beyond

14. _____ occasionally

15. ✔ inside

16. _____ crying

17. _____ speak

18. ✔ upon

19. ✔ outside

20. _____ bitterly

PRACTICING 2

In the blank provided, write an appropriate preposition.

1. My grandmother used to tell me stories ___*about*___ life in Japan.

2. ___*Throughout*___ the semester, I have received A's and B's in my course work.

3. I never fell in love ___*until*___ I met Sammy.

4. We spoke about it ___*for*___ over an hour.

5. ___*Because of*___ her stubbornness, she never made up with her brother.

6. As they say, "Too much water has run ___*under*___ the bridge."

7. You know very well that he slashed the tire ___*out of*___ pure spite.

8. A big brown bear kept coming ___*toward*___ our tent.

9. I am tired ___*of*___ his constant lying.

10. ___*In spite of*___ the rain, the dance was great fun.

Prepositional Phrases

A preposition is always followed by a noun or pronoun called its **object**. Together, the preposition and its object form a **prepositional phrase**, as illustrated below.

PREPOSITION	+	OBJECT	=	PREPOSITIONAL PHRASE
beyond		the stars		beyond the stars
inside		the NFL		inside the NFL
except for		them		except for them
with		his help		with his help
into		the room		into the room

PRACTICING 3

Underline the prepositional phrase in each sentence. Some sentences may contain more than one prepositional phrase.

Example: I would hate to fall <u>into the lake</u>.

1. Don't be <u>in a hurry</u> to go <u>up the stairs</u>.

2. The scissors are <u>on the table</u> right <u>before your eyes</u>.

3. <u>Because of his drinking</u>, he lost the job.

4. She's sitting <u>in the first row</u> <u>between JoRay and Harriett</u>.

5. Bob left <u>for school</u> <u>at 9:00</u> A.M.

6. A large part <u>of his salary</u> is used <u>for rent</u>.

7. The burglar hid <u>behind the door</u> <u>in the attic</u>.

8. Put glass <u>in this recycling bin</u> and paper <u>in that one</u>.

9. Margie stood <u>in the cold</u> and yelled, "Hello!"

10. We immediately headed <u>down the street</u> and <u>through the alley</u>.

Frequently Misused Prepositions

Although your speaker's ear is a fairly accurate guide to using prepositions, your ear may mislead you occasionally because of slang and the general informality of talk. Here are some frequently misused prepositions.

ESL Advice!

These rules need to be memorized.

- **beside, besides.** *Beside* means *next to,* whereas *besides* means *in addition.*

  The comb is beside the brush.

  Besides planning the trip, she is also getting the tickets.

- **between, among.** Generally, *between* is used when two items are involved; with three or more, *among* is preferred.

  Between you and me, he is among friends.

■ **due to.** *Due to* should not be used as a preposition meaning *because of.*

Because of (not due to) his speeding, we were all ticketed.

■ **inside of, outside of, off of.** The *of* is always unnecessary.

Stay inside (not *inside of*) the house.
The man stayed outside (not *outside of*) the post office.

Take your foot off (not *off of*) the table.

■ **like/as/as if.** *Like* is a preposition and should always be followed by a noun (the object of the preposition.

He eats like a bear

She walks like a cat.

As is a conjunction and should be followed by a clause.

He eats as a hungry bear might.

She walks as if she were a cat.

Note that this distinction is often overlooked in informal speech and writing (They tell it like it is), but expected in formal writing.

■ **regarding, with respect to, in regard to.** All of these expressions sound pompous. Use *about.*

I want to speak to you about (not *regarding, with respect to,* or *in regard to*) your essay.

■ **through, throughout.** *Through* means *by way of; throughout* means *in every part.*

You drive through Bog Walk to get to Linstead.

People are the same throughout the world.

■ **toward, towards.** Both are correct.

He walked toward (towards) me.

PRACTICING 4

In the blank provided, write *C* if the preposition is used correctly and *NC* if it is not correct. Cross through the errors and write the correct form of the preposition above each error.

1. __c__ Slowly, slowly, the bear moved towards the cabin.

2. __c__ We have remained best friends throughout a decade.

3. __NC__ Brand X tastes good like ~~a~~ cigarette should. *(as a)*

4. __NC__ I am writing this letter ~~in regard to~~ your vacation. *(about)*

5. __c__ Because of his height, he decided not to play basketball.

6. ___NC___ The money was divided ~~between~~ *among* Marge, Alice, and Bob.

7. ___NC___ She whines and complains; ~~beside~~ *besides*, she is always late.

8. ___C___   When you turn off Highway 5, go two miles.

9. ___NC___ Get off ~~of~~ my property!

10. ___NC___ I hope I can learn to write like you ~~do~~.

Frequently Misused Expressions

The expressions with prepositions listed below are also frequently misused.

- **agree on, agree to.** *Agree on* is to be of one opinion, whereas *agree to* requires an action.

  They agreed on the terms of the contract.

  They agreed to get a divorce.

- **angry about, angry with.** *Angry about* is used for anger about a thing; *angry with* is used with people.

  Everyone was angry about the detour.

  If you are angry with Sue, tell her so.

- **differ with, differ from.** *Differ with* means to disagree, whereas *differ from* is to be unlike or dissimilar.

  I differ with you on the death penalty.

  Houses in Boston differ from the ones in Sante Fe.

- **grateful to, grateful for.** You are *grateful to* a person, but *grateful for* something.

  We are grateful to Mrs. Smith.

  We are grateful for the sunshine.

- **independent of, independent from.** *Independent of* is the preferred usage.

  He is independent of any political party.

IN A NUTSHELL

- A preposition shows the relationship between two things.
- Look out for some commonly misused expressions involving prepositions.

PRACTICING 5

In each pair of sentences, check the preferred version in the blank provided.

1. __✔__ (a). Morrison was always independent of other rock bands.

   _____ (b). Morrison was always independent from other rock banks.

2. _____ (a). Joey differs from his father on the subject of taxes.

   __✔__ (b). Joey differs with his father on the subject of taxes.

3. _____ (a). Why should I be grateful to my good health?

   __✔__ (b). Why should I be grateful for my good health?

4. _____ (a). Indeed, we agreed to keeping the doors open.

   __✔__ (b). Indeed, we agreed on keeping the doors open.

5. __✔__ (a). I was shocked at how angry he was with me.

   _____ (b). I was shocked at how angry he was about me.

6. _____ (a). People can differ from each other on how to vote.

   __✔__ (b). People can differ with each other on how to vote.

7 _____ (a). Scottie and Maria agreed on seeing a marriage counselor.

   __✔__ (b). Scottie and Maria agreed to see a marriage counselor.

8. __✔__ (a). We are grateful for getting into the championship finals.

   _____ (b). We are grateful to get into the championship finals.

9. __✔__ (a). Max was angry about the long delay at the airport.

   _____ (b). Max was angry with the long delay at the airport.

10. _____ (a). We agree to several issues, including gun control.

    __✔__ (b). We agree on several issues, including gun control.

PRACTICING 6

Cross out the incorrect preposition in each sentence.

Example: My dreams differ (with, from) my hopes.

1. We could not agree (on, to) the rental contract.

2. The Civic Association was angry (about, with) the builder for cutting down the oak tree.

3. I am grateful (for, to) my student loan.

4. I am grateful (to, for) my landlord for extending the grace period for paying the rent.

5. If you're angry (about, with) the new dorm rules, speak up.

6. They agreed (on, to) the wedding date.

7. We were angry (about, with) having to wait in line.

8. My brother differs (from, with) my father in looks.

9. But when it comes to politics, my brother differs (with, from) my father on many issues.

10. I am independent (of, from) her.

 **Unit Test**

In the blank provided, mark *C* if the italicized preposition or prepositional phrase is used correctly. Mark *NC* if it is not correct. Correct the errors by crossing through them and writing the correct form above each incorrect form.

1. __NC__ Put the book *besides* ^(beside) my bookbag.

2. __NC__ Can't we *agree to* ^(on) a single issue?

3. __C__ Why is he so *angry with* his grandfather?

4. __NC__ Let's share the rent *between* ^(among) *us* four buddies.

5. __NC__ Get *off of* that ladder right now!

6. __NC__   The dean wants to see Mike *in regard to* his grades. *about*

7. __NC__   All children must someday become *independent from* their parents. *of*

8. __C__   Senator Smith *differs with* Senator Brown on how to pay for child care.

9. __C__   I worked *throughout* the semester to learn more about astronomy.

10. __NC__   *Because of* *Due to* her red hair we called her "Red Beauty."

11. __NC__   We parked *outside of* the stadium and walked.

12. __C__   Put the bread basket *beside* the butter.

13. __C__   We walked *through* the parking lot to get to the mall.

14. __C__   She slowly walked *towards* me.

15. __C__   I slowly walked *toward* her.

16. __C__   Matt is *grateful for* the chance to repay the favor.

17. __NC__   First put the groceries *inside of* the house.

18. __C__   She told funny stories *throughout* the evening.

19. __C__   *Between* you and me, I'm glad he won.

20. __NC__   We got a ticket *due to* parking illegally. *because of*

Unit Talk-Write Assignment

The sentences below, on the topic of televised sports, are typical of everyday conversation. Some of the sentences are unsuitable, however, because they use idioms, slang, fragments, and other informalities. A few commit preposition errors. Rewrite each sentence to make it suitable for writing, correcting all the preposition errors in the process. Then write a paragraph on your opinion of sports on television.

TALK

1. Man, can you believe all the sports on TV nowadays? Cool!

WRITE

1. *It is hard to believe all the sports on TV these days. I think it's great.*

TALK	**WRITE**
2. Yeah, man, there's a bunch. Beside, there's more getting on everyday.	**2.** *Yes, there are many. Also, there are more broadcast every day.*
3. Take a sport like football, for instance. During the season, there's games on almost every day of the week.	**3.** *For example, during the football season, there are games on TV almost every day of the week.*
4. Sometimes I can't study due to the number of games that are on.	**4.** *Sometimes I can't study because of the number of games that are televised.*
5. I know what you mean, man. Instead of going outside and enjoying the day, I stay inside of the house all Sunday watching football on TV.	**5.** *I know what you mean. Instead of going outside and enjoying the day, I stay inside the house all Sunday watching football on TV.*
6. What about basketball? If you watch all the college games and pro games through the week, your eyes start to bug out.	**6.** *There are a lot of basketball games, too. If you watch all the college games and professional games throughout the week, your eyes start to hurt.*
7. Yeah, and that's not even the playoffs. Sometimes five or six of my friends will come over, and we'll split the cost of pizza between us and sit there and pig out on basketball.	**7.** *Yes, and it's worse during the playoffs. Sometimes five or six of my friends will come over, and we'll split the cost of a pizza among us and sit there and eat and watch basketball.*

TALK

8. I don't think anybody else watches as much TV through the world as Americans. Especially sports. Not by half.

9. Sometimes my old man gets angry about me for watching so much sports. I tell him I can't help it. I'm hooked.

10. Me, too. What'd we do without it ? It's nothing to be angry with if you're a sports fan.

WRITE

8. *I don't think anybody else watches half as much TV, especially sports, throughout the world as Americans.*

9. *Sometimes my father gets angry with me for watching so much sports. I tell him I can't help it. I'm addicted.*

10. *I am, too. What would we do without it? There's nothing to be angry about if you're a sports fan.*

My Opinion of Televised Sports

_____

_____

_____

_____

_____

_____

_____

_____

_____

_____

_____

Unit Collaborative Assignment

Answers will vary.

A. Form a group. Write ten sentences supporting the following topic. Each sentence should comtain at least one prepositional phrase.

Computers exert a growing influence on our lives.

1. _____

   _____

2. _____

   _____

3. _____

   _____

4. _____

   _____

5. _____

   _____

6. _____

   _____

7. _____

   _____

8. _____

   _____

9. _____

   _____

10. _____

   _____

B. Now go back over the sentences and underline all the prepositional phrases.

Unit Writing Assignment

Write about the influence of computers on our lives. Use ideas from the Unit Collaborative Assignment above and new ideas of your own. Use the Revising Checklist to revise.

Photo Writing Assignment

After studying the following photo, write about the dangers of too much daydreaming or wishful thinking. Give at least one example from your own experience. Use the Revising Checklist to revise.

19

Punctuation You Can Hear

"Charlie, will you please close the door?"

Punctuation marks are the traffic signs of writing. They tell the reader when to slow down, when to speed up, and when to stop. In writing, punctuation marks direct the eye's movement across the page. In spoken sentences, punctuation is heard as pauses, upbeats, and downbeats.

Indeed, you can definitely hear some punctuation marks. For example, say the following sentences out loud:

You are going home.

You are going home?

You are going home!

If you listen carefully to yourself, you will notice that you ended the first sentence on a flat note, the second on an upbeat, and the third on a downbeat. These spoken cues help us tell the difference between a statement, a question, and a command.

In this unit, we will discuss punctuation marks you can hear. These marks include end punctuation (periods, question marks, exclamation points), commas, and apostrophes. You can trust your speaker's ear to help you use these punctuation marks correctly.

> **ESL Advice!**
>
> If you can't hear these punctuation marks, you should memorize the rules.

End Punctuation

All sentences end with a period, a question mark, or an exclamation point. There are no exceptions to this rule.

Period (.)

Use a period after a sentence that makes a statement:

My mother lost her wallet.

Her car is in the garage.

Question mark (?)

Use a question mark after direct questions.

Where did the sunshine go?

Have you seen my pen?

The question mark is not used after an indirect question:

Mary asked where the sunshine had gone.

John wondered if we had seen his pen.

Exclamation point (!)

Use an exclamation point to show intense emotion, such as happiness, surprise, anger, or disgust, or to give a strong command:

What a fabulous day!

Get out of my house!

IN A NUTSHELL

- Use a period at the end of a statement or indirect question.
- Use a question mark with direct questions.
- Use an exclamation point to indicate strong emotion or give a command.

PRACTICING 1

Place the proper punctuation mark at the end of each sentence.

Example: What would you do without me?

1. Is long hair on men attractive to women?
2. I was very happy to hear about his grades.
3. Save the whales!
4. Is she as calm as she seems?
5. They asked whether we would be at home.
6. Watch out!
7. We waited in line for 40 minutes.
8. Are you driving or flying?
9. Using your imagination, describe your ideal vacation.
10. What an incredible bargain.

The Comma (,)

You hear the comma as a half-pause. Sometimes the comma just makes listening or reading easier, but sometimes it is crucial to meaning. Here is an example:

> Trying to escape, Alexander Gordon ran out the door.

> Trying to escape Alexander, Gordon ran out the door.

The huge difference in the meanings of these two sentences depends on where the comma is placed. In the first sentence, *Alexander Gordon* is trying to escape an unknown someone or something. In the second, *Gordon* is trying to escape *Alexander*.

We will cover the hard and fast rules of comma usage.

Place a comma in front of coordinating conjunctions (and, but, or, for, nor, so, yet) that link independent clauses (see pp. 117–120).

> He dodged the cold germs, but he caught pneumonia.

> My mother is an accountant, and my father is her assistant.

> He spoke with authority, so I believed him.

Do not use a comma before *and* if it is not followed by an independent clause.

Incorrect:	He did the laundry, and made dinner.
Correct:	He did the laundry and made dinner.
Correct:	He did the laundry, and he made the dinner.

PRACTICING 2

Answers will vary.

Finish the following sentences by adding another independent clause and a coordinating conjunction. Remember to use a comma.

Example: The house she lived in was small, but it was wonderfully cozy.

1. Be kind to all animals_____

2. I drive by that house daily_____

3. On Christmas we always stay home   _____

4. I sat in the barber's chair   _____

5. I believe life exists on other planets   _____

6. Mother baked bread every Tuesday   _____

7. The book was filled with pictures   _____

8. Most repair people are honest   _____

9. The embers glowed in the fireplace   _____

10. She will probably break down and cry   _____

Use a comma after introductory words, phrases, and dependent clauses at the beginning of a sentence.

Words:	Furthermore, he received a big bonus.
	Well, why don't you move out?
	Louise, I did it.

Phrases:	From the point of view of health, he was perfect.
	Having lost all, I really did not care what happened.
	By the way, your mother called.

Clauses: Because it was raining,
we stayed home.

but

We stayed home because
it was raining.

If I win the lottery, I will buy you the car.

but

I will buy you the car if I win the lottery.

**(Use a comma
after a dependent
clause only if it
comes at the begin-
ning, but not at the
end, of a sentence.)**

IN A NUTSHELL

Use commas after introductory words, phrases, and dependent
clauses at the beginning of a sentence.

PRACTICING 3

Insert commas where needed.

1. Yes, they can use the camping site.

2. As far as I am concerned, everyone is invited.

3. Though feeling awkward, John continued to dance.

4. Okay, I'll work Saturday.

5. Elizabeth, when are you leaving?

6. Moreover, you owe me an apology for being late.

7. From behind the curtain, he could not see his brother.

8. If you study the history of Russia, you will understand why
the peasants rebelled.

9. First of all, none of us knows the future.

10. Scoring 15 points, he led the team.

PRACTICING 4

Insert commas where needed. In the space provided, state the rule that makes the comma necessary.

Correction: Mike, we were truly disappointed in your performance.

Rule: _A comma follows an introductory word._

1. When students succeed in their studies, they bring joy to their teachers.

Rule: _Use a comma after an introductory dependent clause._

2. From the street, we could see the flag at half mast.

Rule: _Use a comma after an introductory phrase._

3. We went to the movies, and then we stopped for coffee.

Rule: _Place a comma in front of coordinating conjunctions that link independent clauses._

4. If they had given us the right directions, we would not have gotten lost.

Rule: _Use a comma after an introductory dependent clause._

5. Furthermore, he had no right to open her mail.

Rule: _Use a comma after an introductory word._

6. Well, why did you lend him the money if you knew he wouldn't repay you?

Rule: _Use a comma after an introductory word._

7. Yes, she is my cousin. No, she does not speak English.

Rule: _Use a comma after an introductory word._

8. He earns a good salary, yet he doesn't have any savings.

Rule: _Place a comma in front of coordinating conjunctions that link independent clauses._

9. Are you stopping at the mall, or are you going straight home?

Rule: _Place a comma in front of coordinating conjunctions that link independent clauses._

10. While we were watching the waves come in, we saw a whale.

Rule: _Use a comma after an introductory clause._

Use commas to separate items in a series.

We ate steak, baked potatoes, and sweet corn.

The thick, juicy steak hit the spot.

You can read a book, watch television, or go to bed.

Up the road, through the woods, and along the river they trudged.

Do not, however, use commas unnecessarily with words in a series.

Do not use a comma before <u>and</u> if only two items are mentioned.

Incorrect: He plays the piano, and the trumpet.
Correct: He plays the piano and the trumpet.

Do not use a comma between modifiers unless you can insert the word <u>and</u> between them.

Incorrect: The old, red rowboat finally sank.
Correct: The old red rowboat finally sank.

You wouldn't say *The old and red rowboat finally sank*, so you shouldn't use a comma.

You would, however, use a comma between the modifiers of this sentence:

A cold, bitter wind blew off the lake.

You could insert the word *and* between the modifiers, and the sentence would still sound right.

A cold and bitter wind blew off the lake.

Do not use a comma before the first item in a series or after the last.

Incorrect: Other reasons not to smoke include, the smell, the expense, and the inconvenience.

Correct: Other reasons not to smoke include the smell, the expense, and the inconvenience.

Incorrect: You can add chocolate chips, raisins, or nuts, to the cookie batter.

Correct: You can add chocolate chips, raisins, or nuts to the cookie batter.

PRACTICING 5

Insert commas as necessary to separate items in a series.

1. They complain morning, noon, and night.

2. Give me some rollers, a hairbrush, and a blow dryer so I can make her look stylish.

3. I will climb the highest mountain, swim the deepest ocean, and struggle through the darkest jungle for a raise.

4. I need a hammer, a saw, and some nails.

5. The punch has 7-Up, lemonade, and sliced oranges in it.

6. Not everyone thought the dinner was tasty, well priced, and nutritious.

7. Pick one from column A, one from column B, and one from column C.

8. Would you like potatoes, rice, or beans?

9. The professor entered the room, piled his books on the desk, and began to hand out our papers.

10. I never watch anything on television except the news, the movie reviews, and the weather.

PRACTICING 6

In the following sentences, strike through the unnecessary commas.

Example: The elderly gentleman took off his hat, and sat down.

1. All of us need love, challenging work, and a sense of purpose, to be happy.

2. Give me some loyal, and amusing friends.

3. The kinds of textbooks I can't stand include, economics, finance, and math.

4. My first/ real bicycle still sits in the attic.

5. Go ahead and serve the hors d'oeuvres, the salad, and the lemonade/ before the guest of honor arrives.

6. Don't you enjoy listening to Elvis Presley/ and the Beatles?

7. Other factors that make for pleasant camping include/ smooth ground, leafy trees, and a running stream.

8. The old/ Ford convertible sat in the garage.

9. My whole family plays tennis/ and basketball.

10. For the picnic, we need/ paper plates, napkins, and ants.

Place commas around parenthetical elements that interrupt the flow of a sentence.

In speaking, it is natural to pause before and after words that interrupt the flow of thought. In writing, this pause is signaled by a comma. These interruptions—called parenthetical elements because they can be included in parentheses without affecting the meaning of the sentence—include any expression, phrase, aside, or other remark not essential to your meaning. The commas, in effect, take the place of the parentheses. Here are some examples:

Expression:	She is, of course, a very thoughtful person.
	Registration for the class is, unfortunately, closed.
	You understand, by the way, that I have no other choice.
Descriptive phrases:	We struggled, cold and wet, to climb the mountain.
	I'll ask Milo, our neighbor, if he wants the tickets.
	The governor, running for re-election, shook hands with everyone.
Nonessential clauses that begin with who, whose, which, when, or where.	Mr. Jones, who wore a striped suit, caught a fly ball at the baseball game.

Here are other examples:

My Aunt Matildah, whose pickled beets won first prize, waved at me.

The Hope Botanical Gardens, where flowers bloom all year long, is open to the public.

My days off, when I get one, are cluttered with chores.

The report, which took two weeks to write, earned Henry a promotion.

All the above clauses contain nonessential information and are therefore punctuated as parenthetical elements by commas.

On the other hand, a clause introduced by *who, whose, when,* or *where* containing information that is *essential* to understanding the sentence is not punctuated by commas:

The man who wore the striped suit got hit by a baseball.

Now the information in the clause is essential to identify who got hit by the baseball—the man in the striped suit, not the man in the gray suit.

Here are some other examples of essential *who, whose, which, when, where* clauses:

The aunt whose pickled beets won first prize is Aunt Matildah.	**(It wasn't Aunt Minnie's beets that won.)**
The Hope Botanical Gardens are where flowers bloom all year long; they are open to the public.	**(The Brooklyn Botanical Gardens do not have flowers all year long.)**
The week when I was away the rains began.	**(The rains did not fall in the weeks when the writer was home.)**
The report that took two weeks to write earned Henry a promotion.	**(It was the report that took two weeks to write, not some other report.)**

Notice in this last sentence *which* changed to *that.* Nonessential clauses referring to things are introduced with the relative pronoun *which,* while essential clauses referring to things are introduced with the relative pronoun *that.* Use commas with nonessential *which* clauses; do not use commas with essential *that* clauses. Here are some more examples:

Commas needed: The band repeatedly played *One Love*, which I'd never heard before.

Commas not needed: The band repeatedly played a song that I'd never heard before.

In the first sentence, the fact that the writer never heard the song before is not important, so the information is set off with *which* and commas. In the second sentence, the main idea is that the writer had never heard the song before, so *that* is used and the information is not punctuated with commas.

Commas needed: My Chevy convertible, which I usually drive to work, is in the garage.

Commas not needed: The car that I drive to work is in the garage.

The first sentence says that the writer's Chevy convertible is in the garage; that he drives this car to work is not essential information to identifying it so the phrase is set off with *which* and commas. The second sentence specifies that the car in the garage is the one the writer drives to work—not the one his wife drives. Since this is essential information, *that* is used and the information is not punctuated by commas.

You can usually "hear" the interruption in a parenthetical element. When you can't, context will tell you whether a clause is essential or nonessential. Consider this sentence:

The job fair, which was held in Sanders Hall, was very successful.

This sentence is fine, if there were only one job fair held. But if there were two job fairs, one held in Sanders Hall and the other in Prentiss Hall, then the above sentence would be written and punctuated this way:

The job fair that (not *which*) was held in Sanders Hall was very successful. (But the one that was held in Prentiss Hall was a flop.)

IN A NUTSHELL

- Use commas to set off expressions and phrases that interrupt a sentence.

- Use commas to set off clauses that contain information not essential to understanding the sentence.

PRACTICING 7

Use commas to set off the unessential interruptions in these sentences. If the sentence is correct, leave it alone.

Example: My uncle Albert, who is my favorite relative, is here tonight.

1. Mr. Clark, of course, is running for mayor.

2. Professor Robinson, whom we really admire, won the Best Teacher Award.

3. The incision, which left a large scar, needed plastic surgery.

4. Any official who takes a bribe should be ashamed.

5. The sky, which was filled with billowy white clouds, made me want to write a poem.

6. Our next door neighbor, who was a nice man, often chatted with me over the fence.

7. My uncle, who served in two major wars, still has his uniforms.

8. The old family home where my brother now lives needs remodeling.

9. Who owns the Honda Civic that is blocking the driveway?

10. Give this ticket to the man who is standing at the gate and to no one else.

PRACTICING 8

Underline the words that interrupt the flow of the sentence, then place commas around them.

Example: My brother, <u>who always hated suits</u>, wants a tuxedo
for his birthday.

1. His father, <u>loved and respected by all members of the family</u>, just turned 85.

2. Her wedding, <u>expected for so many years</u>, took place last month.

3. Peter Dunkin, <u>who is very graceful and coordinated</u>, will be the lead dancer.

4. It is not, <u>by a long shot</u>, my first choice.

5. Old people, <u>often neglected by their families</u>, need community help to remain independent.

6. All the children in our neighborhood considered Harry, <u>the local bakery owner</u>, a great hero.

7. Dr. Jensen, <u>who gave the commencement address</u>, kept her audience entertained.

8. Pizza King, <u>especially on Friday nights</u>, is very busy.

9. All cultures, <u>you realize</u>, are becoming more and more technological.

10. She is, <u>by the way my</u>, aunt.

PRACTICING 9

Using context as your guide, cross out either *that* or *which* in the following clauses and punctuate them appropriately:

I own two sailboats, both sloops. One I race, the other I cruise. The sloop (that, ~~which~~) I race is blue and old. The other sloop, (that, which) I don't race but cruise, is red with green trim. Both sloops are lovely. A sailor once offered to buy the sloop (that, ~~which~~) I cruise for $10,000. I told him he could have the old, blue sloop, (~~that~~, which) I race, for that price, but the sloop (that, ~~which~~) I cruise is not for sale at any price.

Use commas for dates and addresses and in the openings and closings of letters.

Commas to separate items of a date:	My twentieth birthday party took place on Tuesday, March 14, 1999. On July 9, 2004, the whole balance on the car will be due.
Commas to separate items in an address:	Alicia lives at 30 Munson Drive, Detroit, Michigan 40202. Mail the card to 1500 North Verdugo Road, Glendale, California 34525.
Commas in the openings and closings of letters:	Dearest Caroline, Dear Juan, Yours truly, Sincerely,

IN A NUTSHELL

Use commas for dates and addresses and in the openings and closings of letters.

PRACTICING 10

Insert commas where needed below. Some of the entries may require no commas.

1. On Monday, September 4, we celebrated Labor Day.

2. My dear Mrs. Wong,

3. We will stay at the campgrounds from Monday, August 27, to Friday, September 1.

4. We moved from Huntington Beach to La Mirada.

5. Pasquale's Hair Salon has moved to 420 Camden Drive.

6. Her complete address is 489 Rock Road, Apartment 3, Tampa Florida 34555.

7. Sincerely yours,

8. They used to live at 6201 Main Street.

9. She's leaving for Kansas City on Tuesday, January 17.

10. Now she lives at 2322 Chevy Chase Drive, Lansing, Michigan.

11. He was born Saturday, May 7, 1982, in Tucson, Arizona.

12. Send Peter's mail to 933 Andover Street, Worthington, Ohio, 43085.

13. We drove from Jackson Hole to Aspen.

14. Mary was born August 12, 1978, and Kevin was born on February 5, 1983.

15. Is she from Miami, Ohio, or Miami, Florida?

Use commas to set off direct quotations from the rest of the sentence.

A quotation may be either direct—exactly what someone said—or indirect—a report of what someone said.

Direct Quotation: "Forget you ever saw me," he whispered.

Indirect Quotation: He said to forget she had ever seen him.

Direct quotations can be reported in three ways, each requiring commas.

"Forget you ever saw me," he whispered.

"Forget," he whispered, "you ever saw me."

He whispered, "Forget you ever saw me."

Commas and periods always go inside the quotation marks (see p. 391).

PRACTICING 11

First turn the following indirect quotations into direct quotations. Then punctuate the direct quotations in the three ways taught in this section.

Example: She said that she was not going.

"I am," she said, "not going."

"I am not going," she said.

She said, "I am not going."

1. He said that you should try the dip with the banana chips.

"You should," he said, "try the dip with the banana chips."

"You should try the dip with the banana chips, " he said.

He said, "You should try the dip with the banana chips.

2. Mary said that was not what she thought would happen.

"That's not, " Mary said, "what I think will happen."

"That's not what I think will happen, " Mary said.

Mary said, "That's not what I think will happen."

3. Howard remarked that's how the game should be played.

"That's how, " Howard remarked, "the game should be played."

"That's how the game should be played, " Howard remarked.

Howard remarked, "That's how the game should be played."

4. Jennifer added that's what she was taught about the procedure.

"That's what I was taught, " Jennifer added, "about the procedure."

"That's what I was taught about the procedure, " Jennifer added.

Jennifer added, "That's what I was taught about the procedure."

5. Catherine snapped that she thought the movie was boring.

"I, " Catherine snapped, "thought the movie was boring."

"I thought the movie was boring, " Catherine snapped.

Catherine snapped, "I thought the movie was boring."

EAR ALERT

PRACTICING 12

Add commas to set off the quoted material from the rest of the sentence.

1. "Steve has a new job," he announced.

2. "The results," he announced, "speak for themselves."

3. "I have never drunk anything stronger than Coca Cola," he replied.

4. Frederico insisted, "It's a perfect day for the picnic."

5. The clerk said, "Shoes and shirts are required."

6. "I ordered one deluxe pizza," she answered.

7. "I certainly didn't mean any harm," indicated Barry, "but I had to tell the truth."

8. "Let's go downstairs and do the laundry," Linda suggested.

9. "Stacking the books on the shelf," he told Rhonda, "is very time-consuming."

10. "They do not resemble each other one bit," he noted.

The Apostrophe (')

The apostrophe has two uses, to show possession and to indicate a contraction.

Use the apostrophe to show possession.

The chart below shows how apostrophes are used to show possession or ownership. For a singular noun, always add *'s*. However, to form the possessive of a plural noun ending in *s*, add only the apostrophe. If the plural does not end in *s*, add *'s*.

SINGULAR (ALWAYS ADD *'s*)	PLURAL
girl's notebook	girls' notebooks
bus's driver	buses' drivers
child's toy	children's toys
Carl Keith's house	the Keiths' house
Ross's car	the Rosses' car

PRACTICING 13

Turn the phrases below into possessives.

Example: the book of Jack.

Answer: Jack's book

1. the umbrella of Lucy

Lucy's umbrella

2. the fence of the garden

the garden's fence

3. the victory of Luis

Luis's victory

4. the anniversary of the Davises

the Davises' anniversary

5. the seat of the driver

the driver's seat

6. the house of Mel

Mel's house

7. the meager food of the people

the people's meager food

8. the car of James

James's car

9. the treatment of the doctor

the doctor's treatment

10. the complaints of most guests

most guests' complaints

PRACTICING 14

Make the following italicized nouns possessive. First decide whether the noun is singular or plural. Then decide whether you need only an apostrophe or *'s*. Finally, change the singular possessive nouns to plural and the plural possessive nouns to singular.

Example: Max and Sara *Marcus* daughter

Answer: Max and Sara *Marcus's* daughter, the Marcuses' daughter

1. the *Smiths'* law

2. the *lion's* mane

3. the *firefighters'* trucks

4. the *grass's* color

5. the *men's* hats

6. the *bus's* horn

7. the *churches'* bells

8. the *tulips'* petals

9. the police *officer's* promotions

10. *Louis's* suspenders

Use the apostrophe to show an omission in a contraction.

Apostrophes are used to show omitted letters in contractions, such as *don't* (do not) or *isn't* (is not). Contractions are commonly used in informal writing. Here are some common contractions:

can not	can't
could have	could've
could not	couldn't
did not	didn't
do not	don't
has not	hasn't
have not	haven't
he is	he's

I am	I'm
I would	I'd
it is	it's
she is	she's
should have	should've
should not	shouldn't
they are	they're
they are not	they aren't
who is	who's
will not	won't
would have	would've
would not	wouldn't
let us	let's

Don't trust your ear in punctuating contractions. Learn the rule. In speech, we can hear these contractions. What we cannot hear is exactly where the apostrophe goes—where the letter was actually omitted.

couldn't (not could'nt)   **(the apostrophe marks the omission of the <u>o</u>)**

they're (not theyr'e)   **(the apostrophe marks the omission of the <u>a</u>)**

Remember to put the apostrophe exactly where the letter is missing.

PRACTICING 15

Insert contractions in the following sentences whenever possible. Cross out the words being turned into contractions, and write the contraction in the space above the crossed-out word.

couldn't
Example: We ~~could not~~ remember their names.

wouldn't
1. Why in the world ~~would~~ you ~~not~~ want to help out?

Why in the world wouldn't you want to help out?

couldn't
2. We ~~could not~~ have studied harder.

We couldn't have studied harder.

3. Ten years from now it ~~will not~~ **won't** matter in the least.

Ten years from now it won't matter in the least.

4. They ~~were not~~ **weren't** the least excited about being on television.

They weren't the least excited about being on television.

5. If Manny ~~had not~~ **hadn't** eaten, he ~~would have~~ **would've** offended the hostess.

If Manny hadn't eaten, he would've offended the hostess.

6. Surely you ~~could have~~ **could've** been more tactful.

Surely you could've been more tactful.

7. Why ~~are~~ **aren't** they ~~not~~ meeting us at the movie?

Why aren't they meeting us at the movie?

8. If Felice had been polite, we ~~would have~~ **would've** included her.

If Felice had been polite, we would've included her.

9. She ~~should not~~ **shouldn't** have said that.

She shouldn't have said that.

10. ~~Who is~~ **Who's** this funny man?

Who's this funny man?

Do not use apostrophes unnecessarily.

1. Only use an apostrophe with a possessive.

Incorrect: Apple's are on sale this week.

Correct: Apples are on sale this week.

To test whether a noun is possessive or not, turn it into an *of* phrase.

The <u>book's cover</u> is red.   **(book's cover = cover of the book = possessive)**

The library <u>books' are</u> due.   **(books' are = the are of the book = not possessive)**

2. Do not use apostrophes with the pronouns *his, hers, its, ours, yours,* or *theirs.*

Incorrect: The sweater is hers'.
Correct: The sweater is hers.

Incorrect: The cat washed it's face.
Correct: The cat washed its face.

It's is a contraction—short for *it is.* If you unravel the contraction, you get:

The cat washed *it is* face.

This sentence makes no sense.

PRACTICING 16

Correct the following unnecessary apostrophes and insert the missing apostrophes in the following sentences.

1. My father always seems to buy ~~cars'~~ [cars] that are lemons.

2. Its's ~~hers'~~ [hers] to lose and ~~ours'~~ [ours] to win.

3. She made three ~~batches'~~ [batches] of cookies.

4. She gave us our due and asked us to give them ~~their's~~ [theirs].

5. ~~Its'~~ [It's] not what you say, ~~its~~ [it's] what you do that ~~counts'~~ [counts].

6. ~~Johns'~~ [John's] in a bad mood today.

7. My ~~cats'~~ [cat's] very affectionate.

8. How you think about your future can be the ~~key's~~ [key] to success.

9. The job of asking why is not ~~yous'~~ [your's].

10. ~~Cathys~~ [Cathy's] pet ~~projects'~~ [projects] all involve her garden.

IN A NUTSHELL

- Use the apostrophe to show possession.
- Use the apostrophe to mark omitted letters in a contraction.
- Do not use unnecessary apostrophes.

PRACTICING 17

Every sentence below has one apostrophe error. It may be missing an apostrophe (or *'s*) in a possessive or in a contraction. Sometimes the error is an unnecessary apostrophe. Add missing apostrophes (or *'s*), and strike out all unnecessary apostrophes.

1. You should add potatoes and bean's to the stew.

2. Weren't you surprised to see Jenny's boyfriend there?

3. I think the red convertible is John's.

4. The mountain bike is her's.

5. I get two weeks' vacation this year.

6. That shirt is missing two button's.

7. It's not clear whether the party is at Jane's or Bill's house.

8. The job is your's if you want it.

9. Hanging by it's tail, the monkey chattered.

10. The volleyball players' uniforms are purple and white.

PRACTICING 18

Insert an apostrophe where needed. In the line after each sentence, explain why the apostrophe is needed by writing *P* for possessive or *C* for contraction. Some sentences require more than one apostrophe.

1. Many people's attitudes toward taxes have changed. __P__

2. They're sick of having to clean up everyone else's mess. __C, P__

3. Mother's worry is needless. __P__

4. Who hasn't hung up their coats? __C__

5. Doesn't it matter to you that they think you lied? __C__

6. New York's tall buildings amaze visitors. __P__

7. Her essays' titles weren't very imaginative. __P__

8. His father's fishing rod was in the garage. ___P___

9. The company's profits were at an all-time low. ___P___

10. Jeff's uncle is a nice person. ___P___

 Unit Test

In the blank provided, mark *C* if the sentence is correctly punctuated; mark *NC* if it is not correct. Correct the incorrect sentences.

Example: __NC__ When did they leave town.

1. __NC__ What could you possibly want from me!

2. __NC__ She asked when the wedding would take place?

3. __NC__ We bought all kinds of green vegetables, but they rotted.

4. __NC__ You could, of course, do the dishes.

5. __C__ Since you prefer carrot cake, I baked one for you.

6. __C__ Birds fly, dogs bark, and bees buzz.

7. __NC__ Your need to bring a flashlight, a sleeping bag, and some dried food.

8. __NC__ She was, however, unable to follow the directions.

9. __NC__ John, whose last name is Abbott, went first.

10. __NC__ We arrived, worn out but happy, at the summit of the mountain.

11. __NC__ Any mother who loves her child will be concerned with the child's diet.

12. __NC__ Dwight D. Eisenhower, a general in World War II, was also president of the United States.

13. __NC__ We graduated on Saturday, May 16, 1999.

14. __C__ The letter was sent to 926 Mayfair Lane, Columbus, Ohio.

15. __C__ "Let's pledge allegiance to the flag, " he said.

16. __NC__ "None of this would've happened," he said, "if you'd swept the floor."

17. __NC__ That coat is not hers; it's his.

18. __NC__ It's about time for you to grow up and quit whimpering.

19. __NC__ If you aren't sure, don't volunteer the answer.

20. __NC__ It's the Millers' back yard.

 # Unit Talk-Write Assignment

This assignment is about the current fad of body tattooing. The *Talk* column reflects one student's (Merrilee's) spirited defense of her own tattoo. We have deliberately scrambled the punctuation. Rewrite her sentences in the *Write* column, correcting all the punctuation errors, incomplete sentences, and nonstandard English. Then write a paragraph giving your views on the popularity of tattoos today.

Answers may vary.

TALK

1. So I have three tattoos. So what.

2. You can see the one on my shoulder. Its a springing tiger. The others—well theyre off-limits to everyone except my boyfriend.

3. O.K. you guys grow up. Quit your stupid giggling. No Im not a druggie.

WRITE

1. What is wrong with my having three tattoos?

2. You can see the one on my shoulder. It's a springing tiger. The others are off-limits to everyone except my boyfriend.

3. You need to act more mature. Stop giggling. No, I do not use drugs.

TALK

WRITE

4. Im just a modern girl. Thats it. Why do I get tattoos. Its my way of being me Merrilee a special person an individual not just another sheep in a big herd of sheep.

4. I'm just a girl of the 90s. That's the only reason I get tattoos. It's my way of being me, Merrilee, a special person, an individual, not just another sheep in a big herd of sheep.

5. My tattoos which are a form of expressing myself can be compared to the way some people always wear a certain perfume to be recognized by.

5. My tattoos, which are a form of expressing myself, can be compared to the way some people always wear a certain perfume to be recognized by.

6. The tiger, thats on my shoulder, lets the world know that somewhere on the inside Im ready to leap at my enemies and tear them apart.

6. The tiger that's on my shoulder lets the world know that somewhere on the inside I'm ready to leap at my enemies and tear them apart.

7. Maybe I sound mean or something but tigers are gorgeous animals.

7. I may sound mean, but tigers are gorgeous animals.

8. And I think of myself as having a tigers courage.

8. I think of myself as having a tiger's courage.

9. Dont laugh everybody likes to be special.

9. Don't laugh. Everybody likes to be special.

10. In this robot world we need to establish our individuality.

10. In this robot world, we need to establish our individuality.

_____

_____

_____

_____

_____

_____

_____

_____

_____

_____

Unit Collaborative Assignment

A. Dictate the following sentences to a chosen partner using pauses, upbeats, and downbeats to indicate the necessary punctuation. The goal of this exercise is for your partner to insert the appropriate punctuation mainly by ear, based on your reading.

1. Call me again, you lovely man.

2. Were you startled to see her?

3. I took his advice and went to see her.

4. I'll have scrambled eggs, fried potatoes, and toast.

5. He told his soldiers, "This is your time to achieve glory."

6. Sit down, take a breath, and then give the answer.

7. Did you really see an eagle?

8. Mrs. Gooch, our student advisor, said, "This should be (y)our goal."

9. Lee's car is a really sleek machine.

10. Mr. Nelson's dog, which now weighs more than I do, almost knocked me over.

B. Punctuate the following sentences, using the same approach as in exercise A, with your partner now doing the dictating.

1. Run for your life!

2. How can you help our neighborhood?

3. My father's stamp collection, however, will go to my sister.

4. Benjamin Franklin made his fortune as a printer, editor, inventor, and a statesman

5. When did you move to South Dakota?

6. Adam's home is his castle.

7. They're so much alike.

8. "I'm leaving at noon," said Millie.

9. "Where are you going," she asked, "and why can't I go with you?"

10. Shouldn't you be getting ready to leave?

Unit Writing Assignment

Write a paragraph about what your best friend means to you. Include a conversation that is typical of your relationship. Be specific and focus particularly on the rules of punctuation we have just covered. Use the Revising Checklist to revise.

Photo Writing Assignment

This photo is a still from *Shane,* a classic western. Westerns (sometimes called "oaters," used to be very popular but have lately given way to other kinds of movies. What kinds of movies are popular now? In your opinion, why have these types of movies replaced Westerns? Which kinds of movies do you particularly like? What are some of your favorite films? Consider these questions as you write a paragraph giving your views on movies. Check that you have punctuated your sentences correctly. Use the Revising Checklist to revise.

20

Punctuation
You Can't Hear

"I drank tea for breakfast; then I ate a muffin."

Your ear may often tell you when a pause means a comma or an upbeat means a question mark. At other times, your ear is of little use in identifying the correct punctuation. For certain punctuation marks, you must simply learn the rules. In this unit, you will learn how to use the punctuation marks we generally can't accurately hear:

- semicolon
- colon
- dash
- quotation marks
- parentheses

Semicolon (;)

The semicolon has a beat somewhere between a period and a comma—too fine for most of us to hear. It is a punctuation mark more commonly associated with writing than with speaking. In writing the semicolon has two main uses.

Use a semicolon to join two closely related, complete thoughts not connected by a conjunction, such as and, but, or, for, or nor.

The winds were as high as 50 mph; tiles flew off our roof.

Bats were roosting in the attic; the renters still stayed.

Notice the close relationship between the thoughts expressed in both sentences. In the first sentence, the tiles flew off the roof because the winds were high. In the second, the renters stayed in spite of the bats. So closely related are these thoughts that both sentences could have been written with a coordinating conjunction.

The winds were as high as 50 mph, so tiles flew off our roof.

Bats were roosting in the attic, yet the renters stayed.

PRACTICING 1

Place a semicolon between the two thoughts in thought in each of the following sentences.

1. I ate a muffin; then I drank some orange juice.

2. A camel can go for weeks without water; it stores water in its hump.

3. He sat listening to the conversation at the next table; it made him chuckle.

4. Bertha had to leave the movie; all the bloodshed made her sick.

5. I dislike shopping during the holidays; people are so rude and in such a hurry.

6. You have a good attitude; you will do well on your new job.

7. Don't blame him for being silent; he was scared out of his wits.

8. I find most poems hard to understand; they don't make sense.

9. Sit quietly in the room; you will hear mysterious whispers.

10. He loves movies; he probably rents three or four videos a week.

Use a semicolon between two complete thoughts joined by the transitions however, thus, therefore, consequently, moreover, furthermore, nevertheless, or otherwise.

We are behind schedule; however, we can work overtime.

She loved to go to the theater; moreover, she felt she had acting talent.

Note that a comma comes after the transition.

IN A NUTSHELL

- Use a semicolon to connect two complete thoughts not separated by *and, but, or, for,* or *nor.*

- Use a semicolon between two sentences joined by the transitions *however, thus, therefore, consequently, moreover, furthermore, nevertheless,* or *otherwise.* Use a comma after the transition word.

PRACTICING 2

Insert a semicolon after each of the following incomplete statements. Then either using a transition word from the preceding Nutshell box or your own phrasing, finish the statement so that it represents a complete idea and reflects the grammatical use of a semicolon. Be sure to place a semicolon before the transition word, if you use one, and a comma after it.

Answers may vary.

Example: He said he was hungry

He said he was hungry; however, we had no food to give him.

1. Annie was bogged down with homework _____

; therefore, she couldn't go to the party.

2. He was told to turn left at the gas station _____

; however, he turned right.

3. He received a scholarship _____

; furthermore, his name was in the school paper.

4. He had to get some rest _____

; otherwise, he would become jumpy and cranky.

5. They could find only red balloons _____

; *consequently, the decorations clashed with the tablecloths.*

6. Hand me my book _____

; *otherwise, I can't do my homework.*

7. There were five children in my family _____

; *therefore, I never felt lonely.*

8. The waiter was young _____

; *nevertheless, he served with polite efficiency.*

9. They did not lead an exciting life _____

; *thus, they did not attract friends.*

10. It occurred to him that he should join a church _____

; *however, he could not decide which church to choose.*

PRACTICING 3

Place semicolons where needed. Use commas after transitional words.

1. Poverty means being tired; moreover, it means being tired day after day.

2. Yesterday my battery went dead; consequently, I am walking to work today.

3. Educated people tend to be open-minded and curious; uneducated people tend to be closed-minded and set in their ways.

4. American families are dominated by television; it stunts our minds.

5. I like her a lot; however, I love you.

6. Betty loves her neighborhood; nevertheless, she wishes it were safer.

7. People who walk two miles every day feel better; they can also eat a dessert now and then.

8. Stand tall; be proud.

9. Large, leafy trees provide shade; they also need much water.

10. He was utterly generous; he gave money to everyone in town.

Colon (:)

The colon has several uses. One of the most common is to introduce a list. A colon so used always follows an independent clause.

> These are the people who will sit at the head table: the mayor, all City Council members, the trustees of the College, and the master of ceremonies.

If the list is not introduced by an independent clause, do not use a colon.

Incorrect:	The chief ingredients are: parsley, sage, rosemary and thyme.
Correct:	The chief ingredients are parsley, sage, rosemary and thyme.

PRACTICING 4

Mark each of the following sentences *C* for correct or *NC* for incorrect. Correct the errors by inserting a colon if it is missing or crossing it out if it is used incorrectly.

NC **1.** On my soccer team are: Mark, Billy, Theodore, and Juan.

C **2.** Flying a kite requires these elements: a kite, string, and a stiff breeze.

NC **3.** You are: a monster, a leech, and a worm.

C **4.** But you are many people to me: my lover, my confidante, my best friend.

NC **5.** These difficult words are: lie, lay, sit, set, rise, and raise.

C **6.** There are three kinds of people in this world: workers, dreamers and doers.

NC **7.** I need to find: a needle, a spool of thread, and a thimble.

NC **8.** For our camping trip, we took: a pup tent, two sleeping bags and a compass.

C **9.** I have accessorized my car with these items: a funny bumper sticker, a convex rearview mirror, and a psychedelic paint job.

NC **10.** She wore: a headband, cutoff jeans, and dirty tennis shoes.

Colon (:)

A colon can also be used to introduce a quotation, or further explanation.

Quotation:	This is what S. J. Lee had to say about heaven: "What a pity that the only way to heaven is in a hearse!"
Further explanation:	When police violate the law, they encourage contempt for the law: People simply will not obey laws that the people in authority do not obey.

If the material after the colon is a complete sentence, begin with a capital letter. If the material after the colon is not a complete sentence, do not use a capital, as in the following example.

Further explanation:	Soccer teaches players at least one useful skill: a sense of balance.

Use a colon after the salutation in a formal letter, to set off the subtitle of a book, between chapter and verse of the Bible, and to separate hours from minutes in time.

Here are some examples.

In a form letter:	Dear Mrs. Jones:
Title and subtitle:	The Mother Tongue: English and How It Got That Way
Chapter and verse of the Bible:	Proverbs 6:34
Hours from minutes:	5:30 P.M.

IN A NUTSHELL

- Use a colon after an independent clause to introduce material that follows, such as a list, a quotation, or a further explanation.
- If the material after the colon is a complete sentence, begin with a capital letter.
- Use a colon after the salutation in a formal letter, to set off the subtitle of a book, between chapter and verse of the Bible, and to separate hours from minutes in time.

PRACTICING 5

Add colons where they belong. Capitalize after the colon if necessary.

1. This is what John F. Kennedy said about poverty: "If a free society cannot help the many who are poor, it cannot save the few who are rich."

2. Here is the author's name: David Halberstam.

3. Today's typical home office contains several necessary machines: a computer, a duplicator, a fax , and a telephone.

4. Recently I read: *Have a Word on Me: A Celebration of Language.*

5. There is one positive result from having a migraine headache: the next day you feel better than ever.

6. It was 11:30 P.M. before I finally got to bed.

7. Dear Prof. Gonzalez:

8. There is one thing stronger than all the armies in the world: it is an idea whose time has come.

9. These are the items I would like you to bring to the picnic: ketchup, mustard, potato chips, hot dog buns, and pickles.

10. Who said the following: "Whoever named it necking was a poor judge of anatomy"?

11. Ever since elementary school, Marcie had dreamed of owning a particular kind of dog: a Dalmatian.

12. Don't forget the most important qualities: compassion, loyalty, and diligence.

13. I'll never forget her advice: "Paint as birds sing."

14. She said the quotation came from Psalms 23:6.

15. Fighting boredom is not easy: It requires patience, understanding, and endurance.

The Dash (--)

The dash—is often typed as two hyphens (--). It is spoken as a short pause, like a comma. A dash is used in writing to signal a sudden break in thought or to emphasize a side comment or an afterthought. Here are some examples:

Sudden break in thought:	He would like to be polite—just as we would—but he interrupts constantly.
	I spoke at length to the class—at least, it seemed long to me—but they listened attentively.
Side thought:	Democracy is based on sharing the good things in life—especially power.
	I would hate myself—and so should all children who have had good mothers—if I neglected my mother now that she is old.
Afterthought:	Stay away from Ben—unless you're looking for trouble.
	If you want to be imaginative, you have to be willing to tolerate criticism—even ridicule.

Don't overuse the dash, or your style will seem breathless.

IN A NUTSHELL

- Use the dash to emphasize a sudden break in thought or to add a side comment or afterthought.
- Do not overuse the dash.

PRACTICING 6

Use dashes to set off sudden breaks in thought, side thoughts, and afterthoughts in the sentences that follow:

1. You owe me $10.00. Oh, I'm sorry I thought you were someone else.

2. I asked her I begged her to pay the bills on time.

3. Do you blame others‾especially society‾for the way your marriage turned out?

4. I need a new computer‾or at least a few more chips for memory.

5. She's not my biological mother‾not that that makes any difference.

6. We rounded the curve‾a whole carload of us.

7. We would all sit in the living room‾Uncle Charlie, Auntie Mae, and Big Ned‾listening to the radio.

8. Bring me a needle and‾no, just sit down and read to me.

9. I can now see what he was trying to tell me‾that it would not be easy.

10. Looking at me or through me‾I couldn't exactly tell which‾he seemed like a ghost.

Quotation Marks (" ")

One of the two main written uses for quotation marks is to indicate a person's exact words—called a **direct quotation.**

Use quotation marks to indicate a person's exact words.

Direct quotations can be reported in a number of different ways, all requiring quotation marks.

> She said, "You know I love you."
>
> "You know I love you," she said.
>
> "You know," she said, "I love you."
>
> "You know I love you," she said. "I miss you."

Begin every quotation with a capital letter.
Do not, however, use a capital letter for the second part of a divided quotation that is *not* a full sentence.

> "I became a librarian," he explained, "because I love books."

Here the second part of the divided quotation is not a full sentence, so a comma is used after *explained*, but no capital letter.

> "Put the book on the table," the librarian said. "I'll shelve it later."

Here the second part of the divided quotation is a full sentence. A period follows *said* and a capital letter.

Do not use quotation marks in indirect quotations.

An indirect quotation—rewording what someone has said—does not require quotation marks. Often an indirect quotation word is announced by the word *that*. Here are some examples:

Direct quotation:	Jane said, "Dad will be down in ten minutes."
Indirect quotation:	Jane told us that Dad will be down in ten minutes.
Direct quotation:	Mom warned us, "Stay away from the poison ivy."
Indirect quotation:	Mom warned us to stay away from the poison ivy.

IN A NUTSHELL

- Use quotation marks to indicate a person's exact words.
- Begin every quotation with a capital letter.
- Do not use a capital letter for the second part of a divided quotation that is not a sentence.
- Do not use quotation marks in indirect quotations.

PRACTICING 7

Add the required quotation marks.

Example: "I'm calling you," said the salesman, "because you filled out our form."

1. "Try to look at it my way, through the corner of your eye," said Audrey.

2. "You know I love ice cream," said David. "Chocolate is my favorite."

3. "When have I ever asked you to make dinner?" she asked.

4. "Watch out," she murmured. "I'm going to tickle you."

5. Jenny asked, "Has the mailman arrived yet?"

6. "You can't remember the sermon," interrupted Mr. Smith, "because you were not in church when it was delivered."

7. "It's not a bad feeling to be kissed," she laughed. "It's actually a good feeling."

8. Letting his arms droop, he answered, "Oh, I'm just tired."

9. "If I don't get a bath soon," Agnes declared, "I'll start itching all over."

10. He said, "I like coming here because the place makes me happy."

PRACTICING 8

Place quotation marks only around the exact words of the speaker; leave the sentence unchanged if the quotation is indirect.

1. We asked ourselves, "How long will they be gone?"

2. Rachel asked him if he would return before sunset.

3. Aaron asked his mother if her boss had been rude again.

4. Marge promised that she would make a special effort to speak loudly enough for Grandma to hear.

5. "Tell us about the accident," we said.

6. She insisted that she didn't care a bit.

7. "Don't use that snippy tone with me," she warned.

8. "If you can't afford to travel, read books," he said.

9. "I've tried desperately to keep the truth from you," she cried.

10. She told him that the sunsets in Hawaii were spectacular.

PRACTICING 9

Change each of the following indirect quotations into a direct quotation in three ways: with the speaker indicated before the quoted words, after the quoted words, and interrupting the quoted words. Check your punctuation.

Example: He explained that Celia was his aunt and Stephen was his cousin.

He explained, "Celia is my aunt, and Stephen is my cousin."

"Celia is my aunt, and Stephen is my cousin," he explained.

"Celia is my aunt," he explained, "and Stephen is my cousin."

1. She explained that it was the funniest bumper sticker she'd ever seen.

She explained, "This is the funniest bumper sticker I have ever seen."

"This is the funniest bumper sticker I have ever seen," she explained.

"This is," she explained, "the funniest bumper sticker I have ever seen."

2. My landlady told us we'd have to move.

My landlady told us, "You will have to move."

"You will have to move," my landlady told us.

"You," my landlady told us, "will have to move.

3. He said that he hated Godzilla movies.

He said, "I hate Godzilla movies."

"I hate Godzilla movies," he said.

"I hate," he said, Godzilla movies.

4. My aunt said that she lost all her money in the Savings and Loans' crash.

My aunt said, "I lost all my money in the Savings and Loans' crash."

"I lost all my money in the Savings and Loans' crash," my aunt said.

"I lost all my money," said my aunt, "in the Savings and Loans' crash."

5. She told us bluntly that nothng we said or did would change her mind.

She told us bluntly, "Nothing you said or did will change my mind."

"Nothing you said or did will change my mind," she told us bluntly

"Nothing you said or did," she told us bluntly, "will change my mind.

Using other punctuation with quotation marks.

- Commas and periods always go inside quotation marks.

  He said, "I am not going."

  He said, "I am not going," and then added, "at least, not today."

ESL Advice!

If you learned English either in Britain or a British colony, you were taught an entirely different way of using quotation marks. In that case, you'll have to memorize the American rules.

- Question marks and exclamation points go either inside or outside, depending on the sentence.

  Inside: "Is he just making a wild guess?" Larry asked.

  Outside: Who just said, "He's making a wild guess"?

In the first example, the spoken words make up a separate question; in the second example, the spoken words are part of the question.

  "Watch out!" Karen cried.

  Karen, stop saying, "Watch out"!

In the first example, the spoken words make up a separate command; in the second, the spoken words are part of the command.

IN A NUTSHELL

- Always put periods and commas inside quotation marks.
- Question marks and exclamation points go either inside or outside quotation marks, depending on the sentence.

PRACTICING 10

The sentences that follow use other punctuation marks in connection with quotation marks. In the space provided, mark *C* if the sentence is correctly punctuated and *NC* if it is not. Correct the sentence if it is incorrectly punctuated.

Example: _NC_ "Are you happy"? she asked.

Correction: "Are you happy?" she asked.

1. _C_ The teacher said to Leo, "Explain your answer."

2. _NC_ Was it Snoopy who asked, "Do you like dogs"?"

3. _NC_ She screamed, "I love that story"!"

4. _NC_ Who said, "I think; therefore, I am?"?

5. _C_ "Get off my lawn!" she screamed.

6. _C_ What is the meaning of "Blessed are the poor"?

7. _NC_ Stop telling me to "shut up!"!

8. _C_ She loudly cried, "Give me some air, please!"

9. _C_ "No, never!" she insisted.

10. _C_ He asked, "Have you actually read that book?"

Use quotation marks to indicate titles of short works.

Use quotation marks to indicate the titles of short works, such as magazine articles and short stories. Underline (or italicize) the titles of long works.

SHORTER WORKS	LONGER WORKS
magazine article—"Easy Desserts"	magazine—<u>Healthy Eating</u>
newspaper article—"Hurry Up and Relax"	newspaper—<u>The Atlanta Journal</u>
song—"Summer Wind"	book—<u>David Copperfield</u>
poem—"Mary Had a Little Lamb"	poetry collection—<u>Leaves of Grass</u>
book chapter—"The Darkness Appears"	movie—<u>The Truman Show</u>
editorial—"Education at the Crossroads"	television show—<u>60 Minutes</u>

IN A NUTSHELL

- Use quotation marks to indicate the titles of short works.
- Underline (or italicize) the titles of longer works.

PRACTICING 11

Add quotation marks and underline as required.

Example: "Rules for Aging" is an essay that appears in an
anthology titled <u>Readings for Writers</u>.

1. Chapter 1 is titled "Mattie Michael."

2. My sister was going to read the book <u>The Littlest Angel</u>.

3. <u>Titanic</u> was a good movie.

4. One of my favorite songs is "Gimme Shelter" by the Rolling
Stones.

5. She searched through the book <u>Great Italian Recipes</u>.

6. <u>People</u> magazine is filled with juicy gossip.

7. The <u>San Francisco Chronicle</u> is a fine newspaper.

8. Did you see the movie <u>A Perfect Murder</u>?

9. The <u>Taming of the Shrew</u> is my favorite Shakespeare play.

10. My wife likes to watch reruns of <u>Seinfeld</u> on television.

Parentheses ( )

Use parentheses for side comments that illustrate a point or add information. They are also used to enclose numbers when you list items.

To illustrate a point:	Curiosity (the kind exemplified by Edison and Newton) is one mark of intelligence.
	My brother and his friend (the best man at his wedding, actually) were both rushed to the emergency ward.
To add information:	The Ritz-Carlton hotels train their managers in Total Quality Management (TQM).
	The average person (the so-called "reasonable man") used to be defined as male by the English language.
	Brad Anderson (b. 1924) is my favorite cartoonist.

| | The author explains precisely how the team works (see p. 53). | **(Place the period *after* the parentheses in references.)** |
| **With numbers:** | Here are the rules: (1) Keep your room clean, (2) be on time, and (3) don't complain about the food. | |

IN A NUTSHELL

- Use parentheses to add an illustration or side remark to a sentence.
- Use parentheses with numbers.

PRACTICING 12

Add parentheses where needed.

1. Edward M. Kennedy (b. 1932) is the only surviving brother of President John F. Kennedy.

2. Read the chapter on civil rights (pages 85–98).

3. The chapter on moving westward (pp. 25–36) will be on the test.

4. It was freezing weather (13 degrees Fahrenheit).

5. The National Endowment for the Arts (NEA) may have its budget severely slashed.

6. Make a list of goals and divide them into three categories: (1) immediate goals, (2) short term goals, and (3) long term goals.

7. Maya Angelou (b. 1928) writes about the black experience in America.

8. Define "cajole" and "ascendancy" (see paragraph 5).

9. There are five types of microorganisms: (1) bacteria, (2) algae, (3) fungi, (4) protozoa, and (5) viruses.

10. By noon, twelve of us sat there (the number required for jury)

Unit Test

Use what you learned in this unit to correctly punctuate the following passage.

Russell Baker (1925–present) began his career in journalism in 1947 as a staff member of the Baltimore Sun. Today, his newspaper articles have been collected in book form for two reasons: they are simple, and they reveal life as many of us have experienced it. The other day, I asked my classmate Deanna, "Do you ever read Russell Baker?" She answered, "Of course not. I hate reading in my spare time." I pointed out to her that she would enjoy Baker's essay entitled "Meaningful Relationships." I said, "It discusses the modern approach to love." "Are you crazy?" she asked me. "Why would I waste my time reading about love when I can see a movie about love?" "Look, I replied, "Reading is good for you." I left the room thinking to myself, "What a superficial person you are. You probably don't even read the Baltimore Sun, your local newspaper."

Unit Talk-Write Assignment

For this assignment, you are a fly on the wall listening to a conversation between two students about their older relatives. Your job is to correct each sentence by putting in the appropriate punctuation marks that can't be heard, all of which have been covered in this chapter. Be sure to insert quotation marks and to put other marks where they belong in the quotation. Some sentences may be punctuated more than one way.

Answers may vary.

TALK

1. I have a special aunt Jimmy said who is something of an artist she does macramé

2. Roberta replied and I have a special uncle who is missing a leg however that doesn't stop him from being a blue water sailor

WRITE

1. *"I have a special aunt," Jimmy said, "who is something of an artist: she does macramé."*

2. *Roberta replied, "And I have a special uncle who is missing a leg; however, that doesn't stop him from being a blue water sailor."*

TALK

3. My aunt is crotchety she's 87 but strong furthermore she still keeps a sense of humor and often likes to tell off color jokes Jimmy added

4. This is amazing gushed Roberta my uncle is much the same way he was in the war which war I don't know but he didn't like it much too noisy dirty disorganized and regimented he said

5. My aunt's macramé is much in demand said Jimmy for all the work she does on her pieces it takes her nearly a week to finish one she sells them for very little

6. My uncle has no hobby like that said Roberta he just likes to talk a lot about the good old days otherwise he's likely to be found on the lake he goes there a lot sailing by himself. He says sailing is a good hobby it has action danger the outdoors and the feeling of the wind in his hair

WRITE

3. "My aunt is crotchety: she's 87 but strong; furthermore, she still keeps a sense of humor and often likes to tell off-color jokes," Jimmy added.

4. "This is amazing," gushed Roberta. "My uncle is much the same way. He was in the war—which war I don't know, but he didn't like it much—too noisy, dirty, disorganized, and regimented, he said."

5. "My aunt's macramé is much in demand," said Jimmy. "For all the work she does on her pieces, it takes her nearly a week to finish one; she sells them for very little."

6. "My uncle has no hobby like that," said Roberta. "He just likes to talk a lot about the good old days; otherwise, he's likely to be found on the lake; he goes there a lot, sailing by himself. He says sailing is a good hobby—it has action, danger, the outdoors, and the feeling of the wind in his hair."

TALK

WRITE

7. You wouldn't catch my aunt dead on the lake said Jimmy she's afraid of the water she won't even take baths, only showers

7. *"You wouldn't catch my aunt dead on the lake," said Jimmy. "She's afraid of the water; she won't even take baths, only showers."*

8. Jimmy then went on to talk about the special things he loves in his aunt her sharp tongue her individuality her strong will she's afraid of nothing he added but water

8. *Jimmy then went on to talk about the special things he loves in his aunt: her sharp tongue, her individuality, and her strong will. "She's afraid of nothing," he added, "but water."*

9. Roberta added some of her uncle's traits 1 his sense of adventure 2 his eagerness to learn and 3 his willingness to take risk even at his age she told the story of the time her uncle capsized his sailboat on the lake, and when the lake police tried to help, he asked them don't you have anything better to do

9. *Roberta added some of her uncle's traits: (1) his sense of adventure, (2) his eagerness to learn, and (3) his willingness to take risks even at his age. She told the story of the time her uncle capsized his sailboat on the lake, and when the lake police tried to help, he asked them, "Don't you have anything better to do?"*

10. Jimmy sighed I'm going to miss my aunt when I move on to four-year college she'll be too far away for a drop-in visit

10. *Jimmy sighed, "I'm going to miss my aunt when I move on to a four-year college; she'll be too far away for a drop-in visit."*

11. Gosh my uncle already lives far away from me he's in the next state and I hardly ever see him replied Roberta

11. *"Gosh, my uncle already lives far away from me. He's in the next state and I hardly ever see him," replied Roberta.*

TALK

12. My aunt is a special person in my life remarked Jimmy I hope she lives long enough for my own kids if I have any to get to know her

WRITE

12. *"My aunt is a very special person in my life,"* *remarked Jimmy. "I hope she lives long enough for* *my own kids—if I have any—to get to know her."*

_____

_____

_____

Unit Collaborative Assignment

A. Choose a partner to whom you dictate the following sentences. See if your partner can write them down with the correct punctuation.

1. "Whose book is this?" she asked Tom.

2. Ten years ago we heard, "Learn word processing." Now we hear, "Get on the Internet."

3. "You backed into my car!" she cried.

4. Did you see the movie Face Off?

5. The title of the poem is, "How Tall Is the Mountain?"

B. Reversing the process, have your partner dictate the following sentences to you. Write them down with correct punctuation.

1. I did a report on the book <u>Cold Mountain</u>.

2. We knew who he meant when he said, "She's gone."

3. The title of the essay is "I Want a Wife."

4. "What is her real name?" he muttered to himself.

5. Who said, "Give me liberty or give me death"?

Unit Writing Assignment

Imagine that you are disturbed about a critical remark someone made about your best friend. Recreate the incident, and include an imaginary conversation between you and your friend's critic. The point is to punctuate correctly. Be especially careful to use quotation marks where they belong. Use the Revising Checklist to revise.

Photo Writing Assignment

The following photo shows someone reading intently. Write a paragraph about the importance of books or the importance of reading. Or, if you have read a good book lately, write about it. When you have finished writing, get together with a classmate and check each other's punctuation. Use the Revising Checklist to revise.

21

Capitalization

"Jimmy, will you please jimmy
open the door?"

Because uppercase (capital) and lowercase letters sound the same, your ear cannot help you with capitalization: *Jimmy,* the name, sounds the same as *jimmy,* the verb (which means to force open). To capitalize correctly, you must know the following rules:

- Capitalize the first word in a sentence or direct quotation.

- Capitalize after a colon if what follows is a full sentence.

- Capitalize names of individual persons and the word *I.*

- Capitalize family relationships used as names.

- Capitalize the names of nationalities, religions, races, tribes, and languages.

- Capitalize the names of companies, clubs, political groups, and other official organizations.

- Capitalize names of commercial products.

- Capitalize the names of specific places, including monuments.

- Capitalize areas of the country.

- Capitalize abbreviations of familiar organizations, corporations, people, countries, time, and titles.

- Capitalize the names of the days of the week, months, holidays, and religious occassions.

- Capitalize historical eras and events.

- Capitalize titles of books, magazines, essays, poems, stories, plays, articles, films, television shows, songs, and cartoons.
- Capitalize titles used in front of a person's name.
- Capitalize specific college courses.
- Capitalize the opening and the first word of the closing of a letter.

We will discuss each rule of capitalization separately.

Capitalize the first word in a sentence or direct quotation.

Jimmy was 17 years old.

He said, "My dad's the greatest."

"They realized," she admitted, "that they were wrong."

Notice that in the third example, *They* is capitalized because it begins a new sentence; however, *that* remains lowercase because it is part of the first sentence.

PRACTICING 1

Correctly capitalize the following sentences.

1. He set several goals. first, he would get his degree. then he would buy a new car.

2. "Perhaps," she suggested, "your father could help you. he has money."

3. He scoffed, "my dear fellow, you must have been living on the moon."

4. an open mind can lead to indecision. it can be worse than a closed mind.

5. Get out of my way! don't just stand there!

Capitalize after a colon if what follows is a full sentence.

These are the words he spoke: "We must love our country."

but

These are the items we need: a wheelbarrow, a shovel, and a large sack.

(*Note:* See also Unit 20, pages 383.)

PRACTICING 2

Correctly capitalize the following sentences. Cross out any unnecessary capitals and replace them with lower case letters.

Example: Dear Sir: ~~w~~We have never met, but I am interested in your product.

1. Do the following: ~~g~~Get some ice, set out some glasses, and pour some lemonade.

2. Listen to me carefully: ~~d~~Don't swim immediately after eating.

3. He has many talents: playing the accordion, tap dancing, and singing the blues.

4. This is the program for today: ~~w~~We take out the garbage and clean up the cabins.

5. To become a freelance writer, here is what ou need: talent, an agent, and luck.

Capitalize names of individuals and the word I.

It was Mary, not Miss Muffet, who had a little lamb.

The name of my sociology teacher is Mathilde Johnson.

Nicknames are also capitalized:

He was known in the neighborhood as Big Thumb Bob.

PRACTICING 3

Capitalize the names of individuals in the following sentences.

1. Even foreigners are familiar with the name ^G̲george ^W̲washington.

2. Because of his large size, his own mother called him ^J̲jumbo.

3. Henry ^H̲hadley, ^M̲marguerite ^W̲woolley, and ^I̲isabelle ^L̲lopez gave speeches in favor of recycling cans.

4. George ^H̲herman ^R̲ruth was ^B̲babe ^R̲ruth's real name.

5. All of a sudden, ^B̲billy kissed ^E̲erika. I know because ^I̲i saw him.

Capitalize family relationships used as names.

I'm glad that Uncle Bryan is happily married.

Every Saturday I take a box of cookies to Grandmother Trudy.

Don't make so much noise, or you'll wake up Mother.

However, do not capitalize *mother, father, grandmother, grandfather, uncle, aunt, cousin,* and so forth when these terms are preceded by *my, your, our,* or any other possessive word.

Hand Grandpa his walking stick.

Hand your grandpa his walking stick.

IN A NUTSHELL

- Capitalize the first word in a sentence or direct quotation.

- Capitalize after a colon if what follows is a full sentence.

- Capitalize names of individual persons and the word *I*.

- Capitalize family relationships used as names.

PRACTICING 4

Write *C* in the blank if the sentence is correct. Capitalize the other sentences correctly.

1. _____ My Ďad is a completely self-made man.

2. _____ He looked at Åunt Martha's purse and wondered what was in it.

3. __*C*__ My grandmother came over from Ireland in 1920.

4. __*C*__ My cousin Gerty never speaks to my cousin Bob.

5. _____ Please give Ṁother my love and tell her to quit working so hard.

Capitalize the names of nationalities, religions, races, tribes, and languages.

The nationalities of my three best friends are Korean, Armenian, and Brazilian.

He is Roman Catholic, and she is Buddhist.

Carolyn Mazloomi is a famous African-American artist.

The patterns in Navajo rugs have specific meanings.

Which language sounds more beautiful to you—Italian or French?

PRACTICING 5

Fill in the blanks as indicated.   Answers will vary.

Example: In high school, I took (language) <u>Spanish</u>.

1. My neighbors are (nationality) _____.

2. I was brought up in the (religion) _____ faith.

3. I can't imagine ever learning (language) _____.

4. Occasionally, a questionnaire will ask me my race. I am (race) _____.

5. The (nationalities) _____, _____, and _____ create a melting pot in many large cities.

Capitalize the names of companies, clubs, political groups, and other official organizations.

I prefer to buy gas from Union Oil.

The May Company has huge sales every year.

My father's family has always belonged to the Democratic Party.

My parents encouraged me to join the Girl Scouts.

"Olé" is the name of our Spanish Club.

My car is insured with Allegiance Insurance company, and my medical plan is with Kaiser.

PRACTICING 6

Capitalize as necessary in the following sentences.

1. My mother wants me to pledge *A*lpha *S*igma, a sorority that stresses grades.

2. The advantage of working for a company like *L*incoln *S*avings is that you get benefits.

3. My parents' building is controlled by the *L*os *F*eliz *T*owers *H*omeowners *A*ssociation.

4. Sometimes extreme *D*emocrats are the same as extreme *R*epublicans.

5. My history professor has decided to run for the *N*ew *Y*ork *S*tate *A*ssembly.

Capitalize the names of commercial products.

Why not buy Dove soap? It is as good as more expensive soaps.

Do not capitalize types of products.

A good breakfast consists of oatmeal, fruit, and skim milk.	**(These are merely types of products, not brand names.)**

but

Quaker Oats cereal is low in fat.

(Quaker Oats is a brand name, but cereal is a type of food.)

PRACTICING 7

Capitalize the names of commercial products in the following sentences.

1. I love ^R reese's candy because the peanut butter and chocolate combination is delicious.

2. If I have to have breakfast, then give me ^J jimmy ^D dean sausages and eggs.

3. Dandruff is helped by ^H head and ^S shoulders shampoo.

4. In the 1940s, ^F fords and ^C chevrolets were the most popular cars.

5. On a hot day, nothing tastes better than ^C carnation strawberry ice cream.

Capitalize the names of specific places, including monuments.

It was a small town in the Imperial Valley called El Centro.

Let's visit the Grand Canyon and Yellowstone National Park.

The Taj Majal is one of the world's great wonders.

I attend Glendale Community College, which has about 15,000 students.

Just walk straight down Broadway; then turn right on Monroe Boulevard, and look for Virgil's Hardware Store.

Do not capitalize the names of places that are not specific:

He walked down the street toward the hardware store.

but

He walked down Elm Street toward Ace Hardware.

- Capitalize the names of nationalities, religions, races, tribes, and languages.

- Capitalize the names of companies, clubs, political groups, and other official organizations.

- Capitalize names of commercial products.

- Capitalize the names of specific places, including monuments.

PRACTICING 8

Correct the capitalization errors in the following sentences.

Examples: I love Murietta because it's such a sleepy little town.

            M

            I love murietta because it's such a sleepy little town.

1. The capital of Jamaica is Kingston.

2. Keeping Grant's Tomb beautiful is not as easy as it seems.

3. A millionaire once wanted to buy the famous Rock of Gibraltar.

4. President Kennedy was killed by a sniper in Dallas, Texas.

5. Once I had a job as a busboy at the Hilton Hotel in New York.

Capitalize areas of the country.

When we lived in the South, I spoke with a drawl.

The Southwest has become a popular source of interior decor and food.

They moved to the East Coast.

Do not capitalize compass directions or areas of the country used as adjectives.

Drive south on Hill Street until it crosses Allen Drive, and then turn west on Allen.

She has a southern drawl.

We like southwestern food.

PRACTICING 9

In the blank provided, fill in an area of the country or a compass direction. Capitalize correctly.

Example: My favorite poet lives in the <u>South</u>. (or Midwest, or East, etc.)

1. To the _____ of us were three steep, muddy hills.

2. Our wagons crept along slowly, always moving toward the

_____.

3. In December we moved to _____.

4. I'd like to live in the _____.

5. Head _____ on Maple, then _____ on Elm

Road.

Answers will vary, but capitalization should be consistent, as follows:
1. no cap
2. cap
3. cap
4. cap (e.g., the Rockies) or no cap (e.g., the desert)
5. no caps

Capitalize abbreviations of familiar organizations, corporations, people, countries, time, and titles.

Organization: CIA, FBI, IRS

Corporation: IBM, NBC, ITT

People: JFK, FDR, LBJ

Countries: USA, UK (United Kingdom)

Time: 10:00 A.M., 1:15 P.M.

Titles: Milton Freedman, Sr.,
Jean Smith, M.D.,
Ana Chang, D.D.S.,
Pasqual Mancina, Ph.D.

PRACTICING 10

Complete the following sentences with an appropriate abbreviation.

1. President John F. Kennedy was called _____JFK_____.

2. Under Stalin, Russia was part of the _____USSR_____.

3. The Young Women's Christian Association is referred to as

the _____YWCA_____.

4. If you're a dentist, you will place _____*D.D.S.*_____ after your name.

5. An intelligence quotient is also called _____*IQ*_____.

Capitalize the days of the week, months, holidays, and religious occasions.

My birthday falls on Tuesday this year.

The best time to see the fall colors is in October or November.

Have you picked out your Halloween costume yet?

We celebrate both Christmas and Hanukkah.

The seasons of the year, however, are not capitalized.

I'm always joyful in the spring.

PRACTICING 11

In the space provided, mark *C* if the sentence is properly capitalized and *NC* if it is not. Then correctly capitalize the sentence.

1. __*NC*__ The $\overset{A}{\text{african-}}\overset{A}{\text{american}}$ holiday $\overset{K}{\text{kwanza}}$ is celebrated from $\overset{D}{\text{december}}$ 26 to $\overset{J}{\text{january}}$ 1.

2. __*NC*__ I get confused because $\overset{F}{\text{february}}$ has only 28 days except for $\overset{L}{\text{leap}}$ $\overset{Y}{\text{year}}$.

3. __*NC*__ Monday, $\overset{W}{\text{wednesday}}$, and $\overset{F}{\text{friday}}$ I have a body-building class.

4. __*C*__ Do we get the day off on Veteran's Day?

5. __*NC*__ I gain three pounds every $\overset{E}{\text{easter}}$.

Capitalize historical eras and events.

During the Middle Ages, women were adored but given no legal power.

The Modern Age has given us some great jazz musicians.

The Depression of the 1930s left my grandparents poor.

No one wants to have World War III.

The Battle of Little Big Horn was an important event in history.

IN A NUTSHELL

- Capitalize areas of the country.
- Capitalize abbreviations of familiar organizations, corporations, people, countries, time, and titles.
- Capitalize the days of the week, months, holidays, and religious occassions.
- Capitalize historical eras and events.

PRACTICING 12

Correctly capitalize the following sentences.

1. My personal favorites are poets from the ^Rromantic ^Aage.

2. Would you have been happy as a woman in the ^Vvictorian Age?

3. The Battle of Fort Sumter officially began the ^Ccivil ^Wwar.

4. Many famous movies have been made about ^Wworld ^Wwar II.

5. The ^Ssixties were a crazy time.

Capitalize titles of books, magazines, essays, poems, stories, plays, articles, films, television shows, songs, and cartoons.

Book:	I enjoyed *Tom Sawyer* by Mark Twain.
Magazine:	I always read *Time* magazine.
Essay:	My essay is entitled "Women in Politics: Onward and Upward."
Poem:	The poem "The Waltzer in the House" is about a mouse.
Story:	"Flowering Judas" is Katherine Anne Porter's best short story.

Play:	He was very good in *Death of a Salesman*.
Article:	I read an article entitled "Coming to Grips with Kingston."
Film:	Each year the film version of *Gone with the Wind* is shown without losing its popularity.
Television show:	We always watch *Law and Order* on Mondays.
Song:	I love the way Nat King Cole sings "Mona Lisa."
Cartoon:	People complain that "Peanuts" has gotten stale.

(For more on the use of italics and quotation marks in titles, see Unit 20, p. 385.)

Notice how words are capitalized in titles. The beginning word is always capitalized. The first word after a colon is also always capitalized. Certain words are not capitalized, however, unless they come at the beginning.

Do not capitalize:

■ The article *a, an,* or *the* unless it is the first word

■ The coordinating conjunctions *and, but, yet, or, nor, so, for*

■ Short prepositions such as *of, from, by, in, up,* or *out.*

Capitalize, however, prepositions of five or more letters, such as *about, among, between, behind, through, though,* and *without.*

PRACTICING 13

In the following sentences, capitalize all words that should be capitalized, and change any incorrect capitals to lower case.

Example: I wish that cartoon "Calvin *And* Hobbes" appeared in [*and*] the *New York times* but that newspaper doesn't publish any comic strips. [*Times*]

1. On the back page of today's newspaper was a mysterious

article, titled "A Car Is born—again." [*B*] [*A*]

2. My sister wrote a song about rock climbing—"Take Me

With You Up To The Top." [*w*] [*u*] [*t*] [*t*]

3. You can learn much about nature by watching ^t The ^D discovery ^C channel on television.

4. KCBS is showing a television special—"Travels ^w With Chuck Henry."

5. In the eleventh grade, we were asked to write a report on Hemingway's *For whom ^t The ^B bell Tolls*.

Capitalize titles used in front of a person's name.

President Abraham Lincoln, Mayor Cheryl Dixon, Senator Dianne Feinstein, General Colin Powell

Mrs. Milford, Mr. Franklin, Ms. Hightower, Dr. Dorsey

but

Abraham Licoln, the sixteenth president of the United States; Cheryl Dixon, mayor of Cedartown; Dianne Feinstein, senator from California; and Colin Powell, retired general

PRACTICING 14

In the blank in front of each sentence, mark *C* if the sentence is correct and *NC* if it is incorrect. Correct by writing above the word.

1. __C__ President Lincoln was called "Honest Abe."

2. __NC__ Pass the message to Mr. Brown and ^M miss Hurst.

3. __C__ I wish that a strong woman would become governor of our state.

4. __C__ I greatly admire Vice-President Al Gore.

5. __NC__ Perhaps ^A assemblywoman Waters would give the speech.

Capitalize specific college courses.

I'm hoping for a passing grade in Calculus 101.

but

Most freshmen find calculus a difficult subject.

The Introduction to Marine Biology course includes a field trip to Baja.

but

Courses in marine biology are popular today.

Language courses are always capitalized.

I'm taking Spanish C22.

I'm taking Spanish again this year.

PRACTICING 15

Capitalize the names of specific college courses.

1. If I fail ~~e~~*E*conomics 103, I cannot graduate next June.

2. Charles loves ~~a~~*A*stronomy, but he hates the night labs.

3. He is majoring in ~~e~~*E*nglish.

4. I am taking geography, ~~r~~*R*ussian, and theater.

5. Professor Jenkins teaches a humanities course called ~~t~~*T*he ~~h~~*H*uman ~~s~~*S*truggle C421.

Capitalize the first word of the opening and the closing of a letter.

Dear Sir,

My dear Lily,

Dear Dr. Lopez,

Sincerely,

Sincerely yours,

Best regards,

Love and kisses,

PRACTICING 16

Write a brief letter to an imaginary bank, reporting that someone is using your credit card without permission. Capitalize correctly the opening and closing and the sentences in the body of the letter.

Letters will vary.

_____

_____

_____

_____

_____

_____

_____

_____

_____

_____

_____

_____

_____

_____

_____

_____

_____

_____

_____

_____

_____

IN A NUTSHELL

- Capitalize titles of books, magazines, essays, poems, stories, plays, articles, films, television shows, songs, and cartoons.
- Capitalize titles used in front of a person's name.
- Capitalize specific college courses.
- Capitalize the first word of the opening and the closing of a letter.

☑ Unit Test

Correct all the capitalization errors in the following paragraph.

I want to say something about glenacre, my home town. picture in your mind a middle-class neighborhood in california, nestled against the san rafael mountains. my parents moved here on a bright monday in may. i was ten years old and happy as a clam to be out of new york. from our house malibu beach is one hour west; mt. baldy is one hour east; beverly hills is one hour north.

glenacre is an international neighborhood, filled with armenians, iranians, vietnamese, koreans, and hispanics. The most famous monument, standing in a bank patio, is a bronze statue entitled "wild horses." the u.s. post office is always crowded with people standing in line to buy stamps or pick up packages because we are a town of people with relatives living elsewhere.

In an election year, the republican candidate always gets more support than the democratic one. I suppose this is because we are conservative property boosters who value private enterprise. a handful of people run the city—from the city council to the chamber of commerce. they all know each other and get reelected when it's time to choose the local politicians.

^Wwe have an old movie theater, called "^Tthe ^Ccapitol," that features classics like ^Ccasablanca and ^Iit ^Hhappened ^Oone ^Nnight. ^Yyou might say that my town is old-fashioned and out-of-step with modern ways. ^Wwell, maybe so, but I'm happy here. ^Aas my mother said just the other day, "^Iit's a safe place to bring up a family."

Unit Talk-Write Assignment

When students were asked, "What has the computer contributed to society?" most spoke glowingly about the magic of word processing, doing research through the Internet, and communicating by e-mail. But one student worried that computers were causing a generation gap. His ideas, are expressed in the *Talk* column. Rewrite his comments in the blanks provided in the *Write* column. Be sure to capitalize correctly throughout. Then write a short paragraph agreeing or disagreeing with this student's ideas.

Answers will vary.

TALK

Sorry, guys, but I see a black cloud on the horizon. Hey, sure computers are awesome for us, but what about for mom, dad, grandma, and grandpa? You can bet that I don't want to go back to typewriters, library shelves, and letters sent only through post offices. I'm with you when you rave about how it is to order paperbacks through Amazon.com and how much time is saved by surfing the internet for sources on your History or Psychology paper. But do your parents or, for that matter, your grandparents know how to use a computer? Here's my point: I'd hate to see technology divide young from old. We're not talking about the problem like at the early part of the last Century when some women could drive while others couldn't. That's peanuts compared to the rift computers are causing. My mom can't even use the ATM. Her sis, aunt Birdie, sits at the computer and practically has the shakes from being so nervous. One of our elderly neighbors, dr. Manley, sees the computer as satan trying to destroy the world—or something. My point is that some older people are unbelievably

WRITE

I'm sorry, but I see a black cloud on the horizon. Of course computers are awesome for us, but what about for Mom, Dad, Grandma, and Grandpa? You can bet that I don't want to go back to typewriters, library shelves, and letters sent only through post offices. I agree with you when you say how wonderful it is to order paperbacks through Amazon.com and how much time is saved by surfing the Internet for sources on your history or psychology paper. But do your parents, or, for that matter, your grandparents know how to use a computer? I'd hate to see technology divide young from old. This problem is different from the one at the early part of the century when some women could drive while others couldn't. That is trivial compared to the rift computers are causing. My mom can't even use the ATM. Her sister, Aunt Birdie, sits

TALK

threatened by computers. Not all of them sit right down, learn it, and then go on their merry way to use the software quicken for paying bills, excel for keeping track of business, and the latest microsoft word version for writing things. All kinds of things have come between people—religion, politics, race. The computer is doing the same. It's making a society of knows and know-nots. What needs to happen is that the older generation needs to be talked into learning how to use computers. Once they have, there'll be no stopping them. They'll see how hot it is.

WRITE

at the computer and shakes from being so nervous. One of our elderly neighbors, Dr. Manley, sees the computer as Satan trying to destroy the world. Some older people are very threatened by computers. Not all of them sit right down, learn it, and then go on easily to use the software Quicken for paying bills, Excel for keeping track of business, and the latest Microsoft Word version for writing. All kinds of issues have come between people—religion, politics, race. The computer is doing the same. It's making a society of Knows and Know-Nots. The solution is that the older generation needs to be talked into learning how to use computers. Once they have, nothing will stop them. They'll see how valuable it is.

Unit Collaborative Assignment

A. Dictate the following sentences to a partner. Then check to see if there are any capitalization errors.

1. I always wished I could meet Jerry Lewis in person.

2. Yesterday I read a newspaper article entitled, "Be Kind to Your Neighbor."

3. My maternal grandparents are Baptists, but my mother converted to Islam when she married Dad.

4. My gas credit card is with Wells Fargo Bank.

5. When it's cold, I love to sit and sip Hershey's hot cocoa.

6. My favorite junk food is Coke and Twinkies.

7. Photographers love Rainbow Ridge in Arizona.

8. The second Sunday in May is important because it is Mother's Day.

9. Dear Mr. Nolan: Thank you for your order. Sincerely yours, Janet Johnson

10. Jerry failed geography but did very well in Spanish.

B. Now, turn the tables and have your partner dictate the following sentences to you. Try to avoid any capitalization errors.

1. Why would anyone send greeting cards for Groundhog Day?

2. My family is taking a trip to Montana, where we plan to visit Glacier Park.

3. Dear Mrs. Grant, Please excuse Jeffrey from gym class. Yours truly, Frank Alpert.

4. Sometimes I have nothing but a can of Campbell's soup for dinner.

5. My sister gave me her old Honda as a birthday gift.

6. We hiked through the Blue Ridge Mountains.

7. My grandmothers tells us stories about the Roaring Twenties.

8. If you're in business, it is important to join the Rotary Club.

9. I love my Angora cat.

10. Promise that you will not tell Grandpa George.

Unit Writing Assignment

Write a paragraph describing where you went on your last vacation or on a school outing. Describe what you saw and how the experience affected you. Be sure to capitalize correctly.

Photo Writing Assignment

After looking at the following photo of a national landmark, write a paragraph describing any national landmark you have seen pictured or personally visited. State the location of the landmark, and tell something of its history, mentioning, for example, individuals involved in discovering or designing the site. Be sure to use the proper capitalization. Use the Revising Checklist to revise.

22

How to Use
the Dictionary

dic•tion•ar•y (dik′ shän er′ ë), n., pl. –aries. 1. a book containing a selection
of the words of the language, usually arranged alphabetically, giving
information about their meanings, pronunciations, and origins.

The modern dictionary is a useful tool for the writer. It tells not only what words mean, but how they are used, spelled, hyphenated, pronounced, and often how they came into being. For anyone who writes in standard English, the dictionary is a vital tool.

Among the good desk dictionaries are the following:

American Heritage Dictionary

The Random House Dictionary of the English Language

The Random House Unabridged Dictionary: Print and Electronic Versions

New Webster's Dictionary

The New International Webster's Dictionary of the English Language: Encyclopedic Edition

Most good dictionaries give more or less the same kind of information about words. Typically, this information includes the following:

- Spelling
- Word division
- Pronunciation

- Grammatical uses

- Meanings

- Usage labels

- Origin

- Synonyms

Here is a sample dictionary entry from the *American Heritage Dictionary* (Houghton-Mifflin Company):

> **sand•wich (san'wich) n.** 1. Two or more slices of bread with meat, cheese, or other filling placed between them. 2. An arrangement resembling an edible sandwich; for example, two slabs of one material holding a slab of different material between them, as in certain electronic devices. **tr v.** *sandwiched, wiching, wiches.* 1. To insert tightly between two things. 2. To place in tight, alternating layers. 3. To fit between two other things that allow little time: *sandwich a meeting between two others.* [After the Fourth Earl of Sandwich (1718–92), for whom sandwiches were made so that he could stay at the gambling table without interruptions for meals.]

Spelling

A prime function of the dictionary is to tell us how a word is spelled. If there is more than one acceptable spelling, the preferred spelling is given first. Next comes the plural spelling of irregular nouns and verbs. If the noun or verb is regular, no spelling is given. Because *sandwich* has a regular plural—*sandwiches*—it isn't spelled. On the other hand, if you look up the word *goose*, you will find that the plural—*geese*—is given because it is irregular. If a verb is irregular, the dictionary will also list its principal parts. For instance, our dictionary lists the principal parts of the irregular verb *to go* as follows: present participle, *going*; simple past, *went*; past participle, *gone*.

If you do not know how to spell a word, pronounce it slowly, even in several ways, and then look them all up. Chances are that one will be right. If you are a really bad speller, you might check *The Bad Speller's Dictionary,* published by Random House, whose entries are organized to help the bad spellers find words they can pronounce but can't spell.

PRACTICING 1

The words listed are spelled incorrectly. Pronounce them first and then look up each word in the dictionary. Write the correct spelling in the blanks provided.

1. accidently   *accidentally*

2. potatos   *potatoes*

3. Febuary   *February*

4. labratory   *laboratory*

5. lightening   *lightning*

6. disasterous   *disastrous*

7. heighth   *height*

8. mischeivous   *mischievous*

9. goverment   *government*

10. sophmore   *sophomore*

Word Division

A good dictionary will show how a word is divided into syllables. The end of each syllable is marked by a dot (•). Look again at the word *sandwich.* It has two syllables, **sand•wich**. The word *preparation*, on the other hand, has four: **prep•a•ra•tion**.

Knowing how a word is divided helps you to pronounce it correctly and tells you how to break it at the end of a line. You may break any word by inserting a hyphen at the end of a convenient syllable.

sand-wich

not

sa-ndwich

prepara-tion or prep-aration or prepa-ration

not

pre-paration

If you must break a word that won't fit at the end of a line and don't know where to put the hyphen, check your dictionary.

PRACTICING 2

Draw a vertical line between the syllables of the words listed below.

Example: sau/sage

1. decent   *de/cent*

2. brutality   *bru/tal/i/ty*

3. anatomy   *an/at/o/my*

4. calculate   *cal/cu/late*

5. controversial   *con/tro/ver/si/al*

6. foliage   *fo/li/age*

7. glimmer   *glim/mer*

8. gunfight   *gun/fight*

9. likelihood   *like/li/hood*

10. penalty   *pen/al/ty*

Pronunciation

Another basic function of the dictionary is to give the pronunciation of words. Pronunciation is given in parentheses after the listing of the word. For example, the dictionary tells us that *sandwich* is pronounced this way:

san' wich   **(the *d* is silent)**

Pediatrician is pronounced this way:

pe' de æ trish' an

Two recurring sounds in English are the æ combination and the *schwa*, an upside down *e*. The combined æ sound is what we find in words like P*a*t, fl*a*t, and s*a*ck. The *schwa* is the unaccented sound in words like *a*bout, gall*u*p, and circ*u*s. You will find these symbols on many pages of your dictionary.

PRACTICING 3

Copy the pronunciation information given in your dictionary for the following words. Then pronounce the words out loud.

See dictionary for pronunciation symbols/spellings.

1. mahogany _____

2. telegraph _____

3. commentary _____

4. realtor _____

5. spaghetti _____

6. voluntary _____

7. lieutenant _____

8. silicone _____

9. pachyderm _____

10. realization _____

Grammatical Uses

Dictionaries also list the various grammatical uses of a word. Our example lists *sandwich* as a noun (*n.*) and a transitive verb—a verb requiring an object (*tr. v.*). Here are the grammatical labels commonly used:

adj.	adjective
adv.	adverb
conj.	conjunction
interj.	interjection
intr. v.	intransitive verb
n.	noun
pl.	plural
prep.	preposition
pron.	pronoun
sing.	singular
tr. v.	transitive verb
v.	verb

PRACTICING 4

Consult your dictionary and list the various grammatical uses for the following words. Then use each word correctly in a sentence.

Example: quake   <u>intransitive verb, noun</u>

<u>Louis quakes every time he speaks in public.</u>

1. quarrel _____

noun, intransitive verb—I never <u>quarrel</u> with my father.

2. skid _____

noun, intransitive verb—The car went into a frightening <u>skid</u>.

3. talkative _____

adjective—I like <u>talkative</u> people.

4. for _____

preposition, coordinating conjunction—The gift was <u>for</u> my sister.

5. inmate _____

noun —She was an <u>inmate</u> at a mental hospital.

6. nest _____

noun—He climbed into the tree to get a better look at the <u>nest</u>.

7. record _____

noun, intransitive verb—The ticket went on his driving <u>record</u>.

8. tonight _____

adverb, noun—<u>Tonight</u> will be the ideal time to see her.

9. tomato _____

noun—The <u>tomato</u> was red and juicy

10. too _____

adverb—While he was growing up, his mother gave him <u>too</u> much money.

Meanings

A chief function of the dictionary is to define words. If a word has more than one meaning—many do—each meaning is numbered and listed, starting with the most common.

The most common meaning of our example, *sandwich*, is *two or more slices of bread with meat, cheese, or other filling placed between them.* Another meaning is *an arrangement resembling an edible sandwich.* For example, one of the last steps in making a quilt is to make a sandwich (that is the term quiltmakers use) by putting cotton batting between the finished quilt top and the fabric that will be the quilt bottom; now the quilt is ready to be sewn together. A third meaning is *to fit tightly between two things.* Thus, a car between two trucks on the highway may be said to be *sandwiched* between them.

The primary meaning of *cricket* is *an insect*; a secondary one is *a low wooden footstool*; and a third is *a game played with a ball and a bat.*

PRACTICING 5

Look up in your dictionary the primary and secondary meanings of the words listed below. Give only the meanings for the part of speech listed, not all the meanings for the word.

Dictionaries will vary.

Example: fleece, n.

Answer: 1. the coat of wool covering a sheep, 2. any of various soft or woolly coverings.

1. grade, v.t.

(1) to arrange in grades; sort, (2) to make level or evenly sloping, (3) to give a grade

to, (4) to assign a grade

2. costly, adj.

of great cost or value; not cheap; dear, valuable, expensive

3. governess, n.

a woman who teaches and trains a child, especially in a private home

4. leotard, n.

a close-fitting garment worn especially by dancers and people doing exercises

5. nervous, adj.

(1) spirited, (2) of, relating to, or made up of nerve cells or nerves, (3) easily excited

or annoyed, (4) timid, apprehensive, (5) uneasy, unsteady

6. persist, v.i.

(1) to go on resolutely or stubbornly in spite of difficulties; persevere, (2) to

continue to exist

7. red herring, n.

a diversion intended to distract attention from the real issue

8. simple, adj.

(1) not combined with anything else, (2) not other than; mere, (3) not complex;

plain, (4) absolute, (5) straightforward, artless, (6) unadorned, (7) lacking education,

experience, or intelligence, (8) developing from a single ovary

9. tattle, n.

rumor, hearsay, gossip

10. whimper, n.

a low, whining, plaintive or broken sound

Usage Labels

College writing requires the use of standard English. By now you know that standard English is accepted as universal by dictionaries and respected authorities. In other words, dictionaries have the final say on whether words are standard or nonstandard. Sometimes a dictionary simply labels a word *nonstandard*. Other times it also tells us specifically in what way a word is nonstandard. These are the other labels dictionaries use:

> ***nonstandard:*** language not accepted by most educated people
>> **Example:**   irregardless (Irregardless of the weather, we'll stay home. Instead, use *regardless*.)

> ***informal or colloquial:*** conversational, appropriate for casual communication
>> **Example:**   gonna (I'm gonna go for a walk. Instead, use *going to*.)

> ***slang:*** informal, often humorous, words used by various groups
>> **Example:**   flunk (Pete flunked math. Instead, use *failed*.)

regional: words limited to a particular region

    Example: goober for peanut (in the South)

usage problem: a word that is often misused

    Example: snuck (The cat snuck in the room. Instead, use *sneaked.*)

Because language is always changing, you should consult a recent dictionary for any word you think might not be standard English.

PRACTICING 6

Use your dictionary to label each italicized word below as *standard, nonstandard, informal* or *colloquial, slang,* or *regional.*

Example: My problem with studying is that I love to *goof* around.

    Slang

1. His car is a *heap.*   slang

2. I *ain't* scared of the dark.   nonstandard

3. They *reckon* that by tomorrow it will rain.

    regional

4. The plumber *repaired* the leaking faucet.

    standard

5. Many neighbors *brung* food to the family.

    usage problem

6. That bike *rocks!*   slang

7. Mary looks *real* pretty in her graduation picture.

    informal

8. What kind of *pop* do you want? We have Pepsi and Diet Coke.

    regional

9. Americans *sure* like football.   informal

10. He's such a *dude.*   slang

Origin

A good desk dictionary (not a portable) will often include the origin or **etymology** of a word. For example, we learn from the entry that *sandwiches* were first made for the British Earl of Sandwich, after whom they were named, to allow him to continue gambling without breaking for meals.

PRACTICING 7

Dictionaries will vary.

Using a desk dictionary, look up the origins of the following words.

1. silhouette, n.

Named for Etienne de Silhouette, 1767 French controller general of finances, in

reference to his petty economies.

2. lunatic, n.

From the Latin luna meaning moon; based on the belief that lunacy fluctuated with

the phases of the moon.

3. sinister, adj.

From the Latin for left side, which represented being unlucky, unfavorable, or

illegitimate.

4. pasteurized, adj.

Named for Louis Pasteur, who invented the process.

5. magnanimous, adj.

From magnus, meaning great, and animus, meaning spirit.

6. peer, n.

From per, meaning equal.

7. paradise, n.

From the Latin and Greek words for an enclosed park of Iranian origin.

8. cabbage, n.

From the Old North French for head.

_____

9. arrowroot, n.

From arrow (from the Latin for arch or arc) and root (from various origins meaning

root) —together, a plant with an arrow-shaped root.

10. cute, adj.

Short for acute, meaning severe.

_____

Synonyms

The **synonym** of a word is another word whose meaning is similar. For example, *chilly, cool, frigid,* and *frosty* are listed in the dictionary as synonyms for *cold.* In most dictionaries, the synonyms of a word are listed after its definition and labeled *syn.*

Sandwich has no synonyms listed. *Erase,* however, does. Its synonyms in our dictionary are listed as *expunge, efface, delete, cancel,* and *blot.* Synonyms can be helpful, but you must use them carefully. After all, a *cool* morning is hardly the same as a *frosty*—or a *frigid*—one.

PRACTICING 8

With the help of a dictionary, list two synonyms for the following words:

Answers will vary.

1. dark (adjective) — *dim* — *dusky*

2. inflexible (verb) — *stiff* — *unyielding*

3. careful (adjective) — *cautious* — *deliberate*

4. fat (adjective) — *plump* — *stout*

5. lawyer (noun) — *attorney* — *solicitor*

6. circle (verb) — *orbit* — *circumnavigate*

7. fault (noun) — *defect* — *failing*

8. glib (adjective) — *articulate* — *vocal*

9. promise (noun)   *oath*   *pledge*

10. sour (adjective)   *rancid*   *acidic*

IN A NUTSHELL

A good dictionary gives the following information about words:

- spelling
- word division
- pronunciation
- grammatical uses
- meanings
- usage labels
- origin
- synonyms

Unit Test

The paragraph that follows contains words that are nonstandard, colloquial, and slang. It also contains some words that are misspelled. Rewrite all sentences that aren't in standard English and correct all misspellings. If a sentence is correct, mark "C" below.

1. Fred irritiates the heck out of me. 2. He is forever bragging about his grades. 3. But yesterday I gave him something to worry about: I whipped him good in a biology examination. 4. Once he even ripped me off a dollar by not paying up when we made a bet that I won. 5. Sometimes I wonder why I bother to remain his friend and to socialice with him on campus and at parties. 6. He ain't never going to become the sort of friend I respect and admire. 7. So why do I hang out with him? 8. Fred doesn't give a hoot about me, and I should distence myself from him. 9. My mom agrees with me; she don't like Fred. 10. Here comes Fred. Who's that cute chick with him?

1. *Fred really irritates me.*

_____

2. *He is always bragging about his grades.*

_____

3. *But yesterday I gave him something to worry about: I did better than he did on*

a biology examination.

4. *Once he even cheated me out of a dollar by not paying what he owed when we*

made a bet that I won.

5. *C*

6. *He isn't ever going to become the sort of friend I respect and admire.*

7. *So why do I spend time with him?*

8.. *Fred doesn't care about me at all, and I should distance myself from him.*

9. *My mother agrees with me; she doesn't like Fred.*

10. *I see Fred coming. Who's that pretty young woman with him?*

Unit Talk-Write Assignment

What follows in the *Talk* column is an ungrammatical, incomplete attempt at defining "glass ceiling." Your assignment has several parts. First, turn the *Talk* column into complete sentences written in standard English and spelled and punctuated correctly. Use your dictionary if you need help. (Every sentence has at least one misspelled word.) Then, find out—from the dictionary, teachers, friends, and any other available source—just what the term "glass ceiling" means. Finally, write a paragraph on "glass ceilings." Begin with a one-sentence definition, which will function as your topic sentence. Then, expand on your definition with reasoning and examples. If you need help with spelling or word meaning, check your dictionary.

Answers may vary.

TALK

1. What's this "glass ceiling" busness I keeps hearing about?

2. Betes me what it means.

3. I know it has something to do with womin's jobs.

4. Something about being shovved back down by men when they gets too hotsy totsy.

5. Can you imagine someone trying to get through a glass cieling?

6. Maybe that be the point; glass cielings are tricky, man.

7. I wish peoples wouldn't use words like them without splaining.

8. The reason this come to mind is that yestday I hear someone say that some Air Force woman had gone through the glass cieling because she was to be the pilat on a space shuttle.

9. I guess the glass cieling is what keep women in jobs where they make less money.

10. But why not call it an iron cieling or a sement cieling?

WRITE

1. What's this "glass ceiling" business I keep hearing about?

2. (Beats me) I don't know what it means.

3. I know it has something to do with women's jobs.

4. It is about women being pushed (shoved) back down by men when they get too ambitious.

5. Can you imagine someone trying to get through a glass ceiling?

6. Maybe that is the point; glass ceilings are tricky.

7. I wish people wouldn't use words like those without explaining.

8. The reason this came to mind is that yesterday I heard someone say that an Air Force woman had gone through the glass ceiling because she was to be the pilot on a space shuttle.

9. I guess the glass ceiling is what keeps women in jobs where they make less money.

10. But why not call it an iron ceiling or a cement ceiling?

Unit Collaborative Assignment

Pair up with a partner. Working together, use your dictionaries to turn this paragraph into standard English. Also, find and correct the spelling errors (there are seven).

Most college campuses are filled with various personality types. There are the jocks, the nerds, the party animals, the lab rats,/the do-gooders. *[and]* My ~~favorit~~ *[favorite]* is the nerd. Computer ~~sceince~~ *[science]* programs seem to grow nerds. My theory is that nerds spend so much time at a keyboard they ~~beccome~~ *[become]* iso-lated. They turn into geeks ~~that ain't got~~ *[who have]* no social contact with people out-side their computer circle.

A sure way of ~~identifing~~ *[identifying]* a nerd is by ~~appearence~~ *[appearance]*. A nerd just does not know how to dress ~~cool~~ *[fashionably]*. His pants are always too short, usually hitting just above the ankle. His shirts are buttoned up to the collar, but the buttons are never in the right button holes. Then, too, the nerd's shirts are never ~~stuck~~ *[tucked]* inside his pants, but hang half in and half out, looking quite sloppy. (I say "his," but there are just as many ~~femmale~~ *[female]* nerds today.) A nerd never inquires about the ~~wether~~ *[weather]* before dressing. You can count on the fact that if it is a hot day, he will wear a sweater; whereas if it is a cold day, he will wear shorts. Nerds wear tee-shirts that say "My parents went to Disneyland, and all I got was this lousy tee-shirt." This, of course, is the nerd's ~~yucky~~ *[unsuccessful]* attempt ~~at being cool~~ *[to be fashionable]*.

Nerds always dress opposite to the established styles. They don't do this to rebel the way punks do. They just don't know better. When the surfer look is popular, they wear leather jackets. When the preppy look is in, they wear disco clothes. Most important of all, though, a nerd is always com-fortable in polyester. Sometimes, I'm a nerd, but then that's a ~~diffrent~~ *[different]* story.

Unit Writing Assignment

In a good dictionary, find a word with an interesting origin (etymol-ogy). In a paragraph, explain this origin and tell how knowing the origin helps you better understand the word. Use the Revising Check-list to revise.

Photo Writing Assignment

The following photograph shows a baseball game in progress. Write a paragraph explaining the basic rules of the game to someone who has never even heard of it. Or, if you wish, you can explain the basic rules of another sport or any board or card game. Be sure to explain any words that are unique to the sport or game or have a different meaning from their meaning in common usage. For example, in discussing baseball, you should explain the special meanings of *ball* and *strike*. Use the Revising Checklist to revise.

23

Spelling Rules

Before the existence of dictionaries, words were spelled entirely by ear or by whim. *Slow* might be spelled *sloe, slo,* or *slough*. With the appearance in the eighteenth century of the first English dictionary, however, spelling gradually became standardized to the point that children today compete in spelling bees.

Even if we never get skilled enough at spelling to enter a spelling bee, we can all become better spellers by observing some simple rules.

Tips for Improving Your Spelling

1. Sound out words. For instance, the word *government* contains an *n* if you say it aloud slowly. The word *find* has a final *d* sound and should not be spelled *fine*. Saying a word out loud can definitely help you to spell it correctly.

2. Make up your own memory tricks for remembering the spelling of problem words. For example, *cemetery* is spelled with all *e*'s because it is so eerie; the *principal* is your *pal*; after-dinner *dessert* has two *s*'s because it is doubly good.

3. Use a dictionary regularly. Looking up a word not only helps you with the spelling of that particular word, it helps you develop a sense of how words are spelled. That is, you begin to develop a feeling for the English language and for its spelling rules and exceptions. (See the list of dictionaries on page 421.)

4. Keep a list of words that you often misspell and use it when you proofread your writing. For some reason, everyone has trouble with certain words. Make a list of your particular spelling weaknesses—words you often misspell—and put it in your dictionary. Be sure to check the spelling of these words when you proofread your paper.

Using a Spell Checker

For those lucky enough to write using a computer, the first rule of spelling is simply this: Use the Spell Checker. The second rule is this: Remember that Spell Checkers go only so far. Although they catch such misspellings as *heighth* for *height,* and *ocasion* for *occasion,* they don't tell you if you've incorrectly used *its* for *it's* or *their* for *there* or *they're.* Neither do they tell you whether you've spelled a name correctly. This is very important if you're writing a letter of application for a job: You do not want to misspell the name of the company.

PRACTICING 1

The following paragraph contains a number of words that are incorrectly spelled. Find the words and correctly spell them using context as your guide.

Spelling checkers are useful but they can all so *(also)* make miss steaks *(mistakes)*. If you depend on spelling checkers too much, your writing will contain many arrows *(errors)*. These will be very hard to fine *(find)*. The individual words may be correctly spelled, but in the context of your right in *(writing)* they will be wrung *(wrong)*. For example, I've already maid *(made)* several bad spelling errors in this paragraph, yet my spelling checker tells me that there are no missed takes *(mistakes)*. Can you sea watt *(see what)* I've done rung *(wrong)*? If you have a sharp aye *(eye)*, ewe *(you)* should find thirteen misspelled words.

Rules for Spelling

You will become a better speller if you follow certain simple spelling rules. However, spelling in English is not always as clear-cut as we would like; nearly every rule has an exception. Nevertheless, learning the rules, and the exceptions, can still help you become a better speller.

As you go over the rules, bear in mind the difference between vowels and consonants.

| **Vowels:** | a, e, i, o, u, and sometimes y |
| **Consonants:** | All other letters of the alphabet |

Using ie and ei

Remember the age-old rule: "*i* before *e* except after *c* or when sounded as *ay* as in *neighbor* or *weigh*":

        niece

        relieve

        believe

but

        ceiling

        receive

        deceive

EXCEPTIONS

either	leisure	species
caffeine	neither	their
financier	seize	weird
foreigner	science	
height	society	

ESL Advice!

If your background is British, remember that there are significant differences between American and British rules of spelling, for example, in the use of the final *-our* or *-or* (Br. *colour,* Am. *color*).

PRACTICING 2

Place a check mark in front of the correct spelling in each word pair.

1.___✔___ **(a).** reign

   _____ **(b).** riegn

2._____ **(a).** yeild

   ___✔___ **(b).** yield

3.___✔___ **(a).** perceive

   _____ **(b).** percieve

4._____ **(a).** preist

___✔___ **(b).** priest

5._____ **(a).** recieve

___✔___ **(b).** receive

6.___✔___ **(a).** weigh

_____ **(b).** wiegh

7._____ **(a).** cheif

___✔___ **(b).** chief

8.___✔___ **(a).** society

_____ **(b).** soceity

9.___✔___ **(a).** vein

_____ **(b).** vien

10._____ **(a).** breif

___✔___ **(b).** brief

PRACTICING 3

Underline the correct spelling of the word in parentheses.

1. Drinking too much (<u>caffeine</u>, caffien) makes you jittery.

2. His (conciet, <u>conceit</u>) makes him unpopular.

3. Every one of our (nieghbors, <u>neighbors</u>) is quiet after 10 P.M.

4. The (<u>weight</u>, wieght) of the fruit does not determine its taste.

5. (Niether, <u>neither</u>) Paula nor Manuel was at the scene.

6. He was (<u>heir</u>, hier) to a huge fortune.

7. Were you (<u>relieved</u>, releived) to see her leave?

8. It is difficult to (beleive, <u>believe</u>) him.

9. A good (freind, <u>friend</u>) is like pure gold.

10. How could they have (decieved, <u>deceived</u>) us so thoroughly?

Changing y to i

When you add an ending to a word that ends in a consonant plus *y*, change *y* to *i*:

fry + ed = fried

worry + es = worries

happy + ness = happiness

merry + ly = merrily

EXCEPTIONS

decry	decrying (but decried)
horrify	horrifyingly
lady	ladylike
carry	carrying
cry	crying (but cried, crier)
worry	worrying (but worried, worrier)

PRACTICING 4

Combine the following words with the endings to their right and write the words in the blanks provided.

Example: study + es = _studies_

1.	marry	+	ed	=	married
2.	hazy	+	ily	=	hazily
3.	hurry	+	ed	=	hurried
4.	terrify	+	es	=	terrifies
5.	purify	+	ing	=	purifying
6.	bury	+	ing	=	burying
7.	stay	+	ed	=	stayed
8.	copy	+	es	=	copies
9.	worry	+	ing	=	worrying
10.	cry	+	ed	=	cried
11.	marry	+	ing	=	marrying
12.	happy	+	ly	=	happily
13.	delay	+	ed	=	delayed

| **14.** mercy | + | ful | = | *merciful* |
| **15.** juicy | + | er | = | *juicier* |

The final silent *e*

When you add endings that start with a vowel, such as *-al*, *-able*, *-ence*, or *-ing*, drop the final *e*. When you add an ending that starts with a consonant, such as *-ment*, *-less*, or *-ly*, keep the final *e*. Here are some examples for you to study:

bride + al = bridal

like + able = likable

emerge + ence = emergence

take + ing = taking

manage + ment = management

love + less = loveless

polite + ly = politely

EXCEPTIONS

argue + ment = argument

courage + ous = courageous

judge + ment = judgment

manage + able = manageable

nine + th = ninth

notice + able = noticeable

true + ly = truly

PRACTICING 5

Write *C* next to the word that is spelled correctly.

Example: pleasureable _____   pleasurable __*C*__

1. desirable   __*C*__   desireable   _____

2. endureable   _____   endurable   __*C*__

3. abatment   _____   abatement   __*C*__

4. measureless	_c_	measurless	_____
5. dosage	_c_	doseage	_____
6. writing	_c_	writeing	_____
7. forcful	_____	forceful	_c_
8. believable	_c_	believeable	_____
9. exerciseing	_____	exercising	_c_
10. completely	_c_	completly	_____
11. excitment	_____	excitement	_c_
12. sameness	_c_	samness	_____
13. hopless	_____	hopeless	_c_
14. continuous	_c_	continueous	_____
15. arrangment	_____	arrangement	_c_

Doubling the final consonant in one-syllable words

To add *-ed*, *-ing*, *-er*, or *-est* to a one-syllable word, double the consonant if it is preceded by a single vowel:

    pin + ed = pinned

    trim + ing = trimming

    thin + er = thinner

    sad + est = saddest

PRACTICING 6

Add the indicated endings to the words listed below and spell them correctly in the blanks provided.

Example: drop (ed) *dropped*

1. dip (ing) *dipping*

2. top (ing) *topping*

3. trim (ing) *trimming*

4. big (est) *biggest*

5. knit (ing) *knitting*

6. run (er) *runner*

7. stop (ed)   *stopped*

8. hot (est)   *hottest*

9. slap (ed)   *slapped*

10. beg (ed)   *begged*

11. skip (ing)   *skipping*

12. fit (ed)   *fitted*

13. clip (ing)   *clipping*

14. flip (ed)   *flipped*

15. strip (ing)   *stripping*

Doubling the final consonant in multisyllable words

To add *-ing* or *-ed* to words of more than one syllable, double the final consonant if the following is true:

- The stress is on the final syllable:

  ad-mit′

  be-gin′

  de-fer′

- The last three letters consist of a consonant/vowel/consonant:

  admit

  begin

  defer

Therefore,

  admit + ed = admitted

  begin + ing = beginning

  defer + ed = deferred

Now, consider these words:

tra′vel = traveling   **(Do not double because the accent is on the first syllable: tra′-vel.)**

benefit = benefited   **(Do not double because the accent is on the first syllable: be′-ne-fit.)**

repeat = repeating   **(Do not double
                                            because the last three
                                            letters do not fit the
                                            consonant/vowel/
                                            consonant pattern.)**

PRACTICING 7

In the blank on the right, add *-ed* and *-ing* to the following words.

Example: commit   _committed_   _committing_

	ED	ING
1. deter	deterred	deterring
2. label	labeled	labeling
3. expel	expelled	expelling
4. omit	omitted	omitting
5. travel	traveled	traveling
6. evict	evicted	evicting
7. occur	occurred	occurring
8. rebel	rebelled	rebelling
9. begin	begun	beginning
10. control	controlled	controlling

PRACTICING 8

Underline the correct word in parentheses.

Example: Twice John (travelled, <u>traveled</u>) across the country by motorcycle.

1. John politely (<u>deferred</u>, defered) to those in authority.

2. He (predictted, <u>predicted</u>) sunshine, but it rained.

3. Believe me, they were all (<u>profiting</u>, profitting) from the experiment.

4. While we were (<u>unwrapping</u>, unwraping) the box, they left.

5. If he had (<u>returned</u>, returnned) on time, the fire would have been detected.

6. (Submiting, <u>submitting</u>) meekly to mean bosses is difficult.

7. The new puppy (<u>resisted</u>, resistted) anyone who came near his bone.

8. The short order cook was (refered, <u>referred</u>) to Burger King by my mom.

9. Jim did not believe in (enlistting, <u>enlisting</u>) in the army.

10. Have you (<u>relented</u>, relentted) after your decision to leave?

Forming plurals

1. Most words form their plurals by simply adding -*s*:

SINGULAR	PLURAL
dog	dogs
umbrella	umbrellas
mother	mothers
book	books

However, there are a few exceptions that you should master. For example, words ending in -*s*, -*ss*, -*z*, -*x*, -*sh*, or -*ch* form their plurals by adding -*es*, an extra syllable for easier pronunciation.

SINGULAR	PLURAL
lens	lenses
kiss	kisses
buzz	buzzes
box	boxes
wash	washes
church	churches

PRACTICING 9

Form the plurals of the following words.

1. boy   *boys*

2. peach   *peaches*

3. bump   *bumps*

4. fox   *foxes*

5. business   *businesses*

6. fix   *fixes*

7. bush   *bushes*

8. wish   _wishes_

9. sun   _suns_

10. letter   _letters_

11. lurch   _lurches_

12. bus   _buses_

13. flash   _flashes_

14. tax   _taxes_

15. farmer   _farmers_

2. If a word ends in an *o* preceded by a vowel, add *-s*:

rodeo	rodeos
patio	patios
zoo	zoos
radio	radios
video	videos

If a word ends in an *o* preceded by a consonant, add *-es*:

hero	heroes
potato	potatoes
echo	echoes
buffalo	buffaloes

EXCEPTIONS

alto	altos
grotto	grottos
memo	memos
motto	mottos
photo	photos
piano	pianos
solo	solos

PRACTICING 10

Form the plurals of the following words.

1. zero   *zeroes (or zeros)*

2. rodeo   *rodeos*

3. mosquito   *mosquitoes*

4. halo   *halos*

5. zoo   *zoos*

6. tomato   *tomatoes*

7. domino   *dominoes (or dominos)*

8. radio   *radios*

9. tornado   *tornadoes (or tornados)*

10. motto   *mottos*

PRACTICING 11

Sentences will vary. Correct plural versions follow.

Write a sentence using the plurals of the following words.

1. buffalo

buffaloes

_____

2. photo

photos

_____

3. antipasto

antipastos

_____

4. soprano

sopranos

_____

5. hero

heroes

---

6. potato

potatoes

---

7. memo

memos

---

8. video

videos

---

9. patio

patios

---

10. lingo

lingoes

---

3. For most words ending in *f* (or *fe*), change the *f* to *v* and add *-es*:

SINGULAR	PLURAL
half	halves
calf	calves
leaf	leaves
wife	wives

EXCEPTIONS	
roof	roofs
safe	safes
chief	chiefs
proof	proofs

PRACTICING 12

Form the plurals of the following words.

1. brief   *briefs*

2. hoof   *hooves*

3. yourself   *yourselves*

4. knife   *knives*

5. wife   *wives*

6. thief   *thieves*

7. chief   *chiefs*

8. proof   *proofs*

9. leaf   *leaves*

10. mastiff   *mastiffs*

11. self   *selves*

12. wolf   *wolves*

13. life   *lives*

14. wharf   *wharves*

15. half   *halves*

4. Some words form irregular plurals:

SINGULAR	PLURAL
woman	women
foot	feet
ox	oxen
mouse	mice
index	indeces
appendix	appendeces
criterion	criteria
analysis	analyses

PRACTICING 13

Form the plurals of the following words.

1. tooth   *teeth*

2. child   *children*

3. goose   *geese*

4. louse   *lice* _____

5. man   *men* _____

6. foot   *feet* _____

7. ox   *oxen* _____

8. mouse   *mice* _____

9. species   *species* _____

10. alumnus   *alumni* _____

5. Compound nouns—made up of two or more words—form their plurals by adding *-s* to the main word. If a compound noun is written as a single word, make the ending word plural:

SINGULAR	PLURAL
boyfriend	boyfriends
eyeglass	eyeglasses
grandchild	grandchildren
bookshelf	bookshelves

EXCEPTION	
passerby	passersby

If the compound noun is written as separate or hyphenated words, make the main word plural:

SINGULAR	PLURAL
bus stop	bus stops
jump shot	jump shots
rule of the road	rules of the road
mother-in-law	mothers-in-law
man-of-war	men-of-war

PRACTICING 14

Form the plural of the following compound nouns.

1. rule of thumb   *rules of thumb* _____

2. right-of-way   *rights-of-way* _____

3. sergeant major   *sergeants major* _____

4. attorney general   *attorneys general* _____

5. attorney-at-law   *attorneys-at-law* _____

6. secretary of state   *secretaries of state* _____

7. eyesore   *eyesores*

8. daughter-in-law   *daughters-in-law*

9. storybook   *storybooks*

10. storm window   *storm windows*

11. jumping jack   *jumping jacks*

12. son-in-law   *sons-in-law*

13. jack-of-all-trades   *jacks-of-all-trades*

14. home plate   *home plates*

15. jukebox   *jukeboxes*

6. Some words have the same spelling for singular and plural:

SINGULAR	PLURAL
deer	deer
fish	fish
sheep	sheep
species	species
series	series
moose	moose

PRACTICING 15

Turn the following words into plurals and then write a sentence using the plural.

Sample: fish   *fish*

The boys caught three fish with their homemade rods.

1. series   *series*

_____

2. sheep   *sheep*

_____

3. person   *persons*

_____

4. moose   *moose*

_____

5. tie   *ties*

_____

6. deer   *deer*

_____

7. virus   *viruses*

_____

8. species   *species*

_____

9. virtue   *virtues*

_____

10. household   *households*

_____

PRACTICING 16

The following announcements were taken from actual church bulletin boards. Correct the misspelled or mistyped words.

1. The pastor would appreciate it if the women of the congregation would lend him their electric ~~girdles~~ *griddles* for the pancake breakfast next Sunday morning.

2. The audience is asked to remain seated until the end of the recessional.

3. Deacon Clark is on vacation. ~~Massages~~ *Messages* can be given to the church secretary.

4. The third verse of "Blessed Assurance" will be sung without musical ~~accomplishment~~ *accompaniment*.

5. A song fest was ~~hell~~ *held* at the Methodist church Wednesday.

6. Prayer and ~~medication~~ *meditation* will follow Wednesday's potluck supper.

7. The choir director invites any member who enjoys ~~sinning~~ *singing* to join the choir.

IN A NUTSHELL

Most words form their plurals by adding -*s*. Many exceptions exist. When in doubt, check the dictionary.

Unit Test

Circle the word in each pair that is correctly spelled.

1. leafs   (leaves)
2. (receive)   receive
3. (committed)   commited
4. expeled   (expelled)
5. potatos   (potatoes)
6. (benefited)   benefitted
7. gooses   (geese)
8. feets   (feet)
9. (echoes)   echos
10. (writing)   writting
11. noticable   (noticeable)
12. (admitted)   admited
13. sliming   (slimming)
14. (yield)   yeild
15. (saddest)   sadest

Unit Talk-Write Assignment

The *Talk* column presents a conversation between two students, Jan and George, on whether it's better to live in a small town or a big city. First, rewrite the *Talk* column into complete sentences in standard English. Be sure to correct all the spelling errors you find. Then write a well-developed paragraph stating your opinion and supporting it with evidence from your own experience.

TALK

Jan: Living in a small town is so wierd.

George: No weigh! I used to live in a town so small I knew the names of all the dogs. I loved it.

Jan: No, in small towns, the soceity is too pusshy. Everyboudy nose your bussiness.

George: I don't think so. I like the way people in small towns percieve each other. Nobody's a chief. Everyone's a bottle washer.

Jan: Yeah, wright! Like living in a restaurant. You said it!

George: That's not what I mean. I mean the nieghbors are friendly.

Jan: There's just a samness that's borring. Plus, everybody's chucked together like potatos in a sack. I destest it.

George: So, what'd you get in a city? Greif on the streets, not nowing the person next door?

Jan: Yeah, but at least you can come and go as you please. Their's something to be said for that.

George: There's something to be said for feeling foriegn where you live?

WRITE

Jan: Living in a small town is strange (weird).

George: No, it isn't. (No way.) I used to live in a town so small I knew the names of all the dogs. I loved it.

Jan: No, in small towns, the society is too pushy. Everybody knows your business.

George: I don't think so. I like the way people in small towns perceive each other. Nobody's in charge. Everyone's a worker.

Jan: You're right about that—it's like living in a restaurant.

George: No, I mean the neighbors are friendly.

Jan: There's just a sameness that's boring. Plus, everybody is crowded together like potatoes in a sack. I detest it.

George: So, what did you get in the city? There is trouble (grief) on the streets, and you don't know (knowing) the person next door.

Jan: Yes, but at least you can come and go as you please. There's something to be said for that.

George: Is there something to be said for feeling foreign where you live?

TALK

WRITE

Jan: Well, a big city makes me feel free, not penned up and surrounded by bunch of watchdogs. Sorry, but that's my openion.

Jan: A big city makes me feel free, not restricted and surrounded by people watching me. I'm sorry, but that's my opinion.

George: A small town makes me feel loved, not penned up. Listen, I gotta go. You're too crochety today, anyhow.

George: A small town makes me feel loved, not restricted. I have to go now. You're too argumentative today, anyway.

Jan: Yeah, later. Meantime, I'll just sit here and enjoy being ingured by all the passer-bys. City life! It's fabuluous! Look at me! I'm unknown! I'm free!

Jan: I'll see you later. In the meantime, I'll just sit here and enjoy being injured by all the passersby. City life is fabulous! Look at me! I'm unknown! I'm free!

George: Bye!

George: Goodbye!

Jan: Bye!

Jan: Goodbye!

Unit Collaborative Assignment

Work with a partner. First read the spelling rule, and then think of examples of the rule. Use one of your examples in a sentence.

Example:　"*I* before *e* except after *c*."

Answer:　Tomorrow I will *receive* my history grade.

1. When you add an ending to a word that ends in a consonant plus *y*, change *y* to *i*.

   _____

   _____

2. When you add *-ed, -ing, -er,* or *-est* to one-syllable words, double the consonant if it is preceded by a single vowel.

   _____

   _____

3. To add *-ing* or *-ed* to words of more than one syllable, double the final consonant if (1) the stress is on the final syllable, or (2) the last three letters consist of a consonant/vowel/consonant.

   _____

   _____

4. Most words form their plurals by simply adding *-s.*

   _____

   _____

5. Words ending in *-s, -ss, -z, -x, -sh,* or *-ch* form their plurals by adding *-es,* an extra syllable for easier pronunciation.

   _____

   _____

6. When you add endings that start with a vowel, such as *-as, -able, -ence,* or *-ing,* drop the final *e.* When you add an ending that starts with a consonant, such as *-ment, -less,* or *-ly,* keep the final *e.*

   _____

   _____

7. Some words ending in *o* form their plurals by adding *-es.*

_____

_____

8. For most words ending in *f* (or *-fe*), change the *f* to *v* and add *-es.*

_____

_____

9. Some words have the same spelling for singular and plural.

_____

_____

10. Some words form irregular plurals.

_____

_____

 Unit Writing Assignment

Many people criticize the programming on television. Others say that television can be a positive force. Write a paragraph supporting one of the following topic sentences:

1. Television is a negative influence on people.

2. Television helps educate people.

Be sure to follow the spelling rules in this unit. Use the Revising Checklist to revise.

Photo Writing Assignment

The following photo shows students campaigning for their causes on campus. What cause do you support? Write a paragraph explaining why one of your causes is important to you. What do you do to support this cause? Make sure your spelling follows the rules outlined in this unit. Use the Revising Checklist to revise.

24

Commonly Misspelled Words

....

"Are you quite quiet?"

....

English spelling is difficult. Words are often not spelled the way they sound. *Raccoon* sounds like it should have a *k* but doesn't. *Threw* sounds like *through* but is spelled differently. *Though, cough,* and *through* look like rhyming words but are actually not pronounced at all alike. Given that English has a vocabulary of over 400,000 words, it's a wonder that we spell as well as we do.

Some words—called **homonyms (also called homophones)**—sound exactly alike but have different spellings and meanings. Other words are not exact homonyms but are similar enough to be often confused. Study the following examples:

Homophones:	altar (a raised platform in church)	alter (to change)
	The minister stood at the *altar*.	I can *alter* your jacket.
	it's (short for "it is")	its (possessive pronoun)
	It's getting late.	The rabbit is in *its* nest.
Confusing words:	accept (to receive with consent)	except (excluded)
	I *accept* your money.	Everyone left *except* Fred.

advice (a noun)   advise (a verb)
She asked for   They *advised* her to
advice.   study.

Homophones and Frequently Confused Words

Learn the meaning and spelling of these homophones and frequently confused words. Errors in spelling can change the meaning of writing. *Angel* spelled correctly will still confuse your reader if you really meant *angle.*

- **accept**—to take or receive/**except**—excluding, other than, but for

  I *accept* the gifts.

  Everyone was there, *except* you.

- **access**—a means of approach/**excess**—too much

  He had *access* to the computer.

  Ann wore an *excess* of jewelry.

- **advice**—recommendation (noun)/**advise**—to caution, to warn (verb)

  My *advice* is to remain silent.

  We *advise* you to remain silent.

- **affect**—to influence, to change/**effect**—to bring about (verb); consequence, result (noun)

  Breaking up with Barry *affected* my grades.

  They were able to *effect* some improvements in the hospital kitchen.

  One *effect* of regular exercise is increased energy.

- **alter**—to change/**altar**—a raised platform in a church

  She will *alter* the dress.

  At the *altar*, they said, "I do."

- **bare**—without covering or clothing/**bear**—to bring forth; to endure (verb); an animal (noun)

  The trees were *bare* of leaves.

  Please *bear* with me one more minute.

  The *bear* strolled past the campground.

- **berry**—a kind of fleshy fruit/**bury**—to place in the ground

  My favorite *berry* is the raspberry.

  Let's *bury* the garbage in the back yard.

- **capital**—value of goods, money; a principal city/**capitol**—a building in which lawmakers meet

  My grandfather would not part with any of his *capital*.

  The *capital* of Ohio is Columbus.

  The students toured the new state *capitol*.

- **cite**—to quote/**site**—place or scene/**sight**—ability to see

  The lawyer could *cite* a dozen laws.

  What a perfect *site* for a public park!

  At seventy, she had the *sight* of a youngster.

- **course**—a path; subjects taken in school/**coarse**—rough in texture

  He followed a different *course* through the woods.

  Helen signed up for two *courses* in history.

  The texture of the linen was *coarse*.

- **desert**—a dry land (noun); to abandon (verb)/**dessert**—something sweet served at the end of a meal

  I spent the weekend in the *desert*.

  He vowed he would never *desert* his troops.

  I always check the *dessert* menu first.

- **fairy**—a tiny superhuman being/**ferry**—a boat used for transportation across water

  A *fairy* helped Cinderella go to the ball.

  They crossed the Sacramento river in a *ferry*.

- **forth**—forward/**fourth**—next after third

  He said, "Go *forth* and play hard."

  I am the *fourth* child.

- **gulf**—deep chasm/**golf**—game

  We could see across the gulf.

  My grandfather loves to play golf.

- **its**—possessive form of it/**it's**—contraction of it is

  The dog chased *its* tail.

  It's a hot day.

- **lose**—to misplace or come to be without/**loose**—to be free from restraint

  You're going to *lose* your hat in this wind.

  The cattle were let *loose* on the range.

- **passed**—went by/**past**—an earlier time; beyond

  I *passed* her in the hall.

  Forget the *past*; live for today.

  I drove *past* your house.

- **piece**—part of a whole/**peace**—opposite of war

  Would you like a *piece* of chocolate cake?

  Everyone wants *peace* in the world.

- **personal**—private, intimate/**personnel**—employees

  This is my *personal* diary.

  Go directly to the *personnel* office.

- **principal**—first in rank; the chief or head/**principle**—an accepted rule or belief

  She's the *principal* of our elementary school.

  I have my *principles*.

- **quiet**—making no noise; peaceable/**quite**—completely or entirely

  They were *quiet* all night.

  I am *quite* confused.

- **right**—correct, fitting, proper (adj.) privilege, prerogative (noun)/**write**—to form letters on a surface/**rite**—a formal or ceremonial act or practice

  Don't bother unless you expect to be *right*.

  To see your bank balance is your *right*.

  Please *write* me a postcard.

  The *rite* of Baptism is observed in many churches

- **hole**—an opening through something/**whole**—complete

  They hid the money in a deep *hole*.

  Max ate the *whole* lemon pie.

- **sole**—only; the bottom of the foot/**soul**—the spirit

  I was the *sole* member of the team to go.

  The *soles* of my feet itch.

  Music is good for the *soul*.

- **their**—ownership/**there**—in that place/**they're**—contraction of they are

  This is *their* boat.

  My car is over *there*.

  They're friendly people.

- **to**—a preposition; part of any infinitive/**too**—also, excessively/ **two**—second

  He went *to* the beach.

  I'm going *to* walk the dog.

  First Julie wept; then Meg wept, *too*.

  Don't eat *too* much ice cream.

  I have *two* dogs.

- **who's**—contraction of *who is*/**whose**—the possessive case of *who*

  Who's talking about us?

  I know *whose* coat that is.

- **your**—the possessive case of *you*/**you're**—contraction of *you are*

  This is *your* choice.

  You're quite welcome.

These are, of course, not the only homophones—English is riddled with many others. These are just some you are most likely to encounter.

IN A NUTSHELL

Watch out for homophones—words that sound exactly alike but have different spellings and meanings—and words that are easily confused.

PRACTICING 1

Underline the correct word in the parentheses.

Example: Mr. Murphy is the (forth, <u>fourth</u>) person in line.

1. They cut down all the trees, making the plot look (bear, <u>bare</u>).

2. He was the (<u>sole</u>, soul) survivor of the airplane crash.

3. All I want is a (quite, <u>quiet</u>) evening at home by the fire.

4. All (there, <u>their</u>) relatives showed up for the wedding.

5. They were forced to (except, <u>accept</u>) twenty extra guests.

6. They must hire extra (<u>personnel</u>, personal) for the job.

7. If they only understood (<u>their</u>, they're) limitations.

8. The (passed, <u>past</u>) is behind us; don't worry about it.

9. I had apple pie for (desert, <u>dessert</u>).

10. Don't (<u>lose</u>, loose) your place in line.

PRACTICING 2

In the space provided, mark *C* if the sentence is correct and *NC* if it is not correct. Write the correct word over any italicized word that is incorrect.

Example: ___*NC*___ As a mother, she could not *bare* to watch her
son being punished
<small>(bear written above *bare*)</small>

___*C*___ 1. Everyone is going to the game *except* Joe.

___*C*___ 2. My sister always gives me good *advice*.

___*C*___ 3. The nuts should be *coarsely* chopped.

___*C*___ 4. We're going hiking in the *desert*.

___*NC*___ 5. Was I happy I ~~*past*~~ accounting! <small>(passed written above)</small>

___*NC*___ 6. We went to ~~*they're*~~ open house last Sunday. <small>(their written above)</small>

___*NC*___ 7. I'm afraid ~~*its*~~ too late for that. <small>(it's written above)</small>

___*C*___ 8. Don't make the knot too *loose*.

___*C*___ 9. If *you're* not the owner, who is?

___*NC*___ 10. ~~*Who's*~~ jacket is this? <small>(Whose written above)</small>

PRACTICING 3

Each sentence below is preceded by a pair of homonyms. Insert the correct word in each blank in the sentence.

1. witch/which

___Which___ ___witch___ in *The Wizard of Oz* was the

good ___witch___?

2. plain/plane

The ___plane___ landed on the ___plain___.

3. warn/worn

Let me ___warn___ you that those socks are ___worn___ and may have holes in them.

4. wore/war

The general ___wore___ the medals that he won during the ___war___.

5. heal/heel

She is hoping that the cut on her ___heel___ will ___heal___ soon.

PRACTICING 4

Write a sentence for each of these homophones.   Answers may vary.

1. piece

Give him a _piece_ of pie.

___

peace

Let us hope for _peace_.

___

2. advice

"Be tolerant" is the _advice_ he gave.

___

advise

We must _advise_ them to take notes.

___

3. affect

That screaming affects the game.

_____

effect

John's drinking had a bad effect on his grades.

_____

4. bare

Her bare arms were sun burned.

_____

bear

"Bear your burdens proudly"he suggested.

_____

5. site

Many New York tourists have visited the site where the Twin Towers used to stand.

_____

sight

What a site for a homesick girl—to see Dad and Mom waiting at the airport!

_____

6. gulf

Her words created a gulf between them.

_____

golf

He did not have enough money or time to play golf.

_____

7. berry

The basket contained one big red berry.

bury

Hurry up and bury those bones.

8. fairy

I wish I had a fairy godmother.

ferry

It cost $20 to cross the river by ferry.

9. right

You will know instinctively what is right.

write

Why don't you write her an e-mail?

10. hole

Giving them more money is like pouring sand into a hole.

whole

Our whole life is spent wondering what the future holds.

Commonly Misspelled Words

Below is a list of words that are commonly misspelled. If you regularly have trouble with any words on this list, memorize the correct spellings.

accidentally

acquaintance

acquire

address

already (not to be confused
    with *all ready*)

all right (always two words, just
    like *all wrong*)

answer

anxious

arithmetic

athletics

attendance

awful

awkward

believe (not to be confused
    with *belief*)

breathe (not to be confused
    with *breath*)

business

calendar

cemetery

changeable

chief

choose (not to be confused
    with *chose*)

conscience (not to be confused
    with *conscious*)

daily

definite

dependent

design

device (not to be confused
    with *devise*)

disappearance

embarrass

environment

especially

exaggerate

exercise

existence

familiar

fascinate

finally

foreign

forty

fragrant

friend

fulfill

government

harass

height

hindrance

incredible

independent

interesting

irresistible

judgment

library

literature

maintenance

mathematics

medicine

million

miracle

miscellaneous

mischief

necessary

neighbor

noticeable

nuisance

occasion

occur/occurrence/occurred

offered

parallel

peculiar

politics

possess

practically

precede

preferred

prejudice

preparation

privilege

proceed

receive

recognize

referred/referring

relieve/relief

resemblance

restaurant

reverence

ridiculous

sandwich

seize (not to be confused
   with *size*)

separate

several

similar

sincerely

succeed

surprise

temperature

than (not to be confused
   with *then*)

thorough

tragedy

truly

until

unnecessary

usually

vegetable

visitor

weird

writing

IN A NUTSHELL

You should memorize any words you often misspell.

PRACTICING 5

Each of the following sentences contains a misspelled word from the list above. Write the corrected version in the blank provided.

Example: He has a definate plan for getting a career in broadcast journalism. _definite_____

1. She looked akward giving the speech. _____ _awkward_____

2. The baby suffered from a high temparature. _____ _temperature_____

3. It's January 1, so I need a new calandar. _____ _calendar_____

4. The Senate voted to expand our aid to foriegn nations.
   _foreign_____

5. Why did you refuse to fulfil your promise to a good friend?
   _fulfill_____

6. By speaking so crassly, he does embarass our class.
   _embarrass_____

7. His judgment of people has been sharpened by litareture.
   _literature_____

8. He claimed that thousands of people attended the parade—
   an exageration. _____ _exaggeration_____

9. Stop being such a baby and take your medecine.
   _medicine_____

10. His driving priviledges were taken away. _____ _privileges_____

11. Don't be rediculous! That's a fake orange. _____ _ridiculous_____

12. In preperation for the swim meet, she ate lots of pasta.
    _preparation_____

13. The restoraunt serving the best fries is MacDonalds.
    _restaurant_____

14. Broadway and Lincoln are paralell streets. _____ _parallel_____

15. The hero siezed the controls and safely landed the spaceship. _____*seized*_____

PRACTICING 6

Cross out the incorrectly spelled word in parentheses in each of the following sentences.

1. Spinach is my favorite (vegetable/~~vegtable~~).

2. Wait (~~untill~~/until) late afternoon to go to the beach.

3. I have better grades in English than I do in (~~mathmatics~~/mathematics).

4. It's (all right/~~alright~~) to cry when you're sad.

5. Her (~~temprature~~/temperature) was normal, but she felt warm.

6. Evelyn runs a successful(business/~~busness~~).

7. She has (definite/~~defnite~~) ideas about how to manage her money.

8. Joan has been my (~~freind~~/friend) since second grade.

9. Don't complain about the (government/~~goverment~~) if you don't vote.

10. Use your good (judgment/~~judgement~~) when you vote.

11. A (~~pecular~~/peculiar) smell is coming from the refrigerator.

12. I think it's coming from the (vegetable/~~vegitable~~) bin

13. Let's (~~seperate~~/separate) the twins in school so their teachers won't be confused.

14. For the sake of peace, the neighbors will have to overcome their (prejudice/~~predjudice~~) against newcomers.

15. You have (~~finaly~~/finally) completed this exercise.

PRACTICING 7

Circle the correctly spelled word in each of the following pairs.

1. fourty/(forty)

2. (literature)/litrature

3. (practically)/practicly

4. (receive)/recieve

5. sevral/(several)

6. sincerly/(sincerely)

7. (calendar)/calender

8. (address)/adress

9. necessry/(necessary)

10. nieghbor/(neighbor)

11. (precede)/preceed

12. truely/(truly)

13. (ridiculous)/rediculous

14. pratically/(practically)

15. (noticeable)/noticable

Unit Test

The paragraph that follows contains 16 spelling errors mentioned in this unit. Correct each error.

    In the ~~passed~~ *past*, my relationship with my teachers was always ~~quiet~~ *quite* hostile. They always seemed to treat me like a criminal instead of just the insecure, ~~akward~~ *awkward* schoolboy that I was. For instance, my ~~arithmatic~~ *arithmetic* teacher once told my parents that they might consider ~~chosing~~ *choosing* a ~~diffrent~~ *different* school for me since I was so difficult to handle. At the time I found that suggestion ~~incredable~~ *incredible*. I didn't think my teachers were using ~~there~~ *their* best ~~judgement~~ *judgment* and most compassionate instincts to help me ajust to school. It seemed I couldn't do anything to please my teachers. Even my perfect ~~attendence~~ *attendance* didn't ~~altar~~ *alter* the fact that just the ~~site~~ *sight* of me annoyed them. My very ~~existance~~ *existence* seemed a threat to their way of teaching. I truly ~~beleived~~ *believed* that they were

predjudiced against me and prefered the more pleasant and agreeable

students who simply sat at desks and treated the teachers with great

~~reverance~~ *reverence*. But today, I look back and realize that in actuality I was just a

~~peculiar~~ *peculiar*, cynical student while my teachers were conscientious and com-

mited to their jobs. Today, I like most of my teachers because I understand

what a difficult task they have.

 ## Unit Talk-Write Assignment

Asked to say what they thought were life's simple pleasures (romance excluded), students in an English class came up with the list reproduced in the *Talk* column. First, rewrite each item as a complete sentence, correcting any misspelled words. Then choose one of the topics listed or a simple pleasure of your own and write a paragraph.

Sentences will vary.

1. State what the pleasure is (e.g., "I love to play pick-up basketball. . .").

2. Describe the pleasure in detail.

3. State why it gives you pleasure.

4. Check your paragraph for spelling errors.

TALK

1. Sleeping grate at knight.

2. Playing ketch with my dog.

3. Picking while flours.

WRITE

1. *I enjoy sleeping <u>great</u> at night.*

_____

_____

2. *Playing <u>catch</u> with my dog is fun.*

_____

_____

3. *I like picking <u>wild flowers</u>.*

_____

_____

TALK

WRITE

4. Riding in my ant's convertible.

4. *Riding in my <u>aunt's</u> convertible is exciting.*

5. Having a bear with a friend.

5. *I look forward to having a <u>beer</u> with a friend at the end of the day.*

6. Shearing secrets with a girlfriend.

6. *<u>Sharing</u> secrets with a girlfriend relieves my stress.*

7. Going cite seeing in a new city.

7. *Going <u>sight</u> seeing in a new city is adventurous.*

8. Eating my favorite desert.

8. *I enjoy eating my favorite <u>dessert</u> any time of day.*

9. Excepting a challenge.

9. *<u>Accepting</u> a challenge takes courage.*

10. Watching a knew program on TV.

10. *Sometimes I like watching a <u>new</u> program on TV.*

11. Walking in the rein without an umbrella.

11. *Walking in the <u>rain</u> without an umbrella seems crazy, but it's fun.*

12. Fixing my family there dinner.

12. *I don't mind fixing my family <u>their</u> dinner.*

13. Laying on the grass and watching the clouds.

13. *I like to spend time with my children <u>lying</u> on the grass and watching the clouds.*

TALK

WRITE

14. Eating a hot fudge Sunday topped with nuts.

14. Eating a hot fudge <u>sundae</u> topped with nuts is a wonderful experience.

15. Watching my wife comb her blonde hare.

15. I love watching my wife comb her blonde <u>hair</u>.

16. Celebrating the forth of July.

16. Celebrating the <u>Fourth</u> of July is one of my favorite events of the summer.

17. Enjoying a quite day in my garden.

17. Enjoying a <u>quiet</u> day in my garden is very relaxing.

18. Watching my brother moe the lawn.

18. I get tired just watching my brother <u>mow</u> the lawn.

19. Taking a coarse in night school.

19. I'm thinking about taking a <u>course</u> in night school.

20. Watching Monday nite football.

20. I like inviting some friends over and watching Monday <u>Night</u> Football.

Unit Collaborative Assignment

A. Read the following sentences aloud, asking a partner to spell the words in italics. Confirm that the spelling is right or correct it.

1. Jane's *past* work has always been excellent.

2. I have had *quite* enough trouble from you.

3. We had cookies for *dessert*.

4. *They're* over *their* limit of credit.

5. You have a hole in the *sole* of your shoe.

6. She has red hair, and she is *awkward*.

7. Lately the weather has been *changeable*.

8. What is your *height* and weight?

9. They were guilty of more than *mischief*.

10. Although they were twins, they always chose *separate* friends.

B. Now reverse your roles.

1. You give me *too* much trouble.

2. If she does not *accept* this time, I will still ask her out again.

3. I could not *bear* so much pain again.

4. This is the *fourth* football game we've won!

5. I hated the big *hole* in John's sock.

6. The dance floor looked *irresistible*.

7. Our *neighbor* picks up our newspaper when we're gone.

8. A camping trip requires much *preparation*.

9. *Seize* the next opportunity to do a kind deed.

10. She always tries to *fulfill* her promises.

Unit Writing Assignment

Your neighborhood action committee wants to raise money to buy children's play equipment for the park. You have been asked to write a description of the project and ask for donations. Your letter will be mailed to everyone in town, so you'll want to watch your spelling. Use the Revising Checklist on the inside cover.

Photo Writing Assignment

The following photo shows a graduation exercise. Discuss the value of this ceremony with a classmate. You might ask yourselves these questions: What is the value of the tradition? What would happen if it were discontinued? Is the tradition worth the time and effort it requires? Begin with a discussible topic sentence, which you will then prove. Check your spelling carefully and use the Revising Checklist to revise.

READINGS

In these readings, you will see put into practice many of the techniques and principles you have learned so far in this book. We strongly advise you to read the headnote that precedes each reading, and to take the comprehension test, Understanding What You Have Read, before going on to the questions under Thinking About What You Have Read.

Help for Your Reading

You can improve your reading with a few commonsense techniques. Here are some suggestions to help you read the selections in this book.

1. Scan the whole piece before you read.

Before you begin to actually read an essay, short story, or poem, casually look it over. Pay attention to the title—especially in the case of poems and short stories. The title is often a clue to the meaning of the piece. Turn the pages of an essay to see its major divisions, if any. Some essays are subdivided by heads; others appear as solid blocks of print. Scanning the heads as you turn the pages will tell you what an essay is about and what points it covers. Note the number of pages. What you are doing is looking over the essay as if it were a map for an upcoming trip. You are finding out how far you have to go and what kind of ground you have to cover.

2. Read the headnote first.

The **headnote** is the paragraph that precedes each writing selection. It gives you a general idea of what the reading is about and any surprises or twists you should look for. The headnote may also alert you to the work's main points. Through the headnote, the editors can whisper advice in your ear as you get ready to tackle the selection.

3. Write your reactions in the margins of the pages.

Get rid of the old-fashioned idea that writing in a book is a sin. If the book belongs to someone else or to the library, writing in it is *definitely* a sin. Otherwise, writing in a book is not sinful, but useful. Feel free to underline words or ideas. Scribble your reactions in the margin as you read. Writing down your reactions helps you become an active, rather than a passive, reader. When you react to a piece of writing, you involve yourself in it and are likely to get its point better than if you simply sit and read between snores. If a description is particularly sad, you might note: "This passage is gloomy." If the author's opinion annoys you, show your irritation by jotting down your reaction, whether it be, "That's a typical closed-minded opinion," or simply, "Rubbish." Another good use of marginal writing is to summarize in a phrase what the whole paragraph is about, so that when you reread, you can go straight to your summaries.

4. Underline key ideas.

All writing consists of two parts—a point and its proof. As shown in this text, most nonfiction paragraphs make a point and then try to prove it, using facts, examples, or reasons. To understand a paragraph, you must know its main point, usually found in the topic sentence. The topic sentence can be the opening sentence of a paragraph, or, less commonly, the closing sentence. An alert reader learns, therefore, to pay special attention to opening and closing sentences. Underlining the topic sentence is an excellent way to help you keep the main idea in mind as you read the rest of the paragraph. Consider this passage:

The best way to make sure that you don't die a pauper is to begin a systematic savings account early in life. Even if you put away only $10.00 a month at the start, the act of saving some money every month of the calendar starts a habit that, if continued, can eventually make you, if not wealthy, at least secure. With no savings, a person usually is unable to retire. It is a pathetic situation in our country that people who have earned good wages all of their working days often retire without a penny. They become dependent on their children or the state for food and board. If you have a pension plan, so much the better, but even then, an additional nest egg of savings will give added comfort in your retirement.

The topic sentence is the key to the meaning of the paragraph. The rest of the paragraph supports and explains the topic sentence.

Also pay close attention to *signal words*, words that announce some important idea. Here are some examples, with the signal words underlined:

Most important, however, is the temperature of the metal.

Particularly relevant is how the mother gorilla shows affection to her baby.

A major reason for the country's downfall was love of luxury.

Above all, we recommend exercises to strengthen the muscles of the abdomen.

Most noteworthy is the senator's stand on the tobacco industry.

These signal words are clues to ideas the author considers particularly important.

5. Think about what you have read.

Every paragraph or so, stop and think about what you have just read. Make a mental summary—preferably aloud—to be sure you fully understand what you are reading. If you have trouble doing this, read the passage again, and perhaps even a third time, until you understand it.

6. Look up unfamiliar words in the dictionary.

Often **context**—surrounding words or sentences—will suggest a word's meaning. In the paragraph below, notice how context tells what the word *interloper* means:

Just a few days after the police barricaded Pennsylvania Avenue to car traffic, in order to protect the White House from dangerous intruders after the Oklahoma City bombing, the first of two *interlopers*—a psychologist—climbed the White House fence. In front of dozens of shocked tourists, the man rushed across the White House lawn. A few days later, another intruder hoisted himself over the fence and was immediately handcuffed and hustled into a guard house. While neither man seemed to have a clear motive and did not seem intent on assassinating the President, the incident caused concern among the White House police.

What is an *interloper*? The context of the paragraph tell us that it means the same as *intruder*—one who barges into a place uninvited.

Sometimes context tells us all we need to know about the meaning of a word. Consider this sentence: "The cows had to be herded back to their *byre* for milking." Although you may have no idea what the word *byre* means if you see it standing alone, in the context of this sentence, you are sure it must mean something like "barn," "stable," or "cowshed."

7. Reread.

Your first reading of an essay, short story, or poem will provide a general picture of the work. You will understand its broad outline, get its main idea, and absorb its general point of view. But in order to become a better writer, you must read, and reread, line by line and even word by word. Poems, especially, need rereading because so much meaning is contained in relatively few words. So rid yourself of the idea that five minutes before class starts you can skim the reading assignment and know it. Good writing requires careful rereading.

An Object

Tortillas

José Antonio Burciaga

In Burciaga's words, the common tortilla takes on the life of a theater prop, a piece of clothing, and—most importantly—a symbol of Mexican life. Burciaga not only describes the most familiar use of the tortilla, but also informs us of its important history, reaching back to the Mayan civilizations and their mythology. The author even suggests ways of eating tortillas and creating works of art with them. In addition to serving as a basic food staple over the centuries, the tortilla has risen to the high rank of a cultural badge for the Mexican people. As you read, think about what details the author uses to give the tortilla such cultural importance.

1 My earliest memories of tortillas is my Mamá telling me not to play with them. I had bitten eyeholes in one and was wearing it as a mask at the dinner table.

2 As a child, I also used *tortillas* as hand warmers on cold days, and my family claims that I owe my career as an artist to my early experiments with *tortillas*. According to them, my clowning around helped me develop a strong artistic foundation. I'm not so sure, though. Sometimes I wore a *tortilla* on my head, like a *yarmulke*, and yet I never had any great urge to convert from Catholicism to Judaism. But who knows? They may be right.

3 For Mexicans over the centuries, the *tortilla* has served as the spoon and the fork, the plate and the napkin. *Tortillas* originated before the Mayan civilizations, perhaps predating Europe's wheat bread. According to Mayan mythology, the great god Quetzalcoatl, realizing that the red ants knew the secret of using maize as food, transformed himself into a black ant, infiltrated the colony of red ants, and absconded with a grain of corn. (Is it any wonder that to this day, black ants and red ants do not get along?) Quetzalcoatl then put maize on the lips of the first man and woman, Oxomoco and Cipactonal, so that they would become strong. Maize festivals are still celebrated by many Indian cultures of the Americas.

4 When I was growing up in El Paso, *tortillas* were part of my daily life. I used to visit a *tortilla* factory in an ancient adobe building near the open *mercado* in Ciudad Juárez. As I approached, I could hear the rhythmic slapping of the *masa* as the skilled vendors outside the factory formed it into balls and patted them into perfectly round corn cakes between the palms of their hands. The wonderful aroma and the speed with which the women counted so many dozens of *tortillas* out of warm wicker baskets still linger in my mind. Watching them at work convinced me that the most handsome and *deliciosas tortillas* are handmade. Although machines are faster, they can never adequately replace generation-to-generation experience. There's no place in the factory assembly line for the tender slaps that give each *tortilla* character. The best thing that can be said about mass-producing *tortillas* is that it makes it possible for many people to enjoy them.

5 In the *mercado* where my mother shopped, we frequently bought *taquitos de nopalizos*, small tacos filled with diced cactus, onions, tomatoes, and *jalapeños*. Our friend Don Toribio showed us how to make delicious, crunchy *taquitos* with dried, salted pumpkin seeds. When you had no money for the filling, a poor man's *taco* could be made by placing a warm *tortilla* on the left palm, applying a sprinkle of salt, then rolling the *tortilla* up quickly with the fingertips of the right hand. My own kids put peanut butter and jelly on

tortillas, which I think is truly bicultural. And speaking of fast foods for kids, nothing beats a *quesadilla*, a *tortilla* grilled-cheese sandwich.

Depending on what you intend to use them for, *tortillas* may be made **6** in various ways. Even a run-of-the-mill *tortilla* is more than a flat corn cake. A skillfully cooked homemade *tortilla* has a bottom and a top; the top skin forms a pocket in which you put the filling that folds your *tortilla* into a taco. Paper-thin tortillas are used specifically for *flautas*, a type of taco that is filled, rolled, and then fried until crisp. The name *flauta* means *flute*, which probably refers to the Mayan bamboo flute; however, the only sound that comes from an edible *flauta* is a delicious crunch that is music to the palate. In México *flautas* are sometimes made as long as two feet and then cut into manageable segments. The opposite of *flautas* is *gorditas,* meaning *little fat ones*. These are very thick small *tortillas.*

The versatility of *tortillas* and corn does not end here. Besides being **7** tasty and nourishing, they have spiritual and artistic qualities as well. The Tarahumara Indians of Chihuahua, for example, concocted a corn-based beer called *tesgüino*, which their descendants still make today. And everyone has read about the woman in New Mexico who was cooking her husband a *tortilla* one morning when the image of Jesus Christ miraculously appeared on it. Before they knew what was happening, the man's breakfast had become a local shrine.

Then there is *tortilla* art. Various Chicano artists throughout the South- **8** west have, when short of materials or just in a whimsical mood, used a dry *tortilla* as a small, round canvas. And a few years back, at the height of the Chicano movement, a priest in Arizona got into trouble with the Church after he was discovered celebrating mass using a *tortilla* as the host. All of which only goes to show that while the *tortilla* may be a lowly corn cake, when the necessity arises, it can reach unexpected distinction.

Vocabulary

yarmulke (2)   bicultural (5)
maize (3)   concocted (7)
infiltrated (3)   whimsical (8)
absconded (3)   host (8)
aroma (4)

Understanding What You Have Read

Check the correct answer in the blank provided.

1. The author's earliest memory of tortillas is
    _____ **(a).** the odor they produced while baking.
    ✔ **(b).** his mother telling him not to play with them.
    _____ **(c).** using them as flying saucers.
    _____ **(d).** that they tasted terrible.

2. Tortillas predate
    _____ **(a).** horses.
    _____ **(b).** the wheel.
    _____ **(c).** the founding of Mexico City.
    ✔ **(d).** the Mayan civilizations.

3. What do the author's children place on their tortillas?

_____ ✔ **(a).** Peanut butter and jelly.

_____ **(b).** Chocolate syrup.

_____ **(c).** Ice cream.

_____ **(d).** The hottest jalapeños.

4. What is a *flauta*?

_____ **(a).** A girl who flouts customs.

_____ **(b).** A flirtatious girl.

_____ ✔ **(c).** A tortilla that is filled, rolled, and fried until crisp.

_____ **(d).** An act of disobedience.

5. What segment of society has used tortillas when they were short of materials?

_____ ✔ **(a).** Artists.

_____ **(b).** Nurses.

_____ **(c).** Football players.

_____ **(d).** Cleaning women.

Thinking About What You Have Read

1. What is the author's formal definition of a tortilla? In which paragraph does he state it?

2. Why do you think the author uses terms like *mercado, masa, deliciosas,* and *jalapeños?* Do these terms make the essay difficult to understand for readers who do not know Spanish? Why or why not?

3. Besides serving as a basic food, what other functions have tortillas served over the centuries of Mexican history? Why does the author mention these other functions?

4. What does the author have against machine-made tortillas? Do you agree or disagree? Give reasons for your answer.

5. What humor does the author use throughout his essay? Point to some specific instances. What does the humor add?

Writing Assignments

1. Write about a food that is particularly representative of your ethnic background. Describe the food and explain how it is used among your family and friends. Use details that allow your reader to see the food and taste it.

2. Describe your favorite food with details that will show your reader why you like it.

The Ritual of the Grill

Bonny Thomson Belgum

This essay highlights a custom special to most Americans—the Fourth of July bar-becue—which brings together families and friends. In describing the process, the author goes into great detail and also muses about the possible greater meaning of barbecuing as ritual. As you read, try to imagine being at a barbecue, watching the meat sizzle on the grill, hearing the conversation, and feeling the mood of the celebration. How important are barbecues and picnics on the Fourth of July? What, if anything, do you like about them?

1   The Fourth of July means only one thing to the American male: raw meat. Forget fireworks, flags, family, even potato salad. These elements only serve as accessories to the main event: the tray of raw meat.

2   The oohs and ahs issuing forth from the guests gathered around the grill far exceed any to be elicited by the spectacular fireworks display the sated group will later attend. The pride a child feels while wielding a sparkler cannot touch the self-satisfaction of the "chef" as the meat hits the grill and the first sizzle is heard.

3   It is further lost on this horde that the myriad women bearing covered dishes—each dish reflecting days of meticulous preparation—might more appropriately be called "chef." The women's 12-tiered tortes simply cannot compete with 16 ounces of bleeding bovine flesh. No, their tortes and other delicate creations are regarded merely as condiments, much as mus-tard, to enhance the grilled wonder.

4   If I understand the procedure correctly, you drop the meat onto the grill with a long fork. After a while, you spear the meat with the long fork and flip it over. Lather, rinse, repeat, basically. Then the cooked meat is speared yet again and dropped onto a platter or onto the paper plate of the next in line. Miracle complete.

5   So, I am forced to ask, what is the big deal? Is it that raw meat is the only food the guests, who are kept outdoors, can see and therefore believe is truly theirs to eat? Is it the chef's apron, replete with a clever saying like "Don't bother the cook" that elevates his status? Or the utterly unneces-sary oven mitts that perhaps remind one of boxing and by association raise the perceived testosterone level of the fork-holder?

6   Could it be too much beer?

7   Maybe it's all about fire. The ritual begins with a bag of coals. There is much heated discussion about the most efficient and artful way to arrange the briquets. This turns out to be your basic pile. The coals are then doused, way beyond the recommended dosage, with lighter fluid. The match is lit. The flames erupt. They—the blaze and the men—simmer down to half an hour of glowing and smoking until the Moment of Raw Meat, when the flames rally and burst forth in enthusiastic response to the spray of animal fluids and A-1 sauce.

8   Perhaps the mystical cookout is simply an expression of the male pre-occupation with the power of fire, a fascination summoned forth by a primal survival instinct. That theory strikes me as more plausible, and far more accessible to the logical mind, than the notion that grilling meat is even a skill, much less an act of unbridled admiration.

9   So, then, men grill in order to survive. In order that we all may survive. And for that I am grateful.

Vocabulary

accessories (1)
elicited (2)
meticulous (3)
bovine (3)
replete (5)
testosterone (5)
doused (7)

mystical (8)
summoned (8)
primal (8)
plausible (8)
accessible (8)
unbridled (8)

Understanding What You Have Read

Check the correct answer in the blank provided.

1. What one thing does the Fourth of July mean to the American male?

   _____ **(a).** A vacation from work.

   _✔_ **(b).** Raw meat.

   _____ **(c).** Reaffirmation of our country's independence.

   _____ **(d).** Spending considerable money.

2. Fireworks, flags, family, and even potato salad are considered

   _____ **(a).** the main ingredients of the celebration.

   _____ **(b).** what the Fourth of July is all about.

   _____ **(c).** necessary for taking photos.

   _✔_ **(d).** mere accessories.

3. What is the first step in barbecuing the meat?

   _✔_ **(a).** Dropping the meat on the grill with a long fork.

   _____ **(b).** Singing "American the Beautiful."

   _____ **(c).** Handing everyone a paper plate.

   _____ **(d).** Sprinkling salt and pepper on the meat.

4. Which of the following items is not mentioned?

   _____ **(a).** The chef's apron.

   _____ **(b).** Oven mitts.

   _____ **(c).** Beer.

   _✔_ **(d).** Ice cream sundaes.

5. In barbecuing, heated discussion is held about

   _____ **(a).** having good weather.

   _____ **(b).** keeping the smoke out of the guests' eyes.

   _✔_ **(c).** arranging the briquets.

   _____ **(d).** lighting the match.

Thinking About What You Have Read

1. How does the writer feel about the ritual she describes? Does she admire it? Hate it? Make fun of it? Find it delightful? Support your answer with details from the essay.

2. Why does the writer consider the women the real chefs of the barbecue? Do you agree with her comment? Why or why not?

3. What does the author mean when she states, "Maybe it's all about fire."

4. In paragraph 8, the writer refers to "a primal survival instinct." What other example of this instinct can you offer?

5. What meaning does the Fourth of July hold for you? Do you have a special Fourth of July ritual? Describe it in detail. If you have no ritual, explain why.

Writing Assignments

1. Write a paragraph about one of your family rituals that holds an important place in your life. Include a description of the ritual and an explanation of its importance to you.

2. In one paragraph, state what the word *ritual* means (look it up in the dictionary if you are not completely sure about its definition). Support your definition with two or three examples of important rituals with which you are familiar.

The Cello

Lorena Bruff

"The Cello" is a modern poem. As you can see, it has no traditional rhyme or poetic rhythm. It is short and to the point. Yet it has a haunting quality to it. As you read this poem, ask yourself these questions: What is the poet actually talking about? Is she talking about a cello or about a person? How can you tell? What point is she really trying to make?

THE CELLO

To tell you   **1**
the truth
I never
wanted to be
a cello.

When I was
wood
I had
my own song.

Lorena Bruff

Understanding What You Have Read

Check the correct answer in the blank provided.

1. What is a cello?
   _____ **(a).** It is a musical instrument played with the lips.
   _____ **(b).** It is a percussion instrument.
   _____ **(c).** It is something used in chemistry experiments.
   __✔__ **(d).** It is a musical instrument played with a bow.

2. Who is speaking in this poem?
   __✔__ **(a).** The cello.
   _____ **(b).** We can't tell.
   _____ **(c).** A person who plays the cello.
   _____ **(d).** None of the above.

3. What is a cello made of?
   _____ **(a).** Metal.
   __✔__ **(b).** Wood.
   _____ **(c).** Clay.
   _____ **(d).** Cotton.

4. What would you say is the mood of the cello?
    _____ **(a).** It is happy.
    _____ **(b).** It is optimistic.
    __✔__ **(c).** It is sad.
    _____ **(d).** It is in love.

Thinking About What You Have Read

1. What do you think the stanza "when I was / wood / I had / my own song" means?

2. What was the cello before it became a cello? How can "wood" have its own song?

3. What is this poem actually about? About whom do you think it was written? A cello, or a person?

4. How could the complaint of the cello be summed up in a single sentence? Write a single sentence explanation of the meaning of this poem.

Writing Assignments

1. Write a paragraph comparing yourself to any musical instrument you think you are like.

2. Write a paragraph about a time you had to sing a song (or play a role) you felt was really someone else's, not your own.

A Place

The Hole at Alcatraz

Jim Quillen

This brief essay is taken from the memoir of an inmate who, at age 22, was sentenced to forty-five years in Alcatraz, the island prison in San Francisco Bay, now closed except for tourist visits. The author describes the "hole," an isolation cell where troublesome prisoners were kept. Bear in mind the youth of the writer at the time of his experience. What does his description of the hole tell you about him as a person? Try to imagine yourself in a place where the food is the same day in and day out, where your living quarters consist of a bed, a toilet, and a sink, and where you are totally isolated from the rest of the world.

A day in the hole was like an eternity. The day would start at 6:30 A.M. when the lights were turned on and a nerve-jangling bell was rung. This was soon followed by a guard unlocking the outer sound-proof door and shouting for you to stand up. After being accounted for, the guard would leave, closing the outer door again. The light remained on and you were to prepare for breakfast. A short time later your door would again open and a tray was passed through the narrow slot in the inside barred door. This was your morning meal. **1**

Although one received the same food as the mainline, it was all dumped together in an unappetizing lump. Bread was buried in the oatmeal, prunes dumped on top and no milk or sugar was allotted. A cup of warm coffee completed the meal. This was typical of how food was served in the hole. True, nutritional value was adequate, but the unappetizing manner in which it was served soon made one lose his desire to eat. **2**

After approximately twenty minutes your tray was collected. If you could not stomach the meal, you had best dump it down the toilet, in order to prevent missing what might be a better noon meal. Shortly after your tray was collected, your door would open up again and you would be instructed to roll up your blanket, pillow and mattress and set them in the three-foot space separating the inner and outer doors. The guard would step out, relock the outer door and open a metal peep slot and watch until you complied. After you returned inside the inner door, it was again relocked and the lights were turned off, leaving you in total darkness for the remainder of the day, except for meals. **3**

There was nothing in the cell except a cold metal bed frame, a toilet, a sink and you. There was total silence because of the outer sound-proof door. It was also very cold, because of the limited clothing you were allowed. Inmates were given a pair of shorts, socks and coveralls. These were inadequate to keep one warm, because the steel walls and floor of the cell retained the cold. **4**

Worse than being cold, though, was the total feeling of isolation from the world. Being unable to see or hear is a very awesome experience to someone who has no physical impairment. Since total silence and darkness were to be my constant companion for twenty-four hours of each day of solitary confinement, it was imperative to find a way to keep my mind occupied, somehow! I invented a game simply to retain my sanity. I would tear a button from my coveralls, then fling it into the air, turn around in circles several times and, with my eyes closed, get on the floor on my **5** hands and knees and search for the button. When it was found, I would repeat the entire routine over and over until I was exhausted, or my knees were so sore I could not continue.

When I could no longer hunt the button, I would pace back and forth **6** between the toilet and the door. I would continue these routines until evening, since it was too cold to just sit and pacing helped pass the time. If not for the interruption of meals, it would have been easy to confuse night and day.

After the evening meal, our bedding was returned and I would get into **7** bed and hope to fall asleep quickly. Nineteen consecutive days was the maximum time an inmate could be confined in solitary. If he behaved, he was not usually returned. If he still persisted in creating a problem, however, he was taken out, fed a full meal, allowed to brush his teeth and then returned to solitary for another nineteen days.

Vocabulary

complied (3)
impairment (5)
imperative (5)
pace (6)

Understanding What You Have Read

Check the correct answer in the blank provided.

1. At what time would a day in the hole begin?

    _____ **(a).** Dawn.

    _____ **(b).** 4 A.M.

    ✔ **(c).** 6:30 A.M.

    _____ **(d).** Midnight of the day before.

2. How many doors did the hole have?

    _____ **(a).** One.

    _____ **(b).** Three.

    _____ **(c).** Four.

    ✔ **(d).** Two.

3. How did the prisoner pass the daylight hours?

    ✔ **(a).** He played a game of finding a button with his eyes closed.

    _____ **(b).** He daydreamed.

    _____ **(c).** He recited poetry.

    _____ **(d).** He thought about murdering the rat who had sent him there.

4. What made the food in the hole so unappetizing?

    _____ **(a).** It was served cold.

    _____ **(b).** It was not seasoned.

    _____ **(c).** It was always raw.

    ✔ **(d).** It was lumped together.

5. What was the maximum stay given a prisoner in the hole?
    __✔__ **(a).** Nineteen days.
    _____ **(b).** Six months.
    _____ **(c).** Three months.
    _____ **(d).** Two weeks.

Thinking About What You Have Read

1. What effect do you think confinement in the hole would have on an inmate? How do you think being locked in the hole would affect you?

2. Aside from punishment, what other aim do you think was behind confinement in the hole?

3. Do you think confinement in the hole is cruel and inhuman punishment? Why or why not?

4. Based on the author's description of how he passed the time in the hole, what can you say about him and his personality?

5. In the last paragraph, the author writes that he would go to bed hoping to fall asleep quickly. What does this statement tell you about him and about being in the hole?

Writing Assignments

1. Write a paragraph about a time when you felt lonely.

2. Write a paragraph giving your opinion about keeping prisoners in solitary confinememt.

Letter from Tokyo

Michael A. Lev

Every country has its own way of adapting to and dealing with the world—its own culture. The episode that Lev, the Tokyo foreign correspondent for the Chicago Tribune, *recounts here is a classic example of what can happen when the expectations of two cultures clash. Lev, with the point of view of a typical American, cannot understand why he can't get lettuce and tomato on his cheeseburger. On the other hand, the Japanese restaurant owner cannot understand why Lev doesn't follow the rules. As you read this piece, try to imagine how Lev must have seemed to the Japanese, with their entirely different way of looking at things.*

TOKYO—The day of the naked cheeseburger could have turned ugly. **1** The ex-New Yorker in me wanted to scream and yell. But the journalist in me recognized a chance to gain insight into Japanese society, or at least to have a classic native experience—like being in Manhattan and getting accosted by an arrogant panhandler.

It was lunch time, and my Japanese interpreter, Naoko Nishiwaki, and **2** I were in a Tokyo hamburger restaurant called One's. Naoko ordered the One's burger, and I picked the cheeseburger.

When our food came, Naoko's hamburger looked fabulous—a thick, **3** juicy patty heaped with fresh lettuce and tomato. My cheeseburger was naked. It looked sad. In halting Japanese, I called over the proprietor.

"Excuse me." I said. "My cheeseburger doesn't have lettuce or tomato. **4** Can I have some, please?"

She gave me a quizzical look. **5**

"No." **6**

No? My pulse immediately quickened beyond my Japanese fluency **7** level, and Naoko was forced to begin interpreting. "Just bring some lettuce and tomato. I'll pay for it."

Sorry. The cheeseburger doesn't come with lettuce and tomato. **8**

I didn't back down, so she got tough. "Cheeseburgers don't get lettuce **9** and tomato; that's not how they come," she said, adding, "Even for a child, we wouldn't do anything different."

Her final offer: If you don't want the cheeseburger, I'll take it back and **10** make you an One's burger.

"That's absurd. Just cut me some tomato slices and bring them on a **11** napkin "

The woman got so excited that even Naoko had trouble deciphering her. **12** The tomato and lettuce aren't the right size for the cheeseburger, she argued. They won't mesh properly with the cheese.

She grabbed my cheeseburger from me. She returned later with a **13** freshly cooked One's burger and a dirty look.

I label this run-in with Japanese inflexibility the "kir effect" because of **14** what happened to Masao Miyamoto, an author and social critic I know.

Miyamoto went to a hotel bar, saw an open bottle of white wine on dis- **15** play and ordered a glass. Sorry. he was told, white wine isn't on the menu. It's used to make kir, a wine cocktail with cassis. Thinking quickly, Miyamoto ordered a kir—hold the cassis.

Long negotiations ensued with the waiter, with the maitre d', with the **16** assistant manager. Finally, he got his drink, but he was told to please never come back.

These moments of exasperation reflect a culture in which order reigns. **17** It is a cliché, but it's true: Japan is a group-oriented society. If everyone did their own thing, this tiny over-populated archipelago would descend into chaos, the thinking goes.

In some ways, it's a great system. Riding a bicycle in Tokyo is a pleasure, even on crowded sidewalks. The rule is, ring your bicycle bell once and pedestrians ahead will step to the side. Works every time. **18**

Just don't question the rules. While buying an expensive cellular telephone, the salesman asked for my Japanese residency card. I had my temporary card with permanent ID number but had not yet received the credit card size permanent card with photograph. **19**

"Sorry," he said. "Come back when you have it." **20**

"But it's the correct ID number," I explained. "I just have it on a sheet of paper instead of on a credit card." **21**

He continued to pack up the paperwork. I insisted that he call headquarters. I needed the phone, didn't he need the sale? He returned sucking his teeth and shrugging. "It would be a little difficult," he said, using the Japanese phrase for "impossible." **22**

If I were Japanese, I would have been expected to apologize and leave the store for causing trouble. Instead, Naoko, who has lived in America and understands our strange ways, went to work. There were belabored discussions by telephone with several parties and then a visit to the local telephone company office. Proposals. Counteroffers. Liberal use of the phrase "a little difficult." But I finally got my phone. **23**

Miyamoto sees the issue in harsh terms: Japanese society does not teach or tolerate independent thinking. All decisions are reached by consensus. Everything is done by the book. **24**

I was stopped for speeding not long ago. Instead of producing a Japanese or an American driver's license, I showed my international driver's license. The cop had never seen one before. I knew he was impressed with how official it looked. But he was confounded by the identification numbers. They didn't correspond with the number of blank spaces on his speeding-ticket form. **25**

Would he risk filling out a messy ticket with numbers that didn't fit in the boxes? **26**

No way. He let me go. **27**

Vocabulary

accosted (1)	archipelago (17)
quizzical (5)	belabored (23)
deciphering (12)	consensus (24)
exasperation (17)	confounded (25)

Understanding What You Have Read

Check the correct answer in the blank provided.

1. What did the author want that caused such a scene in the restaurant?

   _____ **(a).** He wanted a bottle of ketchup.

   _____ **(b).** He wanted sushi.

   _____ **(c).** He wanted Jamaican pepper sauce.

   __✔__ **(d).** He wanted lettuce and tomato on his cheeseburger.

2. What name does the author give to Japanese inflexibility?

    _____ **(a).** Mulishness.

    _____ **(b).** The kamikaze principle.

    __✔__ **(c).** The kir effect.

    _____ **(d).** The anti-American practice.

3. What, according to the author, is a cliche, but true?

    __✔__ **(a).** That Japan is a group-oriented society

    _____ **(b).** That there is a streak of wildness in the Japanese.

    _____ **(c).** That the Japanese love sports.

    _____ **(d).** That the Japanese emphasize individual rights

4. What is the rule for riding a bicycle on the sidewalk in Tokyo?

    _____ **(a).** Bicyclists have the right-of-way.

    __✔__ **(b).** Ring your bicycle bell once and pedestrians will step to the side.

    _____ **(c).** Shout, "Look out!"

    _____ **(d).** Hire a guide to go ahead of you.

5. Why did the Japanese cop not give the author a speeding ticket?

    _____ **(a).** Because he felt sorry for the author.

    __✔__ **(b).** Because the author's license number would not fit on the speeding ticket form.

    _____ **(c).** Because the author was unfamiliar with the rules of the road.

    _____ **(d).** Because the author talked him out of it.

Thinking About What You Have Read

1. The author writes in the first paragraph that the "ex-New Yorker" in him wanted to scream and yell. What do you suppose an ex-New Yorker is like? Why do you think he mentions where in the United States he used to live?

2. What basic rule of American business did the author's experience at the hamburger restaurant run counter to?

3. The author writes, "While buying an expensive cellular telephone, the salesman asked for my Japanese residency card." The sentence contains a grammatical error that this book has taught you how to correct. What is it? How would you correct the sentence?

4. What is your opinion of the author's complaints about Japanese society? Do you think them reasonable, or do you think him fussy? Explain your answer.

5. In paragraph 23 the author writes that his interpreter had lived in America and understood "our strange ways." What does he mean by "strange ways"?

Writing Assignments

1. Write a paragraph about a time someone did not behave the way you thought he or she would.

2. Write about any unpleasant encounter you had with a difficult salesperson.

The Monkey Garden

Sandra Cisneros

The most striking aspect of this short story is the imagery. The narrator is obviously exaggerating the fabulous aspects of a garden she remembers from her youth in a Chicago neighborhood. You will need to pay close attention to what happened in the garden when the boys stole Sally's keys and wouldn't give them back unless she kissed each of them. This incident affected the narrator in a special way. Imagine yourself in her position and see if you can figure out what bothered her.

1 The monkey doesn't live there anymore. The monkey moved—to Kentucky—and took his people with him. And I was glad because I couldn't listen anymore to his wild screaming at night, the twangy yakkety-yak of the people who owned him. The green metal cage, the porcelain table top, the family that spoke like guitars. Monkey, family, table. All gone.

2 And it was then we took over the garden we had been afraid to go into when the monkey screamed and showed its yellow teeth.

3 There were sunflowers big as flowers on Mars and thick cockscombs bleeding the deep red fringe of theater curtains. There were dizzy bees and bow-tied fruit flies turning somersaults and humming in the air. Sweet sweet peach trees. Thorn roses and thistle and pears. Weeds like so many squinty-eyed stars and brush that made your ankles itch and itch until you washed with soap and water. There were big green apples hard as knees. And everywhere the sleepy smell of rotting wood, damp earth and dusty hollyhocks thick and perfumy like the blue-blond hair of the dead.

4 Yellow spiders ran when we turned rocks over and pale worms blind and afraid of light rolled over in their sleep. Poke a stick in the sandy soil and a few blue-skinned beetles would appear, an avenue of ants, so many crusty lady bugs. This was a garden, a wonderful thing to look at in the spring. But bit by bit, after the monkey left, the garden began to take over itself. Flowers stopped obeying the little bricks that kept them from growing beyond their paths. Weeds mixed in. Dead cars appeared overnight like mushrooms. First one and then another and then a pale blue pickup with the front windshield missing. Before you knew it, the monkey garden became filled with sleepy cars.

5 Things had a way of disappearing in the garden, as if the garden itself ate them, or, as if with its old-man memory, it put them away and forgot them. Nenny found a dollar and a dead mouse between two rocks in the stone wall where the morning glories climbed, and once when we were playing hide and seek, Eddie Vargas laid his head beneath a hibiscus tree and fell asleep there like a Rip Van Winkle until somebody remembered he was in the game and went back to look for him.

6 This, I suppose, was the reason why we went there. Far away from where our mothers could find us. We and a few old dogs who lived inside the empty cars. We made a club-house once on the back of that old blue pickup. And besides, we liked to jump from the roof of one car to another and pretend they were giant mushrooms.

7 Somebody started the lie that the monkey garden had been there before anything. We liked to think the garden could hide things for a thousand years. There beneath the roots of soggy flowers were the bones of murdered pirates and dinosaurs, the eye of a unicorn turned to coal.

8 This is where I wanted to die and where I tried one day but not even the monkey garden would have me. It was the last day I would go there.

9 Who was it that said I was getting too old to play the games? Who was it I didn't listen to? I only remember that when the others ran, I wanted to

run too, up and down and through the monkey garden, fast as the boys, not like Sally who screamed if she got her stockings muddy.

I said, Sally, come on, but she wouldn't. She stayed by the curb talking to Tito and his friends. Play with the kids if you want, she said, I'm staying here. She could be stuck-up like that if she wanted to, so I just left. **10**

It was her own fault too. When I got back Sally was pretending to be mad . . . something about the boys having stolen her keys. Please give them back to me, she said punching the nearest one with a soft fist. They were laughing. She was too. It was a joke I didn't get. **11**

I wanted to go back with the other kids who were still jumping on cars, still chasing each other through the garden, but Sally had her own game. **12**

One of the boys invented the rules. One of Tito's friends said you can't get the keys back unless you kiss us and Sally pretended to be mad at first but she said yes. It was that simple. **13**

I don't know why, but something inside me wanted to throw a stick. Something wanted to say no when I watched Sally going into the garden with Tito's buddies all grinning. It was just a kiss, that's all. A kiss for each one. So what, she said. **14**

Only how come I felt angry inside. Like something wasn't right. Sally went behind that old blue pickup to kiss the boys and get her keys back, and I ran up three flights of stairs to where Tito lived. His mother was ironing shirts. She was sprinkling water on them from an empty pop bottle and smoking a cigarette. **15**

Your son and his friends stole Sally's keys and now they won't give them back unless she kisses them and right now they're making her kiss them, I said all out of breath from the three flights of stairs. **16**

Those kids, she said, not looking up from her ironing. **17**

That's all? **18**

What do you want me to do, she said, call the cops? And kept on ironing. **19**

I looked at her a long time, but couldn't think of anything to say, and ran back down the three flights to the garden where Sally needed to be saved. I took three big sticks and a brick and figured this was enough. **20**

But when I got there Sally said go home. Those boys said, leave us alone. I felt stupid with my brick. They all looked at me as if I was the one that was crazy and made me feel ashamed. **21**

And then I don't known why but I had to run away. I had to hide myself at the other end of the garden, in the jungle part, under a tree that wouldn't mind if I lay down and cried a long time. I closed my eyes like tight stars so that I wouldn't, but I did. My face felt hot. Everything inside hiccupped. **22**

I read somewhere in India there are priests who can will their heart to stop beating. I wanted to will my blood to stop, my heart to quit its pumping. I wanted to be dead, to turn into the rain, my eyes melt into the ground like two black snails. I wished and wished. I closed my eyes and willed it, but when I got up my dress was green and I had a headache. **23**

I looked at my feet in their white socks and ugly round shoes. They seemed far away. They didn't seem to be my feet anymore. And the garden that had been such a good place to play didn't seem mine either. **24**

Vocabulary

twangy (1)
porcelain (1)
hiccupped (22)

Understanding What You Have Read

Check the correct answer in the blank provided.

1. What relationship exists between the title and the story?
    _____ **(a).** The narrator loved to go to the zoo and watch the monkeys.
    _____ **(b).** The garden was named after a famous African monkey.
    _____ **(c).** The narrator's house was next to a garden that housed many monkeys.
    ✔ **(d).** The garden that seemed so fabulous to the narrator used to house a monkey.

2. The children went to the garden so that they
    ✔ **(a).** could get far away from their mothers.
    _____ **(b).** could sunbathe in the nude.
    _____ **(c).** could play basketball.
    _____ **(d).** could have picnics.

3. Somebody started the lie that the monkey garden
    _____ **(a).** was filled with poisonous snakes.
    ✔ **(b).** had been there before anything else.
    _____ **(c).** was owned by an Arabian prince.
    _____ **(d).** was to be replaced by an elementary school.

4. Feeling that Sally was in danger from Tito and his friends, the narrator
    ✔ **(a).** ran to complain to Tito's mother.
    _____ **(b).** called 911.
    _____ **(c).** took her dog and ran after Tito.
    _____ **(d).** ran to ask Sally's mother for help.

5. What happened that kept the narrator from ever going back to the garden?
    _____ **(a).** The ugly monkey came back.
    _____ **(b).** She almost got raped in the garden.
    _____ **(c).** One day she just felt too grown-up to play in the garden.
    ✔ **(d).** Sally seemed to enjoy kissing the boys.

Thinking About What You Have Read

1. The description of the garden is that of a child's fantastic memory. What kind of garden do you think it really was? Give a realistic, rather than fantastic, description.

2. What is the meaning of the entire story? Try to summarize it in one complete sentence.

3. Why was the narrator so utterly miserable over Sally's behavior? What do you think was at the heart of her despair?

4. Is the portrayal of Tito and his gang realistic? Do young boys really act the way they did? Give an example from your own background to either support or refute this portrayal.

5. At what point in the story do we get a hint that Sally will play along with the boys? Point to a specific passage.

Writing Assignments

1. Write about an imaginary place in your past. If you cannot think of one, make it up. Provide vivid details like those in "The Monkey Garden."

2. Write about a time when you became disillusioned with a friend because of something he or she did. Describe your reaction in vivid language to make your reader understand how you felt.

An Animal

Snakes

Michael Ondaatje

What makes this brief essay fascinating is the mystery associated with it. Why did the grey cobra lead such a charmed life? Snake stories tend to interest most readers because secret powers have been attributed to this reptile by many ancient myths and folklore. As you read, look for humor as well as mystery.

1   The family home of Rock Hill was littered with snakes, especially cobras. The immediate garden was not so dangerous, but one step further and you would see several. The chickens that my father kept in later years were an even greater magnet. The snakes came for the eggs. The only deterrent my father discovered was ping-pong balls. He had crates of ping-pong balls shipped to Rock Hill and distributed them among the eggs. The snake would swallow the ball whole and be unable to digest it. There are several paragraphs on this method of snake control in a pamphlet he wrote on poultry farming.

2   The snakes also had the habit of coming into the house and at least once a month there would be shrieks, the family would run around, the shotgun would be pulled out, and the snake would be blasted to pieces. Certain sections of the walls and floors showed the scars of shot. My stepmother found one coiled asleep on her desk and was unable to approach the drawer to get the key to open the gun case. At another time one lay sleeping on the large radio to draw its warmth and, as nobody wanted to destroy the one source of music in the house, this one was watched carefully but left alone.

3   Most times though there would be running footsteps, yells of fear and excitement, everybody trying to quiet everybody else, and my father or stepmother would blast away not caring what was in the background, a wall, good ebony, a sofa, or a decanter. They killed at least thirty snakes between them.

4   After my father died, a grey cobra came into the house. My stepmother loaded the gun and fired at point blank range. The gun jammed. She stepped back and reloaded but by then the snake had slid out into the garden. For the next month this snake would often come into the house and each time the gun would misfire or jam, or my stepmother would miss at absurdly short range. The snake attacked no one and had a tendency to follow my younger sister Susan around. Other snakes entering the house were killed by the shotgun, lifted with a long stick and flicked into the bushes, but the old grey cobra led a charmed life. Finally one of the old workers at Rock Hill told my stepmother what had become obvious, that it was my father who had come to protect his family. And in fact, whether it was because the chicken farm closed down or because of my father's presence in the form of a snake, very few other snakes came into the house again.

Vocabulary

magnet (1)
deterrent (1)
pamphlet (1)
poultry (1)

ebony (3)
decanter (3)
absurdly (4)

507

Understanding What You Have Read

Check the correct answer in the blank provided.

1. What at the family home of Rock Hill was a greater magnet to the snakes than the garden?
    _____ **(a).** The turtles.
    _____ **(b).** The geese.
    _____ **(c).** The fireplaces.
    __✔__ **(d).** The chickens.

2. Certain sections of the walls at Rock Hill showed signs of
    _____ **(a).** splattered food.
    _____ **(b).** earthquake damage.
    __✔__ **(c).** shotgun holes.
    _____ **(d).** pink paint.

3. Once the author's stepmother saw a snake coiled asleep
    __✔__ **(a).** on her desk.
    _____ **(b).** in her washing machine.
    _____ **(c).** on her bed.
    _____ **(d).** on her ironing board.

4. What happened each time the stepmother would shoot at the grey cobra?
    _____ **(a).** The snake would slither out of range.
    __✔__ **(b).** She would miss or the gun would jam.
    _____ **(c).** Someone could be heard praying.
    _____ **(d).** She would faint from fear.

5. Finally, one of the old workers decided that the grey cobra
    _____ **(a).** had no taste for eggs.
    _____ **(b).** was too old to do any harm.
    __✔__ **(c).** was really the author's father returning from the dead to protect the family.
    _____ **(d).** deserved to be handed over to the local zoo.

Thinking About What You Have Read

1. What does the ping-pong ball incident indicate about the author's father?

2. What incident, other than finding a snake in your house, could cause the same kind of family excitement described in paragraphs 2 and 3? Give a specific example.

3. Judging from the details offered by the author, what kind of woman was the author's stepmother? List some of her traits.

4. What do you suppose gave the old worker the idea that the snake was the father returned from the grave?

5. Why do you think few other snakes came into the house again?

Writing Assignments

1. Write about something that happened in your life that you have never been able to fully explain.

2. Write a paragraph describing how you feel about snakes. Do they frighten you? Are you repulsed by them? Do you like them? Do you consider them interesting? Do they have a special meaning for you?

The Revolt of the Elephants

Ingrid E. Newkirk

This is an argument in favor of freeing captive elephants. The author argues with the passion of a true believer. Her point is simple: It is wrong to hold elephants in captivity solely for the entertainment of humans. She tries to convince us that the elephant is not just a dumb animal, but a sensitive creature capable of almost human feelings. As you read, notice her use of examples and the contrast she draws between the lives of a wild elephant and one that has been captured, trained, and put to work in a circus.

The elephants are mad and they're just not going to take it anymore. Three times this summer a "circus elephant" has run amok and hurt her captors. In New York, an elephant named Flora crushed the skull of a Moscow Circus interpreter minutes before a planned appearance on the "Live With Regis and Kathy Lee" show. In Honolulu, a 21-year-old African elephant named Tyke trampled her trainer to death and injured a dozen spectators as she tore out of the Circus International tent. She was shot dead in the street. **1**

Last summer, Janet, an old elephant who had been kept on repeated doses of drugs to calm her down, tore out of the Great American Circus ring in Florida, carrying a box full of children on her back, and was shot 47 times by an off-duty police officer before she died. These spectacularly hideous attacks made headlines; many others did not. **2**

Circus proprietors have been too busy counting their money to do more than slug or drug uppity elephants. Now the pachyderms' polite protestations have turned nasty. How much human blood will mingle with that of the elephants before their struggle for freedom is successful? **3**

Sound farfetched? Consider this. Elephants have the largest brains of any mammals on Earth. They are creative and altruistic. Imagine what it must be like for them to be told what to do, courtesy of a bullhook, every moment of their lives. They live more than 70 years in their homelands but their average life in captivity is reduced to 14 years; because of stress, traveling in boxcars and being stabled in damp basements, many captive elephants have arthritis, lame legs and tuberculosis. **4**

Left to their own devices in their homelands, elephants are highly social beings; aunts babysit, mothers teach junior life skills such as how to use leaves and mud to ward off sunburn and insect bites, babies play together under watchful eyes, lovemaking is gentle and complex, and elephant relatives mourn their dead. They draw pictures in the dirt with twigs and rocks. **5**

Life under the big top means: Pay attention to your trainers, don't falter even if you feel tired or ill, obey, obey, obey. It means leg chains between acts, the loss of warmth from your father and mother, no long-term friends. **6**

Behaviorists tell us elephants cry from loss of social interaction and from physical abuse. If you wonder how they keep from going mad, they don't. **7**

Rani was the first captive elephant I ever met. Every single day for years she stood outside the Asoka Hotel in New Delhi, India, from sunrise to late at night, waiting to be prodded into action whenever a tourist fancied a ride. One day I asked Ram, her owner, where Rani had come from, and he explained that young elephants are taken from their families and "broken." He described how they must be chained and beaten until they learn to listen and behave. Several years ago, a National Geographic television special about elephants in the wild and in servitude showed men carrying out exactly that barbaric, inhumane system. **8**

Rani died long before I had learned that elephant calves in the wild stay **9** at their mothers' sides for a decade or longer; the elephants grieve and mourn, cradling their lost relatives' skulls in their trunks and swaying back and forth; that they communicate subsonically at frequencies so low humans cannot detect them without sophisticated equipment.

There are 2,000 to 3,000 "Ranis" held captive in the beast wagons **10** of circuses and in private collections. Sometimes, they stop behaving like windup toys and crush the bones and breath out of a keeper, make a break for it, go berserk. Most simply endure.

It is now a criminal offense to confine elephants, big cats and, in most **11** cases, primates in circuses visiting the Australian Capital Territory. Seven municipalities in Western Australia have banned circuses from using government land. Animal acts have also been banned or restricted in Sweden, Denmark, and the United Kingdom.

What are we waiting for before we grant elephants the freedom we **12** have taken from them? Perhaps the tragedies of the summer will be lesson enough for us to demand that legislators ban captive animal performances and to redirect our children's attention to entertainments that avoid exploitation. As a society that prides itself on being civilized, we would be far richer for the "loss" of captive beasts.

Vocabulary

amok (1)	behaviorists (7)
proprietors (3)	servitude (8)
pachyderms (3)	subsonically (9)
altruistic (4)	berserk (10)
bullhook (4)	exploitation (12)
falter (6)	

Understanding What You Have Read

Check the correct answer in the blank provided.

1. What has happened to elephants "three times this summer"?

_____ **(a).** Elephants have escaped.

_✔_ **(b).** Elephants have run amok.

_____ **(c).** Elephants have been freed by animal rights activists.

_____ **(d).** Elephants have died of loneliness.

2. What is the average life span of an elephant in captivity?

_____ **(a).** Ten years.

_✔_ **(b).** Fourteen years.

_____ **(c).** Seventy years.

_____ **(d).** Five years.

3. Left alone in their homeland, what are elephants like?

_✔_ **(a).** They are highly social beings.

_____ **(b).** They are disorganized.

_____ **(c).** They are loners.

_____ **(d).** They long for the company of people.

4. How are elephants broken for servitude?
   ___✔___ (a). They are chained and beaten.
   _____ (b). They are given electric shocks.
   _____ (c). They are deprived of food.
   _____ (d). They are treated with great kindness.

5. How do elephants communicate with one another?
   _____ (a). They do not communicate.
   ___✔___ (b). They communicate subsonically.
   _____ (c). They bellow.
   _____ (d). They tap on the ground with their feet.

Thinking About What You Have Read

1. The author opens her essay by declaring that "The elephants are mad and they're just not going to take it anymore." What evidence does she provide for this statement?

2. In paragraph 5 the author talks about the behavior and lifestyle of elephants in the wild. How does this discussion help in her argument against the captivity of elephants?

3. Do you agree that animals should be treated humanely? Give reasons for your answer.

4. In some countries it is now a criminal offense to confine elephants, big cats, and primates in circuses. What is your opinion of this regulation?

5. What do you think is the obligation, if any, of humans toward animals?

Writing Assignments

1. Write a paragraph about the way circus animals should be treated and why.

2. If you have a pet, write a paragraph on how you treat that pet. If you have no pet, write a paragraph on how you would treat one if you had one.

Sport

Jimmy Carter

This poem, by a former President of the United States, is a moving last farewell to a beloved pet. Some readers have criticized the way the dog's life was ended. However, no one has questioned the writer's sincere affection for his friend. He most certainly loved his dog. As you read the poem, ignore the fact that it is written in poetic form and concentrate only on the meaning and feelings expressed.

Yesterday I killed him. I had   **1**
known
    for months I could not let
him live. I might
    have paid someone to end it,
but I knew
    that after fifteen years of
sharing life
    the bullet ending his must
be my own.   **10**
    Alone, I dug the grave,
grieving, knowing
    that until the last he trusted
me.
    I placed him as he'd been
some years ago
    when lost, he stayed in place
until I came
    and found him shaking,
belly on the ground,   **20**
    his legs too sapped of
strength to hold him up,
    his nose and eyes still
holding on the point.
    I knelt beside him then to
stroke his head—
    as I had done so much the
last few days.
    He couldn't feel the tears
and sweat that fell   **30**
    with shovelfuls of earth.
And then a cross—
    a cross, I guess, so when I
pass that way

513

I'll breathe his name,
and think of him alive,
and somehow not remember
yesterday.

Vocabulary

sapped (21)

Understanding What You Have Read

Check the correct answer in the blank provided.

1. How did the speaker put the dog to death?
    _____ **(a).** By lethal injection.
    _____ **(b).** By drowning.
    _____ **(c).** By poisoning.
    __✔__ **(d).** By shooting.

2. Who witnessed this act of euthanasia?
    _____ **(a).** The speaker's mother.
    __✔__ **(b).** No one.
    _____ **(c).** His sister.
    _____ **(d).** A visiting uncle.

3. Why didn't the speaker pay someone to do it?
    __✔__ **(a).** Because he loved the dog.
    _____ **(b).** Because no one was available.
    _____ **(c).** Because he wanted to save the expense.
    _____ **(d).** Because his mother ordered him to do it.

4. What did the speaker do after he euthanized the dog?
    _____ **(a).** He wept on his wife's shoulder.
    _____ **(b).** He offered a prayer.
    __✔__ **(c).** He dug a grave.
    _____ **(d).** He visited his minister.

5. What had the speaker done to the dog many times lately?
    _____ **(a).** He had scolded him.
    _____ **(b).** He had taken walks with him.
    _____ **(c).** He had watched birds with him.
    __✔__ **(d).** He had stroked his head.

Thinking About What You Have Read

1. How does the title of this poem relate to its content?

2. What does the anecdote about losing the dog and finding him later, "his nose and eyes still/holding on the point," say about the animal? How does the speaker seem to regard this behavior? How do you regard it?

3. What would have happened to the speaker if he had done to a suffering human being what he did to the dog? What is your view of this double standard?

4. What are the speaker's feelings during this final act he is performing? How do you know?

5. The speaker says he put a cross over the dog's grave. What is your view of the appropriateness of this gesture?

Writing Assignments

1. Write a paragraph about the real or imagined loss of a pet. Try to describe your feelings at the time.

2. Write a paragraph agreeing or disagreeing with the idea of mercy killing for people who are painfully and hopelessly sick.

A Person

A Brotherly Bond That Beat the Odds

Bill Paschke

Many of us regard sports either as a waste of time or as the couch potatoes' favorite excuse for drug. But sometimes sports can also be the glue cementing two people together. This article, by a sportswriter, describes a relationship that grew between a little boy and his "Big Brother." Along the way we meet two memorable characters whose only thing in common was a mutual love for sports.

1 He was so small. Expecting to meet a little boy, I had just been introduced to a stick figure.

2 His jeans hung loosely around dental-floss legs. His T-shirt swallowed the rest.

3 I reached for his hand, and grabbed him clear up to his elbow. I had just agreed to be Andrew's "Big Brother," yet there was nothing there.

4 A commitment of three hours a week, each week, for the next year?

5 What could an active 22-year-old man possibly do with a 7-year-old shadow?

6 What could we ever share besides an awkward stare?

7 I had been told that Andrew was suffering from cystic fibrosis, a genetic predator that kills young. But an overeager counselor whispered, "Don't worry, you can't tell."

8 One look at Andrew's stunted growth and I could tell. One ugly cough, and I could hear.

9 I had just met a boy to whom I was morally bound for the next year, yet I couldn't figure out how to spend the first minute.

10 "So, um, what do you like?" I finally asked this little thing hugging his mother's legs.

11 It was then I realized I had missed something, two eyes, flickering under a mop of blond hair, eyes now bigger than all of him.

12 "Sports," he said, his small voice booming, and I'll remember this as long as I remember anything. "I like sports."

13 We like it, hate it, embrace it, denounce it, talk about it for hours, watch it for weekends, rip it for days. We teach with it, blame it, try fruitlessly to play it and hopelessly to understand it.

14 The one thing we never do, it seems, is pause and be thankful for it.

15 For me, for sports, this day works as well as any.

16 This is trying to be a Thanksgiving sports story, but not about sports as names and numbers, winners and losers.

17 It's about sports as language, as one of this country's most important means of communication, spanning generations, crossing economic classes, giving our diverse people something in common.

18 It's about how sports connected me with Andrew.

19 I wasn't trying to save the world. I was trying to save myself.

20 I had just graduated from college and was working in the swamp bureau for a newspaper in Fort Lauderdale, Fla. I was covering bowling and shuffleboard and hoping for the day when somebody would consider me good enough to cover high school football.

I lived in a one-room apartment with a bed in the wall and roaches on **21** the ceiling. My life lacked any sense of order or importance. I figured the Big Brothers & Sisters program would give that to me.

I met Andrew Fishbein at a Christmas party in 1980. **22**

He said he liked sports. **23**

"What do you know?" I said. "So do I." **24**

On our second visit, I tentatively dumped a pile of baseball cards on **25** the floor. He dropped to his knees and ran them through his hands like money.

"Do you know how to play?" I asked. **26**

He didn't, so I taught him a game I had learned when I was young. Soon **27** we were sprawled out on the carpet, shouting together at little pieces of cardboard, big and little now shoulder to shoulder.

And so the language of our relationship had been established, the cur- **28** rency set.

We played soccer as long as his clogged little lungs could handle it. **29** We pitched baseball until it was time to go home for his medicine.

I was promoted to covering high school basketball, so he attended his **30** first live sports event, Boyd Anderson High versus Dillard High., sitting next to me in the stands, cheering as if it was the Bulls and the Jazz.

Sports was like this for us. A language of laughter and lessons, a **31** bridge between distant lives.

A year passed, my formal commitment to Andrew ended, but our visits **32** continued. Sports had given us a new world—big enough for only two—that neither was willing to leave. There was always another miniature golf course to play, another pretend Super Bowl to enact with a rubber football on the scrubby field behind his townhouse.

Then in the fall of 1983, I landed a job as far from that world as Andrew **33** thought possible. I was going to cover the Seattle Mariners, 3,500 miles away,

I still remember watching Andrew collapse in tears on the floor of his **34** mother's townhouse. To him, I was just another man who had come and gone.

"You'll come see me, I'll stay in touch, I promise," I said quickly. "I'm **35** covering baseball, remember?"

I'm sure he didn't believe it. I don't know if I believed it. **36**

But it was baseball, remember? Within a year, Andrew, by then 10, had **37** worked up the courage to fly cross-country by himself to spend long summer days with me and my wife.

Or more to the point, to spend an afternoon with the Mariners, running **38** the outfield during batting practice, hanging out in the clubhouse, chaperoned by an unforgettable pitcher named Roy Thomas.

As we grew older, through vastly different situations on different sides **39** of the country, it was sports that gave us both the incentive to keep our relationship strong.

At least three times a year, we would get together, seemingly always to **40** watch a sporting event or to hang out near a sporting event I was covering. Our reunions were, therefore, usually marked by big happy crowds, and our separations usually occurred against the echoes of cheers.

When Andrew was 13, a basketball assignment took me close enough **41** to Florida so I could give the toast at his bar mitzvah, a wonderful celebration of manhood for a child not expected to live long past his 18th birthday.

When Andrew graduated from high school, another milestone for a kid **42** whose lungs and digestive system were weakening by the day, he received a congratulatory phone call from Orel Hershiser.

I've never asked an athlete for anything like that before or since. But **43** Hershiser never held it over my head because he understood the death sentence hanging over Andrew's.

Cystic fibrosis is a genetic, terminal disease affecting about 30,000 **44** children and adults. It causes the body to produce an abnormally thick mucus that clogs the lungs and obstructs the pancreas, affecting everything from breathing to digesting.

The language of sports, of course, includes none of those words. It's **45** about life, and I privately rejoiced that the topic of Andrew's prognosis never came up. We were too busy arguing who was better, the Dolphins or Seahawks, the Heat or Lakers.

Many times, for a boy who underwent daily chest-pounding therapies and **46** biannual lengthy hospital stays, sports was also the language of healing.

Despondent over his situation as a freshman at the University of **47** Florida, Andrew once swallowed enough pills to kill himself. Fortunately, a fraternity brother found him in time.

When I was finished being furious, I bought him World Series tickets, **48** and we stayed up all night in Atlanta, talking about comebacks.

It was his first of three World Series games, one baseball All-Star game, **49** one Super Bowl, one national college football championship, one NCAA regional basketball championship.

He has been with me everywhere from Seattle to St. Petersburg, with **50** stops in places like Cincinnati, New Orleans, Charleston, S.C., and even Dodgertown.

He has survived two major surgeries—half of his lungs have been **51** removed—with that same language.

Sitting at his hospital bedside, I would read him the sports pages. **52**

Phoning his room, from across the country, I would ask which game he **53** was watching, and turn my TV to the same game, and we would shout at it together, even if he couldn't always shout.

The years passed, and I became a balding middle-ager, and the stick **54** figure became a strong, handsome adult. Yet we stayed together until, at some point, it stopped being all about sports and started being somewhat about us.

That point was reached this fall, when I was scheduled to fly to Boston **55** to cover what became one of the most dramatic Ryder Cup golf tournaments in history.

I flew to Jamaica instead. It was there, on a beach, that his mother and **56** I gave Andrew away at his wedding.

On Wednesday, he flew to join me for this Thanksgiving with his new **57** bride, Sigrid. Sure enough, the little guy has finally rumbled his way out of the corner and back up field.

Andrew is 26. He is a successful real estate agent. He undergoes **58** countless daily therapies and painstaking hospital stays, but he works out at a gym, and is cut like a body builder. Scientific advancements have pushed the median age of an individual with CF to 31, and here's betting he doubles it.

Today he will hug my wife as if she is his second mother, which she is. **59** He will roll around the floor with my three children like one of their favorite uncles, which he is.

And with me? What do you think? **60**

Today we'll watch football, eat turkey, watch football, watch more foot- **61** ball, then fall asleep in front of the TV while watching everything replayed in 30-second video bites on the highlight show.

Some might call us lazy sports nuts. We just call ourselves brothers. **62**

Vocabulary

predator (7)	incentive (39)
denounce (13)	congratulatory (42)
diverse (17)	prognosis (45)
tentatively (3)	biannual (46)
currency (28)	despondent (47)
scrubby (32)	painstaking (58)
chaperoned (38)	median (58)

Understanding What You Have Read

Check the correct answer in the blank provided.

1. What was the writer's initial impression of the boy?
   _____ **(a).** That he was big for his age.
   _____ **(b).** That he had startling red hair.
   _____ **(c).** That he was uncommonly bold.
   __✔__ **(d).** That he was a stick figure.

2. What disease did the boy suffer from?
   _____ **(a).** Parkinson's disease.
   _____ **(b).** AIDS.
   _____ **(c).** Multiple sclerosis.
   __✔__ **(d).** Cystic fibrosis.

3. What useful function does the writer see in sports?
   _____ **(a).** It provides employment for many people.
   _____ **(b).** It helps make some star athletes very rich.
   __✔__ **(c).** It gives a diverse people something in common.
   _____ **(d).** It contributes to the renewal of old neighborhoods.

4. What baseball team was the writer assigned to cover?
   _____ **(a).** The New York Yankees.
   __✔__ **(b).** The Seattle Mariners.
   _____ **(c).** The Atlanta Braves.
   _____ **(d).** The Texas Rangers

5. What did the boy do that enraged the writer?
   __✔__ **(a).** He tried to kill himself.
   _____ **(b).** He eloped.
   _____ **(c).** He disobeyed his mother.
   _____ **(d).** He tried to kill the writer.

Thinking About What You Have Read

1. This piece came from a newspaper. What characteristic of its paragraphing makes its journalistic origin obvious?

2. What does the author mean in paragraph 20 that he was "working in the swamp bureau?"

3. Aside from describing the relationship that emerged over the years between the writer and the boy, what else does this article do?

4. In paragraph 31, the author writes: "Sports was like this for us. A language of laughter and lessons, a bridge between distant lives." What is wrong with this paragraph? How could you fix this error with different punctuation?

5. What main point about sports does the writer prove in the extended example of his relationship with Andrew?

Writing Assignments

1. Write a paragraph about any personal hobby or passion that would work to bond you to someone else.

2. Write a paragraph about the importance of sports either in your own life or in the life of your family.

Two Roads Converged in a Wood

Jenijoy La Belle

*The essay that follows was written as a newspaper column for Father's Day. A daughter paints a loving portrait of the father about whom no "greeting card can speak." Ask yourself what greeting cards are likely to say about a father as opposed to what the author actually says. Do you think the writer is **romanticizing** her father—picturing him as better than he is—or telling the truth? What does she find admirable about her father? How does she express this in a way that no greeting card could? A tribute to a father on Father's Day can easily become sticky with sentimentality. How does the writer avoid that trap?*

1   It was easy to choose a card for Mother's Day. I knew the one my mother would like because I'm like my mother. Now, I stand perplexed in front of the Father's Day display.

2   My father, Joy La Belle, was a meter reader for 25 years. Most meter readers finally move into office positions, but my father liked being outdoors. He retired in 1976. By that time, he figured he'd walked around the world twice (more than 50,000 miles) on his job. He weighed 125 pounds when he started, 125 when he stopped. He was bitten by dogs only four times. You can still see German shepherd teeth marks on his right arm.

3   Once he retired, my father could turn his full attention to his real career. Almost 60 years ago, he bought a tract of wooded land near Olympia, Wash. He began building a house on a hill overlooking a waterfall. But a winter storm crushed the unfinished frame. My newly married parents moved into a tiny cabin and lived there for several years without electricity or running water. When my brother and I were born, my father added rooms and handcrafted furniture. Eventually, my father built five dwellings in the woods. For each, he cleared just enough for construction. The green light of the forest filters through the windows. Since several houses have walls of glass, the woods almost move into the living rooms. My father has no use for curtains. Like Thoreau* at Walden, he has "no gazers to shut out but the sun and moon." What they gaze in on is beautiful and true, in harmony with nature.

4   I came to appreciate my father's life more fully when I met him in literature. I found him in Robert Frost's† poems and Thomas Hardy's‡ novels—a straightforward, hard-working man with a quiet wisdom deeper than that of more articulate men. My father watches and waits. He doesn't talk much, but his silence is wonderful to listen to.

5   I work with words, my father with wood. And yet we communicate. He doesn't write me letters, but sometimes in the fall I receive a large envelope full of yellow maple leaves. When my favorite madrona tree died, he carved from it a "writer's block" to keep on my desk. In days when no words come, I pick it up, feel its smoothness and know that somewhere my father is driving nails or patiently planing and sanding. These are also ways of giving form to ideas.

---

*Henry David Thoreau (1817–1862), American author and novelist who escaped the city to spend more than two years in a cabin on Walden Pond in Concord, Massachusetts.

†Robert Frost (1874–1963), American poet.

‡Thomas Hardy (1840–1928), English novelist and poet.

What is unspoken is not unexpressed. One morning when he thought **6** I was asleep, I heard my father walk softly into the kitchen near my room and begin slowly unloading the dishwasher. I lay in bed, listening to how gently he lifted out each pan, each glass. Like the stealthiest thief in reverse, he returned the silverware to its drawer. He took 20 minutes to do what he could have done in five, just to let me dream. Once in a while, we are lucky enough to be awake when love performs its silent testaments.

My father is 81. Not only do he and my mother still live quietly in the **7** woods; they belong to it. Slender as is his frame, my father remains a powerful man. His arms are sinewy from years of chopping trees and raising roof beams. He works every day, digging stumps, laying a brick floor with precision, repairing the steps to the waterfalls, creating a bridge from a white fir that had fallen over the creek.

Knowing what to leave alone is as important as knowing what to do. **8** Every few months, someone offers my father a small fortune to timber his forest. "Why would I want to cut down the trees?" my father asks. A doctor tells him about an operation for his fingers, which have become gnarled into a fist. "I can still hold a hammer," my father says. And he can.

My father is a happy man—not from trying to be, but because he lives **9** at the center. He understands how to simplify the complexities of life. He does something each day toward clearing his own path through the wilderness, within and without. There is at the core of his being a mysterious strength I will never fully comprehend, nor to which any greeting card can speak.

Vocabulary

perplexed (1)	testaments (6)
tract (3)	sinewy (7)
articulate (4)	gnarled (8)
planing (5)	timber (8)
stealthiest (6)	comprehend (9)

Understanding What You Have Read

Check the correct answer in the blank provided.

1. What did the author's father do for a living before he retired?

_____ **(a).** He was a lawyer.

_____ **(b).** He was a physician specializing in elderly care.

_____ **(c).** He flew planes for a large business.

__✔__ **(d).** He was a meter reader.

2. What can you see on the right arm of the author's father?

__✔__ **(a).** Bite marks from a German shepherd dog.

_____ **(b).** A burn scar from a plane crash.

_____ **(c).** A tattoo of Uncle Sam.

_____ **(d).** A Nazi death camp identification sign.

3. When did the author first come to appreciate her father's life?
   _____ **(a).** When she saw how hard he had to work.
   _____ **(b).** When she met his brother.
   _✔_ **(c).** When she met him in literature.
   _____ **(d).** When she joined the Air Force.

4. What testament of love did the author witness her father perform?
   _____ **(a).** He shot a bear for her.
   _____ **(b).** He bought her a car for her graduation.
   _____ **(c).** He threw himself between her and a rattlesnake.
   _✔_ **(d).** He unloaded the dishwasher silently so she could sleep.

5. What offer does the father receive every few months?
   _✔_ **(a).** Someone offers him a small fortune for his timberland.
   _____ **(b).** Someone offers him a job in the home office.
   _____ **(c).** Someone offers to marry him.
   _____ **(d).** Someone offers him a million dollars for his life story.

Thinking About What You Have Read

1. The author admits that she finds it easy to buy a greeting card for her mother, but hard to buy one for her father. What explanation can you give for this difference? What impact do you think being a daughter rather than a son has on this dilemma?

2. The author says she is like her mother. Reading between the lines, what do you think her mother is like?

3. Why did the father build walls of glass without curtains? What is your reaction to his attitude? Do you agree or do you prefer to feel protected by walls and curtains? Explain your answer.

4. In your own words, how would you describe the author's father? What does the author mean when she states that her father's "silence is wonderful to listen to"?

5. What fact about the author's father seems at odds with her portrayal of him as a man who lived off the woods and was a source of "mysterious strength"?

Writing Assignments

1. Write a paragraph about a "silent testament" of love you have witnessed.

2. Write a paragraph about someone you admire.

Barbie Doll

Marge Piercy

*The title of a poem must never be ignored because a poem begins with its title, not its first line. Since this poem is about society's unhappy tendency to judge people, especially women, solely by their looks, the reader who does not know what a Barbie doll is misses the biting commentary of its title. Notice the **ironic**—opposite of what is expected—ending of the poem and the description at the end of the unhappy "girl-child" as a made-up doll.*

This girlchild was born as usual   1
and presented dolls that did pee-pee
and miniature GE stoves and irons
and wee lipsticks the color of cherry candy.
Then in the magic of puberty, a classmate said:
You have a great big nose and fat legs.

She was healthy, tested intelligent,
possessed strong arms and back,
abundant sexual drive and manual dexterity.
She went to and fro apologizing.   10
Everyone saw a fat nose on thick legs.

She was advised to play coy,
exhorted to come on hearty,
exercise, diet, smile and wheedle.
Her good nature wore out
like a fan belt.
So she cut off her nose and her legs
and offered them up.

In the casket displayed on satin she lay
with the undertaker's cosmetics painted on,   20
a turned-up putty nose, dressed in a pink and white nightie.
Doesn't she look pretty? everyone said.
Consummation at last.
To every woman a happy ending.

Vocabulary

puberty (5)   wheedle (14)
dexterity (9)   putty (23)
coy (12)   consummation (23)
exhorted (13)

Understanding What You Have Read

Check the correct answer in the blank provided.

1. What did someone say to the "girlchild" that made her defensive?
   _____ (a). That she looked powerful.
   _____ (b). That she had a potbelly.
   _____ (c). That she had two different colored eyes.
   __✔__ (d). That she had a great big nose and fat legs.

2. What did the "girlchild" do after that remark?
   __✔__ (a). She went around apologizing.
   _____ (b). She went on a strict diet.
   _____ (c). She saw a psychiatrist.
   _____ (d). She moved out of town.

3. When was the damaging remark made?
   _____ (a). At the senior prom.
   __✔__ (b). During puberty.
   _____ (c). At a birthday party.
   _____ (d). By her first date.

4. What aspect of the girl wore out "like a fan belt"?
   _____ (a). Her sense of humor.
   _____ (b). Her patience.
   _____ (c). Her faith.
   __✔__ (d). Her good nature.

5. What did everyone say about her in the casket?
   _____ (a). That she looked asleep.
   _____ (b). That she looked unnatural.
   _____ (c). That she had on too much makeup.
   __✔__ (d). That she looked pretty.

Thinking About What You Have Read

1. What is the significance of the toys given to the "girlchild"?

2. Had the girl been born a boy, what do you think would have been an equivalent cutting remark to "You have a great big nose and fat legs"?

3. In lines 7–9 the poet tells that the girl was "healthy, tested intelligent / possessed strong arms and back, / abundant sexual drive and manual dexterity." Why do you think she tells us all this?

4. We are told that the girl was advised to "play coy," "come on hearty, / exercise, diet, smile and wheedle," but we are not told who gave her this advice. Why do you think this information is omitted?

5. It is sometimes said that the type of sexist pressure exerted on this girl simply doesn't occur any more. What is your opinion of this view?

Writing Assignments

1. Write about the most cutting criticism you ever suffered.

2. Write about the pressures to which males are subjected nowadays.

An Event

Last Flight

Isao Matsuo

The terrible drama of the following letter arises from the fact that it was written during World War II by Petty Officer First Class Isao Matsuo of the 701st Air Group just before he took off for a **kamikaze**—*suicide flight—attack. Imagine his parents' agony on receiving this letter. Ask yourself whether Isao's attitude—that it would be a glorious privilege to die for the Emperor—could in any way lessen the pain a parent feels in losing a son. You might compare Matsuo's mission with the suicidal terrorist attacks of September 11, 2001, in New York and Washington DC.*

28 October 1944

Dear Parents;

1 Please congratulate me. I have been given a splendid opportunity to die. This is my last day. The destiny of our homeland hinges on the decisive battle in the seas to the south where I shall fall like a blossom from a radiant cherry tree.

2 I shall be a shield for His Majesty and die cleanly along with my squadron leader and other friends. I wish that I could be born seven times, each time to smite the enemy.

3 How I appreciate this chance to die like a man! I am grateful from the depths of my heart to the parents who have reared me with their constant prayer and tender love. And I am grateful as well to my squadron leader and superior officers who have looked after me as if I were their own son and given me such careful training.

4 Thank you, my parents, for the 23 years during which you have cared for me and inspired me. I hope that my present deed will in some small way repay what you have done for me. Think well of me and know that your Isao died for our country. This is my last wish, and there is nothing else that I desire.

5 I shall return in spirit and look forward to your visit at the Yasukuni Shrine. Please take good care of yourselves.

6 How glorious is the Special Attack Corps' Giretsu Unit whose *Suisei* bombers will attack the enemy. Movie cameramen have been here to take our pictures. It is possible that you may see us in newsreels at the theater.

7 We are 16 warriors manning the bombers. May our death be as sudden and clean as the shattering of crystal.

8 Written at Manila on the eve of our sortie.

Isao

Vocabulary

destiny (1)
hinges (1)
smite (2)
sortie (8)

Understanding What You Have Read

Check the correct answer in the blank provided.

1. The letter is written to Isao's

_____ **(a).** lover.

__✔__ **(b).** parents.

_____ **(c).** brother.

_____ **(d).** squadron commander.

2. The year in which the letter is written is important because it was

_____ **(a).** Shakespeare's year of birth.

_____ **(b).** the year Napoleon died.

__✔__ **(c).** during World War II.

_____ **(d).** during the Vietnam War.

3. In this letter, the writer expresses

_____ **(a).** fear and apprehension.

_____ **(b).** anger and cynicism.

__✔__ **(c).** gratitude and pride.

_____ **(d).** hatred of the emperor.

4. The age of the writer is

__✔__ **(a).** 23.

_____ **(b).** 18.

_____ **(c).** 40.

_____ **(d).** 65.

5. The author writes that he shall fall from the sky like a

_____ **(a).** shooting star.

_____ **(b).** raindrop.

_____ **(c).** white dove.

__✔__ **(d).** cherry blossom.

Thinking About What You Have Read

1. How do you think the parents of this kamikaze soldier will react to his letter? How would your parents react?

2. What seems to be the great ideal for which the soldier is ready to die? Do you consider this ideal worthy of so many young deaths?

3. What religious belief is expressed in paragraph 5? Do you think this would be a comforting belief under the circumstances? Why or why not?

4. What image is used in paragraph 7? How effective is it?

5. What is your opinion about suicide missions? Under what circumstances, if any, would you be willing to attempt such a mission?

Writing Assignments

1. Write an imaginary letter to the parents of a soldier who died in action during some military action. Try to comfort them.

2. Write a paragraph either attacking or defending the idea of suicide missions.

Looking for Love in Cyberspace Isn't as Easy—or Safe—as It Seems

Sharon Whitley

The essay that follows is about the downside of cyberspace technology. It reminds us that perhaps we should stop and think before we plunge headfirst into all of the possibilities that such modern miracles as the Internet and the Worldwide Web offer. Unfortunately, modern advances attract not only the good, the smart, and the altruistic, but also the bad, the smart, and the twisted. This essay should warn you to be alert as you sharpen your computer skills so you are not drawn into schemes that will embarrass or harm you.

1   It started innocently enough. I signed up with an online service and was enjoying sending and receiving e-mail with friends around the country.

2   Like many subscribers, I had submitted a profile that listed the city I live in, my marital status, occupation and hobbies—and noted that I enjoyed people with a sense of humor. In retrospect, I'm glad I didn't list my name.

3   One evening when I signed on, I had e-mail from someone new. "Hi!" the posted message read. "I see that you are also in San Diego and single—and I thought we might be compatible?"

4   The writer—who signed himself Tom—went on to tell a little about himself. He wrote so well I thought he must be a professional.

5   Intrigued, I wrote back to thank him for the message and asked him to tell me more about himself—"to ascertain that you're not an ax murderer or a very gifted 12-year-old kid."

6   Tom wrote back and said he worked for a software company and had been a Navy pilot with nearly 400 aircraft carrier landings in 10 years. He said he was a commercial pilot as well. He told me his hometown, where he went to college and that he had traveled all over the world.

7   My interest was definitely piqued. I had just been on a 24-hour media tour on the aircraft carrier Abraham Lincoln. I wrote back to Tom about the excitement of catapulting off the ship and tail-hook landings.

8   For the next several days, Tom and I exchanged notes—nothing sensual, just friendly. We discovered both our fathers had been World War II pilots.

9   Tom had charm and wit, and I found myself looking forward each morning to his latest note. When I told him that, he responded that he, too, enjoyed mine.

10   This was really fun, and in the back of my romantic mind I thought, wouldn't it be something to actually meet someone this way? I knew of two couples who had met via computers.

11   After a week of information exchange and banter, Tom suggested that we meet "in three-dimension."

12   "It could be for coffee, a drink, or dinner—somewhere nice," he wrote.

13   I wrote back that I'd like that and suggested we meet for a drink after work. We exchanged work numbers and talked on the phone, picking a restaurant. We agreed to meet at 4:30 p.m. the next day.

14   "How will I know you?" he asked.

15   "Look for the hazel-eyed blonde," I said. "I'm 5'5" and I'll be carrying a magazine.

"I'm six feet tall and have brown hair and brown eyes," he said. "Bring **16** your photos and article about your experience on the carrier, and I'll bring some of my Navy stuff to show you."

I looked forward to meeting Tom, thinking that at the very least he **17** sounded like someone who would be an interesting friend.

I arrived at the restaurant at 4:30. No one who might be Tom was **18** there. I waited. And waited. Finally, at 5, I called home to check my messages. No message from him. Shortly after 5, I headed home to e-mail him. I had never been stood up before and felt that there was some explanation.

I wrote him: "Tom, what happened? I was at the restaurant from **19** 4:30–5. Somehow we missed each other. Call me when you get home and we can reschedule."

No call. But one minute later, he replied by e-mail. "SHAME ON **20** YOU. I don't appreciate being lied to. Don't you EVER write to me again."

What? **21**

I had written to him at 5:29. At 5:30 he sent the bizarre note. It **22** was eerie, as though he had just been sitting there, waiting to hear from me.

I was completely baffled. I'm used to meeting strangers at restaurants **23** to interview for articles and have never had trouble connecting. Tom had never shown up. What was going on?

I relayed the experience to friends. "There are a lot of Internet nuts out **24** there. You can't be too trusting," said one. "Look, folks sit behind a computer keyboard and can pretend to be anyone they want. He may have never been a pilot. He could be married. Maybe he gets his kicks and feeds his ego from leading women on."

"He could have been a real nut and have just waited in his car at the **25** restaurant and then followed you home," my brother said.

I thought of a woman I had read about in a newspaper who had fallen **26** in love and become engaged to her cyberspace cupid. Then one day she received a call from the "sister" of her fiancé, who informed her of the man's sudden death.

Later, it turned out, it had been the "sister" all along who had posed **27** on-line as a romantic male suitor.

When I tell my friends my story, I caution them not to list their real **28** names on the member profiles, and to be very careful what personal information they reveal.

Millions of folks out there are signed on-line. And, as in anything, a per- **29** centage of them are not honest or nice. And may even be psycho.

Maybe next time I'll stick with the old-fashioned blind date. **30**

Vocabulary

e-mail (1)	sensual (8)
retrospect (2)	via (10)
compatible (3)	banter (11)
ascertain (5)	three-dimension (11)
piqued (7)	bizarre (22)
catapulting (7)	eerie (22)
tail-hook (7)	

Understanding What You Have Read

Check the correct answer in the blank provided.

1. The author is intrigued with Tom because
   _____ (a). he knows so much about sports.
   _____ (b). he used to sing for an opera company.
   _____ (c). he seems to be quite wealthy.
   __✔__ (d). he writes like a professional writer.

2. Tom claimed to have been
   __✔__ (a). a software company worker and a Navy pilot.
   _____ (b). a graphic artist and hotel concierge.
   _____ (c). chimney sweep and plumber.
   _____ (d). dancer and actor.

3. In the back of her mind, the author thought the following:
   _____ (a). This guy is probably a jerk.
   __✔__ (b). Wouldn't it be something to actually meet someone this way?
   _____ (c). I should not be revealing myself to this stranger.
   _____ (d). I hope he doesn't have a wife and children.

4. When Tom and the author decided to meet at a restaurant, what happened?
   _____ (a). The two of them fell instantly in love.
   _____ (b). His dog attacked her food.
   __✔__ (c). He never showed up.
   _____ (d). He turned out to be most unattractive.

5. According to the author, of the millions of people who are signed on-line,
   __✔__ (a). most should be decent.
   _____ (b). a certain percentage are bound to be bad or psychotic.
   _____ (c). only those who are uneducated will cause trouble.
   _____ (d). no children should be allowed.

Thinking About What You Have Read

1. What advice would you give someone who is starting a relationship through cyberspace?

2. What is the attractive part of meeting someone by computer? List some advantages.

3. What is the disappointing part of the author's experience? What probably made her feel completely dumbfounded?

4. Why didn't Tom show up for the date? Why did he write such a bizarre note? Speculate on your answers to these questions.

5. Given a choice, which method of meeting someone would you prefer—an old-fashioned blind date or computer dating? Give reasons for your answer.

Writing Assignments

1. Write a paragraph describing a blind date experienced by yourself or a friend. Begin with a topic sentence that evaluates the experience.

2. Write a paragraph of advice about computer dating for an audience of college students.

Shame

Dick Gregory

Because most of us can remember someone from our youth who represented all the romance we desired, we can understand the writer's experience even though we may never have been as poor as he was. Allow yourself to soak in all of the details that make this narration so moving and heartrending. Try to imagine yourself in the narrator's place—to understand how his pride was hurt because of a teacher's lack of sensitivity.

I never learned hate at home, or shame. I had to go to school for that. I was about seven years old when I got my first big lesson. I was in love with a little girl named Helene Tucker, a light-complected little girl with pigtails and nice manners. She was always clean and she was smart in school. I think I went to school mostly to look at her. I brushed my hair and even got me a little old handkerchief. It was a lady's handkerchief, but I didn't want Helene to see me wipe my nose on my hand. The pipes were frozen again, there was no water in the house, but I washed my socks and shirt every night. I'd get a pot, and go over to Mr. Ben's grocery store, and stick my pot down into his soda machine. Scoop out some chopped ice. By evening the ice melted to water for washing. I got sick a lot that winter because the fire would go out at night before the clothes were dry. In the morning I'd put them on, wet or dry, because they were the only clothes I had. **1**

Everybody's got a Helene Tucker, a symbol of everything you want. I loved her for her goodness, her cleanliness, her popularity. She'd walk down my street and my brothers and sisters would yell, "Here comes Helene," and I'd rub my tennis sneakers on the back of my pants and wish my hair wasn't so nappy and the white folks' shirt fit me better. I'd run out on the street. If I knew my place and didn't come too close, she'd wink at me and say hello. That was a good feeling. Sometimes I'd follow her all the way home, and shovel the snow off her walk and try to make friends with her Momma and her aunts. I'd drop money on her stoop late at night on my way back from shining shoes in the taverns. And she had a Daddy, and he had a good job. He was a paper hanger. **2**

I guess I would have gotten over Helene by summertime, but something happened in that classroom that made her face hang in front of me for the next twenty-two years. When I played the drums in high school it was for Helene and when I broke track records in college it was for Helene and when I started standing behind microphones and heard applause I wished Helene could hear it, too. It wasn't until I was twenty-nine years old and married and making money that I really got her out of my system. Helene was sitting in that classroom when I learned to be ashamed of myself. **3**

It was on a Thursday. I was sitting in the back of the room, in a seat with a chalk circle drawn around it. The idiot's seat, the troublemaker's seat. **4**

The teacher thought I was stupid. Couldn't spell, couldn't read, couldn't do arithmetic. Just stupid. Teachers were never interested in finding out that you couldn't concentrate because you were so hungry, because you hadn't had any breakfast. All you could think about was noontime, would it ever come? Maybe you could sneak into the cloakroom and steal a bite of some kid's lunch out of a coat pocket. A bit of something. Paste. You can't really make a meal out of paste, or put it on bread for a sandwich, but sometimes I'd scoop a few spoonfuls out of the paste jar in the back of the room. Pregnant people get strange tastes. I was pregnant with poverty. Pregnant with dirt and pregnant with smells that made people turn away, **5** pregnant with cold and pregnant with shoes that were never bought for me, pregnant with five other people in my bed and no Daddy in the next room, and pregnant with hunger. Paste doesn't taste too bad when you're hungry.

The teacher thought I was a troublemaker. All she saw from the front **6** of the room was a little black boy who squirmed in his idiot's seat and made noises and poked the kids around him. I guess she couldn't see a kid who made noises because he wanted someone to know he was there.

It was on a Thursday, the day before the Negro payday. The eagle always **7** flew on Friday. The teacher was asking each student how much his father would give to the Community Chest. On Friday night, each kid would get the money from his father, and on Monday he would bring it to the school. I decided I was going to buy me a Daddy right then. I had money in my pocket from shining shoes and selling papers and whatever Helene Tucker pledged for her Daddy I was going to top it. And I'd hand the money right in. I wasn't going to wait until Monday to buy me a Daddy.

I was shaking, scared to death. The teacher opened her book and **8** started calling our names alphabetically.

"Helene Tucker?" **9**

"My Daddy said he'd give two dollars and fifty cents." **10**

"That's very nice, Helene. Very, very nice indeed." **11**

That made me feel pretty good. It wouldn't take too much to top that. **12** I had almost three dollars in dimes and quarters in my pocket. I stuck my hand in my pocket and held onto the money, waiting for her to call my name. But the teacher closed her book after she called everybody else in the class.

I stood up and raised my hand. **13**

"What is it now?" **14**

"You forgot me." **15**

She turned toward the blackboard. "I don't have time to be playing with **16** you, Richard."

"My Daddy said he'd . . ." **17**

"Sit down, Richard, you're disturbing the class." **18**

"My Daddy said he'd give . . . fifteen dollars." **19**

She turned around and looked mad. "We are collecting this money for **20** you and your kind, Richard Gregory. If your Daddy can give fifteen dollars you have no business being on relief."

"I got it right now, I got it right now, my Daddy gave it to me to turn in **21** today, my Daddy said . . ."

"And furthermore," she said, looking right at me, her nostrils getting big **22** and her lips getting thin and her eyes opening wide, "we know you don't have a Daddy."

Helene Tucker turned around, her eyes full of tears. She felt sorry for **23** me. Then I couldn't see her too well because I was crying, too.

"Sit down, Richard." **24**

And I always thought the teacher kind of liked me. She always picked **25** me to wash the blackboard on Friday, after school. That was a big thrill, it made me feel important. If I didn't wash it, come Monday the school might not function right.

"Where are you going, Richard?" **26**

I walked out of school that day, and for a long time I didn't go back **27** very often. There was shame there.

Now there was shame everywhere. It seemed like the whole world had **28** been inside that classroom, everyone had heard what the teacher had said, everyone had turned around and felt sorry for me. There was shame in going to the Worthy Boys Annual Christmas Dinner for you and your kind, because everybody knew what a worthy boy was. Why couldn't they just call it the Boys Annual Dinner, why'd they have to give it a name? There was shame in wearing the brown and orange and white plaid mackinaw the welfare gave to 3,000 boys. Why'd it have to be the same for everybody so when you walked down the street the people could see you were on relief? It was a nice warm mackinaw and it had a hood, and my Momma beat me and called me a little rat when she found out I stuffed it in the bottom of a pail full of garbage way over on Cottage Street. There was shame in running over to Mister Ben's at the end of the day and asking for his rotten peaches, there was shame in asking Mrs. Simmons for a spoonful of sugar, there was shame in running out to meet the relief truck. I hated that truck, full of food for you and your kind. I ran into the house and hid when it came. And then I started to sneak through alleys, to take the long way home so people going into White's Eat Shop wouldn't see me. Yeah, the whole world heard the teacher that day, we all know you don't have a Daddy.

Vocabulary

relief (20)
mackinaw (28)

Understanding What You Have Read

Check the correct answer in the blank provided.

1. Where did the narrator say he learned shame?
    _____ **(a).** In church.
    _____ **(b).** At home.
    _____ **(c).** On the baseball field.
    _✔_ **(d).** At school.

2. Helene Tucker is a symbol of
    _✔_ **(a).** everything you have ever wanted.
    _____ **(b).** academic achievement.
    _____ **(c).** power.
    _____ **(d).** girlish modesty.

3. The teacher thought the narrator was stupid when in actuality he was
    _____ **(a).** lonely.
    _____ **(b).** ashamed.
    _✔_ **(c).** hungry.
    _____ **(d).** stubborn.

4. "The eagle always flew on Friday" means that
    _____ **(a).** a political rally is about to start.
    _✔_ **(b).** it's pay day.
    _____ **(c).** people were taking off for vacation.
    _____ **(d).** Friday is a time to observe eagles flying in the sky.

5. What did the narrator plan to do in order to impress Helen Tucker?

   _____ **(a).** Give her some red roses.

   _____ **(b).** Take her to the Worthy Boys Annual Dinner.

   _____ **(c).** Attend church regularly.

   __✔__ **(d).** Pretend that his father asked him to pledge $15.00 to the Community Chest.

Thinking About What You Have Read

1. How does his crush on Helen Tucker affect the narrator? Do you consider his reaction believable? Cite a similar experience you or someone you know has had.

2. What about the classroom experience kept the narrator remembering Helene Tucker for decades to come? Do you consider this long-term remembrance healthy? Give reasons for your view.

3. What are some of the details used by the narrator to prove that his family was poor? Point to specific passages.

4. What technique does the narrator use to make the "shame" scene come to life so that you, the reader, can feel the complete humiliation of the event?

5. What seems to be the most shameful aspect of all for the narrator? Why would that be so shameful? Give specific reasons for your answer.

6. How does the narrator maintain a consistent voice and point of view?

Writing Assignments

1. Write about an event in your life that made you feel ashamed and humiliated. Make sure that the details of your narration support your point.

2. Write a paragraph about the importance of elementary school teachers being sensitive to their students' home lives and lifestyles.

A Problem

Señor Payroll

William E. Barrett

Look for the main conflict in "Señor Payroll." Decide who is fighting whom. Once you have clarified the battle lines, concentrate on the story, which is about Mexican gas plant laborers and the two American engineers who are their paymasters. Notice that it is both serious and humorous. As you read, try to identify the major character traits of the laborers and the managers. Compare and contrast these traits.

Larry and I were Junior Engineers in the gas plant, which means that **1** we were clerks. Anything that could be classified as paper work came to the flat double desk across which we faced each other. The Main Office downtown sent us a bewildering array of orders and rules that were to be put into effect.

Junior Engineers were beneath the notice of everyone except the Mex- **2** ican laborers at the plant. To them we were the visible form of a distant, unknowable paymaster. We were Señor Payroll.

Those Mexicans were great workmen; the aristocrats among them were **3** the stokers, big men who worked Herculean eight-hour shifts in the fierce heat of the retorts. They scooped coal with huge shovels and hurled it with uncanny aim at tiny doors. The coal streamed out from the shovels like black water from a high-pressure nozzle, and never missed the narrow opening. The stokers worked stripped to the waist, and there was pride and dignity in them. Few men could do such work, and they were the few.

The Company paid its men only twice a month, on the fifth and on the **4** twentieth. To a Mexican, this was absurd. What man with money will make it last fifteen days? If he hoarded money beyond the spending of three days, he was a miser—and when, Señor, did the blood of Spain flow in the veins of misers? Hence, it was the custom of our stokers to appear every third or fourth day to draw the money due to them.

There was a certain elasticity in the Company rules, and Larry and I **5** sent the necessary forms to the Main Office and received an "advance" against a man's pay check. Then, one day, Downtown favored us with a memorandum:

"There have been too many abuses of the advance-against-wages priv- **6** ilege. Hereafter, no advance against wages will be made to any employee except in a case of genuine emergency."

We had no sooner posted the notice when in came stoker Juan Garcia. **7** He asked for an advance. I pointed to the notice. He spelled it through slowly, then said, "What does this mean, this 'genuine emergency'?"

I explained to him patiently that the Company was kind and sympa- **8** thetic, but that it was a great nuisance to have to pay wages every few days. If someone was ill or if money was needed for some other good reason, then the Company would make an exception to the rule.

Juan Garcia turned his hat over and over slowly in his big hands. "I do **9** not get my money?"

"Next payday, Juan. On the twentieth." **10**

He went out silently and I felt a little ashamed of myself. I looked **11** across the desk at Larry. He avoided my eyes.

In the next hour two other stokers came in, looked at the notice, had **12** it explained and walked solemnly out; then no more came. What we did not

538

know was that Juan Garcia, Pete Mendoza, and Francisco Gonzalez had spread the word, and that every Mexican in the plant was explaining the order to every other Mexican. "To get money now, the wife must be sick. There must be medicine for the baby."

The next morning Juan Garcia's wife was practically dying, Pete Mendoza's mother would hardly last the day, there was a veritable epidemic among children, and, just for variety, there was one sick father. We always suspected that the old man was really sick; no Mexican would otherwise have thought of him. At any rate, nobody paid Larry and me to examine private lives; we made out our forms with an added line describing the "genuine emergency." Our people got paid. **13**

That went on for a week. Then came a new order, curt and to the point: "Hereafter, employees will be paid ONLY on the fifth and the twentieth of the month. No exceptions will be made except in the cases of employees leaving the service of the Company." **14**

The notice went up on the board, and we explained its significance gravely. "No, Juan Garcia, we cannot advance your wages. It is too bad about your wife and your cousins and your aunts, but there is a new rule." **15**

Juan Garcia went out and thought it over. He thought out loud with Mendoza and Gonzalez and Ayala, then, in the morning, he was back. "I am quitting this company for a different job. You pay me now?" **16**

We argued that it was a good company and that it loved its employees like children, but in the end we paid off, because Juan Garcia quit. And so did Gonzalez, Mendoza, Obregon, Ayala and Ortez, the best stokers, men who could not be replaced. **17**

Larry and I looked at each other; we knew what was coming in about three days. One of our duties was to sit on the hiring line early each morning, engaging transient workers for the handy gangs. Any man was accepted who could walk up and ask for a job without falling down. Never before had we been called upon to hire such skilled virtuosos as stokers for handy-gang work, but we were called upon to hire them now. **18**

The day foreman was wringing his hands and asking the Almighty if he was personally supposed to shovel this condemned coal, while there in a stolid, patient line were skilled men—Garcia, Mendoza, and others—waiting to be hired. We hired them, of course. There was nothing else to do. **19**

Every day we had a line of resigning stokers, and another line of stokers seeking work. Our paper work became very complicated. At the Main Office they were jumping up and down. The processing of forms showing Juan Garcia's resigning and being hired over and over again was too much for them. Sometimes downtown had Garcia on the payroll twice at the same time when someone down there was slow in entering a resignation. Our phone rang early and often. **20**

Tolerantly and patiently we explained: "There's nothing we can do if a man wants to quit, and if there are stokers available when the plant needs stokers, we hire them." **21**

Out of chaos, Downtown issued another order. I read it and whistled. Larry looked at it and said, "It is going to be very quiet around here." **22**

The order read: "Hereafter, no employee who resigns may be rehired within a period of 30 days." **23**

Juan Garcia was due for another resignation, and when he came in we showed him the order and explained that standing in line the next day would do him no good if he resigned today. "Thirty days is a long time, Juan." **24**

It was a grave matter and he took time to reflect on it. So did Gonzalez, Mendoza, Ayala and Ortez. Ultimately, however, they were all back—and all resigned. **25**

We did our best to dissuade them and we were sad about the parting. This time it was for keeps and they shook hands with us solemnly. It was **26** very nice knowing us. Larry and I looked at each other when they were gone and we both knew that neither of us had been pulling for Downtown to win this duel. It was a blue day.

In the morning, however, they were all back in line. With the utmost gravity, Juan Garcia informed me that he was a stoker looking for a job. **27**

"No dice, Juan," I said. "Come back in thirty days. I warned you." **28**

His eyes looked straight into mine without a flicker. "There is some mistake, Señor," he said. "I am Manual Hernandez. I work as the stoker in Pueblo, in Santa Fe, in many places." **29**

I stared back at him, remembering the sick wife and the babies without medicine, the mother-in-law in the hospital, the many resignations and the rehirings. I knew that there was a gas plant in Pueblo, and that there wasn't any in Santa Fe; but who was I to argue with a man about his own name? A stoker is a stoker. **30**

So I hired him. I hired Gonzalez, too, who swore that his name was Carrera and Ayala, who had shamelessly become Smith. **31**

Three days later the resigning started. **32**

Within a week our payroll read like a history of Latin America. Everyone was on it: Lopez and Obregon, Villa, Diaz, Batista, Gomez, and even San Martín and Bolívar. Finally Larry and I, growing weary of staring at familiar faces and writing unfamiliar names, went to the Superintendent and told him the whole story. He tried not to grin, and said, "Damned nonsense!" **33**

The next day the orders were taken down. We called our most prominent stokers into the office and pointed to the board. No rules any more. **34**

"The next time we hire you hombres," Larry said grimly, "come in under the names you like best, because that's the way you are going to stay on the books." **35**

They looked at us and they looked at the board; then for the first time in the long duel, their teeth flashed white. "Sí, Señores," they said. **36**

And so it was. **37**

Vocabulary

array (1)	gravely (15)
stokers (3)	transient (18)
Herculean (3)	virtuosos (18)
retorts (3)	stolid (19)
elasticity (5)	tolerantly (21)
veritable (13)	ultimately (25)
epidemic (13)	dissuade (26)
curt (14)	solemnly (26)
significance (15)	prominent (34)

Understanding What You Have Read

Check the correct answer in the blank provided.

1. In the story, management functions as
   _____ (a). a cruel tyrant.
   _____ (b). supporters of communism.
   ✔ (c). a benevolent dictator.
   _____ (d). cold and remote headquarters in the United States.

2. The ending of the story is satisfying because
   _____ (a). the cruel boss was assassinated.
   _____ (b). all of the laborers became rich overnight.

_____ **(c).** Larry and the narrator were promoted.

__✓__ **(d).** the hardworking laborers got their way.

3. The morality of the laborers is based on

__✓__ **(a).** pure and instant needs.

_____ **(b).** their Catholic upbringing.

_____ **(c).** what their loving mothers had taught them.

_____ **(d).** their hatred for their employers.

4. How did the laborers first respond when management informed them that there would be no more pay advances except in a case of emergency?

_____ **(a).** They formed a picket line and refused to work.

_____ **(b).** They worked shorter hours.

__✓__ **(c).** They all came in with emergencies.

_____ **(d).** They fled to the United States.

5. What was the reputation of the stokers?

_____ **(a).** They were known to be lazy.

__✓__ **(b).** They were excellent workers who performed without mistakes.

_____ **(c).** They were frail men who did their best.

_____ **(d).** They were arrogant and demanding.

Thinking About What You Have Read

1. How does the author achieve humor?

2. The ending of the story is ironic; it does not end the way we expected it to under the circumstances described. Why? How would you expect the story to end?

3. The narrator is himself a character in the story. What does this dual role add to the narrative?

4. How do you feel about the morality of the laborers? About the morality of management? Explain the reasons for your views.

5. How is the passing of time indicated? Point to specific passages.

Writing Assignments

1. Write a paragraph describing the work of someone you know. It can be physical work, such as that of a car mechanic, bus driver, firefighter, or carpenter. Or, it can be mental work, such as that of a teacher, lawyer, accountant, or psychologist. Describe the worker's duties and attitude toward the job.

2. Write a paragraph answering the question, "Why are some laborers so poorly paid in our country?"

Talkin' White

Wayne Lionel Aponte

When the author wrote this essay, he was an English major at the University of Rochester in New York. He felt compelled to put down his thoughts because so many Blacks were accusing him of denying his African-American heritage by using what they considered "white talk." His point is that there are many kinds of English, and pride in African-American heritage doesn't require the exclusive use of street slang.

Recently, during a conversation on film at a dinner party, when I was using my best college-educated English, I was asked where I was born. I received a curious look when I replied, with pride, "Harlem." The questioner, whom I had met through a mutual friend, looked at me as if I were a brother from another planet and immediately wanted to know whether I'd lived in Harlem all my life. When I responded, "Yeah, man, I been cold chillin' on Lenox Avenue ever since I was rockin' my fly diapers," he laughed, and I realized his was a nervous laughter, the kind folks use to mask their thoughts. *Has he really lived in Harlem all his life? He talks white* was the thought behind his laughter, and the follow-up question asked after my departure.   **1**

While growing up in Harlem during my not-so-long-ago elementary and middle-school days, I often encountered the phrase "talkin' white." It was usually thrust on people who were noticed because they were speaking grammatically correct English in a community that did not. I've also heard the term applied to people who place themselves above others by verbally showboating with the elocution of a Lionel Trilling or a Sir Laurence Olivier.   **2**

Nevertheless, I've always loved those folks who have mastered the art of manipulating words. Eloquent oratory and masterful writing have stimulated my mind for as long as I can remember. I took great pride in my ability to mimic and to slowly transform the styles of my favorite writers and orators into my own voice. In this sense language is a form of intellectual play for me.   **3**

When I was a child, my reaction to the question "Why do you talk so white?" was to alter my spoken English drastically (once "Ask yo mama" became less effective and after I ran out of money for candy bribes to make the kids like me). Like most children, I wanted to be liked and wanted to blend into each new social circle. But speaking as I did made blending difficult since it brought favorable attention from teachers that, outside the classroom, evoked fierce verbal attacks from my peers. I never could quite understand how talking slang proved I was Black. Nor did I understand why I couldn't be accepted as a full-fledged, card-holding member of the group by speaking my natural way.   **4**

Hearing the laughter, though, and being the butt of "proper" and "Oreo" jokes hurt me. Being criticized made me feel marginal—and verbally impotent in the sense that I had little ammunition to stop the frequent lunchtime attacks. So I did what was necessary to fit in, whether that meant cursing excessively or signifying. Ultimately I somehow learned to be polylingual and to become sensitive linguistically in the way animals are able to sense the danger of bad weather.   **5**

The need to defend myself led me to use language as a weapon to deflect jokes about the "whiteness" of my spoken English and to launch harsh verbal counterattacks. Simultaneously language served as a mask to hide the hurt I often felt in the process. Though over time my ability to "talk that talk"—slang—gained me a new respect from my peers, I didn't   **6** want to go through life using slang to prove I am Black. So I decided "I yam what I yam," and to take pride in myself. I am my speaking self, but this doesn't mean that I'm turning my back on Black people. There are various shades of Blackness; I don't have to talk like Paul Laurence Dunbar's dialect poems to prove I'm Black. I don't appreciate anyone's trying to take away the range of person I can be.

"Talkin' white" implies that the English language is a closed system owned exclusively by whites. But my white friends from Chattanooga, Ventura, California, and New York City don't all speak the same way. Nor do the millions of poor whites working below the poverty line "talk white," as that phrase is interpreted. **7**

But the primary reason I question this peculiar euphemism for "speaking well" is that it has been used tyrannically to push to the periphery of the race people who grew up in the West Indies and attended English schools or who lived in predominantly white environments: They are perceived as not being Black enough, or as somehow being anti-Black. **8**

It hurts to know that many people judge me and others on whether or not we break verbs. If we follow this line of thought, maybe we'll also say that W. E. B. DuBois wasn't Black because he matriculated at Harvard and studied at the University of Berlin. Or perhaps that Alain Leroy Locke wasn't Black because he earned a degree from Oxford University. Or, to transfer the logic, maybe we're not all of African descent since we don't speak Swahili and some "real" Africans do. **9**

If we can take pride in the visual diversity of the race, then surely we can transfer this diversity and appreciation to spoken English. Because all of us don't be talkin' alike—ya know what I'm sayin'? **10**

Vocabulary

encountered (2)
elocution (2)
manipulating (3)
oratory (3)
evoked (4)
marginal (5)
impotent (5)

signifying (5)
polylingual (5)
linguistically (5)
deflect (6)
euphemism (8)
periphery (8)
diversity (10)

Understanding What You Have Read

Check the correct answer in the blank provided.

1. The author of the essay grew up in
   _____ **(a).** the West Indies.
   _____ **(b).** Africa.
   ✔ **(c).** Harlem.
   _____ **(d).** Chicago.

2. According to the essay, what did "talkin' white" mean?
   _____ **(a).** Socializing with white people rather than Blacks.
   _____ **(b).** Speaking in a dull monotone.
   _____ **(c).** Speaking with a British accent.
   ✔ **(d).** Speaking grammatically correct English.

3. For some time the author used Black slang outside of school because

___✔___ **(a).** he wanted to fit in and be liked by fellow Blacks.

_____ **(b).** his teachers advised him to do so.

_____ **(c).** it made him seem physically tough.

_____ **(d).** he knew it well.

4. What does the author mean when he says he became "polylingual"?

_____ **(a).** He used a polished kind of slang.

_____ **(b).** He was always polite.

_____ **(c).** He had more than one wife.

___✔___ **(d).** He could use different kinds of English.

5. What is the main reason the author disapproves of the term "talking' white"?

_____ **(a).** It angers the white community because their language is attacked as inferior.

___✔___ **(b).** It is used as a label to exclude people from the West Indies or Black people who grew up in predominantly white environments.

_____ **(c).** Blacks can never learn to "talk white."

_____ **(d).** Blacks should continue to keep their own slang and resist "talkin' white."

Thinking About What You Have Read

1. What does the author mean when he states (paragraph 3) that "language is a form of intellectual play for me"?

2. Children and teens often ridicule anyone who is different. Did this happen to you or to someone you know? For what reason? Looking back, how do you react to such behavior in yourself or in others?

3. Why do you think the author's classmates ridiculed him and were angry with him when he spoke educated English? Try to put yourself in the classmates' shoes.

4. Do you believe that the English language is a closed system, or that it allows for a wide range of spoken English? Give reasons for your answer.

5. What, if any, advantage is there in learning to speak and write grammatically correct English?

Writing Assignments

1. Write an imaginary letter to Wayne Lionel Aponte telling him your reaction to the experience he had with fellow Blacks who disapproved of his language.

2. Write a paragraph about the diversity of spoken English in our country. Use specific examples.

TV's Distorted Images

Tom Siebert

Every time someone goes berserk with a gun in a public place, the topic again comes up about what effect television programming, with its portrayal of violence, might have had on the crazy behavior. Some people are convinced that television is not merely reflecting behavior in society, but actually causing it. Others hold just the opposite view—that TV only reflects how we behave. In this article, a writer weighs in with the example of Fiji that, until recently, had no television. He finds some surprising results.

1   In the continuing cultural debate over who is to blame for all of our problems, let's yield the floor for a moment to the voice of Fiji's young women.

2   Fiji is a remote South Pacific Island nation, so isolated that until 1995 most islanders did not get television reception. Now, thanks to some persistent capitalists and satellite technology, Fiji gets one channel, mixing a smorgasbord of English-language programming from the United States, England and Australia.

3   Until the arrival of television, eating disorders among the young women—who live in a culture where voluptuously rounded bodies are the norm and plump is preferred—were unheard of. But now, according to the Harvard Eating Disorders Center, that's no longer the case.

4   According to a recent *New York Times* article, Harvard researchers started monitoring impressions high school girls had of their own bodies one month after satellite transmissions began beaming broadcasts into Fiji. In three years, the researchers discovered some alarming shifts in perception and behavior.

5   Surveying a similar number of Fiji girls in 1995 and 1998, and matching them up by age, weight and other characteristics, researchers found that by 1998 almost 30 percent of Fiji's girls tested high-risk for eating disorders, as opposed to 13 percent in the earlier study. Fifteen percent admitted that they had induced vomiting to control weight, almost a five-fold increase.

6   Nearly three-quarters said they had been on a diet at least once, in a culture where three years earlier the word "diet" was used about as much as the word "snow."

7   Perhaps most tellingly, girls who watched television three or more nights per week were far more likely to describe themselves as "too fat" than those who didn't. Or perhaps even more tellingly, two of Fiji's highest rated programs are "Melrose Place" and "Beverly Hills 90210."

8   People in the entertainment business will tell you that what they do only reflects society's behavior; it doesn't instigate it. They will tell you that kids know that what they see is only make-believe, not something for them to imitate. They'll say we don't give people enough credit: People have the strength of free will to make up their own minds.

9   But the facts in Fiji indicate otherwise. No TV, virtually no eating disorders. Three years of TV, lots of anxious girls who feel, in the words of one girl quoted in the *Times,* "I'm very heavy. Sometimes I'm depressed because I always want to lose weight."

10 Clearly, the programming being shown in Fiji did not reflect the culture of the country, but it did induce new behavior. So if three years of one television channel can do this to the young women of Fiji, what's a lifetime of dozens to hundreds of channels doing to America's children? What does seeing 40,000 murders before a kid hits high school do to a young mind?

How about a relentless onslaught of sitcoms in which the kids always have a witty rejoinder for their uncool parents, instead of showing them respect?

How many people on TV go to church or mosque or synagogue? What percentage cheat on a spouse? **11**

If the entertainment industry really didn't think it could affect your behavior, it wouldn't be able to sell advertisements during programs, or get large corporations to pay big money to sneak their products into key scenes in movies or pay sports stars to wear their logos on their uniforms. **12**

Here's a more personal take. I remember a Christmas season when I was eight years old. I had seen a recent episode of "All in the Family" where Archie was listening to a moronic story from Edith and became so disgusted that he mimed filling a gun with bullets and shooting himself in the head to escape her blathering. **13**

I thought this was the funniest thing I'd ever seen. **14**

During Christmas Eve dinner, my loving and wonderful mother was telling a story to friends who were visiting our home. I thought the story was kind of dull, and so to spice things up a bit, I extravagantly mimed the faux suicide just like Archie Bunker, thinking that this was the most hilarious thing in the world and that I would be the center of attention. People did not think it was funny. They were appalled. My mother cried, she was so hurt. It was not a happy Christmas. **15**

Television is that powerful. It can ruin Christmas. It can ruin our society. Right now, it's ruining part of Fiji's. **16**

Vocabulary

remote (2)	relentless (10)
isolated (2)	onslaught (10)
persistent (2)	rejoinder (10)
smorgasbord (2)	moronic (13)
voluptuously (3)	blathering (13)
perception (4)	extravagantly (15)
induced (5)	faux (15)
instigate (8)	appalled (15)

Understanding What You Have Read

Check the correct answer in the blank provided.

1. Where is Fiji?

    _____ **(a).** In the Mediterranean.

    _____ **(b).** In the Red Sea.

    _____ **(c).** In the North Sea.

    __✔__ **(d).** In the South Pacific.

2. Before the arrival of television, what female figure was culturally the norm in Fiji?

    __✔__ **(a).** Plump women.

    _____ **(b).** Average-sized women.

    _____ **(c).** Stick-figure women.

    _____ **(d).** Extremely obese women.

3. What do people in the entertainment business maintain about the effect of television on society?

_____ **(a).** That it decisively influences behavior.

✔ **(b).** That it reflects behavior, but does not instigate it.

_____ **(c).** That it affects only teenagers.

_____ **(d).** That women are most affected by its images.

4. What does the author say television did to Fiji?

✔ **(a).** It induced new behavior.

_____ **(b).** It had no effect.

_____ **(c).** It caused binge eating.

_____ **(d).** It increased the rate of divorce.

5. What popular television program did the author imitate one Christmas to humiliate his mother?

_____ **(a).** Beverly Hills 10210.

_____ **(b).** Melrose Place.

_____ **(c).** Taxi.

✔ **(d).** All in the Family.

Thinking About What You Have Read

1. The author is specific about the programming that Fiji now receives via television. Why is this information important to his point of view?

2. The author attributes the findings about Fiji women to two sources: The Harvard Eating Disorders Center and the *New York Times*. Why do you think he makes a point of quoting his sources?

3. The author is making an argument about the effect of TV on behavior. Read paragraph 8. What familiar tactic of argument is he using here?

4. What illogic is the author accusing the entertainment industry of in paragraph 12?

5. How would you sum up the author's main point about the effect of TV on Fiji Island society? How and where does the author relate this point to TV's possible effect on our own world?

Writing Assignments

1. Write a paragraph about your favorite television show.

2. Write a paragraph about any specific act of behavior that you know TV has caused in you.

An Argument

With Things That People Can Control, Such as Dress, Stereotypes Make Sense

Leonard Pitts Jr.

This column, by a well-known African-American columnist, makes the argument that teenagers who adopt the so-called "gangsta chic" style of dressing are sending a message which the public is wise to heed. Arguing that he is not stereotyping but exercising good sense, the writer makes a strong case for his belief that sometimes it is smart to judge a book by its cover.

1   The subject was gangsta chic—that distinctive style of urban fashion that says, I am here to rob and injure you. I was speaking at a forum in West Virginia a few days ago when it came up.

2   I said what I usually say: It's troubling to me that young men, particularly many young African-American men, would dress in a style that's universally perceived as the uniform of a criminal.

3   Whereupon a black woman rose from the audience, eyes flashing danger signs, mouth full of rebuke. Her own sons, she said, dress like this and she thinks they look darn good. Why should they change? So white folks will like them? White folks are going to think what they want about young black men, regardless. Besides, you can't judge a book by its cover.

4   I'm here to tell you the same thing I told her: Sometimes, you can.

5   Indeed, as she spoke, I was reminded of something that happened to me maybe four years ago. I'm standing on a subway platform waiting for the train. A group of teenage boys is standing nearby, and I'm watching them with a wary eye. You know the type. Loud and profane city kids dressed like street thugs. Hats to the back, shirts hanging open, pants sagging low so you can see their drawers. When the train pulls in, I wait to see which car they board. Then I board another.

6   You will have a hard time convincing me I did not do the right thing. Don't take that as an argument in favor of stereotyping. It's illogical to make sweeping judgments about a person based on some accident of birth or circumstance. None of us can choose the color of our skin, the nation of our origin, the orientation of our sexuality, the ability or disability of our limbs, the religion of our forebears.

7   No, the argument I'm here to make has to do with the things we do control. One of which is dress.

8   I'm sorry, but if I see a woman tricked out as the rapper Lil' Kim was at the MTV video awards—breast exposed, nipple covered by a pasty—i feel justified in assuming she's not on her way to morning Mass. Similarly, the man with the Confederate flag T-shirt is probably not en route to an NAACP meeting. And the guy who walks around wearing white greasepaint on his face, a big red nose and floppy shoes ought to expect that once in a while, people are going to throw cream pies at him.

9   The point being that all of us make judgments all the time based upon how people present themselves. This is only natural.

10   Certainly, we make special dispensation for the fact that young people always dress so as to annoy the old folks. This, too, is natural. From the

flappers of the '20s to the poodle skirts of the '50s, from the tie-dyed hippies of the '60s to the polyester fashion victims of the disco years, kids have always outfitted themselves according to ever-shifting ideas of what constitutes cool.

But gangsta chic is about more than cool. The universal perception **11** and frequent reality is that it's also about sending an implicit threat. It's no accident that the style rose just as rap went West, finding its inspiration—and performers—among black street gangs in South-Central Los Angeles. Indeed, observers say the whole sagging-pants style came out of jails were prisoners are denied belts for security reasons

What does it tell us about their mind-set, their perception of self, that **12** young African-American men from hellish neighborhoods would adopt that style as a badge of honor? And how grotesque is it that kids from the middle class adopt the same style as a statement of fashion?

I often hear such kids insist that dress is neutral and how dare you **13** stereotype them based on what they wear. Fine. It's the argument you would expect them to make. But it's an abrogation of responsibility for adults to encourage them in that delusion. Better to explain to them that what you show to the world, how you allow yourself to be perceived, will have profound implications for the way people treat you. This is a fact of life that has little to do with stereotyping, racial or otherwise.

I mean, I perceived a threat by those boys on the subway platform and **14** acted accordingly. Anyone who thinks that constitutes racial stereotyping needs to understand something.

They were white. **15**

Vocabulary

chic (1)	dispensation (10)
perceived (2)	implicit (11)
rebuke (3)	grotesque (12)
wary (5)	abrogation (13)
profane (5)	delusion (13)
stereotyping (6)	implications (13)
forebears (6)	

Understanding What You Have Read

Check the correct answer in the blank provided.

1. What does the writer mean by gangsta chic?

   _____ **(a).** Polyester garments.

   _✔_ **(b).** Baggy clothes and belt-less pants worn very low.

   _____ **(c).** Clothes made of tie-die fabrics.

   _____ **(d).** Indian saris that were popular in the '50s.

2. What did the writer do in the subway that might be mistaken for stereotyping?

   _____ **(a).** He refused to talk to badly dressed teens.

   _____ **(b).** He called the police when he saw a group of teens on the platform.

   _____ **(c).** He refused to board the train the teens were on.

   _✔_ **(d).** He made a point of riding in a different car than the teens did.

3. What does the writer say a guy wearing a false red nose and white greasepaint should expect?

_____ **(a).** That he might be hired as a clown.

_____ **(b).** That he might be locked up by the police.

__✔__ **(c).** That someone might throw a cream pie at him.

_____ **(d).** That people would find his get up ridiculous.

4. Where, according to the author, does it gangsta chic come from?

__✔__ **(a).** Prison attire.

_____ **(b).** The movies.

_____ **(c).** The South.

_____ **(d).** Nobody knows.

5. What argument does the writer expect teens to make against his position?

_____ **(a).** That adults don't understand them.

__✔__ **(b).** That dress is neutral and interpreting it otherwise is stereotyping.

_____ **(c).** That teens are usually well spoken and polite.

_____ **(d).** That fraternity dress codes are unfashionable.

Thinking About What You Have Read

1. What message, according to Pitts, does the gangsta chic style send? What is your opinion of this interpretation? What message do you think it sends?

2. What does the saying, "You can't judge a book by its cover," mean? What does that particular saying have to do with this argument?

3. Read paragraph 5 very carefully. What grammatical error that you have been warned against does the writer commit twice? Why do you think he does it?

4. What is odd about paragraph 12? What is the writer doing here?

5. What piece of information about the teens does the author withhold until the last paragraph? Why do you think he does this? How effective a tactic do you think it is?

Writing Assignments

1. Write a paragraph about the clothes you like to wear and what, if anything, you're saying about yourself in wearing them.

2. Write a paragraph either supporting or refuting the author's argument that gangsta chic clothing says, "I am here to rob and injure you."

Who Lives, Who Dies, Who Decides

Evelyn Storr Smart

The title of this essay sums up its theme: Hard choices must be made about terminal illness. As medical science has advanced, it has added years of life for those who would formerly have had only a few months ahead of them. But with the added years have come additional expenses and cruel choices. The author explores what happens in the final harsh days of life. Rather than finding these final days depressing, however, she discovers that they enrich life both for the dying and for their caregivers. What do you think of the author's solution to "open all hearts"? Is it realistic?

1   The problem: Hospice patients, supposedly near death, are living too long.

2   The solution: Operation Restore Trust has been set up by the Health and Human Services Department to combat waste in hospice care. Some hospice providers now fear they may have to repay the government millions of dollars spent on care for those who live longer than the HHS limit of six months. Next on the agenda, physician-assisted suicide.

3   Some people would respond, so who wants to prolong life at that stage anyway? When I was healthy, I would have agreed. I'd just stash some pills, invite my family and friends in to say goodbye, and that would be it.

4   Well, after eight years as a cancer patient, after seven years as a member of a hospice support group, after witnessing more than 100 deaths, I have never once seen a script that resembles the one I'd written for myself.

5   Karen Chapell, a beautiful 42-year-old dying of bone cancer, typifies the metamorphosis that takes place when someone is told she is terminal. Her first concerns were about pain, loss of dignity and the economic burden on her daughter: "When I can no longer take care of myself, I want out. Period." Six months later she needed to use a walker. Four months after that she was in a wheelchair and her hospice support group was helping her with housework. Another two months and she was confined to bed. Her daughter had quit her job to take care of her. After six weeks, she was transferred to a hospice. Her daughter slept in her mother's room, smoothing her brow, moistening her lips. When I visited Karen the day before her death, liver failure had turned her face and bald head a bright orange, her emaciated body was curved in a fetal position, her mouth was hanging open like a baby bird's waiting to be fed. "How do I look?" she whispered. "Beautiful," I answered. And I meant it. Her simple humanity overpowered everything else in the room.

6   "I wouldn't have missed one moment of this ending," she said.

7   Dr. Marion Primomo, a pioneer in hospice care agrees. "Almost all hospice patients who initially request suicide change their minds as soon as they feel cared for. Only one in 1,000 actually follows through."

8   It would be enormously cost effective to assist people to end their lives. The taxpayers would get good value for their money. But do we really want anyone to opt for suicide because it's cost effective? Or because they have no one to care for them?

9   Most people agree, theoretically, that when death is imminent, we should be given only compassionate care. But what if your 25-year-old daughter has third-stage ovarian cancer? Yes, it would be cost effective to

deny her treatment, but it would be even more economical if she were subtly persuaded that a speedy assisted suicide would be in everyone's best interest.

There are no easy answers. The American Medical Assn. is profoundly **10** opposed to doctor-assisted suicide, yet ask any doctor to really levels with you and he will tell you that patients always have been helped to die. Even some ministers support assisted suicide.

But I've come to believe that facing death gives real meaning to our **11** lives. After seven years, I have never seen a lack of dignity in the hospice I am associated with, and most of the patients there remain pain-free and alert up to the last few days. Even those without families are honored and respected by the staff as they undergo the process of closing down.

If we really care enough and open our hearts as well as our pocket- **12** books, it can be done. In a book, "Share the Care: How to Organize a Group to Care for Someone Who Is Seriously Ill," Cappy Capossela and Sheila Warnock wrote about 12 people who gathered around a dying friend, each volunteering to do one thing: pay her bills, bring her dinner once a week, help her bathe. Their friend lived three long and peaceful years, and all were enriched by the experience.

When patients learn to accept the support around them, they almost **13** always choose life instead of death. So should we offer people in the dying process good, palliative, loving care? Or a great big shot of morphine?

Vocabulary

metamorphosis (5)	imminent (9)
emaciated (5)	subtly (9)
fetal (5)	palliative (13)

Understanding What You Have Read

Check the correct answer in the blank provided.

1. What time limit does the Human Services Department allow for dying patients?

_____ **(a).** One year

_____ **(b).** Two years

_____ **(c).** Five years

___✔___ **(d).** Six months

2. What does the author tell us about her own health?

_____ **(a).** She is well.

___✔___ **(b).** She has been a cancer patient for eight years.

_____ **(c).** She has multiple sclerosis.

_____ **(d).** She is suicidal.

3. How many hospice patients, according to Dr. Primomo, actually commit suicide?

_____ **(a).** Most of them

_____ **(b).** Fifty percent

_____ **(c).** More than 75 percent

___✔___ **(d).** 1 in 1,000

4. Although the American Medical Assn. opposes physician-assisted suicide, the author says that most doctors will privately admit

_____ **(a).** Patients are never helped to die.

✔ **(b).** Patients have always been helped to die.

_____ **(c).** Families often have killed their own sick.

_____ **(d).** Patients never ask to be put to death.

5. What has the author come to believe about death?

_____ **(a).** That it is an undignified process.

_____ **(b).** That it is frequently messy.

_____ **(c).** That patients are often in excruciating pain.

✔ **(d).** That facing death gives real meaning to our lives.

Thinking About What You Have Read

1. How would you sum up the author's argument? In a sentence or two, state what she's arguing for.

2. What is a hospice? What does a member of a "hospice support group" do?

3. The author shares her own health history with us and tells us that she has been a member of a hospice support group for seven years. What do these revelations add to her argument?

4. What is the function of paragraph 5 in this argument? What kind of detail does paragraph 5 present?

5. The author writes in paragraph 10 "ask any doctor to really level with you and he will tell you that patients always have been helped to die." According to what you have learned in this book, what is wrong with punctuation of this sentence? What is wrong with the pronoun use?

Writing Assignments

1. Write an essay arguing for or against physician-assisted suicide.

2. Write an essay on any topic associated with death.

Nation's Gun Play Is Dangerous Game

Norman A. Lockman

Gun crimes are always horrifying, but the latest wrinkle, as Lockman points out in this essay, is almost unimaginable: children now settle their school yard disputes with guns. Lockman makes reference to the shooting in West Paducah, Kentucky, which occurred on December 1, 1997. In that incident, a troubled 14-year-old boy killed three of his classmates, all girls, and wounded several others. Other school shootings have followed in Oregon and in Mississippi. The solution, to many thinkers, including Lockman, is to curb the easy availability of guns. Do you agree with this solution? What other proposals could you offer in place of it? As an aside, we might mention that this essay was written before the notorious shooting at the Columbine High School in Littleton, Colorado, which occurred on April 20, 1999.

1   Have you noticed that what we used to call "mass murders" are happening about once a month now somewhere in the United States? A few of them still make the front pages of our newspapers, like the lethal gun-play by the 14-year-old freshman in the hallway of a public school in West Paducah, Kentucky, last Monday.

2   And have you noticed that these "mass murders" are increasingly being committed by kids who are discontented about something trivial? There was one in a Mississippi high school barely a month ago perpetrated by a boy who felt picked on. These disturbed youngsters have switched from pea shooters to pistols to get even.

3   In Wilmington, Delaware, a quiet burg with fewer than 80,000 residents, there have been 100 shootings so far this year, and that is considered an improvement over last year's record 107. Most of the shootings were traced to youths hassling each other over petty drug disputes.

4   Once or twice a week, I can now lie abed at night and hear distant gun play, probably some kid showing off in the wee hours by firing his new toy into the air or out the window of a speeding car. Br-rap-pap! B-r-r-r-r-r-rap-pap-pap! Full automatic. Then silence. No sirens. Which means that nobody got hit, on purpose or accidentally, and nobody close to the gun fire bothered to call the police.

5   What is wrong with us? We are being overrun by irresponsible people with guns and we are too wimpy to do anything about it. Completely cowed by the gun lovers who insist on freedom to infest this society with weapons of mass destruction. How many times do we have to look at pictures of surviving high school kids sobbing and hugging, or hear yet another tale of a disgruntled employee going berserk and turning his workplace into a shooting gallery? How many more times before we stop being cowed and demand some protection from firearms for ourselves and our families?

6   Gun play is causing more deaths in America than AIDS. It's a deadly epidemic with nobody seriously working on a cure. The cure is licensing of all firearms and severe restrictions on the sale and ownership of handguns, and an absolute ban on assault weapons. Let the gun lovers rant about the Constitution; it's macho blather. The Founding Fathers, who recognized real danger to the country when they saw it, would certainly be siding with the gun controllers at this point. They weren't stupid.

7   The gun lovers contend that only irresponsible people misuse guns. And they have to protect themselves against the irresponsible. In fact, most people who own guns are not conscientious gun lovers, they are

casual owners who are careless with their weapons. It's their guns that wind up in the hands of kids like Michael Cameal, who walked off with a neighbor's arsenal and used the .22 automatic before the neighbor even missed his stash.

We should be making it as hard as possible for people—law enforcement people included—to buy and store guns at home. It should be a task far too onerous for an average Joe. Even with such restrictions it would take many years for the gun epidemic to abate in America. Obviously, nobody is going to demand that law abiding civilians turn in their handguns and register their hunting rifles and shotguns (although that's not such a bad idea), but serious gun control has to start somewhere. The laws now on the books aren't nearly tough or effective enough. **8**

While the gun lovers posture the rest of us cower. Aren't you getting tired of cowering? Aren't you tired of your kids cowering—or carrying? Aren't you tired of having to worry about gun play every time you set foot out of doors? Aren't you tired of reading about mass murders being done with guns too easy to get and too easy to use? **9**

Me too. Don't be ashamed to say it. America needs to be disarmed. **10**

Vocabulary

lethal (1)	disgruntled (5)
trivial (2)	berserk (5)
perpetrated (2)	arsenal (7)
petty (3)	onerous (8)
cowed (5)	abate (8)
infest (5)	cower (9)

Understanding What You Have Read

Check the correct answer in the blank provided.

1. What observation does the author make about "mass murders"?
   _____ (a). That they are being increasingly committed in the West.
   _____ (b). That old people are doing them.
   __✔__ (c). That they are being increasingly committed by kids.
   _____ (d). That they are decreasing.

2. By whom does the author say we're becoming cowed?
   _____ (a). By the politicians.
   __✔__ (b). By irresponsible people with guns.
   _____ (c). By mass marketing.
   _____ (d). By television.

3. The author says that gun play causes more deaths in America than
   __✔__ (a). AIDs.
   _____ (b). Smallpox.
   _____ (c). Cancer.
   _____ (d). Heart disease.

4. What do gun lovers contend?

_____ **(a).** That teenages who use guns should be locked up.

_____ **(b).** That hunters never misuse their guns.

___✔___ **(c).** That only irresponsible people misuse guns.

_____ **(d).** That guns are used only for target practice.

5. What does the author propose that we make as hard as possible?

___✔___ **(a).** For people to buy and store guns at home.

_____ **(b).** For hunters to have rifles.

_____ **(c).** For people with a drunken driver conviction to own a gun.

_____ **(d).** For felons to be armed.

Thinking About What You Have Read

1. How does the author introduce his argument on the problem of irresponsible gun use?

2. About "mass murders," the author writes that "a few of them still make the front pages of our newspapers." What tone is he using here?

3. A good argument draws attention to the opponent's position and then tries to refute it. Where does the author do that in this argument?

4. In paragraph 5, the author writes: "Completely cowed by the gun lovers who insist on freedom to infest this society with weapons of mass destruction." What is grammatically wrong with this statement?

5. The author says that the cure for gun violence in America is strict gun control. What is your opinion of this position?

Writing Assignments

1. Write an essay about any incident with a gun that you've either personally experienced or heard about.

2. If you are an opponent of gun control, write an essay arguing against the author's position

Credits

Index

Instructor's Section

Contents

Information for Instructors

Purpose and Content, Additional Activities, Additional Assignments

Part 1: The Paragraph

Part 2: The Sentence

Part 3: Mechanics

INSTRUCTOR'S SECTION

Answers to Various Practices   I-28

Using Writing Talk: Sentences and Paragraphs with Readings

Writing Talk: Sentences and Paragraphs with Readings is a comprehensive textbook that contains a wealth of material and practice opportunities related to sentence-level grammar and mechanics. It also includes sections on the writing process and paragraph structure and development. In addition, there is a selection of short readings at the back that provides students with practice in reading comprehension and stimuli for writing. The best approach is to cover the paragraph material first so that students may begin writing paragraphs early in the term, then teach the grammar and mechanics section, showing the students how the rules apply to the paragraphs they are currently writing. The reading material can provide a nice counterpoint to grammar instruction each week.

Basic writers will not readily understand a writing textbook on their own. They need an instructor to explain, reinforce, and demonstrate the material in the book. The many "Practicing" opportunities in the text are very useful in reinforcing the concepts in the text. Again, students need a teacher's guidance. The practices should either be done in class, or done at home and checked in class. Class time spent on writing is not "wasted" time. Basic writers often need help at the moment they are writing, not later.

Writing Talk: Sentences and Paragraphs with Readings offers many writing prompts and assignments in each unit, and an additional photo prompt at the end of each unit. Students should be doing a little writing every day, and writing a paragraph for evaluation *at least* once a week.

Two suggested schedules follow, one for a 16-week semester, and the other for an 11-week quarter. Both integrate writing, grammar, and reading.

Semester Schedule

PARAGRAPH WRITING	
Week 1	Introduction to Course
	Unit 2: Myths About Writing
Week 2	Unit 3: How to Start Writing
	Unit 4: Moving from Sentences to Paragraphs
Week 3	Unit 5: Writing a Solid Paragraph
	Unit 6: Revising Paragraphs

	GRAMMAR/MECHANICS	**READINGS**
Week 4	Unit 7: The Basic Sentence	Help for Your Reading
		"Tortillas"
Week 5	Unit 8: Building Sentences	"The Ritual of the Grill"
		"The Cello"
Week 6	Unit 9: Avoiding Non-Sentences	"The Hole at Alcatraz"
		"Letter from Tokyo"

	GRAMMAR/MECHANICS	**READINGS**
Week 7	Unit 10: Verbs—An Overview	"The Monkey Garden"
	Unit 11: Regular and Irregular Verbs	"Snakes"
Week 8	Unit 12: Subject-Verb Agreement	"The Revolt of the Elephants"
	Unit 13: Problems with Verbs	"Sport"
Week 9	Unit 14: Using Pronouns Correctly	"At the Core, Why Jordan Is Jordan"
	Unit 15: Pronoun Problems	"Two Roads Converged in a Wood"
Week 10	Unit 16: Distinguishing Between Adjectives and Adverbs	"Barbie Doll"
	Unit 17: Dangling and Misplaced Modifiers	"Last Flight"
	Unit 18: Using Prepositions	
Week 11	Unit 19: Punctuation You Can Hear	"Looking for Love in Cyberspace Isn't as Easy—or Safe—as It Seems"
		"Shame"
Week 12	Unit 20: Punctuation You Can't Hear	"Señor Payroll"
Week 13	Unit 21: Capitalization	"Talkin' White"
	Unit 22: How to Use the Dictionary	
Week 14	Unit 23: Spelling Rules	"Unacceptable Behavior"
	Unit 24: Commonly Misspelled Words	"Faith in the Future of Dreams"
Week 15	Review of problem areas	"Who Lives, Who Dies, Who Decides"
		"Nation's Gun Play Is Dangerous Game"
Week 16	Time for writing or completing essays, reviewing portfolios, taking exams.	

Quarter Schedule

	PARAGRAPH WRITING
Week 1	Introduction to Course
	Unit 2: Myths About Writing
	Unit 3: How to Start Writing
Week 2	Unit 4: Moving from Sentences to Paragraphs
	Unit 5: Writing a Solid Paragraph
	Unit 6: Revising Paragraphs

	GRAMMAR/MECHANICS	**READINGS**
Week 3	Unit 7: The Basic Sentence	Choose 1 or 2 selections from the "An Object" section
	Unit 8: Building Sentences	

	GRAMMAR/MECHANICS	**READINGS**
Week 4	Unit 9: Avoiding Non-Sentences	Choose 1 or 2 selections from the "A Place" section
Week 5	Unit 10: Verbs—An Overview Unit 11: Regular and Irregular Verbs	Choose 1 or 2 selections from the "An Animal" section
Week 6	Unit 12: Subject-Verb Agreement Unit 13: Problems with Verbs	Choose 1 or 2 selections from the "A Person" section
Week 7	Unit 13: Using Pronouns Correctly Unit 15: Pronoun Problems	Choose 1 or 2 selections from the "An Event" section
Week 8	Unit 16: Distinguishing Between Adjectives and Adverbs Unit 17: Dangling and Misplaced Modifiers Unit 18: Using Prepositions	Choose 1 or 2 selections from the "A Problem" section
Week 9	Unit 19: Punctuation You Can Hear Unit 20: Punctuation You Can't Hear	Choose 1 or 2 selections from the "An Argument" section
Week 10	Unit 21: Capitalization Unit 22: How to Use the Dictionary	Unit 23: Spelling Rules Unit 24: Commonly Misspelled Words
Week 11	Time for writing or completing paragraphs, reviewing protfolios, taking exams	

Evaluating Paragraphs

Criteria. Evaluation of writing is always subjective, and no point system or rubric can alter that. However, it is helpful for both instructors and students to have a set of standards or criteria that help define what makes a paper better or worse. *Writing Talk: Sentences and Paragraphs with Readings* suggests that a good paragraph should

- Begin with a topic sentence that expresses a discussible point.
- Stick to its point.
- Prove the point with examples, facts, testimony, reasons, and personal observations.
- Have clear linking of the main points.
- Use standard English.

You may wish to add other criteria to this list or to be more particular about each item.

Grades. After establishing criteria, the next question is what grading scale to use. This is a matter of personal preference; any scale that is used fairly and consistently will be effective. Some instructors, while listing the criteria they are using to evaluate writing, will offer a holistic grade of A to F. Others prefer a point system where each criterion is worth a certain number of points toward a total grade. You may also wish to use a simpler Satisfactory/Needs Revision/Honors system. The number of Satisfactory or Honors papers during the term can contribute to a final passing grade.

How Much to Grade. Next, there is a consideration of how many papers to grade and at what intervals. In general, to make real progress, writing students need to be writing far more than mortal teachers could ever grade. Students may complete two or three paragraphs a week, but not all of these need to be graded. Some instructors use the portfolio system, where students collect their work over the term and select and revise their best pieces to showcase at the end. Students using this system still need feedback and suggestions on their writing during the term, but may not be receiving definitive grades until their portfolio is submitted. Other instructors use a mini-portfolio system where students work for a week or two, then turn in all their work but select only one piece to receive a formal grade. If you wish students to turn in and get feedback on everything they write, the level of feedback doesn't always have to be the same; you may choose to put comments on some papers, grades on others, or just use a highlighter to mark passages that need a student's attention.

Comments. Finally, evaluating writing does call for some commentary as well as a grade. Some instructors prefer to do this during short, individual conferences. Others may write comments on the papers. For the most part, comments should be short and positive. Usually a graded paper is already full of corrections and suggestions and notes about problems. Students can tell from the corrections and their grades if something was wrong. What they need in the comment is to find out what was right.

Responding directly to what a student has written, either in conference or in the final comment, is very beneficial. Comments like, "What a nice tribute to your mother. She sounds amazing," or "I had no idea that could happen to someone while scuba diving," or "I'm glad you were strong enough to get out of that situation," let the writer know that you truly listened to what he/she had to say, and that is the greatest motivation for writing there is.

Two forms for evaluation student paragraphs follow:

Scale

10	Excellent
9	Very good
8	Satisfactory
7	Weak, but acceptable
6	Needs serious improvement
0–5	Unsatisfactory

Criteria

Topic sentence   _____
Focus on topic   _____
Detailed development   _____
Organization and transition   _____
Use of standard English   _____

Total = _____ × 2 = _____ (Grade)

Comments:

	Unsatisfactory	Satisfactory	Honors
Topic sentence	_____	_____	_____
Focus	_____	_____	_____
Development	_____	_____	_____
Organization and transition	_____	_____	_____
Standard English	_____	_____	_____
Overall	_____	_____	_____
Comments:			

Using Computers in a Writing Class

Having students write on computers during class or lab time is advantageous to both students and teachers. If students can write during class time, the instructor can see the writing as it happens—which is the perfect time to correct an error, help someone get over a block, point out that someone is straying off-topic, and so on. This is the greatest advantage, but not the only one. Students' paragraphs are much more legible, which means they do a better job of proofreading and the instructor has an easier job when grading. Also, although we live in "the computer age," basic writing students often do not have access to a computer. For them, writing on the computer teaches them a valuable, marketable skill that they can use later in college or on the job. It also gives them confidence and a sense of validity about their writing. Finally, it makes students much more likely to revise because revision is so easy and doesn't involve the labor of recopying.

Why Not?

The only reason not to have students write on computers is if your college does not have a lab available. If you think you don't have enough time, consider that writing itself is the greatest teacher of writing skills, and "covering material" is secondary. If you don't know how to use a computer yourself, it's very easy to learn, and introductory courses are readily available. If you're afraid the students don't know how, you may be right. However, teaching students to use a computer takes about one hour of class time, and pays off for the rest of the term. If you're afraid the students can't type, you may be right again. Even your students who type with one finger will quickly build up enough speed to finish a draft of a paragraph in about 30 minutes.

How?

Once you have arranged for computer space and time for your students, you need only make sure they know a few things:

- How to open the word processing program.
- How to insert and delete words or letters.
- How to use the Tab key to indent a paragraph.
- How to double space.
- How to use the spell check.
- How to print.
- How to save a document to a floppy disk.
- How to retrieve a document.
- How to close out.

What?

Definitely all paragraphs or essays submitted for evaluation should be done on the computer. Depending on how much class time you can spend in a computer classroom, your students can also do many of the "Practicing" and "Talk Write" activities on computer, as well as a number of the "Additional Activities" in this manual. If you have Internet access in your lab, you may also wish to go as a class to the sites named in the "Internet Assignments" in the manual.

Why Use the Internet in a Basic Writing Class?

There are only a few Internet-related assignments in this manual; more are offered in the manual that accompanies *Writing Talk: Paragraphs and Short Essays with Readings.* The purpose of these assignments is simply to get them on the Net. Many basic writing students have little if any experience on the Internet, and this lack of experience is cutting them off from a vast amount of information and opportunity that more educated people take for granted. They need to learn what's out there and how to get to it.

Why Not?

Again, if the technology is available, there's no reason not to introduce students to the Internet in a basic writing course. You don't have to spend time on it every week—just enough for them to learn how and to search for sites related to a certain topic. "Learning" to use the Internet takes very little instruction, just the opportunity to practice.

Internet Sources for Instructors

National Association for Developmental Education
http://www.umkc.edu/cad/nade/index.htm
     NADE is one of the two national professional organizations for developmental educators. This large site contains information on the organization and its publications, and links to sites related to developmental education.

College Reading and Learning Association
http://www.crla.net/Welcome.htm
     CRLA is the other national professional organization for developmental instructors; this one focuses more on reading and study skills. This site contains information on the organization and its publications, and links to sites related to developmental education.

NADE Discussion Group List
http://www.umkc.edu/cad/nade/nademisc/educdisc.htm
     Part of the NADE site, this is a good list of online discussion groups (listserv) for developmental educators. Subscribing to a listserv will connect you to developmental educators across the country and give you a great opportunity to hear educators share solutions to common problems. You'll get more e-mail than you can read, but you can pick and choose what to open.

ERIC Clearinghouses
http://www.accesseric.org/sites/barak.html
     ERIC is the Educational Resources Information Center. This is the best online source for general education research. It also provides educational materials, services, and coursework in all disciplines. The site is searchable and user-friendly.

Resources for Writing Teachers
http://owl.english.purdue.edu/teachers/introduction.html

This is part of the Purdue University Writing Lab Site. It includes lesson plans for college-level writing instructors, ESL resources, and links to other valuable sites about teaching writing.

The Collaborative Teaching Library
http://www.nmia.com/~nking/collib.html

This site is an electric swap shop featuring new and improving ideas for teaching DADE (Department of Adult and Developmental Education) courses. Well-organized sit with valuable real-life teaching strategies.

Blue Web'n Learning Site Library
http://www.kn.pacbell.com/wired/bluewebn/

This is an enormous collection of links to Web-based tutorials, activities, projects, lesson plans and other resources in many subject areas.

LD Online
http://www.ldonline.org

This is a comprehensive site where you can search for basic information on any specific learning disability, or learn about LD issues in general. Since many developmental students are learning disabled, whether diagnosed or not, this information can be very useful.

Dave's ESL Café
http://www.eslcafe.com

This is an enormous and well-maintained site that will link you to virtually any ESL source or information you might want.

Study Guides and Strategies
http://www.iss.stthomas.edu/studyguides

This is a very large and well-organized collection of links to guides to studying and test-taking.

The Internet Public Library
http://www.ipl.org

This is a searchable source of online books and reference materials.

Peer Editing

Peer editing is very valuable in basic writing classes. It does not hold true that putting unskilled writers in peer editing groups is "the blind leading the blind." A classroom full of students contains a variety of strengths and weaknesses, and this variety will allow students to help one another. Also, research has proven that the student doing the helping or editing profits just as much as the student whose work is being edited. Here are some sample peer editing worksheets.

Peer Editing Instructions, Form A

Read another writer's paragraph, then answer these questions. For each question, answer "yes" or "no" and then write at least one complete sentence to explain or back up your answer.

1. Did the writer begin with a topic sentence that expresses a discussible point?
2. Did the writer stick to his/her point, never getting off-topic?
3. Did the writer prove the point with examples, facts, testimony, reasons, and personal observations?
4. Did the writer provide clear linking of the main points?
5. Did the writer use standard English?

6. Was this paragraph easy for you to understand?
7. Did you enjoy reading this paragraph? Was it interesting to you?
8. Circle all errors or possible errors in this paragraph.

Peer Editing Instructions, Form B

The Writer's Job: The first four questions should be answered *by the writer* on a separate sheet of notebook paper with the writer's name on it.

1. Why did you choose this paragraph to work on? What makes it good?
2. In one short sentence, what is the main point you are trying to make?
3. What two questions or doubts about your paragraph do you have that you would like the readers to answer?

Examples: Did I stay focused on my topic sentence?

Do you understand why the topic is important or does it sound stupid?

Does this paragraph sound funny or serious to you?

Did I give enough details?

4. What is your main weakness in grammar that you would like the readers to check for?

Examples: run-ons, fragments, subject-verb agreement, apostrophes

The Readers' Job, Part 1: The readers of the paper should each answer the following three questions:

1. In one short sentence, what is your understanding of what the writer is trying to say in the paper?
2. Ask one question about the topic that you wish the writer would answer in the paper.
3. Answer the writer's questions (#3). Be as specific as possible.

The Readers' Job, Part 2: The readers of the paper should each make the following notes *directly on the draft.*

1. Write WHAT? any place where you are confused.
2. Write CUT any place where the writer has written something unnecessary or repetitive.
3. Write MORE any place where the writer needs to tell more about a point.
4. Look specifically for whatever grammar problem the writer has mentioned in his/her question #4. If you find a mistake, circle it.

NOTE: Even if someone has already made a note on a paper, if you agree, make the note again.

Five minutes before the end of class, give each paper back to the writer along with the notebook paper with the writer's name on it. Read what was written on and about your own paper and ask questions if you don't understand.

Part 1: The Paragraph

Unit 1: The ESL Student and the Native Speaker

Purpose and Content

This chapter explains the difference between how a native speaker and an ESL student learn and edit English. The author points out that an ESL student does not have the "ear" for language that a native speaker does, and is therefore likely to be confused by homonyms, idioms, and words with multiple meanings or pronunciations. Each of these problem areas is explained in the chapter, and practice in each area is provided. It is emphasized that both native English speakers and ESL student make errors, albeit different kinds, and this textbook is designed for the benefit of both.

Additional Activities

1. Explain to students that different languages have different phonetics. For example, vowels in Spanish have only one consistent sound, while vowels in English have long, short, and other sounds. If you have ESL students in the classroom, ask them to tell some of the different pronunciations of letters or letter combinations in their languages.
2. After completing Practicing 6, and the Unit Talk-Write Assignment, have students come up with as many other idiomatic expressions as they can. Discuss what each one means, and which of the idioms are appropriate for classroom or business writing.
3. Have students who have lived in different regions in America discuss the language differences (pronunciation, idiom, rate of speech) between the regions. You may also wish to have them discuss cultural differences.

Additional Assignments

1. Ask students to write a short paragraph about the difficulties of learning a foreign language. Many students will have some experience taking a foreign language class in school, and of course ESL students will have plenty of experience to draw from. If some students have had no experience with a foreign language, ask them to imagine what the difficulties would be.
2. Internet Assignment: Have students visit Dave's ESL Café at http://www.eslcafe.com. They can explore the site to learn more about what is involved in learning a language. You may wish to have them write a short paragraph about items of interest.
3. In the section on Grammar, the author mentions that "many millions of immigrants have arrived in America knowing absolutely no English and still mastered it sufficiently not only to survive, but to prosper." To encourage thinking about the value of immigration and cultural diversity, have students respond to one of the following prompts:
    (a). What country did your ancestors immigrate from and when? Did they come voluntarily? Do you know any details about what life was like for them when they first came to America?
    (b). How has America benefited from immigration, both over the past several centuries and today?

Unit 2: Myths About Writing

Purpose and Content

This unit is designed to improve students' attitude about writing by disproving common myths about their lack of ability to write. It helps students demonstrate to themselves how much they have to say and how much they already know about standard English. It also clarifies the difference between standard and nonstandard English, and explains the importance of standard English.

Additional Activities

1. Begin with Practicing 5. Then have the small groups share with the whole class their list of difficulties and possible solutions. Record their answers on the board. Additionally, make a class list of fears related to writing and this class, and address each one. Jot down the items on a piece of paper to keep; toward the end of the semester, you can revisit these ideas and see if the students have any new perspectives.
2. After completing Practicing 8, have students collaborate on a list of their own slang/nonstandard terms and then have them write a standard English version of each one.
3. Explain to the students the concept of "code-switching"—that everyone adapts his or her behavior, dress, and speech to fit in with the people he or she is with at the time. Discuss with students how they select clothes appropriate to different occasions, and point out how different styles of English might also be appropriate for different occasions. But just like they need to own one good suit or dress to wear to formal occasions, they also need to be able to speak standard English for formal occasions.

Additional Assignments

1. Paragraph assignment: In place of or in addition to the "Unit Writing Assignment," which asks students what they wish to be doing in 10 years, assign them a paragraph in which they will write about how they are going to achieve those goals, step by step.
2. Paragraph assignment: A myth is something that can't be proven with facts, and often turns out to be untrue. Ask students to write about a myth about anything that they used to believe, but which they later found to be untrue.
3. Paragraph assignment: Have students write a paragraph about why they wish to learn standard English. How will it help them in the future (e.g., in getting or keeping a job, in social situations, in educating their children)?

Unit 3: How to Start Writing

Purpose and Content

This unit teaches students several prewriting techniques including talking, freewriting, brainstorming, and clustering. It also explains and gives examples of topic sentences, and provides practice in writing topic sentences.

Additional Activities

1. Group brainstorming: Put student in groups of three. Give each of the three a different topic, and allow five minutes for brainstorming, clustering or freewriting. Then have students pass their papers to the right, read the new topic, and add to what has already been written by the first two students. Finally, let the students discuss the benefit of collaborative work. You may wish to have them select one of the three topics to write a short paragraph on.

2. Divide class into small groups. Announce a general topic and give students five minutes to come up with as many topic sentences on that topic as they can. Afterwards, write their topic sentences on the board and evaluate each one to determine which ones are most "discussible."

3. Have students do Practicing 6, but tell them when they are writing the two topic sentences about each topic not to label them "good" or "weak" and not to put the weak one first every time, but to mix them up. Then students can exchange papers and see if they can pick out the "good" ones.

Additional Assignments

1. Prewriting assignment: Ask students to choose any topic that interests them and spend 20 minutes prewriting on it: 5 minutes each talking, freewriting, brainstorming, and clustering. It's okay if they come up with many of the same points each time. Then they should evaluate the results of each method. The purpose of this is to let them choose which method works best for them.

2. Topic sentence practice: Ask students to photocopy a page out of one of their textbooks and underline what they think is the topic sentence in each paragraph.

3. Paragraph assignment: Ask students to write a paragraph telling their history with writing. What classes have they taken in the past in which they did writing assignments? What kind of assignments did they do? What did they like or dislike? What were they good at or not so good at? Do they have to write on their jobs? Do they write letters? Songs or poems?

Unit 4: Moving from Sentences to Paragraphs

Purpose and Content

This unit teaches students to support the main ideas of their paragraphs using examples, facts, testimony, reason and logic, and personal observation. Exercises are provided to allow the student to practice developing an idea with each type of support.

Additional Activities

1. When students run out of things to say about a topic, they often add sentences to the end repeating points they've already made. Stress that added development should always come from the points in the middle of the paragraph, not tacked on to the end. The easiest way to add to the main points is to get more specific. Help them understand specificity by looking at the following example and then practicing on the given topics:

Levels of specificity

- Level 1: Older students are often more serious than younger students.
- Level 2 (more specific): In my writing class, the older students are more attentive in class and work harder on assignments than the younger students.
- Level 3: In my Basic Writing class, the four older students who sit in the front row pay close attention to the teacher and take notes. The always have their homework done neatly and completely.
- Level 4: In my Basic Writing class, the four older students who sit in the front row, Joan, Robert, Myra, and Caroline, get to class early every day and by the time the teacher arrives, they have taken out their pens and paper. They take careful notes on everything the teacher says. Robert asks a lot of questions. They always have their homework done neatly and completely. Caroline even types her homework.

Practicing

Here's level 1 on several different topics—students can come up with levels 2, 3, and 4.

- Level 1: During the summer, people play more sports.
- Level 1: There are many different kinds of students at a typical college.
- Level 1: Do unto others as you would have them do unto you.

2. To help students distinguish between facts and opinions, make copies of one or more short movie reviews. Have students decide which statements are opinions and which are facts. Use the review as models of writing that uses facts to support opinions.
3. Put students in small groups and let them write "round-robin" paragraphs where each student writes a topic sentence at the top of a page and then passes it around, where each other student must add an example, fact, piece of testimony, reason, or observation supporting it.

Additional Assignments

1. Testimonial assignment: Give the class one general topic such as education, pets, or health care. Instruct them to find three people who will give them "testimonials" about the topic, and write down briefly what each person says. Then the students should rank the testimonials in order of the expertise of the speaker—for example, a teacher is more "expert" in the area of education than a doctor; a veterinarian is more of an "expert" about pets than a pet owner, but a pet owner is more of an "expert" than someone who doesn't own pets.
2. Paragraph assignment: Give the students the following assignment on music. In order to develop it fully, they will need to have time in advance to carefully listen to the music they will be writing about.

Writing About Music

(a). Choose a general category of music that you like. Describe what the music in that category is like. What makes it different from music in other categories?

- Tell what kind of instruments, vocals, and lyrics this kind of music usually has.
- Choose a specific song in that same category of music that you especially like. Tell the name of the song and the artist.

   (b). Explain how this song fits into its category:
   - Tell what the song sounds like—instruments, vocals, tempo.
   - Tell what the lyrics are about and what they mean. You may include a few lines of the lyrics if you want to.

   (c). Tell why you like the song.

3. Internet assignment: Introduce the class to the Internet. Some may already have experience with it, while others may be novices. Afterward, have students write a paragraph describing their very first Internet experience—what they saw, how they felt.

Unit 5: Writing a Solid Paragraph

Additional Activities

1. Ask students to write a really bad paragraph—one that is repetitive, contains no supporting evidence, wanders off topic, and jumps from point to point with no transition. Focusing on these characteristics will be fun at the time, and help them recognize these problems in their own and others' writing later on.

2. Have students skim "The Hole at Alcatraz" and find the transitional words and phrases that help the reader move chronologically through the day.

3. Do a quick peer editing exercise based on the four criteria mentioned in this chapter. Have students take whatever paragraph they are currently working on and exchange it with another student. Write on the board these four questions:

   (a). Does it have a discussible topic sentence?

   (b). Does it stick to the point?

   (c). Does it prove the point or merely repeat it?

   (d). Are all of the sentences linked so that the reader can easily follow the train of thought?

Have the students write at the bottom of each other's papers a, b, c, and d and beside each put a simple *yes* or *no*. Students should be able to exchange papers several times in about 15 minutes.

Unit 6: Revising Paragraphs

Purpose and Content

This unit emphasizes the writing process and the value of revising a rough draft. It introduces students to the Revising Checklist and gives them plenty of opportunities to practice using it.

Additional Activities

1. Have students apply the Revising Checklist to the paragraph they are currently working on. Ask them to actually write out the answers to each of the questions on the checklist using complete sentences.

2. Assist students in seeing the need for revision by doing one of the following with their rough drafts:
   - Attach a copy of the Revision Checklist. Highlight the one or two areas that need the most work.
   - Highlight problem areas directly on the students' drafts. Let them figure out what's wrong.
3. Begin peer editing, using one of the two forms given in the first section of this manual.

Additional Assignments

1. Revision assignment: Ask students to take the "bad" paragraphs they wrote as an Additional Activity in Unit 1 and revise them into good paragraphs.
2. Paragraph assignment: For this assignment, students must think of a topic that they would like advice about. It could be anything from love to finding an apartment to gardening. They should then ask a person of their choice for advice on the topic, and write the advice down two different ways: (1) Word for word as the person said it, and (2) Revised in standard English with a topic sentence.
3. Internet assignment: Have students use a search engine (http://www.yahoo.com is a good one) to find a site about something that interests them and write a one paragraph summary of what's on the site.

Part 2: The Sentence

Unit 7: The Basic Sentence

Purpose and Content

This unit introduces students to the basic parts of a sentence: subjects and verbs (action, linking, and helping), prepositional phrases, and verbals. It provides many opportunities for students to identify these parts in various types of sentences. Special attention is given to parts of speech, especially verb forms, which are easily confused.

Additional Activities/Suggestions

1. Many of the rules of grammar and mechanics depend upon the writer being able to identify subjects and verbs. This is a *very* important concept for basic writers to learn. Have students under-line the subjects and verbs in *everything they write for the rest of the semester.*
2. After doing the Practicing exercises, have students create their own exercise sentences that contain subjects and verbs, prepositional phrases, and/or verbals. Put the best examples on the board and let the class as a whole identify the parts.
3. Have each student bring a photocopy of a page of a textbook from one of his or her other classes and then ask the students to identify the sentence parts on that page.

Additional Paragraph Assignment

Let students choose one of the following as a topic sentence:

(a). My first semester at college was just like I thought it would be.

(b). My first semester at college was different from what I expected.

Instruct them to write the first half of the paragraph about their expectations—naming at least 3—and the second half about the reality.

Unit 8: Building Sentences

Purpose and Content

This unit shows students how to identify and create simple, compound, and complex sentences. It encourages students to use a variety of sentences, and to expand and enhance sentences with details. It provides practice in building sentences and in improving sentence variety.

Additional Activities/Suggestions

1. Sentence combining exercises have long been used to improve students' writing with great results. There are some good sentence combining practices in this chapter, and you can easily make more by taking any paragraph and separating the clauses and details. For example:

Sentence combining is a technique. This technique has been used before. It has been used for a long time. This technique is supposed to improve writing. The writing is done by students. This technique has produced results. The results have been good.

2. Have students take one of their own paragraphs and label each sentence simple, compound, or complex (you should first explain that there are sentences that are both compound and complex).

3. Put a short kernel sentence on the board and get the whole class to help you add to it until it fills the board.

Additional Paragraph Assignment

Tell students they are all entering a contest to see who has the strangest person in his or her family. The assignment is to write a paragraph about one of the strangest people in their own families, giving convincing examples. If students are comfortable reading each other's papers, they can vote on a winner at the end of the assignment.

Unit 9: Avoiding Non-Sentences

Purpose and Content

This unit teaches students to identify and correct both fragments and run-ons. It provides a comprehensive look at all the common types of fragments and run-ons and contains many exercises in various ways of correcting these problems.

Additional Activities/Suggestions

1. If your students have written paragraphs on computer, have them call up an old paragraph and change it so that it contains deliberate fragments or run-ons. Then have students exchange papers, correct the fragments and/or run-ons, and then compare the corrected paper to the original paragraph.

2. Some students may have more luck identifying fragments and run-ons in their papers by reading the papers backwards sentence by sentence—in other words, reading the last sentence first, then the next-to-last one, and so forth. Let them try this on the "Practicing for Unit Test" exercise or on the "Unit Test."

3. Many students mistakenly believe that a very short sentence is a fragment and a very long one is a run-on. Let students practice writing their own *long* fragments and *short* run-ons to disprove this theory.

Additional Paragraph Assignment

Assign students to write a paragraph about shoes. Give no other specifications—they can write about shoes in any way they wish as long as they have and follow a topic sentence. (It seems like a strange topic, but it always works—another good topic is "hats.")

Unit 10: Verbs—An Overview

Purpose and Content

This unit presents the 12 tenses and discusses problems that students commonly encounter when using the present and past tenses. Special attention is paid to verb endings (-s, -ed, -ing) and the verbs *be, have,* and *do.*

Additional Activities/Suggestions

1. Let students make up and say or write their own sentences in each of the twelve tenses.

2. Discuss the cultural value of verb tenses. We are a culture very much concerned with time; therefore, we have many verb tenses, as do most Germanic and Romance languages. But many Native American and African tribal languages did not have verb tenses, and it is theorized that this is because these cultures operated on a cyclical concept of time rather than a linear one.

3. Plain old practice: Have students write one sentence each containing the following verbs:

1. am	11. having	21. don't
2. is	12. do	22. weren't
3. are	13. does	23. hasn't
4. was	14. isn't	24. haven't
5. were	15. aren't	25. be
6. been	16. wasn't	
7. being	17. weren't	
8. has	18. hasn't	
9. have	19. haven't	
10. had	20. doesn't	

Additional Paragraph Assignment

The two paragraph topics given in the text relate to family of origin. Another assignment on this topic is to ask students to tell the role each family member had in their family of origin, giving each role a name, such as caretaker, clown, boss, baby, and so on. Have the class brainstorm together about possible names for roles, and then have each student write his/her own paragraph.

Unit 11: Regular and Irregular Verbs

Purpose and Content

This unit presents the present, past, and past participle forms of regular and irregular verbs. It cautions students against dropping -ed endings, dropping helping verbs, and using the incorrect form of irregular verbs. An extensive list of irregular verb forms is provided.

Additional Activities/Suggestions

1. Teach students how to look up irregular verb forms in the dictionary under the infinitive form of the verb. Have them look up a familiar word that is on the list in their book, such as *do,* and look at the words immediately following the entry word *do: did, done.* Then have them look up a verb that is not on the list, such as *blow* or *cost,* and tell you what the other forms are and how to use them.
2. Have the class come up with two lists of participles that are commonly used as adjectives: ones that are derived from regular verbs (tired, scared, married) and ones that are derived from irregular verbs (broken, drunk, torn).
3. As the text points out, irregular verbs must be memorized. Teach students good strategies for memorization, including oral repetition, written repetition, flash cards, associations, rhymes, and so on.

Additional Paragraph Assignment

Ask students to write about how college has affected their lives both positively and negatively. Suggest that they separate the effects into positive and negative categories and discuss the most important category—good or bad—last (emphatic order).

Unit 12: Subject-Verb Agreement

Purpose and Content

This unit presents the basic principle of subject-verb agreement and then devotes a separate explanation and practice exercise to each special situation that may cause a student to make an agreement error.

Additional Activities/Suggestions

1. Students must understand how to identify the subjects of their sentences as first, second, or third person as well as singular or plural.

This is important because they may get confused about why "I" is singular but takes a different verb from "he." Use the chart for "Do" to show students that there are really six kinds of subjects. Then take a few students' paragraphs, list all the words they have used as subjects on the board, and let the students classify each subject as one of the six types on the chart.

2. Plain old practice: Have students write one sentence each beginning with the following phrases:

1. There is		**8.** There weren't
2. There isn't		**9.** There has
3. There are		**10.** There hasn't
4. There aren't		**11.** There have
5. There was		**12.** There haven't
6. There wasn't		**13.** Here is
7. There were		**14.** Here are

Have students write a short (six sentences) paragraph about what they usually do on Saturday. Then have them change it from first person to third person and change the verbs to match. This works best on the computer.

Additional Paragraph Assignment

In contrast to the writing assignment in the text, ask students to write about a celebrity—in movies, sports, TV, politics, and so on—who is *not* a good role model for children. Ask them to give specific reasons to back up their assertion.

Unit 13: Problems with Verbs

Purpose and Content

This unit discusses tense shifts; use of *would, could, and should;* double negatives; and active versus passive voice.

Additional Activities/Suggestions

1. Tense shifts occur commonly in written accounts of conversations. Tell students to leave class for 10 minutes, during which time they are to have a short conversation with someone and then immediately write down word for word what was said. The students will then return to class and write a paragraph about the conversation—in the *past tense* (no "then he says" or "she goes" or "I'm like").

2. Plain old practice: Have students write two sentences each containing the following words:

no	never	scarcely
none	hardly	barely

3. To reinforce the difference between active and passive voice, have the whole class together construct a passive voice paragraph about what you did in class yesterday—for example, "The roll was called. The papers were returned. Then the books were opened." Then revise it to make each sentence active.

Additional Paragraph Assignment

By this time students will notice that some of their classmates have stopped attending classes. Ask them to write a paragraph on the three major reasons they believe students drop out of college, whether or not the college should do anything to try to retain these students, and if so, what.

Unit 14: Using Pronouns Correctly

Purpose and Content

This unit explains the usefulness of pronouns, and explains the basic criteria for using pronouns: clear referents, correct agreement, and consistent point of view. It includes sections on indefinite pronouns and non-sexist use of pronouns.

Additional Activities/Suggestions

1. Find a copy of *Anguished English* or *Fractured English* by Richard Lederer. He has some funny real-life examples of unclear or missing referents.
2. To practice consistent point of view, have the class write a brief set of instructions, then turn it into a process description. For example, "Preheat the oven. Assemble the ingredients," becomes "The cook preheats the oven and assembles the ingredients." Or start with the process description and turn it into a set of instructions.
3. Discuss sexism in the English language in general. Ask the students what they think of recent changes in language such as "police officer" instead of "policeman" and "flight attendant" instead of "stewardess." You may even venture into a discussion of some progressive churches that have rewritten prayer books and scriptures to refer to God as "she" or "he or she" or "it."

Additional Paragraph Assignment

Ask students to write as TV critics. Tell them to pick a TV show that has elements that they like and elements that they dislike or think should be improved. Have them write about both the good and bad points of the show, making suggestions for improvement. Students who do not watch TV regularly might write about a movie.

Unit 15: Pronoun Problems

Purpose and Content

This unit explains the correct use of subjective, objective, possessive, and reflexive pronouns. It gives special attention to easily confused words (*its/it's, whose/who's*), the use of *who* or *whom*, and the use of *these, those,* and *them*.

Additional Activities/Suggestions

1. Photocopy a page out of a novel and distribute copies to students. Have them circle every pronoun, and on a separate page list the pronouns and identify them as subjective, objective, possessive, or reflexive.

2. Have students write sets of "mirror" sentences like the following:

He gave the books to me.
He and I offered them a ride.

I gave the books to him.
They offered him and me
a ride.

We asked him and her to
keep it between them.

They asked him and me to
keep it between us.

3. Have each student write five sentences using pronouns, only two of which are correct. Then let students exchange papers and try to decide which ones are right and which are wrong.

Additional Paragraph Assignment

Ask students to literally draw a timeline of the years since they were born and mark on the line times when their lives took important turns or underwent big changes—either good or bad. Ask them to select one of these times to write about in a paragraph.

Unit 16: Distinguishing Between Adjectives and Adverbs

Purpose and Content

This unit explains the difference between adjectives and adverbs, the *-ly* adverb ending, and comparatives and superlatives. Special attention is given to *good/well* and *bad/badly*.

Additional Activities/Suggestions

1. Have the students look in a thesaurus to find synonyms for an adjective such as "pretty." Make a list of all the synonyms on the board, and then have the class tell you the comparative and superlative of each form. Finally, determine whether each word has an adverb form and, if so, what it is.
2. Explain to students that there are certain adjectives and adverbs that are already superlative, such as *unique, perfect,* and *favorite.* These words should not have *more* or *most* in front of them.
3. Photocopy a page of flowery prose and have students make a list of the adjectives and a separate list of the adverbs that they find.

Additional Paragraph Assignment

Ask students to describe the ideal teacher. This fantasy person will probably be a collage of the best traits of their best teachers, so ask them to begin brainstorming by making a list of good teachers they have had, then a list of the qualities of each teacher, then a list of the qualities that appear more than once.

Unit 17: Dangling and Misplaced Modifiers

Purpose and Content

This unit explains what dangling and misplaced modifiers are and offers a variety of ways that they can be corrected. There are a substantial number of practice sentences for students to work on.

Additional Activities/Suggestions

1. As well as containing good examples of unclear referents, Richard Lederer's books *Anguished English* and *Fractured English* contain funny, real-life examples of dangling and misplaced modifiers that students will enjoy.
2. Give students the following phrases to use as modifiers in sentences of their own:
    - with a loud crash
    - barking loudly
    - before passing out the tests
    - tiptoeing carefully
    - easily finishing on time
    - being an experienced mother
3. Have students write sentences practicing using these problematic words:
    - only
    - just
    - even

Additional Paragraph Assignment

Ask students to write a paragraph about two things they can do at the same time, for example, washing clothes and studying; talking on the phone while doing dishes; putting on lipstick while driving; talking on the phone while watching TV. Ask them to explain in the paragraph exactly how they alternate between the two activities so that they can be accomplished at the same time. (They will have to be very careful about misplaced modifiers in this assignment.)

Unit 18: Using Prepositions

Purpose and Content

This unit explains prepositions and prepositional phrases and provides a list of prepositions. It focuses on frequently misused prepositions such as *between, among, through,* and *throughout;* and on frequently misused expressions such as *independent from* and *due to.*

Additional Activities/Suggestions

1. Ask students to take a paragraph they have written earlier in the term, underline all the prepositional phrases, and circle all the prepositions.
2. Preposition errors such as the ones discussed in this chapter often occur in business writing. Look through that pile of memos on your desk and see if you can find real-life examples of these errors to

share with your students—white out the name of the writer, of course.

3. Students for whom English is a second (or third) language will find prepositions very difficult. The web link to "Dave's ESL Café" listed in the first section of this manual has links to sites where ESL/EFL students can get extra practice.

Part 3: Mechanics

Unit 19: Punctuation You Can Hear

Purpose and Content

This unit deals with the easiest punctuation for students to learn, including end-of-sentence punctuation, commas, and apostrophes. It includes a wealth of exercises.

Additional Activities/Suggestions

1. Take a paragraph from any book or essay and retype it with no punctuation whatsoever. Give it to your students to read, and then discuss the difficulty of reading with no punctuation. Then let them try to insert the correct punctuation.

2. Photocopy a short paragraph and have students circle all end-of-sentence punctuation, commas, quotation marks, and apostrophes, and number them. On a separate page, have them write the rule that corresponds with each mark.

3. Divide the class into six groups and assign each group one of the six comma rules listed in this chapter. The group is then responsible for coming up with a five-minute lesson for the class about this rule, including at least three examples that they can put on the board.

Additional Paragraph Assignment

Here are three quotes about writing by famous authors. Ask your students to choose one and respond to it—either agreeing or disagreeing—in a paragraph:

1. "Writing is making sense of life." Nadine Gordimer.
2. "The desire to write grows with writing." Erasmus.
3. "Writing, like life itself, is a voyage of discovery." Henry Miller.

Unit 20: Punctuation You Can't Hear

Purpose and Content

This unit covers the more difficult and sophisticated marks of punctuation such as the semi-colon, colon, dash, quotation marks, and parentheses.

Additional Activities/Suggestions

1. It's important for basic writers to know that they don't have to incorporate all of these marks of punctuation into every paragraph they write. A period can be used in place of most semi-colons, a

comma in place of many colons, dashes and parentheses. Although student writers need to know the rules concerning these marks, they should also know the simpler options.

2. Understanding the difference between direct and indirect quotations can be difficult for students. Here are some extra examples of the differences. Point out the tense differences and pronoun differences in many of the sentence pairs.

DIRECT	INDIRECT
My mother says, "It takes two to tango."	My mother says (that) it takes two to tango.
"I can not believe it!" she said.	She said (that) she could not believe it.
He vowed, "I'm going to find you."	He vowed (that) he was going to find me.
I told her, "I'm not ready."	I told her (that) I wasn't ready.
She asked me, "What time is it?"	She asked me what time it was.
"Who are you?" he demanded.	He demanded to know who we were.
He said, "Don't start without me."	He said not to start without him.
"Be careful—don't drop it," she said.	She said to be careful and not drop it.
"Are you going, too?" he asked.	He asked whether she was going, too.

3. This is a good time to discuss plagiarism and the use of quotation marks to show that a writer has "borrowed" words from another writer.

Additional Paragraph Assignment

Ask students to think of a time in their lives when someone told them something about themselves—good or bad, true or false—that has stuck with them ever since. It might have been someone saying, "I believe in you," or "You're very smart," or "You'll never amount to anything." Ask the students to write about the incident during which the person said this to them, and describe how it has affected them since then.

Unit 21: Capitalization

Purpose and Content

This unit lists all the rules of capitalization, then explains and provides an exercise for each one.

Additional Activities/Suggestions

1. Ask students to look in newspapers and magazines and come up with an example of each one of the capitalization rules listed at the beginning of Unit 20.
2. Have students take any paragraph they've done on computer and *un*capitalize every capital letter. Then let the students exchange papers and put the capitals back in.
3. As a class, make the longest list you can of brand names that are often used generically in casual conversation (e.g., Kleenex, Coke, Clorox).

Additional Paragraph Assignment

Ask students to think of someone who has helped them significantly in some way. Then ask them to write a thank-you letter to that person, describing what the person did and how it has benefited the student. You might offer extra credit to students who are willing to mail their letters.

Unit 22: How to Use the Dictionary

Purpose and Content

This unit is designed to show students how valuable the dictionary is to any writer—and not just for spelling. It explains each major part of a typical word entry and its function.

Additional Activities/Suggestions

1. Assign each student to find one interesting fact in the dictionary and bring it to share with the class.
2. Read aloud or paraphrase for the class Malcolm X's exercise in copying the dictionary and the useful knowledge he gained (from *The Autobiography of Malcolm X*).
3. Compare an entry in your library's Oxford English Dictionary with the same entry in a good desk dictionary and then with the same entry in a 99 cent "office" dictionary to show students the differences.

Additional Paragraph Assignment

Ask students to write about their future career and how they are personally suited for it. For example, a student who wishes to teach kindergarten might believe he/she is suited for it because he/she has patience, creativity, and a love for children. A student who wishes to open a small business may feel that he/she has the appropriate traits of organization, financial aptitude, and ambition.

Unit 23: Spelling Rules

Purpose and Content

This unit offers simple tips and basic rules for spelling patterns that apply to hundreds of thousands of words. Exceptions to the rules are included, and students are given many opportunities to identify misspelled words and to apply the rules to changing word forms.

Additional Activities/Suggestions for Units 22 and 23

1. Using Tip 1: Teach a little phonics. Explain the difference between the sounds of long vowels and short vowels, and explain the spelling patterns that influence these sounds:

    V = vowel, C = consonant

    V + C = short sound (tap)

    V + C + C = short sound (tapped, tapping)

    V + C + V = long sound (tape, taped, taping)

Have students apply these patterns to compare the following word pairs:

write/written

bite/bitten

hoped/hopped

dining/winning

2. Using Tip 2: Assign each student to come up with a memory trick for a troublesome word and share it with the whole class.

3. Using Tip 4: Students need to keep their own lists of words they misspell and add to it throughout the semester. If students are writing on the computer, remind them to have their lists handy when they run the spell-check so that they can add the words they have misspelled to their lists. Encourage students to *memorize* the words on their lists—remind them that during essay exams they won't have a spell-check.

Additional Paragraph Assignment

Ask students to write a paragraph describing changes that should be made either to the high school, middle school, or elementary school that they attended or to the school their children attend.

Unit 24: Commonly Misspelled Words

Purpose and Content

This unit focuses on homophones and easily confused words. It also gives a good list of commonly misspelled words for students to practice and/or memorize.

For Additional Activities/Suggestions, see Unit 23

Additional Paragraph Assignment

Ask students to write a paragraph evaluating their progress as writers this term. In what ways have they improved? What do they still need to work on? How do they feel about writing now? How do they feel about their own abilities and potential?

Part 4: Readings

Suggestions for the Instructor

Reinforcing the Reading Process

To reinforce the suggestions given the students in this chapter, take the students through the process slowly as a group for the first few readings:

1. Give students 60 seconds to **scan** the reading. Then ask what they were able to find out about the piece: topic? length? difficulty? visuals?

2. Have the students read the **headnote** only. Discuss what information they found out there, and what attitude the editor seems to have about the piece.

3. Assign students to write in their books. Ask them to **underline** important points and write occasional **comments** in the margin. Urge them to be selective in what they underline; many students will take a highlighter and proceed to cover the entire page.

Teaching Vocabulary

Have each student turn in a half-sheet of paper (with no name) that contains all the words that student was not familiar with. To keep things really anonymous, all the students must turn in a piece of paper, even if it's blank—then no one knows who's asking about what. Go over all the words on every list with the whole class.

Checking for Understanding

Have students answer the "Understanding What You Have Read" questions. Four out of five is a good score; three out of five is not. Go over the answers with them.

Discussion

Break students up into groups of four or five to discuss the "Thinking About What You Have Read" questions. Then have each group report on *one* of the questions to the class.

Writing

The "Writing Assignments" following each reading ask students to imitate the rhetorical strategies of the reading in their own work. You may wish to review the unit from Part Two on that rhetorical strategy before they write.

Answers to Various Practices

Unit 6

Practice 1

(1)

People should not hurt others by using racial slurs. My first experience with racism changed my perception of the world. A man I didn't know called me, "Damn Jap!" I thought, "Did I hear right?" From the scowl on his face, I must have. But I could not understand what I had done to deserve this ugly label. It was incomprehensible to me that someone who did not know me could make such a demeaning comment when I had done nothing. I was stunned. This incident revealed the sheer power that two words can have and their ability to hurt. Growing up, I knew that a generation before I was born in the United States, my native country had been at war with Japan, the faraway land from which my mother's parents had come. The man who insulted me might have some lingering prejudices from World War II. But I am just as American as anyone in this melting pot of a country, the U.S.A. I thought of myself as a patriotic American, but obviously this man did not see me that way. It was not the last time that I was to hear a racial slur. The point, though, is that I decided to make sure that I myself would not succumb to stereotyping others. I would work hard at appreciating every individual, separate from his or her stereotype.

(2)

Most people learn lessons about their lives from their own mistakes, and some learn from their personal experiences. I believe everybody in this world has had an incident or an experience that taught him or her an important lesson about life, and I am one who has had a memorable experience, which I shall never forget. It happened while I was baby-sitting the Geyer family's four-year-old child, Wally. While eating, he choked on a green bean. His face turned red, then blue, and he kept gasping for air. In my first aid class, I had learned the Heimlich maneuver, and I used it on Wally—grabbing him from behind and vigorously squeezing below his diaphragm, with the result that he spit up the green bean and started to breathe normally. It felt really good to have learned something so useful in class.

(3)

I have a cousin who loves using our family gatherings to discuss the latest family scandals. She enjoys talking about anything bad that has happened to the family. At one Thanksgiving dinner, she went on and on about how terrible it was that Uncle Mark was leaving Aunt Gertrude for another woman. We already felt bad enough about the situation without hearing about the secret phone calls he had been caught making and the expensive gifts that showed up on credit card bills. This cousin uses our family reunions as a pulpit to expose any family wrongdoings. I think when a member of the family has a personal problem, it should stay that way—personal—not broadcast to everyone. Let the people involved work it out themselves or get professional help. Gossiping about the matter only makes it worse.

(4)

It is difficult to look up to a leader who lies and cheats. For example, Richard Nixon never received the full admiration of American citizens after his Watergate affair. If he had just told the truth about breaking into the Watergate apartments to find out what his enemies were up to, he might have recovered his reputation. Similarly, the television evangelist, Jim Bakker, lost all credibility with his audiences once they found out that he had an affair with a prostitute. Finally, even a charismatic leader like John F. Kennedy lost some of his popularity once the newspapers revealed how he had had affairs with various women, including Marilyn Monroe. The public will forgive a popular leader's character faults, but the leader must admit them and show some repentance.

Unit 8

Practice 10

(1)

On Monday nothing seemed right [, but by] Friday Linda was pleased with her life. She had called her mother. ~~Her mother~~ [who] had been feeling sick [, and o]n the phone she sounded chipper. Linda felt relieved. She decided to go camping in the mountains [where h]er friend had a cabin ~~there. She would~~ [and] fish all weekend. She would be alone [which s]he liked ~~being alone.~~ The weekend would cost little [because] she would only have to buy groceries for one. She had enough money [because] she had just gotten a paycheck. She would wear old clothes. ~~She would~~ [,] lounge by the river. ~~She would~~ [, and] sleep late. There would be no alarm clock [, and n]obody would bother her. Linda thought, "Everything turns out for the best."

(2)

Most college students juggle the hours in their day. They play sports and go to parties [, and m]any also have jobs. They try to include serving on committees [,] ~~They~~ perform[ing] volunteer work.~~They~~ [, and] go[ing] to lectures. The many options do evoke a great deal of anxiety. The choices are unlimited [, but t]he hours are limited. Students feel pressured to get good grades [and] ~~They feel pressured~~ to experience life fully. They have to decide how much time they can spare outside of class and work for general enrichment. ~~That decision is not always easy to make.~~ [, which is not always easy to decide.

Unit 9

Practice 13

Two years had passed since I had last seen my grandmother. During this time, her condition had worsened, [and] now she was completely bedridden [, n]o longer able to get up and walk. She babbled without making sense, [and] she had no idea who I was. Her gray eyes stared vacantly [a]s if she were half in another world unknown to me. All I could do was smile at her and hold her hand. Yet, I was struck by the fact that even in this hopelessly deteriorated state, she seemed to want to communicate with me[. S]he wanted a human connection. I decided she was still my kind beautiful grandmother inside, no matter how she appeared on the outside. Today I wonder what it will be like when I am old. Personally, I hope I don't live long enough to be in such a deteriorated condition [, u]nable to recognize loved ones. How frustrating it must be to be senile[, t]o repeat the same questions and to remember nothing. Still, maybe science will some day find a cure for extreme senility[;] I hope so.

Unit Collaborative Assignment

I am a file clerk in the office of one of Denny's restaurants, [so] I am required to file correctly. While this process may seem easy, it can actually become a real problem [i]f the proper filing rules are not followed. Nothing is more confusing and time wasting than lost files.

Here are some basic filing rules to follow: First, you need to know the correct order of the letters in the alphabet [which is s]omething you should have learned in grade school. Second, a file clerk must know that for each of the 26 letters there is a file cut, the file cut [which] is the label part that extends above the rest of the file. These file cuts are right, left, and middle. Third, before you put files in a filing cabinet, you must take the time to alphabetize them so you don't have to jump back and forth [f]rom drawer to drawer. Fourth, while filing, you must never rush[;] otherwise you are likely to misfile [w]hich may cause big trouble because lost files are hard to find later.

Finally, the order of filing is important and can be tricky. For instance, you must file by a person's last name. If two people have the same last name, then use the first name to distinguish between them [t]o stay in proper alphabetical order. For instance, "John Smith," comes after "Agnes

Smith." Furthermore, a space in a name is treated as if the space were not there,[;] for instance, "De Lang" precedes "Derring." Following these simple rules lessens the risk of making filing errors, and in the long run they will save you time and energy.

Unit 11

Practicing 4

What is a real American? Some people have claim[ed] that a real American is a person who is loyal, patriotic, and proud to live in the United States. Other people have suppose[d] that a real American is someone who watches football on Monday nights and eats hot dogs. The definition of a real American changes constantly because different generations have experience[d] different problems, such as war or depression. For instance, during the 1950s when Senator Joseph McCarthy had made everyone paranoid about Communism, a "real American" was someone who was against Communism. Later, in the 1970s, a "real American" was someone who had battle[d] the Vietnamese even though he might have believe[d] that the war was illogical and immoral.

During the later 1970s, a "real American" might have been someone who had purchase[d] an American gas-guzzling car instead of a foreign economical car, just to show that he supported the American economy. Today, the term "real American" is not easy to define because we have not experience[d] a real war or crisis to pull us together. But this is what I think the term means: "A person who wants to change America for the better and will work to do so."

Unit 14

Unit Collaborative Assignment

A.

1. Mary told Felice that Mary's boss was too strict.
2. At the Career Center, the counselors said Judy should be an architect.
3. People who get up will lose their seats.
4. If you have your health, you have everything.
5. Not only was the coat much too tight, but the fact that it was made of cheap material made Irene angry.
6. Merlin walked with a hot dog in one hand and a piece of carrot cake in the other, munching on the cake as he headed down the steps.
7. The form clearly states that you must have a parent's signature.
8. As we walked into the movie, the ushers told us that only the two front rows were unoccupied.
9. Nancy intended to tell her teacher that her teacher had been rude.
10. All the customers wanted their tickets back.

B.

1. Jane told Marguerite that Jane's cousin would be at the meeting.
2. At the market, the vendors said the peaches were ripe.
3. Neither of the girls wants to attend the wedding.
4. All nurses should be gentle with their patients.
5. As one enters the restaurant, a sign says, "No checks, please."
6. Neither of the grocery store checkers ever smiles.
7. The city of Los Angeles has a lot of freeway traffic.
8. All of the volunteers take pride in their service to others.

9. All of the students scored at least 80 on their algebra tests.
10. If you are aware of a problem, you should try to help.

Unit 22

Unit Collaborative Assignment

Most college campuses are filled with various personality types. There are the jocks, the nerds, the party animals, the lab rats, [and] the do-gooders. My ~~favorit~~ [favorite] is the nerd. Computer ~~sceince~~ [science] programs seem to grow nerds. My theory is that nerds spend so much time at a keyboard they ~~beccome~~ [become] isolated. They turn into geeks <u>that</u> [who] ~~ain't got~~ [have] no social contact with people outside their computer circle.

A sure way of ~~identifing~~ [identifying] a nerd is by ~~appearence~~ [appearance]. A nerd just does not know how to dress <u>cool</u> [fashionably]. His pants are always too short, usually hitting just above the ankle. His shirts are buttoned up to the collar, but the buttons are never in the right button holes. Then, too, the nerd's shirts are never ~~stuck~~ [tucked] inside his pants, but hang half in and half out, looking quite sloppy. (I say "his," but there are just as many ~~femmale~~ [female] nerds today.) A nerd never inquires about the ~~whether~~ [weather] before dressing. You can count on the fact that if it is a hot day, he will wear a sweater; whereas if it is a cold day, he will wear shorts. Nerds wear tee-shirts that say "My parents went to Disneyland, and all I got was this lousy tee-shirt." This, of course, is the nerd's ~~yucky~~ [unsuccessful] attempt ~~at being cool~~ [to be fashionable].

Nerds always dress opposite to the established styles. They don't do this to rebel the way punks do. They just don't know better. When the surfer look is popular, they wear leather jackets. When the preppy look is in, they wear disco clothes. Most important of all, though, a nerd is always comfortable in polyester. Sometimes, I'm a nerd, but then that's a ~~diffrent~~ [different] story.